EDUCATION IN
ANCIENT AND MEDIEVAL
IRELAND

By the same author:

Father John Sullivan, S.J. Longmans Green, London 1941.

Newman's University: Idea and Reality. Longmans Green, London, 1951.

The Consecration of Learning: Lectures on Newman's Idea of a University. Fordham University Press, New York, 1962.

EDUCATION IN
ANCIENT AND MEDIEVAL
IRELAND

FERGAL McGRATH S.J.

Studies 'Special Publications'
35 Lower Leeson Street
Dublin 2

LA
641.3
.M32

CONTENTS

<u>Erratum</u>

P.94, line 11 'others during
history' should be omitted

this form in western Europe
of Ireland (Foras Feasa ar

led epochs of Irish
ng two lines inserted:

Keating's History
bout 1640.60

PREFACE

This book was originally planned as a comprehensive history of education in Ireland from the earliest times to the present day. Various reasons, however, induced me to limit its scope. Firstly, two competent comprehensive histories were recently published.[1] Secondly, it appeared to me that in these and other available writings on Irish education the earlier period had been somewhat briefly dealt with. Thirdly, by restricting the work to a limited period, more opportunity would be given for interesting and illustrative detail.

I have relied almost entirely on already published sources. To hunt for educational matter in unpublished manuscripts would obviously be an unending task. It would also require a knowledge of Old Irish and of palaeography which I do not possess. Yet, to a certain extent, this book may lay claim to be based on original documents. As is well known, there were in the last century and the beginning of the present century, in addition to the German scholars, Zeuss, Zimmer, Thurneysen, Meyer, and the Scot Strachan, a large number of Irishmen who devoted themselves with remarkable industry and erudition to the publication of a wide range of documents of every age, Latin, Old, Middle and Early Modern Irish, and Norman-French. It is enough to mention a few of the most well-known names, O'Curry, O'Donovan, O'Reilly, Whitley Stokes, Reeves, Todd, Edward and John Gwynn, Plummer, Calder, O'Grady, Joyce, Hyde, Dinneen, Flower, Best, MacNeill, Macalister, Bergin. This work has been carried on by numerous modern scholars, many still living, whose names appear in the bibliography of this book. It is on this large body of material that I have drawn. Some of it, indeed, has already been utilized by writers on education. I have, however, been at pains to make my examination of it as exhaustive as possible.

I am conscious that almost all the topics I have dealt with have already been explored by experts. This book does not attempt to vie with their works, but aims at gathering together for the use of the general reading public, especially students of education, a quantity of information previously widely scattered. With this in view, I have given copious references for the benefit of those who wish to pursue certain topics further, and I have endeavoured to balance the views of older and modern writers.

My researches have confirmed the truth of a fact commented on by many previous writers, namely that there are serious gaps in our knowledge of early Irish education. This is particularly true of the education of the secular clergy and of the laity during the first centuries of christianity and, to a lesser extent, also during the Middle Ages. I cannot claim to have bridged these gaps entirely satisfactorily, but at least I have endeavoured to collect every scrap of evidence at present available for that task. Future researchers, therefore, may rest assured that any further explanation of these rather puzzling *lacunae* must be sought for in hitherto unedited sources.

It may perhaps appear that this work occasionally strays over the boundary between a history of education and a history of literature. This, however, was at times inevitable. Where direct knowledge of educational activity is missing, the literature of the period is obviously the one source from which indirect knowledge may be gleaned.

In this connection I should like to make an observation and forestall possible criticism. I have naturally been guided by recent works on the history of Irish literature – which will be duly noted – but I have also drawn considerably on older ones, notably O'Reilly's *Irish Writers,* O'Curry's *Manuscript Materials of Ancient Irish History* and *Manners and Customs of the Ancient Irish,* Hyde's *Literary History of Ireland* and Mrs. Stopford Green's *The Making of Ireland and its Undoing.* The writers of these books vary in their degree of documentation. O'Reilly gives no references, O'Curry and Hyde are tantalizingly inconsistent in doing so, Mrs. Green is generally well documented but has occasional lapses. Where possible, I have traced the missing references, but occasionally I have felt justified in accepting statements on the authority of these well-informed and conscientious writers, especially where there is question not of their opinions, but of the existence of documents. I concur with the opinion expressed by Dr. Gearóid Mac Eoin in his preface to the recent reprint of O'Reilly's *Irish Writers,* that there is still wanting a complete history of Irish literature written in accordance with modern principles of criticism and documentation. Much excellent work has been done, but only on limited areas or periods.

The two volumes of *Bibliography of Irish Philology and Literature,* edited by Dr. R. I. Best, have been invaluable in tracing the whereabouts of original and edited manuscripts. But they, however excellent, need to be brought up to date, the second volume having appeared in 1941.[2]

In any historical work extending over a lengthy period, the spelling of personal and place names presents difficulty. In quotations I have kept to that of the authors, regardless of inconsistency. In my own text I have been guided by the consensus of modern Irish scholars, who generally keep to the spelling of the particular periods with which they are dealing, but occasionally substitute modernized forms which have passed into common use.

During the greater part of the writing of this book, I had the constant advice and help of the late Father John Ryan, S.J., Professor Emeritus of Ancient and Medieval Irish History, University College, Dublin. I am glad here to be able to pay a tribute to the memory of this great and kindly scholar, and to express my lasting gratitude to him. At a later stage, I was generously helped by Father Seán Ó Catháin, S.J., Professor Emeritus of Education, University College, Dublin, and Father Diarmuid O Laoghaire, S.J., both of whom read my manuscript and saved me from many errors and omissions.

My thanks are also due to those many experts who were good enough to advise me on special points, Professors D. A. Binchy, James Carney and Brian Ó Cuiv, Dublin Institute for Advanced Studies, Professors Francis J. Byrne, Proinsias MacCana, F. X. Martin, Dr. Art Cosgrove and Dr. Kevin Danaher, University College, Dublin, Professor Aloys Fleischmann, University College, Cork, Dr. Gearóid MacNiocaill, University College, Galway, Professor James Lydon, Trinity College, Dublin and the late Dr. Kathleen Hughes, Cambridge University. I am particularly grateful to the Franciscan Fathers, Dun Mhuire, Killiney, and to the academic staff of St. Peter's College, Wexford, for their hospitality during my examination of their respective archives. A final sincere word of thanks is due to the courteous and helpful librarians of the National Library and the Royal Irish Academy and to Mrs. Marie Conlan for her accurate typing of a difficult manuscript and her help in keeping my unruly footnotes in order.

CHAPTER 1

THE EARLIEST TEACHERS

i. The Evidence of Archaeology

ii. The Druids

i. THE EVIDENCE OF ARCHAEOLOGY

Education may be described loosely, but for our purposes adequately, as the process by which knowledge is imparted to the mind with the twofold purpose of enriching it and of developing in it the power of enriching itself. This process may be the result of various agents. These may be non-intellectual or even inanimate. Thus the child is taught that a cat scratches or that fire burns. This kind of education we more commonly call experience, and we more correctly speak of its effect rather than of its purpose. Education given by intellectual agents, human beings, may be either formal or informal. The boundaries between the two are not strict, but the distinction is clearly observable. Formal education is given by persons who dedicate themselves, either entirely or in part, to that activity. They are the 'teachers' of every description. Informal education is given by all sorts of persons who come into contact with others. The most obvious and outstanding example is that given by parents to their children. (This, incidentally, often crosses the border-line and becomes formal).

When we approach the subject of education in any particular country, we are, of course, mainly concerned with formal education. But we can only commence our study of this at the point when history proper, namely the written record of the past, begins. True, we may find there information going back to long before the actual date of writing. But we ultimately come to the point in time at which all record of formal education ceases. Yet we know that informal education had been going on as long as man existed in the country which we are considering, and we may even surmise that formal education existed before the earliest record of it.

Hence, in making a survey of education, although our work proper begins with the first written records, it is in place to take a brief look at the long period before such records, to consider what evidence we have of man's growth in knowledge during it, to endeavour to discern whatever we can of the various agents, non-intellectual and intellectual, which influenced it, and to fix, with some degree of certainty, the point at which formal education is first discernible.

We shall see later that written records in Ireland commence about the beginning of the seventh century. We have only a handful of manuscripts actually written at that date, but philologists can assign to it the original composition of a considerable number of later ones. Some of these seem to give a more or less accurate, though fragmentary account of events in Ireland as early as the second century B.C. Before that date it is archaeology which comes to our assistance, revealing to us the way of life of our remote ancestors, their habitations, their food, their clothing, their ways of hunting, fishing and tilling the earth, their art, their social organization, their religious beliefs (the last two only in vague outline), and giving us some idea of how this way of life developed in successive ages and of the more notable forces which influenced it.

The summary of the findings of archaeology which follows will be a bare outline, not merely because a more full account would be outside the scope of this work, but also because it will be found that, while an immense amount of information is available concerning the intellectual progress discernible, only very scanty conclusions can be drawn from it as to the way in which education was even informally imparted, and almost nothing as to the existence of formal education. Our survey, therefore, must be considered merely as a setting of the stage for the emergence of formal education as chronicled in our earliest documents.

THE STONE AGE

The first men of whom traces have been found in Europe are those of the palaeolithic or old stone age, about 15,000 years ago. To these metals were unknown, their tools were of stone, bone, horn or wood, and they lived by hunting. No traces of them have been found in Ireland. The first men of whom we do find traces are those of the mesolithic, or middle stone age, about 6,000 B.C., who crossed from Scandinavia to Britain and thence to Ireland. By that time, the recession of the ice age had brought about dense afforestation. The wild deer and horses which had freely roamed the plains had been reduced in numbers, and the density of the forests restricted the movements of the newcomers to the rivers and sea and lake shores, where they could find food. Around Lough Neagh and near rivers and lakes in Roscommon, Limerick and Carlow, traces of their flint instruments have been found, but none of their habitations, which must have been primitive. They had no knowledge of domestic animals, of agriculture or pottery, and their clothing was probably made from the skins of wild animals.

NEOLITHIC AGE

About 3,000 B.C. new settlers, spreading from the Middle East through France, the Low Countries and Britain, began to arrive in Ireland, the men of the neolithic age, still users of stone implements, but differing greatly from their predecessors, since their tools were more perfect. They had learned to cultivate the soil, to clear the forests, to use animals for domestic purposes, cattle, sheep, pigs, dogs, and to manufacture articles of pottery.

Specimens of their tools and pottery (the latter in very small quantities) have been found in various parts of the country, but only at Lough Gur in Co. Limerick are there traces of their habitations, made of walls of turf sods and roofed with rushes. Here, in addition to stone axes and pottery, have been found implements of bone and stone which show that they were acquainted with the arts of spinning wool for clothing and of grinding grain, and also ornaments, beads of bone and stone and bracelets of lignite.

These neolithic men were also the builders of the great stone burial places which are found in Sligo, Meath, the valley of the Boyne and the mountains of Dublin and Wicklow. Little is known of the religious beliefs of the people of this age, but the fact that pottery, beads and tools have been found in these tombs together with the cremated bones of the dead, is generally accepted as a proof that some belief in a future life was then held.

BRONZE AGE

By about 2,000 B.C. the art of extracting metal from ores and moulding it for man's use had become general in Europe and had spread to Ireland. Gold and copper were the first to be discovered, owing to the more noticeable colour of their ores, and almost simultaneously it was found that bronze, an alloy of copper and tin, had a hardness not possessed by pure copper. In the working of Irish copper mines in modern times, traces of prehistoric mining have been come across, and to the early bronze age – up to about 1200 B.C. – belong the bronze axes and gold ornaments, of which many have been discovered and are to be seen in the National Museum, Dublin. This period is also noted for a more elaborate form of pottery, and for the erection of great stone circles which appear to have been connected with religious ceremonies.

In the late bronze age, after 1200 B.C., a greater variety of weapons and tools appears. The most characteristic weapon was a short heavy bronze sword, against which shields of bronze or leather were used. Gold ornaments became more elaborate, for instance the lunula (little moon), a thin crescent shaped plate, or the torque, a collar of gold, formed from a bar twisted in screw fashion and curved into a loop. The ordinary dwelling of this period was probably one of wattle and clay or of rudely hewn logs, surrounded by a stockade to protect the cattle. There was also a peculiar type of dwelling, the crannog, build on an artificial island in a lake. Stone buildings, except of the most rudimentary character, did not come into use until the christian era.

It was probably in this period that the erection of earthen defensive fortifications began, though this continued for many centuries afterwards. These circular earthworks, of which the remains of many thousands[1] are found all over the country, were designated by the name *rath,* and the space enclosed by them was known as the *lios.* They are often called ringforts, but it seems that the majority were not forts in the strict sense, defences against human enemies, but were merely protection for the farmers' flocks and dwellings against wild beasts.

Perhaps a little later may be dated the great stone fortifications, of which perhaps the best-known example is Dún Aonghusa on Inis Mór, the largest Aran island. The name *dún* was a generic one for a fortress, either earthen or stone. The latter was also known as *caiseal* or *cathair.*

IRON AGE. THE CELTS

Meanwhile the use of iron was growing, and about 600 B.C. we find established in central Europe iron-using peoples, speaking a Celtic language, who spread west to Spain, east to Asia Minor and north to Britain and Ireland.[2] In Ireland iron gradually began to be used for all weapons and tools, bronze being mainly reserved for ornament only. The new iron tools made wood more easily worked, and it was more generally used for cauldrons, cups, bowls, pails, canoes, probably even for sea-going vessels. But the use of iron made little change in the economy. The people were mainly farmers. Most of the open land was pasture, but there was considerable tillage, as is shown by the different types of quern for grinding corn which are found in every district.

The Celts were to dominate the country for over a thousand years. The earlier inhabitants, of course, survived, but, by the time of the advent of Christianity in the 5th century, they had taken on the Celtic culture and the Celtic language. The name Gaelic, applied to this culture and language, originated in the fourth century B.C., when the Irish began raiding Roman Britain. The Romans called them *Scotti* and the Britons called them *Gwyddyl.* The Irish adopted this Welsh name for themselves, and gave it the form *Goidil,* which in early modern Irish became Goidhil, modern Irish Gaedhil.[3]

PRIMITIVE APPRENTICESHIP

Whilst the foregoing archaeological findings give us a great deal of information about the steady increase in human knowledge in prehistoric Ireland, it must be acknowledged that they provide us with only the slightest and most general conclusions as to the manner in which that knowledge was acquired and transmitted. We must, of course, conclude that from the earliest ages there existed some form of apprenticeship or analogous form of master-pupil relationship. This at first would have existed only between parents and children, or at most between the older and younger members of local communities. These were largely self-supporting, and the various crafts, the manufacture of articles in wood and leather, basket-work, pottery and the making of primitive furniture and agricultural instruments, would have been handed on from generation to generation.

SPECIALIZATION

Perhaps the earliest indication of some form of specialized craftsmanship is found in the 'factories' for the manufacture of stone axes and other implements. The best known of these is at Tievebulliagh, Co. Antrim, but others have been found at Culban, Co. Derry and in Co. Leitrim and Co. Meath. It might be argued that these 'factories' are merely evidence of the existence in a particular place of large quantities of suitable stones, but the quantity of implements found in various stages of completion suggests the continued presence of workers devoted largely to this craft.

The colonization of Ireland by neolithic man introduced a wide range of fresh knowledge concerning agriculture, the sowing and harvesting of crops, the domesticating of animals and use of their products, the clearing of forests to provide more arable land and pasture. But it made no change in the self-supporting way of life of the people, and hence none in the way of transmission of knowledge.

THE SMITHS

Another new and wide field of knowledge was opened by the coming to Ireland of men conversant with the use of metals, and this brought about far-reaching social changes. In the later bronze age there are found clear indications of the emergence of the first definite specialists, the smiths. The remains of their workshops indicate that they travelled from place to place in response to the need for them, and that their numbers grew rapidly as the quantity of available metal increased. Obviously this would have led to the creation of a more formal system of apprenticeship than had hitherto been known. Its results are clearly seen in the increasing excellence of artistry and craftsmanship in succeeding ages; and the more advanced processes adopted by the metal-workers, casting in sand, wax or metal moulds, welding, soldering, repoussé and embossed work.

Furthermore, the existence of such a body of specialists influenced profoundly the lives of those among whom they lived. For the first time it became necessary to grow surplus crops and to produce surplus hides for the feeding and clothing of the smiths. Large numbers of workers also were drawn away from agricultural pursuits to devote themselves to a variety of occupations connected with the extraction, processing and distributions of metals; miners, transport workers, roadmakers, traders both within the country and outside it, all handing on to the next generation the specialized knowledge of their various occupations.

The discovery of metals had other notable effects besides the creation of specialist employment. It provided for man a greater mastery of the earth's products as a result of the use of larger and more serviceable tools. In the Iron Age it has been noted that there is a great increase in the quantity found of personal ornaments of bronze combined with enamel and glass, which seems to indicate a higher degree of prosperity and a greater amount of leisure. Again, in the same period a great advance seems to have been made in the use of wood. The new tools made for greater ease and better craftsmanship in the making of cups, bowls, dishes, otter and deer-traps, spindles, canoes, specimens of all of which have been found in considerable numbers.

INFLUENCE OF OTHER CULTURES

Now and again, experts have been able to detect, in varying degrees of certainty, the influence of other cultures on that of prehistoric Ireland. Thus, some have found Aegean and Scandinavian influences in the tumuli of New Grange. In the late bronze age it has been noted that in the north-eastern part of the country designs are found obviously influenced by those of the English mountain range system, whereas in the west, south and midlands, the influences come from Iberia, Brittany or the extreme south of England.

But, as we have already acknowledged, all these evidences of educative influences in prehistoric Ireland, whether formal, informal or merely resulting from the impact of inanimate forces, are exceedingly scanty and of the most general kind. Nevertheless, it is clear that they form an essential propaedeutic to our study, since it is from them that we become acquainted with the content of man's knowledge at the moment when in ancient Ireland the records of its transmission begin.[4]

ii. THE DRUIDS

THE BOOK OF INVASIONS

Now let us see what history proper, that is written history, has to tell us about the earliest teachers of Ireland. There is an ancient chronicle, purporting to give the origins of the Irish race, *Lebor Gabála Erenn,* the Book of the Takings, or Invasions of Ireland. Large fragments of this work are found in the *Book of Leinster,* the *Book of Lecan* and the *Book of Ballymote,* and about the year 1630 a version of it was compiled at the monastery of Lisgoole in Co. Fermanagh by the Franciscan scholar, Brother Michael O'Clery and his helpers, Fearfasa O'Mulconry, Cucoigry O'Clery, Cucoigry O'Duigenan and Gillapatrick O'Luinín. They drew on ancient books now lost, most of which were written about A.D. 1,000, but contained traditions going much further back.[5]

Lebor Gabála is a mixture of prose and verse, and evidently had a pedagogic purpose. The verses are obviously a mnemonic summary of the facts contained in the prose passages. This chronicle was widely known from the Middle Ages on. It was relied on by the Annalists and by Keating to supply the beginnings of Irish history. Part of O'Clery's version was published by Macalister and MacNeill in 1916, and in 1938–41 Macalister published a critical edition and translation of the entire work, based on the various redactions.[6]

Having summarized the history of the world from Adam to the time of Christ, *Lebor Gabála* goes on to enumerate the various 'invasions' or immigrations by which Ireland was populated. About 300 years after the Deluge, one Parthalon with his followers came to Ireland from Greece. Three centuries later came Nemid and his three sons from Scythia. They were shortly harassed by the Fomorians, a race of pirates. In a great battle both races were almost exterminated, but three Nemidian leaders escaped. Beothach with his followers went to northern Europe, Simeon Breac to Greece, Britan Mael to the island of Anglesey. The descendants of the first two returned eventually to Ireland, those of Simon Breac under the name of Firbolgs, then those of Beothach under the name of Tuatha Dé Danann. The latter established themselves as masters of most of the country at the great battle of Moytura, near Cong in County Mayo.

The last colonization of Ireland was by the Milesians (sons of Miledh) who were said to have come from Spain about 1,530 B.C. and conquered the ruling Tuatha Dé Danann. From the three sons of Mileadh, Heremon, Heber and Ir, all the royal clans of later Ireland were descended.

It is impossible to decide how much of this account of the early immigrations is pure romance, invented by writers of the Christian age to give to the Irish people a respectable background of antiquity comparable to that provided by the epics of Greece and Rome, and how much is based on real events, however coloured by poetic fancy.

It is, however, not improbable that the Milesians of the chronicles were identical with the Celts, and that the Spain from which they came was a term loosely used to designate any lands beyond the sea. If this is true, the ancient tradition, at least at this stage, would coincide with the findings of archaeologists.[7]

What interests us in these records of the most ancient times is the uniform mention of men entitled Druids. The probable derivation of the name is from two Celtic roots *dru,* abundance, superior, excess, and *vid* knowledge. The old Irish form was *druí* (modern Irish *draoi*), of which the dative was *druid* corresponding to the English druid.[8]

Parthalon is said to have brought with him three druids, the roots of whose names signify Intelligence, Knowledge, Inquiry.[9] The Nemidians had druids who pitted their spells against those of the Fomorians.[10] The druids of the Tuatha Dé Danann cast a pall of darkness over the druids of the Firbolgs, so that their own people could settle without interference on the lands of Ireland.[11] On their journey from Spain, Caicher, the chief druid of the Milesians, revealed to them that Ireland was their destination. 'What place is that "Ireland"?', asked the young prince Lamfhind, son of the chief, Agnomain. 'Further than Scythia it is', said Caicher. 'It is not ourselves who shall reach it, but our children at the end of three hundred years from today.'[12]

THE RED BRANCH CYCLE

Coming now to the point at which legend becomes more closely linked with authentic history, we find the events in what is called the 'Heroic' or 'Ultonian' cycle of tales, since it deals mainly with the heroes of Ulster. It is also called the 'Red Branch' cycle, from the name of one of the palaces of King Conor Mac Nessa, which was also applied to his followers, the Heroes of the Red Branch (known commonly but misleadingly, under the influence of the poet Moore, as 'Red Branch Knights'). The civilization depicted in these tales is that of the late Iron Age, which dates from the fifth century B.C. on, and is known as La Tène from the name of a famous site in Switzerland. It probably reached Ireland in the second century B.C.[13]

The greatest and longest of these sagas is *Táin Bó Cuailnge,* the Cattle-raid of Cooley, a district of Ulster situated in the present county of Louth, into which Oilioll and Medb (Meadhbh) king and queen of Connacht, led their followers to carry off the famous Dun Bull. This epic tale was probably first written down in the seventh or eighth century, but may have been transmitted orally during several preceding centuries. The oldest manuscript of it which we possess (an incomplete one) is found in *Lebor na hUidre,* the *Book of the Dun Cow,* compiled about A.D. 1100, and preserved in the Royal Irish Academy. There is a complete version of the *Táin* in the *Book of Leinster,* compiled only fifty years later than *Lebor na hUidre,* and preserved in the library of Trinity College, Dublin. Both of these invaluable sources for the study of ancient Irish literature will be considered in due course.

In *Lebor na hUidre,* the *Book of Leinster* and in various other collections there are many stories which are either foretales to or sequels of *Táin Bó Cuailnge,* or which are woven around the same personages as figure in it, and also a number of miscellaneous tales. Many of these are described in detail by O'Curry[14] and Hyde,[15] and a full list of the readily available translations is given by the latter. In the *Book of Leinster* there is a list of the types of these tales which the various classes of *filid* had to know. They are thus classified: Destructions and Preyings, Courtships, Battles, Caves, Navigations, Tragedies or Deaths, Expeditions, Elopements, Conflagrations, Irruptions, Visions, Loves, Hostings, Migrations. A list is then given of some two hundred of such tales.[16]

In these sagas of the heroic age we find again constant mention of the druids. It may be noted here that scholars have been divided in their opinions as to the historical value of these ancient tales. In the nineteenth century it was generally held that, though generously embellished with imaginative details, they were based on actual events in the lives of actual personages. Modern scholars generally hold that they are pure romance. But all acknowledge that the picture they draw of Irish civilization as it existed shortly before the Christian era is a correct one, and agrees in many points with what is known of the civilization of the neighbouring Gauls and Britons before the Roman invasion.[17] It may be accepted therefore that the druids so constantly mentioned in these sagas, however imaginary are the events in which they figure, played a real part in ancient Irish civilization, the main features of which can be to some extent discerned.

One of the earliest appearances of the druids is in the story of Eochaid Airem, king of Ireland about 100 B.C., and his queen Etain, *Tochmarc Etaine,* the Wooing of Etain. A mysterious stranger appeared at the court of Tara, and spirited the queen away by a trick. The king sent his chief Druid, Dallan, to find her. 'And the Druid deemed it a grevious thing that Etain should be hidden from him for the space of one year, and thereupon he made three wands of yew; and upon the wands he wrote an ogham; and by the keys of wisdom that he had, and the ogham, it was revealed to him that Etain was in the fairy mound of Bri Leith,' [a hill lying to the west of Ardagh, in Co. Longford], and that Midir, one of the Tuatha De Danaan and, according to one version, her former husband, had borne her away.[18]

The greatest figure in the *Táin* is the nephew of King Conor Mac Nessa, Cú Chulainn, who withstood the invasion of Ulster by the forces of the other four provinces of Ireland. It is related how, as a boy, he was invested with his arms, 'two spears and a sword and a shield', whereupon the king's druid, Cathbad, uttered the prophecy that 'a boy who took arms on this day would be splendid and renowned, but short-lived and transient.' To which the young hero replied: 'It is a wonderful thing if I am but one day and one night in the world, provided that my fame and my deeds live after me.'[19]

The wooing by Cú Chulainn of Emer, the daughter of Forgall, Monarch of Lusk, in the present Co. Dublin, is one of the romantic tales contained in the *Lebor na hUidre.* Cú Chulainn later, under the influence of a fairy spell, deserted his wife for 'Fand of renowned beauty.' Emer at first contemplated direct action and 'had knives made for her to kill the maiden.' But she thought better of this, and appealed to King Conchobar, who sent a band of poets 'and the druids of Ulster' to arrest Cú Chulainn. He endeavoured to resist, but 'the druids gave him a drink of forgetfulness. The moment he drank the drink, he did not remember Fand and all the things he had done. There were, too, drinks of forgetfulness of her jealousy given to Emer, for she was in no better condition.'[20]

On one occasion when, as it happened, Cú Chulainn lay grievously ill at the royal palace of Emain Macha, 'there was, now, a meeting of the four great provinces of Erinn held at this time to see if they could find a person whom they would select, to whom they would give the sovereignty of Erinn', vacant for seven years. The choice was made by the magical means of a 'bull-feast'. One of the assembly ate of the flesh and broth of a bull. He fell asleep and 'a charm of truth was pronounced on him by four Druids'; and he saw in a dream the shape of the man who should be made king, a youth with two red stripes about his body, who was standing at the sick-bed of a man in Emain Macha. This proved to be Lugaidh Reo-Derg (the red-striped) who was the pupil of Cú Chulainn and at the moment was 'solacing his tutor'.[21]

DRUIDS IN THE CHRISTIAN ERA

In the chronicles of the early ages of christianity in Ireland, references to the druids are frequent. The *Tripartite Life of St. Patrick,* so-called because it contains three semi-historical homilies on the saint, is a document dating from at latest the tenth century, and, as is usual in these medieval writings, embodying traditions of a much earlier age. In the seventeenth century the Franciscan scholar Colgan had in his possession three very ancient copies of this work which have been lost. The oldest surviving Ms., in the British Museum, dates from the fourteenth or fifteenth century. It was edited with a translation by Dr. Whitley Stokes in 1887.[22]

In this ancient history of St. Patrick it is related that the saint came to Ireland in the fifth year of the reign of 'a certain fierce heathen king' Loegaire, son of Niall, who had his royal residence at Tara. He had at his court druids of shom the chief were named Lochru and Lucatmael. They foretold that 'an evil-lawed prophet would come hither over sea to their land...and that he would cast the kings and lords out of their realm, and would destroy all the images of the idols'. Seeing in vision the tonsured head of this interloper, they nicknamed him 'adzehead'.

> Adzehead will come over a furious sea
> His mantle head-holed, his staff crook-headed...
> Adzehead will come who will build cities,
> Who will consecrate churches, pinnacled music-houses,
> Many conical caps [of belfries], a realm round croziers'.[23]

The king, with the druids, goes out to kill Patrick, but Lochru, at the prayer of the saint, is raised in the air and dashed to the ground. The other druid, Lucatmael, attempts to poison Patrick, and brings down darkness over the land. Patrick then challenges the druid to a contest in power. A hut is built, into which enter the druid, clad in Patrick's chasuble, and Benen, the saint's disciple, clad in the druid's tunic. The hut is set on fire. Benen is unscathed, but the druid's tunic is destroyed. The druid perishes, but Patrick's chasuble is untouched by the flames.[24]

All these marvels are recounted in almost identical words in another ancient homily on St. Patrick, that contained in the *Lebor Brecc*.[25]

Then there is the well-known story how St. Patrick 'when the high-tide of Easter drew nigh', thought there was no better place to celebrate it than at Tara' the chief abode of the idolatory and druidism of Ireland.' Loegaire, with other kings and chiefs, had come to celebrate 'the high-tide of the heathen, to wit, the feast of Tara.' At the bidding of the king's druids, all fires were extinguished, and it was forbidden, under pain of death, to kindle any fire before the pagan fire was lighted on the hill of Tara, But Patrick 'struck the pascal fire' at *Ferta Fer Féice* (The Graves of Fiacc's men) near Slane, whereupon the druids warned the king that 'unless it is quenched on the night on which it was made, it will not be quenched till doomsday'.[26]

CHAPTER 2

THE EARLIEST TEACHERS (continued)

    i. The Druids of Gaul
    ii. The Irish Druids

i. THE DRUIDS OF GAUL

Who, then, were these druids? It may be remarked at the outset that we are helped in answering this question by the fact that druidism is found flourishing among the Celts of Gaul[1] for at least three centuries before the Christian era.[2] Much information is given concerning it by Greek and Latin writers in the first century B.C. and after. It is obvious that druidism came to Ireland with the Celtic invaders, and must have preserved many of the characteristics which it displayed in its country of origin, though, as will be seen, certain differences developed.[3]

The chief authors who have written about the druids of Gaul are Posidonius, (c. 135 – c. 50 B.C.), Julius Caesar (102 – 44 B.C.), Strabo (c. 63 B.C. – after A.D. 12), Diodorus Siculus (flourished under Julius Caesar and Augustus, lived to at least 21 B.C.), Pomponius Mela (flourished c. A.D. 43) and Lucan (c. 39–65 A.D.). Of these Caesar is the most informative, but there are evidences that he and other later writers drew upon the work of Posidonius.[4]

THE LEARNED CLASS

These writers are unanimous in depicting the druids as the learned class of the Celts of Gaul, philosophers and theologians. Pomponius Mela calls them 'teachers of wisdom' who 'profess to know the size and shape of the world, the movements of the heavens and of the stars, and the will of the gods'.[5] Caesar seems to echo the words of Pomponius when he describes the druids as holding 'many discussions as touching the stars and their movements, the size of

the universe and of the earth, the order of nature, the strength and
the powers of the immortal gods'.[6] We must remember, however,
that Caesar had lived long in Gaul and was an accurate observer,
and hence must have been satisfied that this description was confirmed by what he himself had heard and possibly witnessed. Strabo
states that 'the druids, in addition to natural philosophy, study
also moral philosophy',[7] whilst Diodorus Siculus calls them
'philosophers and theologians who are held in much honour.'[8]

LAWYERS AND JUDGES

The druids were, however, not merely scholars. They were also
lawyers and judges. According to Caesar, 'it is they who decide in
almost all disputes, public and private, and if any crime has been
committed...or there is any dispute about succession or boundaries,
they also decide it, determining rewards and penalties.'[9] Strabo
agrees that 'they are entrusted with the decision, not only of private
disputes, but of public disputes as well,' and adds that 'in former
times they even arbitrated cases of war.'[10]

DRUIDS NOT PRIESTS

Many writers, both past and recent, have represented the druids
of Gaul as being priests.[11] This view, however, appears to be based
either on a preconceived notion or else on a doubtful interpretation
of two passages from Caesar. In one of these he states that the druids
'are concerned with divine worship, the due performance of sacrifice,
public and private, and the interpretation of ritual questions'[12] and
in the other that the Gauls 'sacrifice human victims or vow to do
so, employing the druids as ministers for such sacrifice'.[13] The first
passage need mean no more than that the druids were commonly
witnesses at sacrifices (*rebus divinis intersunt*). The second may mean
that the druid who was present was commonly called upon to
immolate the victim. It need not necessarily mean that such
immolation was an essential function of the druid. This interpretation is strongly borne out by the fact that nowhere in the
classical writings are the druids referred to as priests.[14]

From what has been recorded, however, it is clear that the druids
were much concerned with religion, both in theory and practice. It
is possible that some modern writers who refer to them as priests
use the word merely in this loose sense, not in the strict sense of
offerers of sacrifice or ministers of liturgy.[15]

PRETERNATURAL POWERS

The druids are generally represented as being endowed with
preternatural powers, divination: a general term for the discovery
of the unknown; prophecy: the foretelling of future events; augury:

the discovery of the unknown or future events by means of some material phenomenon, such as the flight of birds. It is, however, notable that no great stress is laid on this characteristic of the Gaulish druids. Caesar, for instance, does not allude to it. Those writers who do so pass over it rapidly and without giving details. Timagenes, a Greek historian of Alexandria, who wrote in the first century B.C., speaks of the druids' 'searchings into secret and sublime things'.[16] Cicero asserts that Divitiacus, the chief of the Aedui and a close friend of Caesar, was a druid and given to 'the practice of divination'.[17] And in the 1st century A.D., we have Tacitus who represents the druids of Britain as encouraging their people to resist the conquering Romans 'with the prophetic utterances of an idle superstition',[18] and Dio Chrysostom, who tells us that the druids 'concern themselves with divination and all branches of wisdom'.[19]

ORGANIZATION

Caesar is the only writer who speaks of the druids as an organized body. There is a chief druid 'who has the highest authority among them'. At his death, he is succeeded by some other prominent druid, by voting if there are several of equal standing. Once a year, they meet in conclave. 'Thither assemble from every side all that have disputes, and they obey the decisions and judgments of the druids.'[20]

DRUIDS THE SOLE LEARNED CLASS

A number of the classical writers seem to indicate that among the Gauls there were other intellectual classes besides the druids. Strabo distinguishes the bards 'singers and poets', the *vates* (*ouateis*), 'diviners and natural philosophers', the druids who 'in addition to natural philosophy, study also moral philosophy'.[21] According to Diodorus Siculus, the three classes are bards 'composers of verses', druids 'philosophers and theologians' and diviners, 'who tell the future by watching the flight of birds and by observation of the entrails of victims'.[22] Ammianus Marcellinus, citing Timagenes, has the same classification as Strabo: bards, who celebrate the deeds of great men 'in epic verse accompanied by the sweet strains of the lyre', *euhages* (the *'vates'* of Strabo), who 'explain the high mysteries of nature', and druids 'men of great talent...uplifted by searchings into secret and sublime things.'[23]

In spite of the unanimity of these writers as to the existence of three distinct learned classes, it is more probable that there was in reality only one class, the druids, and that the distinction existed only between the various functions they exercised. This is the view of Kendrick, who discusses the matter fully and concludes 'that these names were originally synonymous and referred to a single class of people'. He points out that in the extracts from these various writers 'the functions of druid, diviner and bard are inextricably mixed.'[24] There is, in addition the significant fact that Caesar speaks of only one intellectual class.

MAGICIANS

In the popular concept of the druids much prominence is given to their power of magic, a mysterious ability to transform the things of nature, or to use them to produce more than ordinary effects. It is remarkable that this power is not alluded to at all by the earlier writers. It is Pliny who first gives prominence to it and he is imitated by his successors. The picture drawn by Pliny is probably the most familiar, the constant meeting of druids in groves of oak trees, cultivated for the sake of the mistletoe which grows upon them, the ritual cutting of the mistletoe with a golden sickle by the white-robed priest, and the sacrificial slaughter of two white bulls. 'They believe', says Pliny 'that the mistletoe, taken in drink, imparts fecundity to barren animals, and that it is an antidote for all poisons'.[25]

Pliny has other instances of the magic practised by the druids, herbs which must be gathered in certain ways and which protect both men and cattle from 'every kind of evil'.[26] His most startling story is of a species of serpent's egg, which must be caught only in a cloak and may be tested 'by seeing if it floats against the current of a river, even though it be set in gold'. This remarkable egg, a specimen which Pliny claims to have seen, 'is said to ensure success in law-suits and a favourable reception with princes'.[27]

Pliny is alone in giving details of the magical powers of the druids, though they are alluded to by some other writers. Hippolytus, for instance, in the early 3rd century describes the druids as 'seers, prophets and magicians'.[28]

The general view of modern scholars is that the marvels described by Pliny are simply 'travellers' tales', and that the tendency of the later Roman writers to emphasise the magical powers of the druids was due to the growing hostility of Rome towards them and the desire to denigrate them. Yet the evidence available goes to show that, in the period of their decline, the druids did dabble in magic as a substitute for the authority they had formerly held as men of learning and administrators of the law.

EDUCATORS

From what has been established as to their character, it is obvious that the druids must have taken steps to hand on their learning to their successors. It is remarkable that very few of the Greek and Latin writers who deal with the druids have anything to say about them as educators. However, the testimony of Caesar is clear that they imparted education not only to their own neophytes, but also to others. Having mentioned that they were exempt from taxation and military service, he goes on to say:

'Tempted by these great rewards, many young men assemble of their own accord to receive their training, many are sent by friends and relations. Report says that in the schools of the druids they learn by heart a great number of verses, and therefore some persons remain twenty years under training'.[29]

Much the same account of the druids as educators is given about the middle of the first century by Pomponius Mela – his words, indeed may have been borrowed from Caesar.

'They teach many things to the nobles of Gaul in a course of instruction lasting as long as twenty years, meeting in secret either in a cave or in a secluded dale'.[30]

This secrecy may have been due to the Roman repression of the druids. On the other hand, it may be an invention of Pomponius Mela, who, like the other later writers, tends to discredit the druids by surrounding them with an atmosphere of mysterious gloom.

THEIR TEACHING

It has already appeared that the teaching of the druids comprised both natural and moral philosophy, the nature of the universe and of the gods. Little is known of their secular teaching, but almost all who have written about them declare that their central moral teaching was the immortality of the soul. Caesar states that 'the cardinal doctrine which they seek to teach is that souls do not die, but after death pass from one to another',[31] Strabo, that they assert 'that men's souls and also the universe are indestructible'.[32] According to Pomponius Mela, 'one of their dogmas has come to common knowledge, namely, that souls are eternal and that there is another life in the infernal regions.'[33]

Earlier writers merely state in general that the druids teach the immortality of the soul. Later authors hold that this immortality involved transmigration. Diodorus Siculus, writing about 8 B.C. says: 'The Pythagorean doctrine prevails among them (the Gauls), teaching that the souls of men are immortal and live again for a fixed number of years in another body.'[34] Lucan, writing early in the first century A.D. thus addresses the druids: 'And it is you who say that the shades of the dead seek not the silent land of Erebus, and the pale halls of Pluto; rather, you tell us that the same spirit has a body again elsewhere, and that death if what you sing is true, is but the mid-point of long life.'[35]

It is, however, noteworthy that there is no indication anywhere of any inculcation by the druids of ethics or morality. This is, of course, merely an argument from silence, but its cogency is increased by the fact that the druids' teaching concerning a life to come was in no way connected with the idea of reward or punishment.[36]

ORAL TEACHING

Caesar alone gives the information that the teaching of the druids was entirely oral. His statement is confirmed by the fact that Origen, in the third century A.D. remarks that nothing survives of their writings. Caesar's account of their teaching is of interest and worth citing in full.

'And they do not think it proper to commit these utterances to writing, although in almost all other matters, and in their public and private accounts, they make use of Greek letters. I believe they have adopted the practice for two reasons – that they do not wish the rule to become public property, nor those who learn the rule to rely on writing and so neglect the cultivation of the memory; and in fact, it does usually happen that the assistance of writing tends to relax the diligence of the student and the action of the memory'.[37]

ii. THE IRISH DRUIDS

Approaching the study of the Irish druids, we at once notice a striking difference between what we know of them and what we know of their Gaulish contemporaries. Our knowledge of the latter comes entirely from outside observers, Greek and Latin writers, whereas our knowledge of the former is entirely from native sources. This fact renders our knowledge of the Irish druids the more reliable, since it is based on direct testimony, but, on the other hand renders it less satisfactory, since the Irish writers were not concerned to give to outsiders a systematic account of the druidic system, but merely incorporated into their writing, according to their literary or historical needs, the doings and sayings of particular druids. O'Curry, writing a century ago, emphasized the scattered nature of the available information, 'vast numbers of allusions to the Druids to be found in our older Mss., which...it would be quite impossible to unfold at full length.'[38] Since his day, many texts have been edited and made more easily available, yet our knowledge of the druids, though fuller than a hundred years ago, still remains fragmentary.

STRESS ON THE PRETERNATURAL

The first impression made on us as we gather together the scattered references to the druids in ancient Irish literature is the stress laid on their powers of divination, prophecy and magic. Thus, at first sight, the picture given to us of druidism in Ireland seems to differ from that given of druidism in Gaul, in which these powers receive comparatively little emphasis.

We have already seen how these preternatural powers are ascribed to the druids in the oldest traditions contained in the *Lebor Gabála,* the *Táin Bó Cuailnge* and the early chronicles of Christianity. The same emphasis prevails throughout the ancient writings. O'Curry and Joyce devote many pages to these preternatural activities of the druids, their use of the 'fluttering wisp' of straw or grass, which, flung into the face of a victim, rendered him insane,[39] their power of saving an army from defeat by surrounding it with a mysterious fire,[40] the showers of fire they could call down,[41] their predictions from the observation of clouds,[42] from rods of yew inscribed with Ogam letters, from dreams, from their knowledge of lucky and unlucky days.[43]

As we have already seen, the druids persisted as a recognizable body during at least the first century of the Christian era in Ireland. It is noteworthy that in this period also they are represented as diviners and magicians.

In the life of St. Ciarán of Clonmacnois it is related that one day before his birth, his parents, Beoit and Darerca were riding in a chariot, and the noise of the wheels was heard by Lugbrann, the druid of Crimthann, king of Ireland. The druid called to some servants of the king who stood by: 'Look, my lads, who is there in the chariot: for here is "noise of chariot under king" [a common proverbial phrase]'. Seeing only Beoit and Darerca in the chariot, 'the lads laughed at the druid', who rebuked them. 'The child that lies in that woman's womb will be a mighty king: and as the sun shineth among the stars of heaven, so will he shine on earth in miracles and marvels that cannot be told'.[44]

Druids figure prominently in the early life of St. Brigid. On one occasion her father Dubthach was driving in his chariot with his bondmaid Broicsech who was to be the mother of Brigid. They passed the house of 'a certain druid named Maithgen' who prophesied that the bondmaid would 'bring forth a daughter, conspicuous, radiant, who will shine like a sun among the stars of heaven.' Yielding to the jealousy of his wife, Dubthach sold the bondmaid to a poet, who in turn sold her to a druid of Tirconnell. This druid made a great feast to which he invited the king of Conaill whose wife was expecting a child. The druid foretold that 'the child which should be brought forth on the morrow at sunrise, and neither within the house or without, would out-go every child in Ireland.' That night the queen bore a dead child, but in the morning at sunrise, the bondmaid bore a child when one of her footsteps was outside the house, one within. The child thus born was brought to the presence of the queen's child, who was restored to life. The druid travelled with his bondmaid and her infant into Connaught when, in a dream, he saw 'three clerics in shining garments, who poured oil on the girl's head: and thus completed the order of baptism in the usual manner', giving to the child the name Brigid.

When Brigid was a grown girl, the druid and his wife went one day to the dairy where their daughter was helping her mother, and demanded to have 'a great hamper eighteen hands high to be filled with butter.' The girl had only 'the making of one churning and a half' but, at her prayer, the butter increased so that 'if the hampers which the men of Munster possessed had been given to her, she would have filled them all'. Whereupon the druid freed Brigid's mother, presented to Brigid the butter and cows, which she gave to the poor and needy, received baptism and 'remained until his death in Brigid's company.'[45]

The question naturally arises why in the Irish writings there is this peculiar stress on the preternatural powers of the druids. In the case of the Gaulish druids we find this emphasis only in later writers, and we have consdiered that it may be due either to the fact that, as their power as teachers and judges declined, the druids actually did come to depend more on the supposed preternatural powers, or to the growing hostility of the Romans which led them to represent the druids in the most unfavourable light. It is possible that the Irish druids also suffered a decline in influence and sought to reinforce it by claiming preternatural powers. This would be more likely to have happened on the advent of Christian learning. But it is also possible that the narration of the preternatural gave more scope to the imaginative genius of the early chroniclers, and hence found a greater place in their writings. The question is an obscure one, and does not seem to have been considered by any of the recognized writers on the subject of Irish druidism.

IRISH DRUIDS NOT PRIESTS

We have already seen that, in spite of a few indications to the contrary, the main weight of evidence goes to show that the Gaulish druids were not priests in the strict sense of the word. The matter is even clearer in the case of the Irish druids. A few writers, indeed, refer to them as priests,[46] but do not examine the question fully and give no reasons to justify their view, which is rejected by the vast majority of authoritative scholars. Hyde says: 'The druids, as far as we can ascertain, do not seem to be connected with any positive rites or worship; still less do they appear to have been a regular priesthood.'[47] Joyce, while accepting the view that the Gaulish druids were priests, goes on to say: 'The Irish druids were not; they were merely wizards and learned men.'[48] O'Curry, dealing with the idol-worship of the pre-christian Irish, mentions in particular the great idol called Crom Cruach, which stood in the plain of Magh Slecht (the Plain of Adoration) in Co. Cavan, and which was overthrown by St. Patrick. 'But it is remarkable,' he notes, 'that we find no mention of any connexion between this Idol and the Druids, or any other class of priests, or special idol-servers. We have only record of the people, generally, assembling at times to do honour to the idol creation'.[49] MacNeill indeed holds that 'they interested themselves in matters of religion' but it was 'as experts in theology, not as priests'.[50]

THE LEARNED CLASS

In spite of the stress laid in the ancient histories and romances on the preternatural powers of the druids, it is the universal belief of scholars that they were not by any means mere wizards, but that, like the druids of Gaul, they constituted the learned class of society. According to Joyce, 'In pagan times the druids were the exclusive possessors of whatever learning was then known. They combined in themselves all the learned professions; they were not only druids, but judges, prophets, historians, poets and even physicians.'[51] Hyde gives much the same account of the druids, though with reservations. 'Although Irish literature is full of allusions to the druids, it is extremely difficult to know with any exactness what they were...They are frequently mentioned in Irish literature as ambassadors, spokesmen, teachers and tutors. Kings were sometimes druids, so were poets. It is a word which seems to me to have been, perhaps from the first, used with great laxity and great latitude'.[52] Dr. Healy states that they were 'frequently poets and judges'.[53] MacNeill, having given a summary of the philosphical beliefs of the Gaulish druids, implies that such beliefs were held by the Irish druids. 'Except as regards religion, everything that Caesar tells us about Gaul is found reflected in the learning of the Irish druids.'[54]

It is noticeable, however, that O'Curry, whilst giving copious information about the druids, is more reserved than other writers as to their learning. He disclaims any 'endeavour, at present, to suggest any theory of what exactly constituted our own Druidism in ancient Erinn. Perhaps the time is not come for satisfactory inquiry, either into the nature of the Druidical Philosophy, (or "Religion" if it be proper so to call it), or into the details of the rites and ceremonies used by the Druids.'[55]

It is true that we shall search in vain in the ancient writings for any actual mention of the doctrines of the Irish druids. Nevertheless, the view accepted by scholars seems justified on several grounds. Firstly, as we have seen, druidism came to Ireland from Gaul, and it is obvious that the tradition of learning which came with it must have been preserved and transmitted for at least some generations. Secondly, we not infrequently find references to the druids as teachers. Lastly, as we shall see, it was from the druidical body that the well recognized learned classes of Ireland evolved, the *filid* and the brehons.

TEACHERS

That the Irish druids were teachers is claimed by all who have written on the subject. O'Curry says: 'That the Druids shared largely in the instruction of the youth of Eirinn, of all classes, in ancient times, could be shown from innumerable passages in our old writings.'[56] Hyde states that 'they seem to have been teachers above everything else'.[57] It is curious that neither of these able scholars offers much substantiation of this claim. O'Curry contents himself with two instances, and a promise (not fulfilled) to 'make further allusion to the subject'.

The two instances to druids as teachers given by O'Curry are, however, significant. We have already considered the incident in the *Táin* when the druid Cathbad foretold the great but brief glory of the boy Cú Chulainn. The prelude to this prophecy is as follows.

'Cathbad the druid was teaching his pupils to the northeast of Emain (Emain Macha, the capital of Ulster), and eight pupils of the class of druidic learning were with him. One of them asked what omen and presage was for that day, whether it was good or whether it was will.' Their master then uttered a prophecy about a boy who would take arms that day. This was overheard by the boy Cú Chulainn 'as he was playing south-east of Emain'. He demanded to be invested with arms and the druid then declared that the prophecy referred to him.[58]

The second example given by O'Curry of the druids as teachers comes from christian times. It is the familiar and picturesque story told in the *Tripartite Life of St. Patrick* of the daughters of King Loegaire, Ethne the Fair and Fedelm the Ruddy, one of whom had been put by their father under the tuition of two druids who were brothers, Moel and Caplait.[59] St. Patrick, coming to the palace of Cruachan in Co. Roscommon, was sitting at sunrise with his followers at the well of Cliabach on the slopes of Cruachan. The two princesses, coming to the well, saw the 'assembly of the clerics in white garments with their books before them. And they wondered at the shape of the clerics, and thought they were fairy men or apparitions.' Then, entering into conversation, they learned of the God of the christians, whose power and beauty are reflected in the face of nature, and shortly, together with Moel and Caplait, were converted to the christian faith. The relation of the druids to the princesses is emphasized by the statement that Caplait for some time 'contended against Patrick' for he 'had fostered the second girl.'

In the life of St. Colum Cille contained in the *Book of Lismore,* there is an incident in which a druid is depicted as being, if not precisely a teacher, at least a person competent to advise on education. When the time came for the boy to begin to read, his foster-father Ceallach, a priest, consulted a druid as to when exactly this should be. The druid 'scanned the sky', and ordered that an alphabet (aibghitir) should be written on a cake, which the boy ate 'half to the east of a water, and half to the west of a water'. The druid declared that this foretold the boy's future work. 'So shall this child's territory be, half to the east of the sea, and half to the west of the sea, that is, in Ireland.'[60]

CHAPTER 3

PRE-CHRISTIAN WRITING

IRISH DRUIDS. ORAL TEACHING

We have seen that it is generally accepted that the teaching of the Gaulish druids was purely oral. Caesar, in fact, states that they positively prohibited the committing of their teaching to writing.

It may be taken that the teaching of the Irish druids was, if not entirely, at least almost entirely oral. Nowhere in Irish literature do we find this clearly stated, but it is undeniable for three reasons. Firstly, the druids who accompanied the Celtic invaders of Ireland would have naturally carried on and transmitted to their successors the tradition prevailing in Gaul. Secondly, even if the art of writing were known in Ireland before the coming of St. Patrick – a question with which we shall deal presently – it would have been confined to a very few. Thirdly we have ample documentary proof that the poets, historians and lawyers, who evolved from the druidic order, adhered to the system of oral teaching for centuries after the art of reading and the production of books had become common.

NO PROHIBITION OF WRITING

There is, however, no evidence that the Irish druids positively prohibited the committing of their teachings to writing. The only authority to mention this point specifically is Joyce, who, alluding to the Gaulish tradition, says: 'There is no mention of any such prohibition among Irish druids'.[1] However, the absence of such prohibition is indirectly indicated by the various writers who claim that the art of writing was known in Ireland before the coming of St. Patrick.

USE OF WRITING IN PRE-PATRICIAN TIMES

The alphabet used in Irish writings from the sixth century onwards is a modification of the Roman alphabet. All authorities agree that the general use of this was due to the christian missionaries who accompanied St. Patrick. The question, however, whether the art of writing was known to any of the Irish people in pre-Patrician days is a somewhat complicated one.

First of all, it is quite certain that not very long – about five centuries at most – before the coming of St. Patrick, the Irish used an alphabet known as Ogam, based on the Roman alphabet, but employing completely different lettering. This method of writing will be dealt with later. All that need be said here is that, of its nature, it could be used only for short inscriptions or messages, and could not possibly have been the means of composing anything like formal literature. Ogam writing continued to be used in a limited way for perhaps a couple of centuries of the christian era.

Secondly, there are certain arguments which render it at least probable that writing, other than Ogam, was to some extent practised before the time of St. Patrick. It will be noted that some of these arguments are based on the fact that the Irish had cultural relations with the continent before that time, and hence go to prove that the alphabet used by them was that of the Romans. Other more general arguments merely go to show that they had some form of writing, and prescind from the question whether this was the Latin or some older form which is completely unknown to us.

Hyde holds that 'there were probably in Ireland many persons in the fourth century, or perhaps even earlier, who were acquainted with the art of writing'.[2] He bases his belief on the now generally accepted fact that some christian missionaries were at work in Ireland before St. Patrick.

In support of this general argument, which has considerable cogency, Hyde cites Pelagius and Sedulius, of whom the former taught at Rome about the year 400 and the latter, 'the Irish Virgil' flourished in the first half of the fifth century. It is difficult, however, to see how the intellectual ability of these men throw any more than a most indirect light on the state of learning in Ireland. Pelagius was not born in Ireland, though of Irish descent, and Sedulius if, indeed, an Irishman, pursued his studies in Gaul.

As a positive proof of the existence of writing in pre-christian times, Hyde cites the incident in the *Tripartite Life of St. Patrick* when, previous to the ordeal by fire of the saint's disciple Benen, King Loegaire proposed that the books of the druid Lucatmael and those of Patrick should be cast into water or fire, and their truth tested by their escaping unscathed.[3]

Hyde furthermore states that when 'at a later date, St. Patrick determined upon revising the Brehon law code, the books in which it was written were laid before him'. This incident is related in one version of the *Tripartite Life,* 'evil laws were cast forth from them, and the proper ones arranged',[4] and in the Introduction to the great law tract, the *Senchus Mór.*[5] It will be seen later that the incident is probably a tenth century invention, but in any case, in neither account is there any mention of books being laid before Patrick. In the *Senchus Mór* Patrick and his associates are represented as arranging the laws in a book, but nothing is said about the manner in which they existed previously. Each of the 'professors of the sciences in Erin...exhibited his art before Patrick', but whether orally or in written form is not stated.

Approaching this subject, O'Curry acknowledges that 'it is perhaps impossible now to arrive at any certain conclusion as to the nature of the writing in which the records were kept, and history, poetry, and literature preserved among the Gaedhils of Erinn in the ages which preceded the coming of St. Patrick'. He poses the questions whether the ancient Irish had any knowledge of written characters, and whether we find in the ancient writings specific names for book, parchment, pen, ink, page, etc., either in use or having reference to these early ages. He acknowledges that he has not given to the question enough attention to enable him 'to give anything like a full or satisfactory answer to them'. He then proceeds to the consideration of Ogam writing, on which he is on sure ground.

At the close of this appendix, O'Curry returns to the question which he has left unsolved, namely whether, in addition to the Ogam, the ancient Irish made use of any other form of writing. He concludes that such ancient books, which are only known to us by later references, as the *Culmenn,* the *Saltair of Teamhair* and the *Book of Drom Snechta,* were not written in Ogam, which hardly needs to be proved, as, no matter what material was used, the quantity required could have been prodigious. He inclines to the theory proposed by Hyde that there were indeed writings in existence before the time of St. Patrick 'but that they were written in the popular Roman characters of the time, modified, perhaps, as at present; and that these characters were first brought in by the druids and poets who from time to time travelled in pursuit of their studies to the continent, or attended the many distant foreign expeditions which took place from this country, even previously to the period of the Incarnation.'[6]

O'Curry concludes by citing the passage in the *Tripartite Life of St. Patrick,* already referred to, and a similar passage in the annotations of Tírechán, preserved in the *Book of Armagh,* both of which allude to the books possessed by the druids on their meeting with St. Patrick, and accepts these as confirmation of this belief that the druids not only knew the art of writing, but used it to preserve their lore.[7]

Joyce approaches the subject from a different point of view. He briefly mentions the incident, found in the *Tripartite Life* and in

Muirchu Maccu Machtheni's memoir of St. Patrick, which implies that the druids possessed books, and remarks, with some cogency, that it has additional force from being introduced incidentally.[8] He goes on to the consideration of Ogam, which, he implies, could not have been the vehicle of any extended writing.[9] He then sets out the general considerations which go to show 'that there was some form of written literature before the advent of Christianity'.[10] Firstly, there is the fact that shortly after that event, the Irish scholars began to commit to writing in their own language the historical poems, not only of their own time, but also of long preceding ages. This rapid expansion of writing could hardly have taken place without a fairly good previous knowledge of letters. Secondly, the glosses in Irish found in so many continental manuscripts, dating from the seventh century, show that at least by that time Irish was a fully developed language with an elaborate systematic grammar, and that it had fixed forms for its words and their numerous inflexions. Such a complete system could not have been developed without the use of writing, and could hardly have evolved in the comparatively short period from the coming of Christian learning. Thirdly, there is the existence of the very complicated Irish poetical prosody, with its fifty or more technical terms, showing no trace of Latin or ecclesiastical influence. This, again, would have been impossible without the help of writing.

In confirmation of his view, Joyce quotes the statement of a Christian philosopher of the fourth century Ethicus of Istria, who wrote a cosmography of the world with a view to which he travelled through three continents. The brief record of his visit to Ireland begins thus: 'He hastened to Ireland and remained there some time examining their volumes (*eorum volumina volvens.*)[11]

It will be noted that the arguments put forward by Joyce prescind from the question whether the use of letters before the time of St. Patrick – if it existed – derived from Latin culture or was a completely native growth. Joyce acknowledges indeed that nothing in sacred or secular literature gives 'the least hint as to the characters or sort of writing used in the books of the pagan Irish.'[12]

The theory accepted by O'Curry and Hyde, that the Irish had some knowledge of the Latin alphabet before the coming of St. Patrick, is held by a less-known, but interesting writer, Richard Rolt Brash (d. 1876), a Cork builder and architect, who made a considerable study of Ogam inscriptions. He bases his belief on the fact that there was constant communication between Ireland, Gaul and Britain, and between Munster and South Wales. He also envisages the possibility that, even at that early period, Irish scholars may have learned the art of writing on the continent and brought home manuscripts. This knowledge, however, would have been 'confined to the literati alone, and perhaps to a section of them.'[13]

Healy deals very briefly with this matter. As so many authors do, he cites the passage from the *Tripartite Life* in which mention is made of the 'books' of the druids. He adds an argument not proposed by any other authorities for the possession of the art of writing by the Irish druids. Alluding to the fact mentioned by Caesar that, though the Gaulish druids prohibited the committing of their teachings to writing, they knew the art of writing and used it for other purposes, he concludes: 'We must infer that the Irish druids possessed a similar culture.'[14] This is a slightly different argument from that drawn from the intercourse between the Celts of Ireland and the continent. Its value seems somewhat doubtful. It would depend on several unknown factors, whether, for instance, at the time of the Celtic invasion of Ireland the art of writing was known to the Gaulish druids, as it apparently was in Caesar's time, whether among the druids who accompanied the Celtic invaders there were many who possessed this art, and whether they preserved links with their Gaulish brethren.

Bury's view is cautious and balanced.[15] He holds that although Patrick and his followers gave to the Latin alphabet a new position, it must have been already known to the scattered christian communities who existed previously in Ireland. This view is confirmed by the fact that Ogam is practically identical with the Latin alphabet (though using different signs for the letters), showing that the latter must have been in use when the former was invented (how far before the fifth century we do not know). However, it is not impossible that the Irish had some pre-Roman form of writing. Writing was in use among the Celtic Iberians of Spain and the Celts of Gaul before the Roman conquest. But there is no 'clear and authentic' evidence of its existence among the Irish. Bury therefore holds that 'we cannot say whether the introduction of the Latin script originated a written Irish literature, or only displaced an older form of writing in which a literature existed.' He confesses that 'in the mist which rests over the early history of Ireland this is one of the darkest points.'

Later scholars do not accept the view of O'Curry, Hyde and Joyce. Curtis briefly describes the Ireland to which Patrick came as 'a land that had no written literature'.[16] Flower holds that 'no evidence has ever been produced to prove the existence of writing for literary purposes in Ireland before the coming of Christianity'.[17] Professor Ó Fiaich thinks that 'it is extremely doubtful if our ancestors had any method of writing before his [St. Patrick's] time except the Ogham alphabet.'[18]

CONCLUSIONS

To sum up. Firstly, whether or not the druids had the art of writing in pre-Patrician days, their teaching was largely, if not entirely, oral. Secondly, the Ogam script could not possibly have been used for writings of any considerable length. Thirdly, if there was any method of writing in use prior to the Ogam and Latin alphabets, we know nothing whatever about it. Fourthly, we cannot, however, categorically deny the existence of any such method. The fact that we have no writings, either pagan or christian, from before the time of St. Patrick (with the exception of the Ogam inscriptions), merely shows that Ireland, in this respect, resembles other European countries. In Britain, where writing was generally practised from the Roman occupation on, no manuscript has been preserved from earlier than the eighth century. Fifthly, it seems on the whole probable that there was some limited knowledge of the Latin script before it was made commonly known by the Christian missionaries. The strongest arguments for this view are those put forward by O'Curry, Hyde and Brash, namely the existence of Christian missionaries in Ireland and the intercourse between Ireland and the continent in pre-Patrician days. Joyce's arguments are ingenious, but hardly convincing, the rapid adoption of the Latin script by the Irish, and the existence of elaborate grammatical and poetic rules. It does not seem impossible that a body of men who already had a rich oral literary and legal tradition could have acquired, in the course of a century or so, the art of committing that tradition to writing. Nor does it seem impossible that grammatical and poetic structures could have been evolved orally by scholars accustomed through long and severe training to the oral method of communication. Finally, the argument put forward by the older writers based on the possession of books by the druids is of doubtful value. The instances quoted are chronicled in works written in, at the earliest, the tenth century. It seems impossible to decide definitely that they are statements of an acknowledged tradition and not merely poetic details inserted by the historian.

OGAM

The Ogam alphabet consists of fifteen consonants, in three groups of five, and five vowels. The consonants are indicated by strokes above or below a stem-line or diagonally across it, the vowels by notches in the stem-lines. The Ogams which survive are all carved on stone pillars and the stem-line is usually one of the edges of the pillar.

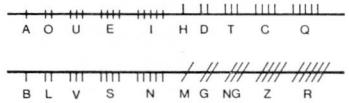

Though the form of the letters is completely original, the letters themselves are taken from the Latin alphabet. This is clear from the fact that they include h and z, which are not needed in writing Irish.[19] The stones on which they are engraved are obviously grave-stones or stones erected to the memory of the dead, and usually give merely the name of the person commemorated, in the genitive case, and his descent. The inscriptions have, therefore, little or no historical value, but they are of great interest to philologists. The language in which they are written is of an older form than that found in the earliest vellum documents, and was possibly archaic even at the time when the stones were erected.

Ogam inscriptions are, as a rule, easily interpreted, since we have two ancient tracts which give a key to the Ogam alphabet. The more valuable of these is included with a treatise on grammar, *Auraicept na n-Éces, The Scholar's Primer,* in the fourteenth century manuscripts, the *Book of Ballymote* and the *Yellow Book of Lecan.* The second tract is found in the twelfth century *Book of Leinster* in a treatise known as *Trefhocal,* a collection of rules for the correction of faulty versification.[20]

Furthermore, a few bilingual inscriptions have been found, one at least in Ireland and several in Wales, in which the same words and names are given in Ogam and in Latin. But centuries of exposure to the weather have rendered many of the inscriptions difficult or totally impossible to decipher.[21]

With few exceptions, each letter of the Ogam alphabet is named from a tree or plant having it as an initial. Thus B=*beith* (birch), C=*coll* (holly), D=*daur* (oak). Hence the alphabet is sometimes referred to in ancient writings as *Beth-luis-nion* from the names of the first three letters B, L, N. Also, since the letters are almost all named from trees, they are called collectively *feada* or 'woods'. It is noteworthy that the order of the letters is totally different from that of the Latin or any other alphabet.[22]

ORIGIN OF THE NAME OGAM

In the treatise on Ogam in the *Book of Ballymote,* the name is asserted to be derived from its inventor, the god Ogma, one of the chiefs of the *Tuatha Dé Danaan.* 'Now Ogma, a man well skilled in speech and in poetry, invented the Ogham'.[23] It has been held by some scholars that the Irish Ogma was identical with the Gaulish god Ogmios, patron of eloquence, of whom a detailed account is given by the second century Greek writer, Lucian. The invention of Ogam by the god is, of course, pure myth. Whether there is any connection at all between Ogam, Ogma and Ogmios is an abstruse question which need not delay us. It is dealt with in detail by Hyde,[24] more briefly by MacNeill, who holds that 'it is impossible to dissociate' the Irish god Ogma and the Gaulish god Ogmios,[25] and by Professor Binchy who believes that the name Ogam 'can hardly be separated from Gaulish Ogmios, Irish Ogma, but the connection is not clear'.[26]

Some three hundred Ogam inscriptions have been discovered, mostly in Cork and Kerry. In Wales, England, Scotland and the Isle of Man another fifty have been found, all in areas where Irish invasions occurred. Those in Scotland are probably the latest in date, as some of them bear Christian symbols.[27]

Ogam inscriptions have been the study of many archaeologists in the past.[28] Amongst these, the most notable and assiduous, though not always the most reliable in his interpretations, was Professor R. A. S. Macalister. In the three parts of his *Studies in Irish Epigraphy* he has recorded and deciphered two hundred and eighty-four Ogams inspected by him in the barony of Corkaguiney, in counties Mayo, Wicklow, Kildare, Cork, Tipperary, Waterford, Kerry, Limerick, Cavan, Offaly and in Scotland and the Isle of Man.[29]

There is almost complete unanimity amongst older and modern authorities that Ogam writing originated in pagan times. Hyde alone seems to dissent when he speaks of the 'yet unproved assumption that Ogam writing is pre-Christian and pagan'.[30] The pagan origin of the inscriptions is indicated by the fact that the name of the dead person's ancestor was often that of a pagan god, and also by the absence of any christian emblem or expression of faith.

In view of the fact that Ogam is based on the Latin alphabet, it is clear that it originated in the later pagan period when some knowledge of Latin culture was beginning to spread. All authorities agree that it lasted on for some time after the coming of christianity.[31] One Ogam, at Church Island, Valentia, Co. Kerry, is imposed on an earlier Christian cross.[32] But with the coming of christianity the Ogam inscriptions apparently fell into bad odour. In some cases, the name of the ancestor, especially if that of a pagan deity, has been effaced.

HISTORICAL RECORDS OF OGAM

In the ancient written records we find constant mention of Ogam writing. Sometimes allusion is made to its use for those obituary inscriptions of which we have examples in the surviving Ogam stones. The longest of the Fenian sagas, though only fragmentary, is *Acallamh na Senórach, The Colloquy with the Ancients,* in which Ossian, son of Finn Mac Cumhaill, and Caoilte, Finn's foster-son are imagined to have met St. Patrick in their extreme old age and to have related to him traditions of the past. Caoilte thus describes the scene after the battle between the Fianna and Clanna Morna under their leader Goll.

'The Fianna came and in excavations of the earth buried those four hundred of Finn's people, the manner in which each one of them was found being with a man of Morna dead under him. Over them their names were written in Ogham, their funeral games were held, and therefore it is that this hill bears the name of *cnoc na laechridhe,* hill of the warriors'.[33]

Again in the *Lebor na hUidre* there is a passage in which Caoilte describes the burial place of Eochaid Airgthech, a usurping king of Ireland in the third century.

'And by his tomb there is a pillarstone, and on the end of the pillar that is in the earth is an Ogham: this is what it says: "Eochaid Airgthech here; Caoilte slew me in an encounter against Finn".'[34]

But there is also mention of Ogam as having been used for purposes other than tomb-inscriptions, and as having been written or carved on materials other than stone. Numerous instances are given by O'Curry and Hyde.[35] Thus in the *Táin* it is related how Cú Chulainn cut from a tree a four-pronged fork, which he then charred, and 'put an Ogam inscription on its side.' This he planted in the way of the advancing army of the men of Ireland, and impaled upon it the heads of four warriors sent to battle with him. This inscribed fork was evidently believed to have some mysterious power. The exiled warrior, Fergus, who fought with the army of Queen Medb, recited over it a lengthy lay in which he exclaimed: 'What inscription is that on its side? Tell us, O druids fair'. King Ailill declared that it would be taboo for the men of Ireland to march on until this fork was removed, a feat which was accomplished by Fergus after superhuman efforts.[36]

Another early mention of Ogam is found in an Ulster story entitled *Loinges Mac nDuil nDermait, The Exile of the sons of Duil Dermait.* These three young men had disappeared mysteriously and Cú Chulainn set out in search of them. On his way, he encountered the son of the king of Scotland who had sailed to Ireland with gifts for King Conchobar Mac Nessa. The prince inscribed on Cú Chulainn's spear an Ogam, by means of which talisman he was enabled to find the island where the youths were held captive.[37]

In the *Book of Leinster* there is found the story of Corc, son of Lughaidh, king of Munster, driven into exile by his father about A.D. 400. The prince took refuge at the court of Feradach, king of Scotland, where he was recognized by Gruibne, the king's poet. The latter noticed that there was an Ogam inscription on the prince's shield and asked him whether he understood it. The prince replied that he did not, whereupon the friendly poet warned him that it must have been inscribed by an enemy, for it contained a message that if Corc arrived by day at the court of Feradach, his head should be struck off before evening, but if he arrived at night, it should be struck off before morning.[38]

Sanas Cormaic, Cormac's Glossary, is a compilation of the ninth or tenth century, generally ascribed to Cormac Mac Cuilennáin, King-bishop of Cashel. This work will be dealt with later. In it the word *fé* is thus explained. 'It was a wooden rod, used by the Gael for measuring corpses and graves...this rod used always be kept in the burial places of the heathen, and it was a horror to everyone even to take it in his hand, and whatever was abominable to them they [the pagans] used to inscribe on it in Ogham'.[39]

It is thus evident that Ogam was commonly used for the writing of brief messages on wood, metal or any other suitable material. Most authorities do not even discuss the question whether it was used for more extended writing, and assume that it was not. The opposite view, however, is held by O'Curry and Hyde.

O'Curry believes that the examples he gives demonstrate that Ogam writing was 'employed to record historical events and even sustained or romantic tales'. The only proofs he puts forward are the frequent references to *Taibhlí Fileadh,* poets' tablets, or *Tamhlorg Fileadh,* poets' staves, and one instance in which the poets of Ulster inscribed the tragic story of Baile, an Ulster prince, and Aillin, granddaughter of the king of Leinster, on *Taibhlí Fileadh* cut from the yew-tree and the apple-tree which sprang up on the graves of the two lovers. O'Curry assumes that these 'tablets' or 'staves' were used for Ogam writing.[40] But in a later passage he gives it as his opinion that the oldest, now lost, books of the Gael were not written in Ogam but 'in the popular Roman characters of the time, modified perhaps, as at present.'[41]

Hyde also makes reference to these poets' tablets or staves and suggests that the poet carried on them 'the whole history and genealogy of his race, and probably the catchwords of innumerable poems and the skeletons of highly-prized narratives'.[42] He cites an instance of the use of the poets' staves even in christian times. In the *Colloquy of the Ancients* it is recorded that St. Patrick was troubled by scruples over the delight he took in listening to the ancient tales of the Fianna, but was reassured by his guardian angels and even encouraged to have these ancient tales recorded '*i támlorgaib filed ocus i mbriatraib ollaman*', which is rendered by O'Grady 'on tabular staffs of poets and in ollaves' words'. Hyde accepts this phrase as indicating the use of Ogam.[43]

Hyde finds positive proof of his view in the concluding words of *The Voyage of Bran*, a romantic verse tale which Zimmer and Kuno Meyer believed to have been first written down in the seventh century.[44] At the end of the sixty-six quatrains of the poem, which describes the search of Bran, son of Febal, for the happy other-world, 'without grief, without sorrow, without death', there is indeed the explicit statement: 'Thereupon, to the people of the gathering Bran told all his wanderings from the beginning until that time. And he wrote this quatrain in Ogam and then bade them farewell'.[45]

But, in spite of the authority of these two scholars, the few scattered instances they give can hardly be thought sufficient to constitute evidence of a real historical tradition, and may well be merely the imaginings of the ancient writers. There is also the overwhelming argument that the cumbrous nature of Ogam would preclude its use for any but short passages. 'If a modern novel were to be written in it', says Professor Ó Fiaich, 'it would require a surface over a mile in length'.[46]

ORIGIN OF OGAM

We have seen that practically all authorities agree that Ogam writing appears in Ireland in the late pagan period, when knowledge of writing had just been introduced, either directly from the continent or through Romanized Britain. But there is considerable difference of opinion as to the authors of the system. Many scholars hold that it was a purely Irish invention. According to Hyde: 'One thing is certain, namely that the Ogam alphabet...is a possession peculiar to the Irish Gael.'[47] Dillon holds that 'it seems more probable that Ogam was invented in Ireland.'[48] Professor Greene says that some time prior to the fifth century when the Latin alphabet came in, 'the Irish had evolved an alphabet of their own'.[49] The argument put forward for this view is the undoubted fact that the vast majority of surviving Ogam inscriptions are found in Ireland, and the remainder in places in Britain known to have been invaded by the Irish. None have been found on the continent.

Amongst those who hold that Ogam was an importation from Gaul are Zimmer, who held that it came through the mercantile traffic between the two countries,[50] Marstrander, who believed that Ogam derived from the old Germanic runes,[51] and T. F. O'Rahilly who seems to be alone in his theory that Ogam was brought in by the original Goidelic invaders.[52]

There are certain internal indications – they can hardly be termed more – that Ogam was an importation from Gaul. Ogam has a sign for the sound ng. This sound was known to the Greeks as *agma,* and was also known to the Roman grammarians. Hence it would seem that the Latin alphabet on which Ogam was based was one which had admitted the Greek *agma.* This points to a continental rather than an Irish origin. Again, as we have seen earlier, the Ogam letters (or more correctly signs) almost all have names taken from trees. The Ogam name for Q is *ceirt* (apple-tree). The old Runic alphabet had such signs, and that for Q has survived in Anglo-Saxon *cueord* and Gothic *questa,* again a slight pointer towards continental origin.

As to the manner in which Ogam could have been imported, the more common view is that suggested by Zimmer, namely that it was through the constant trading intercourse between Ireland and Gaul. This theory is to some extent borne out by the fact that the large majority of Ogam inscriptions are found in Munster, from whose ports there was constant shipping connection with Gaul.

If the theory is accepted that Ogam was imported, the question at once arises how it comes that the surviving inscriptions are all in Ireland or places subject to Irish culture. The following is a tentative answer. We have seen how the Irish used Ogam for sending brief messages cut on pieces of wood. This could have been the original use of Ogam in Gaul. But when it came to making permanent inscriptions on stone, Ogam in Gaul could not establish itself as a rival to the already widely used Latin and Greek alphabets. In Ireland, Ogam had the field almost to itself. The Latin alphabet on which it was based was a newcomer, the Greek alphabet probably utterly unknown.

But another problem remains. Why did the inventors of Ogam, whether Gauls or Irish, hit upon this novel and cumbrous set of symbols instead of adopting the Latin alphabet which they already knew? To Hyde this is 'a complete mystery'[53] and Macalister speaks of 'the difficult – perhaps in some measure insoluble – questions of the time, place and manner of the development of the Ogham script.[54] MacNeill is alone in the surmise – which is worthy of consideration – that the adoption of Ogam was due to the hostility, understandable in view of what had happened in Britain, of the Irish druids towards the Romans and everything connected with them.[55]

Finally, it may be observed that Ogam is unique among the alphabets of the world in this, that the period between its invention and its disappearance was, at most, some five hundred years.

CHAPTER 4

EVOLUTION OF LEARNED ORDERS:
FILID, BREHONS, DOCTORS

EVOLUTION OF THE LEARNED ORDERS

After the first few centuries of the christian era in Ireland, all mention of the druids as such ceases. The question naturally arises how this came about. Did they simply decay and die out, as did their Gaulish brethren, or did they survive in a different form?

Now in the most ancient documents we can trace the emergence of certain well recognized orders of learned men. There were, firstly, the *filid* (nom. sing. *fili;* modern Irish *fili*, nom. sing. *file*). The name is sometimes translated as 'poets', but the *filid*, though they were poets, had also many other functions. They would, perhaps, best be designated by some general title such as 'sage' or 'scholar.' Secondly, there were the brehons (*brithemuin*, nom. sing. *brithem*, from *breth*, to give judgment), the lawyers. Both were included in the generic title *áes dána*, 'men of art.' Thirdly, but at a later date, and with lesser standing, there were the doctors.

It is impossible to give an exact date for the appearance of the two chief learned classes, but it was certainly before the coming of christianity. Much information about the native scholars is to be found in the *Ancient Laws of Ireland,* commonly referred to as the Brehon Laws, which persisted (after the Norman conquest side by side with English law) until the destruction of the old Gaelic order which followed the battle of Kinsale (1601).[1]

The manuscripts which we possess of these laws, preserved mainly in the library of Trinity College, Dublin and the Bodleian Library, Oxford, are as late as the fifteenth or sixteenth centuries. But the text of the laws, as distinct from the many explanatory notes and commentaries of later date, is, by linguistic evidence, as early as the eighth or even the seventh century.[2] As to the date of origin of the laws, no more definite view can be offered than that of Hyde, that 'they appear to have been in great part handed down from time immemorial'.[3]

The most important of these law tracts is the *Senchus Mór,* the *Great Treatise,* placed by Thurneysen in the first half of the eighth century.[4] In the Introduction to this tract we read:

'Until Patrick came, only three classes of persons were allowed to speak in Erin, viz. a Chronicler, to relate events and tell stories; a Poet, to eulogize and satirize, a Brehon to pass sentence from the precedents and commentaries. Since Patrick's arrival, however, each utterance of these professions is subject to the men of the white language, i.e. of the Gospel.'[5]

FUNCTIONS OF THE *Filid*

Earlier writers, by translating the title *fili* as 'poet', have given a restricted impression of the functions of these learned men. All recent scholars, however, have emphasized the wide and varied scope of these functions. The *filid* were guardians of the ancient traditions, history, topography, epics, pedigrees, laws. They were advisers of rulers, witnesses of contracts. By their satires they governed the social conscience. Their knowledge of genealogies was relied on to establish or maintain territorial rights. By their appeal to past glories, they stimulated national pride or martial ardour. They held a recognized and honoured place in the social structure. In a sense, they were poets only in the last place, finding poetry an effective tool for their various functions, especially the type of praise-poetry which they took over from lesser poets, known as bards.

In 1913 an important critical examination was made by Bergin of the work of the *filid.*[6] He pointed out that they were not exceptional in choosing verse as their medium of expression. Verse comes before prose in the literatures of the world. It was, however, a misfortune that the use of verse lasted in Ireland long after the time when other nations had developed a recognized prose style. There is, of course, in old Irish literature a quantity of prose. Apart from such writings as legal and medical tracts, annals, translations, there are the great romantic tales, the greatest treasure of our literary heritage. These show an undoubted power of plain, vivid narrative, but after their anonymous authors, no prose authors emerge until quite modern times.

Bergin recalled and endorsed the view of O'Donovan that the *fili* exercised many of the functions of the modern journalist. He was 'chronicler, political essayist and satirical observer.' It was not necessary that he should be a real poet, though he sometimes was, and his panegyrics were often tainted by insincerity and formality.

But, taken on the whole, what remains to us of the compositions of the *filid* is highly valuable, and that for several reasons. 'They are sometimes emotional lyrics, sometimes moral or didactic essays in verse, sometimes political pamphlets. . . . they are always dignified in style and completely finished. And, as they follow unswervingly the old traditional standards, they form a great linguistic storehouse of classical Gaelic, unimpeachable in vocabulary, morphology and syntax. For the social history of Ireland it would be hard to exaggerate their importance.'

During the time, more than half a century, that has elapsed since the publication of this article of Bergin, much work has been done by Irish scholars in editing and evaluating the work of the *filid*. This activity, and the further light it has thrown on the character and functions of the *filid* has been ably dealt with in a recent article by Professor James Carney.[7] Whilst endorsing in general the views expressed by Bergin, he deals in greater detail with several topics, notably with the relations between the rulers of the hundred or so petty kingdoms (*tuatha*) and the *ollamh,* the *fili* of highest rank, who was attached to each court. The latter had strong bonds of attachment to his royal patron, but with definite limitations. The popular romantic picture of the poet ready to fight and die for his lord on the battlefield is totally unsubstantiated. The person of the *fili* appears to have been sacred – possibly owing to his origin from the semi-priestly druid order – and he was recognized as a non-combatant in war. The praise poetry of the *fili* was believed to bring a blessing on his patron, but, if he turned to satire, he was capable of injuring the prince, even physically. Other issues dealt with by Professor Carney, the number, language, content and antiquity of the poems which remain to us, will be dealt with later in this work.

Fili AND BARD

In modern times the native scholars are sometimes loosely referred to as 'bards', but originally the word *bard* designated an inferior type of poet and is never applied to the true *file*. The *bard* is thus described in the Sequel to the *Crith Gabhlach,* one of the ancient law tracts. 'A bard, now, is one without lawful learning but his own intellect'.[8] He was a poet not trained in the traditional way, but owing his position to his native talent.

This distinction between *file* and *bard* is found as late as 1351, when William O'Kelly, Lord of Hy Many (Uí Maine in southern Roscommon and northern Galway) gave a banquet, or series of banquets for men of learning and some lesser fry 'during Christmas holydays' to which he invited 'all the Irish Poets, Brehons, Bards, Harpers.'[9]

We shall have occasion later to refer again to this gathering, the account of which throws much light on the organization and status of the native scholars. It is recorded in most of the Annals[10] and also in the O'Ceallaigh genealogies in the *Book of Hy Many*.[11] The scene was probably O'Kelly's castle of Gallagh, near Loch Ree in Co. Galway. Among those present was the poet, Gofraidh Fionn Ó Dálaigh, who recorded the event in a poem of fifty-two stanzas, commencing:

> *Filidh Eireann go haointeach*
> The poets of Ireland to one house.[12]

All the learned came, 'jurists of legal decisions; wizards and good poets; the authors of Ireland, those who compose the battle rolls... the musicians of Ireland – vast the flood'. They were lodged in 'sleeping booths....wrought of woven branches on the bright surface of the pleasant hills.' Class distinction was observed. The chroniclers had 'a separate street' of booths, as had the musicians, and the 'bardic companies and the jugglers' had their own 'spacious avenue of white houses'.

O'Kelly did his guests well. 'they were all served to their satisfaction, both good and bad, noble and ignoble, so that they were all thankful to him and to his son Melaghlin'.[13]

FUNCTIONS OF THE BREHONS

The brehons were not primarily judges. The normal court of law in ancient Ireland was the king's court. The brehons were jurists, who elaborated the laws, acted as advisers to litigants, and as assessors and advisers to the kings in court. When, on occasion, they acted as judges themselves, their courts were rather tribunals of arbitration. It may be granted, however, that after the Norman invasion and the introduction of the feudal system, and especially when Irish law was adopted by feudal lords, the court of the brehons tended to supplant the former court of king or chief.[14]

There are numerous passages in ancient Irish literature which make it clear that the judicial function was the prerogative of the king, whether of a great or small *tuath*. One of the clearest of these is found in a passage from the *Book of Ballymote, The Manner of King Cormac's Birth*. In this it is related how Cormac Mac Airt, the great third century ruler, when a boy, came as *dalta*, protégé or pupil, to Tara where a usurper, Lughaidh Mac Con, ruled. The youth was present at a lawsuit in which a 'she-hospitaller Bennaid' was sued because her 'roaming sheep came and ate up the queen's crop of woad.' The king's verdict was that the queen should have the sheep, but Cormac protested that 'the shearing of the sheep is a sufficient offset to the cropping of the woad; for both the one and the other will grow again.' The assembled people applauded Cormac, exclaiming: 'That is the true judgment, a very prince's son it is that has pronounced it,' and Mac Con was driven from the throne.[15]

Mac Neill, who cites this passage, points out how it emphasizes two facts. Firstly, this case is tried by the king, with no suggestion of a brehon's presence. Secondly, the ability to judge fairly is thought to be a natural gift of a lawful prince's son.[16]

FROM DRUID TO *Fili*

The question naturally arises whether these learned classes existed from earliest times side by side with the druids, whom they survived, or were in fact an evolution of the druidic order. The former view seems to have been taken by some of the earlier Irish scholars. Dr. Healy devotes separate sections to the druids, the bards and the brehons, and holding the view we have rejected that they were 'priests of a false and idolatrous religion', thinks that the absence of reference to them in documents of the Christian era was due to the desire 'to remove every trace of their existence from the minds of the people.[17] O'Curry also seems to have held that there was a learned caste distinct from the druids, though overlapping occurred. 'They [the druids] were not connected with the orders of learned men or Profession of Teaching such as before explained. The Druids were often, however, engaged in teaching, as has been seen, and it would appear that kings and chiefs, as well as learned men, were also frequently Druids, though how or why, I am not in a position to explain with certainty at present.'[18]

But all later and contemporary scholars hold that originally the druids constituted the entire learned class. However, in course of time two developments took place. Largely under the influence of christianity the druids renounced all claim to preternatural powers, and emerged as pure *savants,* whilst in this capacity they tended to specialize in some particular branch of learning, law, history, genealogy, poetry and later medicine.

Mac Neill writes: 'With the establishment of christianity, the men of native learning abandoned the description of Druid, closely associated with heathen belief and practice, and became afterwards known as *filid'.*[19] Hyde expresses the same view, though with some reservation. 'These [the bardic institutions] were almost certainly a continuation of the schools of the druids, and represented something far more antique than even the earliest schools of the Christians'.[20] In dealing with the passage from the *Senchus Mór* cited above, detailing the various classes of persons entitled to speak on learned subjects, he points out that it omits all mention of the druids as a separate public body.[21] Professor Myles Dillon, speaking of the coming of Latin learning to Ireland in the train of the Christian missionaries, says: 'The Irish already had a long tradition of native learning, which had grown up in the druidic schools and was preserved by the filid by oral transmission'.[22] Professor Francis J. Byrne says of the *Áes dána,* or 'men of art', the poets, brehons, historians, genealogists: 'They were all originally druids'.[23]

THE EARLIEST *Filid*

In tracing the emergence of the learned classes, the *filid* and the brehons, it is convenient to adopt the division made by Kenney into those who appear before the ninth century and those who flourished after that date.[24] The earlier group consists mostly of shadowy figures, some obviously mythical, others probably real, but obscured by mythical accretions, and generally known to us by the attribution to them of poems or other writings included in document of a later date. A few of the more notable may be mentioned here.

At some remote date before the christian era, we find the figure of Amergin Gluingel, 'White-Knee', who, according to the *Lebor Gabála,* was a son of Mileadh of Spain, and accompanied his father and his brothers, Heber and Ir, on their invasion of Ireland. Three poems are ascribed to him, one being the well-known nature poem or incantation beginning

> I am Wind on Sea
> I am Ocean-wave.[25]

These poems, whether the work of Amergin or not, are extremely archaic. Hyde, in fact, believed that 'they do actually represent the oldest surviving lines in the vernacular of any country in Europe except Greece alone.'[26] Again, in the *Lebor Gabála* there is another remote figure, Ollam Fodla, monarch and lawgiver of Ireland, reputed to have founded a college of scholars at Tara.

> Ollom Fodla, fierce in valour,
> marked out the Scholars' Rampart;
> the first mighty king, with grace,
> by whom the festival of Tara was convened.[27]

Coming to the beginning of the christian era, Adhna was chief poet of Ireland in the reign of Conchobar Mac Nessa over Ulster. He is credited with being the author of some fragmentary law tracts. At about the same time flourished Athairne, a vindictive poet of Beann Éadair (Howth), who at the time of a general proscription of the poets, fled to the protection of Conchobar Mac Nessa in Ulster, and there, with other poets, Forchern, Ferceirtne and Neide, compiled a set of laws known as *Breithre Neimhid,* or laws of the nobles. On the death of Adhna, Ferceirtne was appointed chief poet.[28] We shall refer later to *Auraicept na n-Éces,* a treatise on grammar, to the part-composition of which Ferceirtne has a doubtful claim. His title of chief poet was disputed by Neide, son of Adhna. The contention between the two poets is recorded in a tenth century composition, *Acallamh an dá Shuadh,* the *Dialogue of the Two Sages.* In this it is related how Neide, studying in Scotland, received from a wave a message that his father was dead and that Ferceirtne had usurped the ollaveship. He returned to Emain Macha, where, at the instigation of the malicious poet Bricriú, he disguised his youthful features with a beard of grass, put on the chief poet's robe and seated himself on his chair. The perfidious Bricriú took himself off to Ferceirtne and reported the usurpation. There followed a long disputation between the rivals, which ended when Neide acknowledged 'that Ferceirtne is a great poet and prophet.' He was about 'to cast himself at Ferceirtne's feet', but the latter stayed him, blessed him and foretold that he would be 'famous and adorned in the opinion of Man and God.'[29]

Shortly before the coming of christianity to Ireland, Torna Éces (the learned) was poet and instructor to Niall of the Nine Hostages, who ruled as high king at Tara from 380 to 405, and to Corc, king of Cashel. To Torna are ascribed five poems dealing with his relationship with the kings.[30]

> At times I used to be with Niall, and it was I who bound his hostages
> At times I used to be with Corc, and I was his strong counsellor.

On the arrival of St. Patrick in Ireland, Dubthach ua Lugair was poet and druid of the then High King, Loegaire, son of Niall. In the Book of Leinster three poems are attributed to Dubthach on the triumphs of Enna Censelach and his son, Crimthann, kings of Leinster.[31] Another poem, on the rights and duties of the *filid* is found in *Lebor na Cert,* the eleventh century treatise on the rights of kings.[32] And in the law tract, *Senchus Mór,* a poem on the problem of forgiveness of injury purports to have been written by Dubhthach after his conversion to christianity.

> 'I follow Patrick since my baptism.'[33]

SIXTH TO EIGHTH CENTURIES

In the sixth century, the outstanding figure is Dallán Forgaill, who was chief poet of Ireland at the time of the Convention of Druim Ceat (575) which brought about the reconciliation of the native schools with the new christian civilisation. Dallán celebrated this event by his *Amra* or panegyric of St. Colum Cille, which will be dealt with later. Amongst other poems with which he is credited is a short *Amra* of St. Senán of Inis Cathaig.[34]

In the seventh century there are two clearly defined figures. Senchán Torpéist, a Connacht poet (d. 647) flourished in the reign of King Guaire the Generous. He was a pupil of Dallán Forgaill, whom he succeeded as chief poet of Ireland. In a long prose story, interspersed with verse, called *Imthecht na Tromdáime,* the Proceedings of the great bardic Institution, he is credited, after fantastic adventures, with the recovery of *Táin Bó Cuailnge* after its lengthy loss.[35] Amongst the poems attributed to him is a lament on the death of his master Dallán Forgaill.[36] In 678 or 679 died Cenn Faeled Fodhlumtha, some of whose poems are preserved in the various Annals and in the *Lebor Gabála.*[37] We shall consider later the part played, according to many authorities, by this warrior and scholar in the fusion of the christian and pagan cultures and in the beginning of writing in Irish, also his claim to be author of the law tract *The Book of Aicill* and, at least in part, of *Auraicept na n-Éces.* In the early eighth century occurs the name of Ruman Mac Colmáin (d. 742) 'adept in wisdom, chronology and poetry' according to the *Annals of the Four Masters,* and called 'the Virgil of the Gaedhil' by Oengus Ceili Dé, the monastic scholar of the same period, in his calendar of the Irish saints.

We may freely grant that a good deal of doubt exists about these early men of learning. Modern scholars vary in their judgments as to their authorship of the poems or other works ascribed to them, and sometimes even as to their historical existence. Detailed discussion of such matters belongs to the history of Irish literature. For our purposes it is sufficient to note that from the earliest recorded times we find the tradition of the existence of these poets (in the wide sense already explained) and jurists. Whether all of them actually existed and whether the compositions attributed to them were really their work, are matters of secondary importance. What concerns us is that this tradition could not have come into being unless there were a solid foundation for it.

This conviction is reinforced by the fact that from the ninth century on, we have reliable records of a very large number of these scholars. Their deaths are recorded in the Annals, and numbers of their writings have come down to us and have been published by

experts who accept their authenticity. We shall have occasion later
to refer to many of them. It is enough here to note that at all periods
in our enquiry into educational activity we must take cognizance
of this body of men, their large numbers, their high status and
their great influence.

In the period with which we are concerned, from the introduction
of christianity to the early sixteenth century, the *Annals of the Four
Masters* alone have obituaries of some 150 *filid* and brehons,
besides numerous physicians and musicians. These are only the
most outstanding figures, and there must have been hundreds of
minor ones. In his *Primer of Irish Metrics* (27–58) Kuno Meyer
gives a list of the known native scholars from the earliest times to
the 18th century. They total over a thousand.

INDIVIDUAL SCHOLARS

It will be seen later that by about the year 1200, the native culture
was almost entirely in the hands of a large number of scholar
families, who transmitted their learning from generation to
generation. It is also obvious that this development must have been
going on for a considerable time previously. But at the date with
which we are concerned, there was, as yet, no sign of it. O'Curry
gives a list, taken from the *Book of Ballymote,* of some forty poets,
historians and lawyers of the earliest ages, and, in his succeeding
chapters, deals in detail with the scholars we have mentioned and
many others, ending with Flann Mainistrech, head master of the
great school of St. Buite (Monasterboice), who died in 1056.[38] All
of these appear as individual, independent figures, whose pupils,
when they had them, were recruited by choice, and not by claims
of relationship.

'CLOSED CORPORATIONS'

The native Irish schools have by some writers been compared
to the universities of later times. They were, indeed, similar, in
being institutions of higher learning, but there was one essential
difference. The Irish schools aimed exclusively at the production of
professional scholars, and did not provide education for the people
at large. It will be seen later that the monastic schools admitted a
certain number of young men not destined for the priesthood or
religious life. But, until their final extinction in the seventeenth
century, the native schools retained their strictly professional
character. Dr. Healy refers to them as 'closed corporations'.[39]
Eleanor Hull states that 'the old schools aimed at the production
of a limited number of learned men who usually adopted the learned
professions because their fathers and grandfathers had been filí and

brehons before them'.[40] Only one writer holds the contrary opinion, Joyce, who says: 'The Bardic schools were the least technical of any: and young laymen not intended for professions attended them...to get a good general education'.[41] He offers no proof for this opinion, and there seems to be no evidence to support it.

There are, indeed, in the ancient records indications that even in the pre-christian age some of the ruling class were on an intellectual level with the professional scholars, but they are few and uncertain. Thus Cormac Mac Airt (A.D. 275–300) is represented as being not only a great ruler who made Tara the capital of Ireland, built the five great roads of Ireland running north, south and west of Tara, and established a standing force of warriors, the Fianna, but also as being a man of learning and a legislator. One of the ancient law tracts, the *Book of Aicill,* a treatise on criminal law, is attributed in part to him. The Introduction to this tract begins: 'The place of this book is Aicill (the old name of the hill of Skreen near Tara) close to Teamhair, and its time is the time of Coirpri Lifechair, son of Cormac, and its author is Cormac'.[42] An imaginative account is given of how the book came to be written at Aicill, and it is stated that whatever part of it is not the work of Cormac is the work of Cenn Faeled, a figure of the seventh century whom we shall meet later. The *Annals of the Four Masters* (A.D. 266) attribute to Cormac another extant work. 'It was Cormac who composed *Teagusc-na-Righ* [Instruction of Princes] to preserve manners, morals, and government in the kingdom.' The text of this work is found in the *Books of Leinster, Ballymote* and *Lecan.* It is written in the form of a dialogue in which Cormac imparts to his son, Cairbre, a wealth of advice and information on the customs and pagan moral principles of the day.[43] Cormac is also credited with the authorship of, or at least the inspiration of one of the great lost books, the *Saltair of Tara.* Frequent mention is found of this work, which evidently dealt with history and genealogy. The *Annals of the Four Masters* (A.D. 266) state that 'it was this Cormac, son of Art, also, that collected the Chroniclers of Ireland to Teamhair, and ordered them to write the chronicles of Ireland in one book, which was named the Psalter of Teamhair'. In a poem of the eleventh century poet Cuan Ó Lochain are found these lines:

> Cormac, the prudent and good,
> Was a sage, a file, a prince,
> He compiled the Saltair of Temur.
> In that Saltair is contained
> The best summary of history.[44]

The seventeenth century antiquary, Roderic O'Flaherty, states[45] that a collection known as Ó Dubhagan's Book of Hy-Many, compiled in the fourteenth century, contains a poem of 183 distichs in honour of Cormac, in which it is recorded that he endowed three schools at Tara, one in which the art of war was taught, and one each for the study of history and law. O'Donovan failed to find this book in any of the great libraries,[46] but O'Flaherty describes the poem in such detail, even quoting the opening line 'Temor o' th' kings is Cormac's royal seat', that at least its former existence cannot be doubted.

Though these various attributions of learning to Cormac are of interest, it is impossible to draw any definite conclusion from them. The writings cited all belong to periods many centuries after Cormac's own era (e.g. *Teagasc Ríogh* has clear reference to christian teaching). Therefore three different explanations of them are possible. Though clearly not the work of Cormac, they might possibly be developments or enlargements of such work. Or they might be evidence of old traditions concerning the intellectual gifts of this third century ruler. Or again they might be purely poetical inventions, expressing the later writer's idea of what a great king should be.

The same doubt exists about the numerous poems found in the great cycle of the Fenian tales, which are attributed to Fionn Mac Cumhaill, leader of King Cormac's militia, his sons, Oisín and Fergus Finnbheoil (the Eloquent) and his kinsman Caeilte Mac Ronain.[47] In short, it may be briefly said that we simply do not know whether, at this early age, there were, outside the ranks of the professionals, what would then be known as learned men.

It would, however, be a mistake to think of the great mass of the people as uneducated. From the poets and historians they constantly heard the traditions and legends of the past, and eagerly memorized them and recited them. They had, moreover, a home education in crafts and accomplishments. We can get a very good idea of what this was from the detailed laws laid down as to the duties of foster-parents. These evidently reflect what was the common instruction which parents would give their children. In the *Senchus Mór* it is laid down that the boys of the lower ranks of society are to be taught 'the herding of lambs and calves and kids and young pigs, and kiln-drying, combing and wood-cutting', while the girls are to learn 'the use of the quern and the kneading trough, and the use of the sieve.' Sons of chieftains of higher rank were to be taught 'horsemanship and brann-playing [*brannuidecht,* a game akin to chess] and shooting and chess-playing and swimming. . . . when there is water fit for swimming on the land of his father, or his grandfather or his foster father.' The girls of this rank were to be instructed in 'sewing and cutting-out and embroidery.' Foster parents who neglected any part of the prescribed curriculum were to be fined two-thirds of the fosterage fee.[48]

CHAPTER 5

TRAINING AND STATUS OF SCHOLARS

Approaching the consideration of the education of these native scholars, we may recall the warning issued a century ago by that great pioneer of Irish learning, Eugene O'Curry.

'It would be futile, at this distance of time, and considering the destruction and dispersion that for ages have befallen our ancient Books, to attempt to find or to give any close and detailed account of the exact state of education in this country before...the establishment of Christianity in it, in the fifth century.'

O'Curry goes on to say that it is mainly through the study of the ancient poets, historians and lawyers that we can form an idea of what their education must have been.[1]

However, there is a certain amount of information to be gleaned here and there concerning the training given in the ancient schools. Furthermore, when we consider the extraordinary output of the *filid*, of which we have evidence for over a thousand years, we cannot but admit the value of even a scanty knowledge of the methods which went to produce it.

GRADES OF *Filid*

There was regular course of training prescribed for the *filid*, in which there were seven ascending grades, the members of each having their distinctive title, *Fochluc, Mac fuirmid, Dos, Cana, Cli, Anruth, Ollamh*. There was also a preliminary course with three minor grades, *Ollaire, Taman, Drisac*. The whole course lasted twelve years and to each year specified studies were allotted.

There are two principal sources of information about these grades. The first is three tracts of the Brehon Laws, the *Senchus Mór*, the chief collection of these ancient laws, the *Crith Gablach*, 'The Branched Purchase' and the *Uraicecht Becc*, 'small Primer', both of the last two dealing with social ranks and organization.[2] The second source is a treatise on versification, found in the *Book of Ballymote*. This gives not only the grades and courses but also examples of the types of versification at the various stages. It was known to O'Curry, who gives a digest of the relevant passages in his *Manners and Customs of the Ancient Irish,* published in 1873,[3] but the entire document was published with annotations by Thurneysen in 1891.[4] He pointed out that O'Curry was mistaken in giving to it the title *Lebhar Ollamhan,* the Book of the Ollamhs. In the *Book of Ballymote* it follows on the treatise so entitled, but is a separate work. Joyce, who deals very fully with this subject in 1903, appears to have relied on O'Curry's digest.[5]

THE PRESCRIBED COURSES

Owing to certain differences in terminology, it is somewhat difficult to compile from these two sources a clear scheme of the work to be done in the seven grades. However, that which is given by Joyce is a reasonably good synthesis, and is here summarized.

1st Year. Elementary grades, *Ollaire, Taman, Drisac.* Course of study: 50 Ogams, (probably here meaning brief literary or scientific maxims); the grammatical treatise known as *Auraicept na n-Éces* (to be referred to later); 20 Tales, of which the *Ollaire* had 7, the *Taman* 10 and the *Drisac* 20.

2nd Year. I. *Fochluc.* Course of study: 50 Ogams along with the 50 of the *Drisac;* 6 easy lessons in philosophy; specified poems; 30 Tales, in addition to the 20 of the *Drisac.* (In each grade the number of Tales includes those of the preceding grade).

3rd Year. II. *Mac Fuirmid.* Course of study: 50 Ogams more than the *Fochluc* (i.e. 150); six minor lessons of philosophy; Diphthongal combinations; specified poems; 40 Tales.

4th Year. III. *Dos.* Course of study: The *Bretha Nemed,* or Law of Privileges (a law tract); 20 Poems of the species called *Eman;* 50 Tales.

5th Year. IV. *Cana.* Course of study: Critical study of Gaelic articles, adverbs, and other points of grammar; 60 Tales.

6th Year. V. *Cli.* Course of study: The secret language of the poets (an abstruse form of composition); 48 poems of the species called *Nath;* 70 or 80 Tales.

7th, 8th, 9th Years. VI. *Anruth.* Course of study:

7th Year, the *Brosnacha,* collections of writings attributed to the *Saí,* or professor; Bardism, i.e. the special style of bardic poetry.

8th Year, Prosody, or the Versification of the Poets; Glosses, the meaning of obsolete or obscure words; knowledge of *Teinm Laeghda, Imbas Forosnai* and *Dichetal do Chennibh,* the two first being rites which gave the gift of prophecy, the third being the utterance of an extempore prophecy or poem; *Dinnsenchus* or Historical Topography of Ireland; all the chief Historical Tales.

9th Year. A number of compositions known as *Sennat, Luarca, Nena, Eochraid, Sruith* and *Duili Feda.* During these three years 175 Tales.

10th, 11th, 12th Years. VII. *Ollamh* (also called *Éces,* scholar, or *file*).

10th Year. An additional number of the compositions of the 9th year.

11th Year. 100 of the compositions called the greater and lesser *Anamuin,* the former of which were composed only by an *Ollamh.*

12th Year. 120 *Cetals,* addresses or orations; the four Arts of Poetry. (Nothing is known of these 'Arts', except that they are attributed to various poets).

O'Curry warns us that the titles given to the various kinds of composition to be studied 'are merely arbitrary, and quite incapable of any appreciable analysis'.[6] He quotes from the ninth century Cormac's Glossary: 'It was the ingenuity of the poets that invented these names for their compositions, to distinguish their various species, and it was not their nature or character they took into account.'[7]

The same may be said of the titles of the various grades. Inter-pretations of some of them are given in the *Small Primer,* but they are far-fetched and vague. *Anruth,* for instance, is thus explained: 'i.e. *an reidh* "perfectly easy", i.e. it is perfectly easy for him to make the poetry. Or *"ansruth",* a noble stream, i.e. a noble stream of poetry flows from him to every one, and a stream of...wealth from each to him.'[8]

It is clear that these seven grades of learning were universally known and accepted from the earliest recorded times. They are found and discussed in *Cormac's Glossary.*[9] Four centuries later, in 1351, we read in the poem praising William O'Kelly for his famous banquet that 'here [to the banquet] will come the seven orders who put poetry into shape.[10] Keating, in the seventeenth century, describing in his history of Ireland the convention of Druim Ceat, alludes to the orders of *ollamh* and *anruth* as being well known to all. The *filid,* he says, were threatened with explusion because it was so difficult to rule them. 'For the ollamh's retinue numbered thirty, and there were fifteen in the retinue of the anruth, that is the person who was next to the ollamh in poetic rank.[11]

It is, of course, unlikely that the detailed syllabus for each year was at all times and in each bardic school exactly adhered to. The point of interest is that from such a remote age the principle of a graded course of learning was so clearly recognized.

ORIGINAL COMPOSITION

Much of the training consisted in mere memory work. It must be remembered that these schools originated when writing was unknown, or at most known to a handful of scholars, and that, even after the christian missioners had made it more widely known, books were extremely rare. Furthermore, the traditional native lore began to be written only about the beginning of the seventh century.

But the courses also aimed at the ability to compose. O'Curry cites a passage from a manuscript in Trinity College, Dublin, in which it is stated that to attain to the highest degree, that of *ollamh,* the candidate, having passed through all the lower grades, had to submit his own compositions to some *ollamh* of standing, who reported both on the ability of the candidate, but also on his moral character to the king of the *tuath,* who then conferred the degree. The passage is worth quoting in full.

'Question: in what form are degrees (gráda) conferred upon a poet? Answer: He exhibits his compositions to him, that is to an *Ollamh;* and he has the qualifications of the seven orders; and the king confirms him in his full degree, and in what the *Ollamh* reports of him as to his compositions, and as to his innocence and purity. .'[12]

The fact that the final degree was conferred by the king is confirmed by a passage in the commentary on the *Senchus Mór* defining the title *'Suad Filed'.*

'The chief poet, i.e. the learned poet who explains or exhibits the great extent of his knowledge (i.e. who tests his knowledge) by composing a quatrain without thinking, i.e. without studying, i.e. the *'ollamh'* – poet [did this] after his appointment by the king of territories (*rig tuath*).'[13]

LEVEL OF ATTAINMENT

A high level of attainment was demanded of the fully qualified scholar. We have already seen that in his last three years of training he had to master three hundred and fifty historical and romantic stories, and to have acquired the ability to compose a quatrain or short poem extempore on any subject. In addition, he had to know the prerogatives and duties of the High King and the provincial kings. The *Book of Rights* is a treatise on the rights and duties of kings, composed in the eleventh century, but possibly containing matter going back to the beginning of the tenth century. In a tract prefixed to this work, entitled *The Restrictions and Prerogatives of the Kings of Erin,* we read: 'The poet or the learned historian who does not know the prerogatives and prohibitions of these kings (the High King and the kings of Leinster, Munster, Connacht and Ulster), is not entitled to visitation or to sale of his poems.'[14] The *fili* was also expected to be ready to solve disputes regarding the rights of the various *tuatha*. The *Book of Rights* says: 'He is not entitled to visitation in any of the fair provinces of Ireland nor to the circuit of a single *tuath,* if truth be regarded, the poet who cannot distinguish firmly the revenues and burdens and exemption, the portion of each territory he visits.'[15]

VISITATION OF OLLAMH

The 'visitation' alluded to was a procedure which emphasised the high status of the *filid.* The *ollamh* was entitled to tour the country with a retinue of his disciples, calling at the courts of the kings and receiving from them lavish hospitality and gifts, especially for a poem eulogizing the chief himself. According to the Glossary attributed to Cormac Mac Cuilennáin[16] and to the very ancient poem known as *Amra Coluimcille,* (with both of which we shall deal later), the normal retinue was twenty-four, but, possibly by mere poetical licence, we find the record of more lavish followings. Thus in *Imtheacht na Tromdáimhe, The Proceedings of the great Bardic Institution,* we hear how Dallán Forgaill 'rose early, and his steeds were got ready for him, and he took along with him thrice nine Professors to the Dún of the king of Oirgiall.'[17] And in the same work Senchán Torpéist, leaving the court of King Guaire of Connacht, en route for the fortress of the king of Leinster, is represented as thus addressing his late host:

> A year, a quarter and a month
> We have been with you O exalted king.
> Thrice fifty professors
> And thrice fifty students
> Two women, a gillie and a hound with each man
> Were all supplied with food in one mansion.[18]

The ninth century poet, Erard Mac Coise, records such a visit which he paid to Maelrunaidh, lord of Magh Luirg in east Connacht. Among the gifts he received from the prince were a chessboard, a sword, fifty milch cows and thirty steeds 'fit to appear at fairs and assemblies.'[19]

TEACHING METHOD OF THE NATIVE SCHOOLS

There are two well-known detailed descriptions of the method of instruction in the native Irish schools. Both are of a period long after that with which we are now dealing, but all the evidence goes to show that these schools were intensely conservative, and hence it may be taken that the procedure described so vividly by these later writers was more or less the same in the earliest times.

THE CLANRICARDE MEMOIRS

In 1722 there were published in London the *Memoirs of the Right Honourable the Marquis of Clanricarde,* dealing with Irish affairs from about 1500 to 1650. Ulick de Burgh (1604–1652), fifth Earl and Marquis of Clanricarde, was more of an English courtier than an Anglo-Irish chief. Doubts have been expressed about his alleged neutrality during the Confederate Wars of 1641 to 1649, as also about his loyalty to Charles I. In 1650, when Ormond quitted Ireland, he appointed Clanricarde to act as viceroy on behalf of Charles II, but in 1652 Clanricarde came to terms with the parliamentarians, and spent his remaining years in England.

The book published in 1722 was only a small selection from Clanricarde's memoirs, a much fuller version appearing later. What interests us is the 'Digression containing an Account of the Education and Studies of the ancient Irish Fillim, or Poets, and of their work' given in his lengthy Introduction by the anonymous editor. From documents in the Harleian Collection of the British Museum, Dr. Robin Flower identified him as Thomas O'Sullevane (as he spells it), an Irish lawyer practising in London, who, on his own testimony had 'been bred up to literature from his infancy' and had studied in foreign universities. He was a constant habitué of the Harley Library, then being formed by Robert Harley, 1st Earl of Oxford, and gave much advice on Irish matters to Humfrey Wanley, the librarian, who described him as 'a very learned gentleman and the best skilled in the Irish Antiquities of any man I ever knew.'

It is regrettable to have to relate that the last heard of Thomas O'Sullevane was when he wrote to Wanley in 1736 from the Wood Street Counter, where he was imprisoned for debt, mentioning sadly that he was 'putting the best hand to the treatise I designed against the Scottish historians, the publication whereof I am afraid will now be delayed for some time.'[20]

O'Sullevane's minute account in his 'Digression' of what he calls 'a seminary or school for poetry' gives the impression that he must have based it on information from men who, if they had not actually witnessed the operation of such schools, had reliable inherited traditions concerning them. It is generally accepted that the learned caste of poets and historians broke up after the battle of Kinsale and the subsequent ruin of its noble patrons. But this process must have taken some time, and the schools must have lingered on in parts of the country during a considerable part of the century that elapsed before O'Sullevane wrote his account of them.

O'Sullevane points out first the fundamental difference between these schools and those in other parts of Europe, namely that they

were conducted 'by certain families or tribes in every large
territory.' The aims of the education given were 'reading well,
writing the mother tongue, and a strong memory'. The school was
situated 'in the solitary recess of a garden, or within a sept or
inclosure, far out of reach of any noise'. The building was 'a snug,
low hut, with beds in it', without windows and lit only by candle-
light. The students were divided into classes, 'wherein a regard
was had to everyone's age, genius, and the schooling had before,
if any.' The professor appointed a subject, with detailed instructions
as to the use of 'rhimes...syllables, quartans, concord, corres-
pondence, termination and union, each of which were restrained
by peculiar rules.' The students worked on their allotted themes 'each
by himself upon his own bed, the whole day next day in the dark,
till, at a certain hour in the night, lights being brought in, they
committed it to writing'. They then gathered 'into a large room,
where the masters waited, each scholar gave in his performance,
which being corrected, or approv'd of (according as it required),
either the same or fresh subjects were given against the next day.
This part being over, the students went to their meals...and so
after some time spent in conversation, and other diversions, each
retired to his rest, to be ready for the business of next morning.'

THE MASTERS' SUPPORT

'Every Saturday', records O'Sullevane, 'and on the eves of festival
days, they (the students) broke up and dispersed themselves among
the gentlemen and rich farmers of the country, by whom they were
very well entertained, and made much of, till they thought fit to
take their leaves...Nor was the people satisfied with affording this
hospitality alone; they sent in by turns every week from far and
near, liquors and all manner of provision, towards the subsistence
of the academy, so that the chief poet was at little or no charges,
but on the contrary got very well by it, besides the presents made
him by the students upon their first coming, which always was at
Michaelmas; and from thence until the 25th of March, during the
cold season only, did the close study last. At that time the scholars
broke up, and repair'd each to his own country, with an attestation
of his behaviour and capacity, from the chief professor, to those
that had sent him...'

O'Sullevane is at pains to explain that the curious practice of
composing in the dark was 'doubtless to avoid the distraction which
light and the variety of objects represented thereby commonly
occasions. This being prevented, the faculties of the Soul occupied
themselves solely upon the subject in hand.' The course was long
'six or seven years before a mastery or the last degree was conferred'.

Each chief poet depended on 'some Prince or Lord' and was therefore 'under strict ties to him and family.'

O'Sullevane's knowedge of bardic writing was by no means all at second hand. He evidently had a good knowledge of the Irish language. He had read many of the bardic poems, and remarked that 'the greatest beauty of the composition' consisted in 'a certain contexture of corresponding vowels and consonants, so plac'd in every metre, which contain'd four equal sentences or parts, that it made it very taking to such as had a gust in that way'.[21]

O'Sullevane's statement as to the duration of the schools is thus poetically confirmed by the poet Tadhg Óg Ó Huiginn (d.1448) in an elegy on the death of his brother, Fearghal, who kept a school of poetry in Connacht:

To-night the schools disperse: thereby are beds left widowed; the folk of each bed will shed tears at parting.

The men of art ever had a tryst against Allhallowtide; were but one man, i.e. Fearghal, living, their departure would be no dispersal.

O ye who were in his dwelling, in quest of art and residence, well might ye loathe to hear the utterances of the cuckoos.

When the school dispersed, each man went to his own homeland. None cometh since then from his father's house in search of art.[22]

AN OXFORD SCHOLAR'S IMPRESSIONS

The second account of the methods of the native schools was actually written seventy years earlier than that found in Clanricarde's Memoirs, but both refer to about the same period.

In 1570 Edmund Campion, a brilliant Fellow of St. John's College, Oxford, later to be canonized by the Catholic Church as a martyr for the Faith, came to Ireland as the guest of James Stanihurst, Speaker of the Irish House of Commons, and father of Richard Stanihurst, the historian, a former pupil of Campion. Many authors have stated that Campion was brought over to further the project of an Irish university in which Stanihurst was interested. More will be said of this project in due course. It is enough to say that all the evidence goes to show that at this time Campion had been either formally reconciled to the church of his youth, or at least was living as a Catholic, and that his motive in leaving England was to avoid danger to his newly regained faith. Early in 1572 Campion was forced to flee from Ireland to avoid arrest by the Dublin authorities. During his short stay, he had composed two works, *De Homine Academico,* a portrait of the ideal student, and *Two Bokes of the Histories of Ireland.* The latter, written in 1570–71, is a superb piece of Elizabethan English, but is obviously a hasty compilation and is coloured by the views of the English official circle in which he lived. Indeed, when Campion later heard that Holinshed intended to use his history for his *Chronicles* he objected on the ground that it was an immature work. Campion gives a description of the native schools which confirms in many respects that given by Clanricarde, but is less sympathetic in tone.[23]

'Witheowt either preceptes or observation of congruitie, they speake Latten like a vulgar language, learned in their common scholes of leachcraft and lawe, whereat they beginn children, and hold on sixtene or twentie yeares, conning by roate the aphorisms of Hippocrates and the civill institutes [the code of Justinian], and a few other parings of thos twoe faculties. I have seene them wheare they kept schole, tenn in some one chamber, grovelling upon couches of strawe, theire bookes at theire noses, themselves lying flatt prostrate, and so to chante owt theire lessons by peecesmeale, being the most parte lustie fellows of 25 yeares and upwards.'[24]

DARKNESS AS AID TO COMPOSITION

We have noted the testimony of Thomas O'Sullevane and, though somewhat less clear, that of Edmund Campion, that the students in the native schools lay prostrate in the dark during the throes of composition. That this curious practice actually did prevail seems to be borne out by passages from poems composed centuries earlier.

In the *Dindshenchas* (Mod. I. Dinnsheanchas), the eleventh to twelfth-century prose and poetry topographical treatise, there is a poem on the origin of the name Bend Étair (Mod. I. Beann Éadair, Howth), which commences:—

> Though it be dark to me in my bed.
> Though it be a tale of testing and difficult indeed
> [yet] illustrious with profit of laudation
> is every famous plain, every famous fortress.[25]

Again, in the late sixteenth century, the poet Fear Flatha Ó Gnímh remonstrates, probably goodhumouredly, with his friend Fearghal Óg Mac an Bhaird, for having departed from the usual method and made bold to compose extempore, in the open air and on horseback.

1. This is comfortable, O Fearghal Óg; thou hast gotten gifts from the Trinity; without any need of a good teacher for thy verse thou framest fine scholarly art on horseback.

2. Without a grass hut, without hardship, with leave to take delight in lofty invention, a grassy scaur, an airy prospect are thine.

Fear Flatha then goes on to cite a long list of older poets who would not thus transgress the conventional rules of composition. Four verses are particularly significant.

6. Sgolb, that faultless scholar, and the Orthóir, the two pinnacles before thee, never fashioned – thou hast the luck to overstep their rule – a poem without secrecy and darkness.

8. In the beds where prize lyrics are made, the face of Tadhg Óg Ó Huiginn – how unlike is thine! – was wont to be washed by its own drops.

9. As for myself, could I make a poem, I like – a thing which keeps me from error – a barrier to keep out the sunlight, and dim couches to guard me.

10. If I did not close my eyelids between me and the bright rays as a protecting veil against the daylight, it would ruin my artistry.[26]

In his commentary on this poem, Bergin emphasizes the confidence with which this late sixteenth-century poet cites a long line of his predecessors and defends their unchanging methods.

'Ó Gnímh appeals to the authority of Donnchadh Mór Ó Dálaigh, a celebrated religious poet who died in 1244; Giolla Brighde Mac Conmidhe, a poet of the thirteenth century; Aongus Ruadh, son of Cearbhall Buidhe Ó Dálaigh, author of a highly ornate poem on the *pailis* or palace of O'Conor Connacht (1293–1309) at Cloonfree in Co. Roscommon; Sgolb, a nickname for a son of Cearbhall Buidhe Ó Dálaigh; *an tÓrthóir* "the gilder", a sobriquet of Eoghan Mág Craith, a fifteenth-century poet: Gofraidh Fionn Ó Dálaigh died 1387; and Tadhg Óg Ó Huiginn, who died in 1448.'[27]

Another poem, by an unknown writer as late as the seventeenth century, confirms in some points the description of the bardic schools given by O'Sullivan and Campion and intimated by Ó Gnímh. The poet looks back nostalgically to his student days.

The three forges wherein I was wont to find mental delight – that I cannot visit these forges wears away the armoury of my mind.

The house of memorizing of our gentle lads – it was a trysting-place of youthful companions – embers red and shining that was our forge at first.

The house of reclining for such as we, the university of art, poetic cell that kept us from beguilement, this was the forge of our trained *ánruith*.

The house of the critic of each fine work of art was that house of our three forges, which multiplied the clinging tendrils of knowledge, wherein the very forge of science was wont to be.[28]

The purely oral system of education in the native schools gave place after the introduction of christianity to a combined system of oral and written teaching. How this came about will be recorded later.

FRUITS OF NATIVE SCHOLARSHIP

That this elaborate training of the native scholars produced a high level of culture is manifested by the large body of literature which we have inherited from them, and this in spite of the incalculable losses which have occurred in the many troubled epochs of our country's history. If we survey the *corpus* of writing which remains to us from the ancient and medieval periods, it falls roughly into the following categories:

1. Annals, histories, records of families, topographies.
2. Heroic and romantic tales.
3. Narrative, lyric and elegiac poetry.
4. Lives of saints, homilies, translations of religious works.
5. Native law tracts, treatises, mostly translations, on philosophy, medicine and science.
6. Irish renderings of classical and medieval literature.
7. Folklore, proverbs, epigrams and anonymous songs.[29]

A great deal of this writing is, of course, the work not of the *filid*, but of monastic scholars, almost all, for instance under the fourth heading. 'All our existing early manuscripts', writes Flower, 'were written in monasteries and they derive from earlier lost manuscripts which, as far as we can trace their origin, also had a monastic source'.[30] Later we shall consider some of the earliest, from the sixth century on, culminating in the two great eleventh century compilations, *Lebor na hUidre* and the *Book of Leinster*. But it must be noted that these monastic manuscripts contain not only the monks' own compositions, but also many of those of the *filid*, which up to then had been preserved orally.

Then, from the twelfth century onwards, the native scholars are found joining with the monks in committing their compositions to writing.[31] It is not impossible that this change took place somewhat earlier, and that the absence of evidence of it is due to the fact that the way of life of the *filid* conduced less than that of the monastery to the preservation of manuscripts. But the existing evidence seems to indicate a time-lag on their part in the adoption of writing, due doubtless to loyalty to the traditional method of oral transmission. It is only in the latter years of the fourteenth and the beginning of the fifteenth century that we find from the pen of native scholars great compilations comparable to those of the monastic scribes, the *Book of Hy Many*, the *Yellow Book of Lecan*, the *Great Book of Lecan*, the *Book of Ballymote* and the *Lebor Brecc*.[32] It may be noted that these manuscripts, whether of clerical or lay authorship, are not books in the ordinary sense, but miniature libraries containing legend, history and hagiography, bardic and lyric poetry, medical and legal tracts.

To even mention all the important less surviving manuscripts would be beyond the scope of this work. Many of these will be dealt with in later chapters, in so far as they illustrate the activity of both monastic and lay schools throughout the centuries. It may, however, be suitably recorded here that in the article already cited,[33] Professor Carney mentions two thousand as a reasonable estimate of the number of poetical works of the *filid* still extant.

HIGH STATUS OF *Filid*

The esteem in which learning was held in ancient Ireland is manifested by the fact that the *filid* had a social status equal to that of the highest grades of society. Among the ancient laws (popularly, though inaccurately, referred to as the 'Brehon laws') there are two treatises especially which deal with the matter of status, *Uraicecht Becc* (the Little Primer) and *Crith Gabhlach* (the Branched Purchase). The manuscripts of these laws which we possess date only from the fifteenth or sixteenth centuries, but experts agree that the language of their text (as distinguished from the commentaries added later) indicates that they were written down as early as the eighth, possibly even the seventh century.[34]

In these two treatises the various grades of society are clearly defined. There were, first of all, the unfree classes, slaves, tenants of land, inferior craftsmen, and the lower grade of entertainers, 'musicians and sport-makers in general, viz., equestrians and chariot-drivers, pilots and conjurors...and jugglers and buffoons.'[35]

The freemen were mostly landowners, but also included skilled craftsmen, such as chariot-builders, carpenters, 'cloth-figurers', engravers, turners, leather-workers, fishermen, and – alone among musicians – harpers.[36]

Freemen of both kinds were entitled to exercise franchise by voting in court and assembly.[37] The nobles were those who had *déis,* authority over clients and vassals.[38] They were divided into seven grades, the titles of which vary somewhat in the two documents and at various epochs. In the *Uraicecht Becc* they are given as *aire desso, aire échta, aire túise, aire ardd, aire forgill, rí, rí ruireach.*[39] The lower classes of freemen were similarly divided into seven or eight grades.[40]

The distinctive mark of every freeman was his 'honourprice',[41] a valuation of his status. Wrong done to him was assessed according to this price. The extent to which he could become a surety, and even the extent to which his oath was valid, were also measured by it. In practice the honourprice was usually reckoned in cattle but sometimes in other goods or services.[42]

We recall that among the *filid* there were also seven grades, *fochluc, macc fuirmid, doss, cano, clí, anruth, ollum*. In the *Uraicecht Becc* there are frequent references to the honourprices of these various grades, showing that they correspond with those of the nobles. Thus the honourprice for both *aire ardd* and *anruth* was twenty chattels,[43] but in addition the *anruth* had 'food provision of twelve men and fifteen days protection'.[44]

Some of these prescriptions belong to the period when christian learning and the old learning existed side by side. The same high status was accorded to the learned men of both schools. 'The jurist of three languages is equal in *díre* to an *aire túise*.'[45] According to the gloss, the three languages are *Fénechus*, the ancient laws, *filidecht*, the lore of the *filid*, and *légend* (Latin learning). 'A master of *fili* and a master of wisdom (a master jurist according to the gloss) and a master hospitaller, each of these is equal in franchise to the king of one *tuath*. They have thirty chattels (of honourprice) and a month's protection, and eighty cakes for each of them'.[46] 'A second master of handicraft are equal in franchise to an *aire ardd.*'[47]

THE MEDICAL PROFESSION

In addition to the *filid* and brehons, we find mention from a somewhat later date of a definite class of men to whom the title of physician (*liaig* or *suí leighis*) is given.[48] In the *Annals of Ulster* there is recorded in 861 the death of Maelodhar Ua Tindribh 'the most learned physician of the Gaedhil'. In the Brehon Laws there are enumerated the penalties to be paid to his victim by the party guilty of bodily injury. Included in these there is constant reference to allowances for the physician according to the severity of the injury, to the responsibility of the physician for his own carelessness, or even for lack of success during a fixed testing time, and to the fact that there were both 'lawful' (i.e. fully qualified) and 'unlawful' (unqualified) physicians. The latter were recognized by the law, but were bound, before undertaking a case, to give notice of their lesser status.[49]

EIGHTH-CENTURY MEDICO-LEGAL TRACTS

In the earliest legal texts we find that the injurer, instead of merely paying a medical fee, was obliged to undertake the nursing of his victim and the provision of a physician. Two tracts of the eighth century, *Bretha Crólige*, Judgments on Blood-lying, and *Bretha Déin Checht*, Judgments of Dian Checht,[50] are devoted specifically to this obligation, which was known as *othrus* or sick-maintenance.[51] They are of particular interest, not only because they deal fully with the legal obligation, but also because they are our only source of information as to medical procedure at that remote date.

The victim of an injurious attack was to be brought to a private house, not his own. He could bring with him a retinue suitable to his rank; if married, his wife, and he could receive visitors. The house was to be quiet, not disturbed by such noises as the barking of dogs or the grunting of pigs. No games were to be played in it, no children chastised. Three provisions for the peace of the invalid show an intimate knowledge of sick-bed psychology. No fools were to be admitted; the patient was not to be suddenly awakened, and no conversations were to be held across his bed. Details of his diet are given. No salt fish was allowed, no horseflesh or honey, both of which create disorders in the stomach. The permitted fare included salt meat or bacon 'two fingers thick' from New Year's Eve to the first Sunday in Lent, fresh meat in the summer, well-baked loaf bread, and by way of condiments, celery, garlic and other garden herbs. (The tract adds that gardens are specially provided for the benefit of the sick). Ale was permitted on the physician's prescription. One of the victim's relatives was to be always at hand as nurse. It was his duty to move the patient when necessary, hence his title *fer ócaib tócail* (a man who moves [the patient] hither and thither).[52]

It is remarkable that, though the physicians had such a firm status in the eighth century, very little is known about their medical practice during the next four centuries. Speaking of this period, the late Professor F. Shaw thus summarizes our knowledge, or the lack of it. 'The doctors healed especially with herbs and ointments. A few traces remain of an earlier, independent approach to anatomy and physiology; there is some evidence for cupping, blood-letting and trephining; the doctors, however, did not write and the truth is we know virtually nothing about the men themselves and little about the medicine they applied'.[53]

Later we shall see that in the thirteenth century the families of hereditary physicians are almost as fully established as those of *filid* and brehons. And from the fourteenth century on, we have a rich medical literature, which, though almost entirely borrowed, gives some idea of medical practice in the Middle Ages.

The tract *Bretha Déin Checht* also deals with injuries to the person, compensation for such injury and the physician's fees. It does not contain so many interesting details as *Bretha Crólige,* but nevertheless is of considerable value, since it enumerates all the parts of the human body and the various injuries they may sustain, thus throwing further light on medical knowledge as it existed in the eighth century.

GRADES IN MEDICAL PROFESSION

In his introduction to the tract,[54] Professor Binchy discusses the question whether the doctors had the same 'hierarchical and educational pattern' as the *filid* and the brehons. In *Bretha Déin Checht* there is no suggestion of grades. It might, therefore, be thought that the families of physicians, who appeared later, sprang up in imitation of those of the poets and lawyers. Professor Binchy, however, thinks it more probable that there were, from the start, grades among the doctors. Primitive medicine was a form of magic, and was originally in the hands of the druids. When they evolved into the various classes of learned men, it would be natural that distinction of grade would come to be observed among the doctors as among the others. There are, in fact, certain indications that this distinction did exist. In the *Uraicecht Becc*,[55] we find the physician included with the wright, smith, metal-worker, jurist and druid (now reduced to a mere magician) among the *aes dána* 'men of art', who have the status of *daernemed*,[56] and it was recognized that the master of each of these callings was distinguished by the title of *ollamh*. Again, as we have already seen, there is found in the ninth century the title *suí leighis,* professor of medicine, indicating some position of superiority. Finally, there is the distinction made in the law-tracts between the qualified and unqualified physician. All in all, therefore, it seems most likely that there was among the doctors a hierarchy, though not necessarily as elaborate as that which obtained, or was alleged to obtain, in the other professions.

Professor Binchy also draws attention to the fact that the names for so many diseases are found in these early tracts, showing that the study of medicine goes back much further than the learning which came from the East in the fourteenth century. This being so, it is strange that so little traditional medical knowledge is found in the later manuscripts. One possible explanation is that by the time of the fourteenth century a knowledge of the newly-imported Arabic medicine was deemed essential for the reputation of the physician. It was quite otherwise with the brehons, who were tied to their ancient law texts. Or again it may have been that medical teaching had remained entirely oral. Professor Binchy holds that our present knowledge is not sufficient to enable us to give a definite explanation of this curious lacuna.

TRAINING OF DOCTORS

It may be accepted that, from the beginning, there was a regular system of apprenticeship among the doctors. The positive evidence for its existence is, however, meagre. The title of *suí* given to the physician Ua Tindribh obviously puts him on the same footing as the professor of poetry or history. Presumably it is on this assumption that Professor Shaw bases his statement that these early doctors 'had schools'.[57] Joyce holds that 'those intended for the profession were usually educated by being apprenticed to a physician of standing in whose house they lived', but gives no instance of this in the early period. He also states that, according to the Brehon law of sick-maintenance, not only the physician but also his pupils had to be lodged and fed.[59] He gives no reference, but doubtless refers to a passage in the *Uraicecht Becc* in which it is stated that a doctor 'on sick maintenance' is allowed 'refection for four men.'[60] However, apart from these rather vague intimations, the presumption seems justified that without some form of apprenticeship the medical profession could not have secured continuity, and this presumption is confirmed by the emergence of the numerous families of hereditary physicians in the thirteenth century.

CHAPTER 6

THE CHRISTIAN TEACHERS

PATRICK AND HIS SUCCESSORS

St. Patrick's Own Education

When, in the first half of the fifth century, Magonus Sucatus Patricius[1] – to give him his full Romano-British name – came to evangelize the country where he had worked as a slave in his extreme youth, he was adequately enough prepared for his task, though he could not be described as a learned man. In the twenty odd years which had elapsed between his escape from Ireland and his return, he had devoted a considerable time to study, though there is much uncertainty as to where these studies had been pursued and the length of their duration. Most probably they had been chiefly under the guidance of St. Germanus at Auxerre in the present-day department of Yonne in central France, where Patrick was ordained and consecrated bishop, and possibly before that, under St. Honoratus in the island monastery of Lerins, opposite Cannes on the coast of the Alpes Maritimes.[2]

We are, however, able to form an accurate estimate of both the extent and the limitations of Patrick's education from the two documents which all authorities accept as being his authentic compositions. These are his *Confession,* a justification of his episcopate, composed in the evening of his life, and the *Letter* written to rebuke the British chief Coroticus and his soldiers, who had done violence to some of Patrick's neophytes. In both of these the saint disarmingly acknowledges his own intellectual defects. He is 'unlearned', 'rustic'; he has 'not studied like the others, who thoroughly imbibed law and sacred scripture.' 'I blush and fear exceedingly', he protests, 'to reveal my lack of education'. His enemies had belittled him for his ignorance, probably to frustrate his proposed mission to Ireland.[3]

The documents go to show that his self-depreciation was not due merely to excessive modesty. His Latin is inelegant and obscure, even allowing for the fact that fifth century Church Latin had already strayed from classical models. This he explains by the fact that his exile in Ireland during his formative years had rendered Latin 'a tongue foreign to me, as can be easily proved from the savour of my writing'.[4] But his protestation that he had not thoroughly imbibed sacred scripture cannot be accepted. Both the documents are positive catenae of Scripture, either quoted in full or hinted at with the ease of a writer to whose mind they spring instinctively. There is also evidence that he was familiar with the ecclesiastical legislation of his time and with the customary rules of Latin composition.[5]

PATRICK AND THE BREHON LAWS

Some of the older writers, as for instance O'Curry and O'Donovan, adduced as evidence of St. Patrick's learning the tradition that he played a part in the revision of the Brehon Laws after the introduction of christianity.[6] In the Introduction to the great law treatise, the *Senchus Mór,* it is stated that 'what did not clash with the word of God in the written law and in the New Testament, was confirmed in the laws of the Brehons by Patrick and by the ecclesiastics and the chieftains of Erin.... And this is the Senchus Mór'.[7] A later passage gives the names of the nine persons who 'were appointed to arrange this book,' three bishops, three kings, three *filíd.* Of the bishops the first two are Patrick and his disciple Benen.[8] There are two other passages elsewhere in the Laws which similarly imply the influence of Patrick in their christianization.[9]

Modern authorities consider that this episode is a later invention symbolizing the reconciliation of christian and pagan law. 'The actual text of the Senchus Mór', says MacNeill, 'or of the other books of the Ancient Laws of Ireland present no appearance of having been revised in St. Patrick's time or after it from a christian standpoint. The legend has this justification, that the Church in Ireland quickly found a position in complete harmony with the national life.'[10] The passages cited from the Laws, therefore, though they give testimony to the influential position traditionally assigned to St. Patrick, are no indication of his intellectual powers.

TRAINING OF CONVERT CLERGY

The seventh-century monk and bishop, Tírechán, who composed one of the earliest Lives of St. Patrick, tells us that the saint brought with him 'holy bishops, priests, deacons,' young men in minor orders and other candidates for the priesthood.[11] However, from the first, Patrick did not rely solely on these foreign followers, but set about training a native clergy.

This would have been an obvious step in any mission field, but there was a special reason why in Ireland particular care should be given to the training of the clergy. We have seen that the druids were a long-established, highly cultured and influential body. Some, at the outset, were hostile to the new teaching. Others were friendly – indeed recruits for the priesthood were soon to be found among them whose previous education rendered them specially suitable. It was clearly essential that christianity should be presented to both foes and friends in a manner calculated to command intellectual respect.[12] This explains why St. Patrick, departing from the usual model of the continental monasteries, in which scholars were the exception and the large majority of their inmates pious but comparatively unlettered monks, aimed at a numerous cultural élite. It also explains the high intellectual level of the later sixth-century and seventh-century Irish monasteries, which attracted so many foreign students and furnished founders for so many monasteries in other countries.

PATRICK'S YOUTHS

Patrick's first step was to gather around him a number of young men, many of noble birth, who accompanied him on his travels, and whom he instructed on the way, thus constituting 'a kind of peripatetic school.'[13]

There are numerous references to these *pueri Patricii* (Patrick's youths) in the oldest lives of the saint. Thus Tírechán tells how Patrick 'came to the plain of the Liffey and founded there a church and ordained as exorcist Auxilius, one of Patrick's youths',[14] and how the saint laid a curse on two rivers, the Oingae and the Saele 'because two of the youths of Patrick had been drowned'[15] in the latter.

The story of the most famous of these youths, a boy of sixteen named Benen, is vividly told in the *Book of Lismore*. Patrick had been staying with 'a worthy man named Sescnech', and when he was leaving, he 'put his foot into the chariot, and the little boy clasps his two hands around Patrick's foot and this he said: "Let me be along with Patrick, for Patrick is my own father". Said Patrick: "Let the boy be baptized and put into the chariot". And Patrick afterwards said: "That boy will be a successor of mine". And Patrick bestowed a name on him, Benignus, that is Benen'.[16] The *Tripartite Life* has another pleasant anecdote which relates how, when Benen had entered Patrick's service, the boy found his master asleep, and filled his bosom 'with all the odorous flowers which the gillie had found.'[17]

In making an approach to the inhabitants of this remote land, Patrick had one remarkable advantage. Though thirty years had elapsed since his first sojourn in Ireland, he must have retained a considerable knowledge of the language which he perforce had used for some six years at a retentive age. MacNeill also makes the interesting suggestion that 'in the beginning of the fifth century British and Irish Celtic, which afterwards diverged so widely, were near enough to each other to allow the people of one tongue to understand those who spoke to them in the other.'[18] This would have ensured that Patrick, as a youth, could easily have acquired a good grasp of the Irish language. It is also likely that he had imparted at least some rudiments of it to his companions during the long journey from Auxerre. Hence the first instruction in the teachings of christianity could begin at once in Irish.

USE OF BOOKS

But, as soon as his young candidates were capable of it, they would have been introduced to the Latin tongue, on which all education was based at the time. Their instruction was probably oral at the beginning, following the pattern of the druids, the *filid* and the brehons. There is evidence however, that at quite an early stage, use was made of books, presumably at first those brought with them by the missionary band, massbooks, rituals, psalters and the gospels, then copies of these made as needs multiplied, or works specially composed for the purpose of evangelization.

There is a very ancient *Metrical Life of St. Patrick,* claiming to be by St. Fiach of Sletty, whom we shall meet later. Some earlier authorities believed it to be the authentic work of the saint, but it is now held to belong to the eighth century.[19] There are two manuscripts of this poem, both of the eleventh century, one in Trinity College, Dublin, the other in the Franciscan library, Dublin. In the latter there are a number of commentaries, one of which states that when Patrick was about to set out for Ireland, Pope Celestine 'gave many relics to him and books in plenty.'[20] The *Tripartite Life* relates how 'Patrick went into the territory of Uí Maine (East Galway and part of Roscommon) and left there a deacon of his own household, to wit Deacon Justus, and founded Fidarta (the barony of Fuerty, Co. Roscommon). And Patrick left his book of ritual and baptism with him... And in his old age Deacon Justus baptized Ciarán, son of the wright out of the book of Patrick.'[21] From Tírechán we learn that when evangelizing the country round the estuary of the Moy in Co. Mayo, Patrick ordained one bishop Mucnoi and 'gave him seven books of the law',[22] and from Muirchu that when he crossed the Shannon he brought with him not only bells, patens and chalices, but also 'books of the law and the gospels', and left them in the new churches he set up.[23] The use of books soon became common, as is exemplified in the well-known scene depicted in the *Tripartite Life,* when St. Patrick met three young clerics journeying to Rome 'with their books in their girdles', and gave them a hide to make a wallet which would guide them preternaturally on their journey.[24]

THE 'ALPHABET'

Frequent reference is found to a small catechism or outline of the elements of christianity, which St. Patrick usually wrote with his own hand. In Latin it is sometimes called *elementa,* but also *abigitorium,* corresponding to the old Irish *aipgiter* or *abgiter,* an alphabet, not in the usual sense, but in that of a compendium.[25]

A passage in the *Tripartite Life* has a twofold interest, since it makes mention of this 'alphabet' and also shows that Patrick had already entered into friendly relations with the native learned class and won some of them to christianity. Patrick was travelling from Tara to South Leinster where he met with the arch-poet Dubthach, son of Lugair, whom he asked to suggest a candidate for the bishopric of Leinster. He must be 'a comely youth who would be well-born... a man with one wife, unto whom hath been born only one child'. 'Verily', said Dubthach, 'this is not fortunate for me. Fiacc, son of Erc, [St. Fiach of Sletty] he, I think, is a man of that description: [but] he is gone from me into the lands of the Connacht men with bardism for the kings.' At this moment, Fiacc opportunely appeared. Being probably already a catechumen, he was at once accepted by St. Patrick. 'He is tonsured: he is baptized; an alphabet is written for him.' Miraculously, 'he reads his psalms in one day', and 'is ordained in the episcopal rank.'[26]

Having founded some minor churches, Fiacc, by the direction of Patrick, finally established himself at the place associated with his name, Sletty (Sléibhte) about a mile and a half north west of Carlow, on the right bank of the river Barrow, where he died about 510. His church and monastery were almost completely destroyed during the Norse invasions.[27]

THE 'CHURCHES'

The travelling school of St. Patrick was, of course, only a temporary expedient, and the system of education rapidly became more widely extended. Everywhere the saint went he established 'churches', permanent centres of christianity.[28] These were at first very simple in character, a bishop or priest with perhaps one or two helpers, provided with a primitive little church of clay and wood or wattles and a dwellingplace of the same modest character. These clerics evidently adopted from the start Patrick's method of personal tuition for the priesthood. It will be seen later that, even when the monastic system gained such an ascendancy in the sixth century, novices as a rule entered the monastery only in their teens, having received their primary education from some individual cleric or hermit.

With the rapid growth of christianity, it was inevitable that the more important 'churches' should increase in the number of clerics serving them, and that their buildings should take on a more permanent form. Their location, however, followed a different pattern from that observed on the continent of Europe. There the episcopal sees had been established in the cities, close to the seat of secular government. But in Ireland there were no cities, and the centres of government were the dúns of the reigning princes, which were also their private dwelling-places. Other sites, therefore, were chosen for ecclesiastical administration, either because of their convenient location or because of their historic associations. It was, however, remembered that elsewhere in Christendom the bishop ruled in a *civitas,* and hence any larger Irish ecclesiastical settlements came to be known as *civitas,* or the Irish equivalent, *cathair.*[29]

ARMAGH

Probably the earliest, and certainly the most famous of these churches was that of Armagh, of whose foundation Bury says that no other act of St. Patrick 'had more decisive consequences for the ecclesiastical history of the island'.[30] The date of the foundation is uncertain. The *Annals of Ulster* give it as 445, the *Annals of the Four Masters* as 457. The seventh century writer, Muirchu Maccu Machtheni, gives the story in homespun Latin. The local chief, Daire, was 'a rich and honourable man.' The saint asked him for a hill site, bearing the poetic name of Druimm Sailech, the Ridge of the Willows, but this Daire refused and allotted a piece of lower ground for the church. Some time later he sent Patrick a present of a cauldron. The saint exclaimed, 'Gratias agamus', which Daire's servants reported to their master in the garbled form 'Grazacham'. Piqued by this laconic thanks, Daire ordered his men to go and take away the cauldron. Patrick again – as reported by the servants – exclaimed 'Grazacham'. Daire became aware that he was dealing with no ordinary person. 'You are a constant and immovable man', he exclaimed, and gave Patrick the desired hill site.[31]

This is one of those curious stories which, on the one hand, display the characteristics of a folk tale, yet, on the other, have a curious flavour of authenticity. One may perhaps guess that there were two separate incidents. Daire did at first refuse the site and then relented. St. Patrick did thank God for some favour, and – mindful of Job – thanked Him when it was taken away, thus astonishing the pagans. The old chronicler has emphasized both events by fusing them together.

The name Druimm Saileach gave place to that of Ard Macha, the general title of the district, so called because it was believed to be the burial ground of the legendary Macha of the golden hair, foundress of the ancient palace of Emania three centuries before.

So arose the churches and episcopal buildings of Armagh. No doubt at first they were, like those of other settlements, primitive wooden buildings. But as time went on, stone was employed, first for the church, which was therefore known as *daimhliag,* (the stone house).[32] In 1125 we learn that 'the roof was raised on the great *daimhliag* of Ard-Macha, after it had been fully covered with shingles by Ceallach, successor of Patrick, one hundred and thirty years since it had a complete shingle roof before.'[33] Later the same material was used for the *erdamh* or *urdumh* (sacristy or side-chapel),[34] for the bishop's house and, more rarely, for the cells of the other clerics. The whole was protected, as were all dwellings of importance, by a *rath* or *caiseal,* a rampart of earth or stone. This practice continued for many centuries. The *Annals of the Four Masters* allude to 'the *rath* of Ard-Macha' in the years 1020, 1091 and 1092.

ST. PATRICK AND ARMAGH

There is no mention of Armagh in the *Confessio* of St. Patrick, but neither is there of any other foundation, the saint being concerned with his special personal problems. But that St. Patrick himself was the first bishop of Armagh has been unanimously accepted until recent times, when this claim was disputed by some able Irish scholars. This problem is outside the scope of the present work. It may be said briefly that, from the ninth century on, all ecclesiastical sources take Patrick's association with Armagh for granted. The controversy rests on the interpretation of the few earlier documents we possess in which reference is made to Armagh.[35]

THE SCHOOL OF ARMAGH

The Memoir of Tírechán, written probably shortly after Muirchu's Life of St. Patrick, stresses the ecclesiastical primacy of Armagh. This much discussed topic need not delay us.[36] We are concerned with the intellectual ascendancy of Armagh. It may be taken that, in accordance with the usual custom, a school was established simultaneously with the episcopate. It was to be for some seven centuries a great seat of learning, and was to survive danger and even partial destruction in an almost miraculous fashion.

We have no information about the organization or studies of the school of Armagh in its earliest days. Dr. Healy put forward the theory that St. Benen was its first Rector.[37] St. Benen succeeded St. Patrick, a few years before the latter's death, as bishop of Armagh, and may well have directed the school as well as the diocese. But this is a mere surmise, to which weight is not added by Dr. Healy's attribution to Benen of a part in the recension of the Brehon Laws and of authorship of *Lebor na Cert,* both of which claims, as we shall see, are without foundation.

Curiously enough, the first director of the school of Armagh whose identity we know with some degree of certainty is Gildas the Wise, the British historian, author of the historico-polemic work, *The Destruction of Britain* (*De Excidio Britanniae Liber Querelus*).[38] One of his biographers, Caradoc of Lancarvan, a Welsh monk of the twelfth century, states that about 508, hearing that his brother had been put to death by King Arthur, 'Gildas, the historian of the Britons, who was at that time living in Ireland, being rector of the school (*studium regens*) and a preacher in the city of Armagh, 'returned to Wales and was reconciled with the king'.

But from a somewhat later date there is in the various Annals copious evidence that all during its history Armagh produced able scholars. From the eighth to the twelfth century we find constantly recurring the commemorations of the 'scribes' and 'lectors' of Armagh, often with some added laudatory title. Thus we have (726) 'Ferdomnach, scribe of Ard-Macha', (845) 'Ceilearnach, son of Dunchu, scribe and wise man of Ard-Macha, (1040) 'Dunchad Ua Canege, lector of Ard-Macha, the gentlest and most learned', (1071) 'Gillachrist Ua Clothocan, lector of Ard-Macha and chief doctor of the Gaedhil', (1138), 'Maelpadraig Ua Dugain, paragon of the wisdom of the Irish, chief lector of Ardmacha'.[39]

THE BOOK OF ARMAGH

None of the works of the early scholars of Armagh have survived, but one of the most famous of the ancient compilations, *The Book of Armagh,* was made in the monastery of Armagh by the monk Ferdomnach, who died in 845. It contains the oldest known copies of the Lives of St. Patrick by Muirchu and Tírechán, and of the Confession, as well as the sole known example of the entire Latin New Testament as read in Celtic churches.[40]

CHAPTER 7

THE MONASTIC SCHOOLS

Up to the death of St. Patrick it is clear that, though the saint held the monastic state in high esteem, and established some monasteries, the large majority of his churches were entrusted to bishops and priests not bound by monastic vows. But all the larger foundations such as Armagh, Trim and Sletty, were organized in such a way as to make them resemble monastic settlements. The clergy lived with their bishop, surrounded by the protecting *rath* or *caiseal*. It was natural, then, that they should gather into their company a number of recruits for the priesthood, thus constituting a formal and organized ecclesiastical college.

But in the late fifth, the sixth and early seventh centuries, there was an upsurge in the monastic life, remarkable not only for its rapidity, but also for the holiness and abilities of the founders. Merely to enumerate the familiar names of some of the greatest of these gives an idea of the immense spiritual activity that gave to Ireland the title 'island of saints',[1] Enda of Aran (d. c. 530) Ailbe of Emly (D. 521 or 541), Finnian of Clonard (d. 549), Ciaran of Clonmacnois (d. 549), Iarlaith (Jarlath) of Tuam (d. c. 550), Brendan of Clonfert (d. 577 or 583), whose missionary sea-voyages – probably authentic but much embroidered by medieval writers – earned him the title of the Navigator, Colum Cille of Derry, Durrow and Iona (d. 597), Comgall of Bennchor (Bangor) (d. 601), Columban, the great apostle of Gaul, founder of the historic monasteries of Bobbio and Luxeuil (d. 615), Bairre or Findbarr of Cork (d. 630), Fursa, founder of monasteries in Anglia and at Lagny near Paris (d. 630), and the great women founders, Brigid of Kildare (d. 523 or 525) and Ita of Cluain Credail, later Cell Íte (Killeedy) in Co. Limerick (d. 570).[2]

This movement was remarkable, not only for the number and quality of its leading figures, but also because, as a result of it, the abbots of monasteries came to acquire such an important status.

Some of them were bishops, and all of them had a wider influence than bishops, since the abbot ruled over a *paruchia* which comprised not only groups of subordinate monasteries, but also lands attached to them, and probably other districts which looked to the monastery as their chief church, whereas the bishop's *paruchia* was confined to a small territory occupied by a *tuath,* a petty kingdom, or even by a sept, a group within the *tuath.* This state of affairs lasted until the Synod of Rath Breasail in 1111, when, as part of a general movement towards reform, the whole country was divided into twenty-four dioceses under the primacy of Armagh.[3]

Those abbots who were not bishops did not, of course, possess the power of ordaining and confirming. For the administration of these sacraments they had to invoke the aid of some neighbouring bishop, or rely on some member of the community who had received consecration. It is also clear that the abbot, though usually more powerful than the bishop, was always held to be inferior in dignity. Even the secular law recognized this, since it attributed the same 'honour-price' to the bishop as to the king.[4] In the old Irish Litanies the bishops always come first, and are often invoked in groups of seven or more. We shall have occasion later to refer to a ninth-century tract known as *Riagail Patraic,*[5] in which it is stated that every *tuath* or state should have a chief bishop (*prím-eposcp*) whose office it is to ordain and to see to it that the *tuath* has worthy priests.[6]

It is nevertheless evident that the influence of the monasteries and the extent over which it was exercized were very great from the sixth century on. Furthermore, as we shall see, the earliest documents known to us were all produced in the monasteries. It is thus under-standable that the history of the education brought by christianity to Ireland is largely synonymous with the education given by the monasteries. It has, however, already been emphasized that when the christian missionaries arrived, they found in flourishing existence the educational system of the native schools. How this persisted and how it came to terms with the monastic system will be examined later. The question will also be considered how far the education destined mainly for candidates for the religious life was extended to the secular clergy and the laity. For the moment, we will consider the content and methods of this monastic education.

STAGES OF MONASTIC EDUCATION

As a rule, the monasteries did not undertake what we would call primary education. The normal process was this. Up to the age of about seven years, the child remained with his parents, or, more commonly, in accordance with the usual Irish custom, was given for fosterage to relations or friends of his family. Then, if he was destined for the church, he was entrusted to the care of some priest or hermit to begin his education.

Numerous examples of this system are found in the lives of the Irish saints. Thus St. Declan was first entrusted to one Dobran, a relative, who had 'earnestly pleaded of the parents of Declan that they should give the boy to him for fosterage.' On completion of his seventh year, he was entrusted 'by his parents and foster-parents' to the care of Dymna 'a holy and wise man' to 'learn to read.'[7] St. Brendan was fostered for five years by St. Ita, and then passed into the care of Bishop Erc of Alltraigh, who for another five years 'taught him his letters'.[8] St. Colman of Lann Elo (Lynally in Offaly), said by some to have been a nephew of St. Colum Cille, having remained in the care of his own parents 'for a few years', was entrusted to 'a holy old man, Kevin, that he might teach him and nourish him for God.' In turn, Kevin sent him to certain 'holy abbots in his early youth, that he might witness their rule and religious life and learn the scriptures with them.'[9] Later, St. Colman himself undertook the role of tutor. A certain chief had a boy born blind, and had made several attempts to drown the child, which were miraculously foiled. The saint rebuked the unnatural parent, assuring him that this blind child would be the best of his family. Whereupon the chief offered him 'to be brought up for God.' St. Colman baptized him and afterwards 'instructed him in the sacred scriptures and good morals.'[10] A somewhat similar incident occurs in the life of St. Mochua of Balla. St. Comgall of Bangor came to the house of Mochua's father, Becan, and asked how many sons he had. 'Two', said Becan, 'who are to be counted, and a little lame child who is with the sheep and he is not to be counted.' But the discerning saint replied: 'My soul rejoices greatly at this boy.' Someone else was found to mind the sheep, and Comgall took the little cripple, Mochua, off to Bangor,' where he read the Canon of the Old Law and the New Testament, and the ecclesiastical order.'[11]

Oblati

There were, however, not uncommon exceptions to this general rule that primary education was given by some individual teachers. Reference is found to *oblati,* children who, on the completion of their fosterage, were immediately entrusted to the care of some monastic establishment. In the life of St. Magnenn, of Kilmainham, near Dublin, we read of 'an urchin of his *familia* – one that was just seven years old' who asked his venerable superior how piety must be practised. The reply must have been somewhat daunting to a seven year old. 'Early tierce and long none; meat so much as may suffice a little boy: sleep as it were of a captive cast for death;

...much prayer every night as though that night should be one's last;' and a further litany of austere prescriptions.[12]

And in the life of St. Kieran of Saighir we find the familiar figure of a problem child, one Crithid, 'that in good works was no more than a fool; but in bad works of maliciousness, right noxious.' He began his career with St. Ciaran of Clonmacnois, but was transferred to Saighir, when he distinguished himself by putting out 'a certain hold fire'. Next day he suffered a common fate of naughty children in these cautionary tales, being killed by wolves. But his former master, Ciaran, hurried to the scene, brought the boy back to life by his prayers, and, no doubt to the relief of the good monks of Saighir, brought him back to his own monastery.[13]

THE BIBLE AS TEXT-BOOK

The education given by the christian teachers was that which at the time was given all over the European continent and in Britain. It was based essentially on the Latin language, which by the fifth century was the language of society, of the church and of the schools. The Latin bible was the first reading book of the young Irish scholar. As soon as he had mastered the alphabet, a psalter or part of it was put into his hands. When the five year old St. Brendan began his studies with bishop Erc, we are told that 'thereafter to the end of five years he read his psalms.[14] Then there is the intriguing story of the same saint when at the age of six he was left alone in the bishop's chariot 'reciting his psalms by himself.' A 'young girl of royal race' tried to jump up on the chariot and play with the boy, but was repulsed by a flick of the reins. She ran weeping to her parents, and the good bishop condemned his over-zealous pupil to spend a night in a cave.[15] In the life of St. Comgall, we hear of a youth named Aedhan who was cured of leprosy by the saint, and the detail is thrown in that at the time 'he was reading the twelve minor prophets under the guidance of St. Senell.'[16] Of St. Bairre (Findbarr) of Cork we read that as 'a little lad' he learned his psalms from a cleric named Lochan, and later 'read the book of Matthew and the book of the Apostles with Bishop Mac Cuirb', who had baptized him.[17] It is, in fact, clear that in these early Christian days, primary education consisted in the reading, understanding and learning by heart of the Latin scriptures.

The boy who had followed the usual course and received his early education outside the monastery would be well grounded in Latin and in parts of the Scripture. Abbot Jonas, the Italian monk who entered the monastery of Bobbio in 618, probably three years after the death of Columbanus, tells us in his Life of the saint that, before he left home for the monastery he was well grounded in 'grammar, rhetoric, geometry and the scriptures.'[18] In the monastic school he would begin a more advanced course, more detailed study of the scriptures, introduction to other christian and to non-christian authors, and the 'ecclesiastical rules', i.e. dogmatic and moral theology, canon law and ritual.

It should not be imagined, however, that this more advanced classical education was within the powers of the young neophyte in the earliest ages of christianity in Ireland. St. Patrick's own training had been deficient, and in any case the problem in this pagan country was to get the essential truths of christianity expressed in the simplest language. It is only in the sixth century that we find evidence of the type of classical education common in Europe at the time.[19]

STUDY OF PAGAN CLASSICS

In the early Church opinion was at first sharply divided as to the propriety of using pagan authors in the education of youth. Sulpicius Severus, Tertullian, Arnobius, Lactantius and Cassian would have nothing to do with them. But eventually the broader view prevailed that they could be studied for their literary value, and thus enable christian scholars to defend their religion more effectively, whilst a knowledge of the philosophies which they presented would provide a firmer rational basis for the Faith. This was the final attitude of St. Basil, of St. Jerome, who lectured to young students at Bethlehem on the pagan poets, of St. Augustine, whose philosophy was based on Plato, and of St. Ambrose, who constantly quoted and copied Virgil.

The Irish monks appear to have adopted without scruple the more liberal attitude towards the pagan classics. There is no evidence of disapproval of them, and clear evidence that they were at least fairly generally studied. Thus in the extant works of St. Columbanus, comprising letters, sermons, the monastic rule and poems, there are echoes and even direct quotations from Virgil, Horace (whose works were almost unknown on the continent from the sixth to the eighth centuries), Ovid, Juvenal, Martial and Sallust, and of later writers Prudentius, Fortunatus, Juvencus, Ausonius and Claudian. The number of these quotations and the ease with which they are introduced display complete familiarity with the authors. Thus in the five hundred lines of the poems we have thirty-two such borrowings from Virgil, fifteen from Horace and eleven from Ovid. It is quite intriguing to find that in the charming boat-song which Columban seems to have composed on his journey up the Rhine in 611, the Saint has unblushingly lifted from the Georgics a familiar tag, which, with a slight change of order and tense, he renders: *'Labor improbus omnia vincit.'*[20]

In his scholarly and entertaining work, *Columbanus in his own words* (72, 105–8), Mgr. Tomás Ó Fiaich draws attention to J. W. Smit's *Studies on the language and style of Columba the Younger,* published in Amsterdam in 1971, in which the attribution of the poems to Columban of Bobbio is challenged. Smit's book was reviewed in *Latomus,* vol. 31 (1972) by Professor Ludwig Bieler, whose verdict was that its thesis is unproven. Mgr. Ó Fiaich considers the question to be an open one. It is clear, however, that the identity of the author of these poems is irrelevant to the point with which we are concerned.

In Reeves's edition of the *Life of St. Columba* by Adamnán,[21] the ninth abbot of Iona, the claim is made in the index that five quotations from Virgil and one from Horace are to be found in the text. One hesitates to disagree with so erudite an authority, but examination of the few phrases and words indicated make it doubtful that there is question of anything more than an accidental similarity.

STUDY OF GREEK

Many of the older writers, as, for instance, Healy,[22] Hyde[23] and Joyce,[24] held that there was considerable study of Greek from the earliest times in the Irish monasteries. Hyde and Joyce obviously relied largely on a painstaking but somewhat uncritical article, *The Knowledge of Greek in Ireland between 500 and 900 A.D.,* by George T. Stokes, professor of Ecclesiastical History in Dublin University.[25]

The claim made by these writers was subjected at a later date to searching criticism by Mario Esposito in an article 'The Knowledge of Greek in Ireland during the Middle Ages',[26] and modern authorities accept the view of Professor John Ryan that 'beyond the alphabet and some chance words or phrases, there is no evidence that Greek was studied, known or taught in the early monastic schools.[27] It is significant that whereas in 1908 Mrs. Stopford Green could make the unqualified statement that 'Greek was studied in early times,'[28] she felt in 1925 bound to acknowledge that 'though there are signs of some knowledge of Greek among the Irish... there is no evidence of Greek studies until the ninth century'.[29]

We may consider briefly a few of the scattered evidences that in the early monastic period the Greek language was, at least, not utterly unknown. In the medieval *Life of St. Brendan,* it is related that St. Gildas, the British monk who exercised so much influence in giving to the Irish church its predominantly monastic form, gave to St. Brendan a missal 'written in Greek letters.' It was, however, regarded as a miracle that St. Brendan could understand it.[30]

St. Columban (d. 615), in a letter to Pope St. Boniface IV, makes a
play on his own name, the Dove, and gives both the Hebrew and
Greek forms of it.[31] St. Cummian, one of the successors of St.
Brendan in the school of Clonfert, in his celebrated letter (c. 632)
to his friend Segienus, abbot of Iona, on the vexed question of the
correct date of the Easter celebration, cites the opinions of Greek
writers such as Origen, Cyril and Pachomius, in such a way as to
suggest that he was familiar with their writings.[32] St. Aileran, abbot
of Clonard (d. 665) in his only extant work, *Commentary on the
genealogy of our Lord,* discusses the meaning of each name in
Hebrew, Greek and Latin.[33] In a treatise *De Mirabilibus Sacrae
Scripturae* composed in 660 by an Irishman named Augustine, it is
possible that the scripture quotations are taken direct from the
Septuagint.[34] A few Greek words and the Our Father in Greek are
found in Adamnán's Life of St. Columbanus.[35]

It must be acknowledge that these scattered instances, spread
over a couple of centuries, whilst indicating the possibility of some
acquaintance with the Greek language in the early Irish monasteries,
hardly justify even the guarded claim of Professor Stokes that there
was as much Greek known and studied in the sixth to tenth centuries
in Ireland as in Dublin in 1892.[36]

All authorities, however, hold that in the ninth century the
evidence for the knowledge of Greek is much stronger. It has been
suggested that one reason for this may have been the influence of
the Greek Theodore of Tarsus, who came to Canterbury as archbishop (664–690) and set up there a celebrated school. Bede, who
was a contemporary, states that Theodore's pupils learned to speak
Greek fluently. It is a reasonable surmise that Irish monks, who at
this period were travelling everywhere in search of learning or
spiritual direction, found their way to Canterbury and acquired the
language of their mentor.[37] Esposito[38] rejects this theory on the
ground that more than a century elapsed from the time of Theodore
until the ninth century, when Irishmen abroad certainly displayed
a knowledge of Greek. It is not necessary, however, to postulate
that the Irish monks learned Greek directly from Theodore. They
might well have done so at a later date in the school where he had
revived Greek studies.

SEDULIUS SCOTTUS
What is beyond doubt is that, during the ninth century, Irish
scholars are found in the forefront of the cultural revival in Europe,
and that many of them were remarkable for their knowledge of
Greek at a time when its study was generally at a low ebb. Two
stand out in particular, Sedulius Scottus and Johannes Scottus

Eriugena. The former is not to be confused with the much earlier Sedulius who flourished in the first half of the fifth century, author of the *Carmen Paschale,* which can claim to be the first Christian epic. That Sedulius is said to have studied in Gaul and Italy, and to have settled in Achaia. Older authors claim him as an Irishman, but the only proofs they can adduce appear to be his name, which is the common latinized form of the Irish Siadhal, and the fact that there is no evidence of his belonging to any other nation.[39]

The ninth-century Sedulius was one of those many Irishmen who took refuge on the continent during the Norse wars. Nothing is known of his birth and early upbringing, but it is accepted by all authorities that he was Irish. He is consistently referred to as 'Scottus', 'a name which was to become the normal Latin designation of the people of Ireland from the fifth to the ninth century.'[40] Further proof of his Irish origin is provided by the fact that in his poems he constantly refers to Ireland. Again, as in the case of the older Sedulius, there is the likelihood that the name is the latinized form of the Irish Siadhal.

He appears with rather mysterious suddenness as director of studies at the cathedral school of Liège (845–58), becomes famous as scholar, poet and public orator, is received at the court of Aix as instructor to the sons of Lothair I, and is so highly thought of that the Empress embroiders his verses in gold thread on silk. His Latin works include commentaries on St. Paul and St. Matthew, and his poems, of which eighty-three survive, display a wide knowledge of Latin metres and a lyrical strain not commonly found in his age. He clearly possessed some knowledge of Greek. A Greek psalter, now in Paris, has a colophon stating that it is written by his hand, and he constantly goes out of his way to introduce Greek words into his Latin writings. One of his works is a commentary on the *Isagoge* of Porphyry, an introduction to the logic of Aristotle. It is notable that he seems to show a knowledge of the Greek version of this work, although in his day and for at least three more centuries, the *Isagoge* was known in western Europe in the Latin version only. Kenney holds that Sedulius' knowledge of Greek was 'substantial – even if quite limited.'[41]

JOHANNES ERIUGENA

A far greater figure is Johannes Eriugena. Kenney holds him to be, 'with the exception of St. Columbanus... the most important individual that Ireland gave to continental Europe in the middle ages.'[42] In the opinion of Daniel-Rops he was 'one of the greatest scholars and certainly the most penetrating and controlled mind of the epoch'.[43] Of him, as of Sedulius, nothing is known until he suddenly appears on the continental scene, but it is beyond question that he was born and reared in Ireland.[44]

Prudentius of Troyes, though a personal friend, was obliged in his *De Praedestinatione contra I. Scottum* to criticize the doctrine of Johannes.[45] He acknowledges that Ireland (Hibernia) had given to Gaul this most learned of her scholars, but warns his readers against his friend's 'Celtic eloquence'. Johannes himself, on the title-page of his *De Caelesti Hierarchia,* assumes the appellation Eriugena (born in Ireland) which, less common in his day, was often given to Irishmen after the eleventh century, when Scottus came to mean a native of Scotland. From the ninth to the seventeenth century the more common forms of the name was Johannes Scottus. Certain scholars then popularized the form Eriugena, and later usage has sanctioned the pleonasm, Johannes Scottus Eriugena.

About 850 Eriugena is found at the court of Charles the Bald, Charlemagne's grandson, at Laon and Rheims, and becomes a member, some say director, of the palace school. A prolific writer, his best known works are the philosophico-theological treatise *On the Division of the Universe,* and his *Book on Predestination,* in the latter of which he was held to have fallen into unorthodoxy.

He was obviously a competent Greek scholar. In the second half of the fifth century, an unknown Greek writer composed certain obscure mystical treatises which were ascribed to Dionysius the Areopagite, whom St. Paul converted at Athens. These works, whose author became known as the Pseudo-Dionysius, were gradually accepted by Catholic theologians and were widely read by the initiated during the middle ages. In 858, Eriugena was called upon by Charles the Bald to make a new translation of them. A copy of this translation, sent by Charles to Pope Nicholas I, drew from the Vatican librarian, appointed to examine it, an astonished encomium. 'It is also wonderful that this foreigner, who, coming from the ends of the earth, would have had little intercourse with other nations and hence little opportunity of hearing any language but his own, could understand such matters and render them into another tongue.'[46]

Eriugena's *Versio Operum S. Dionysii* had a far greater effect on medieval thought than his original works. It was his text of the Areopagite that was utilized by Albert the Great, St. Thomas, Alexander of Hales and St. Bonaventure, and it contributed in a considerable way to the formation of scholastic terminology.

It is, of course, not impossible that such men as Sedulius and Eriugena acquired their knowledge of Greek after they had left their native country. This view is taken by Esposito with regard to Eriugena.[47] He bases it on the fact that in Eriugena's earliest work,

De Praedestinatione (851), the Irish scholar shows slight acquaintance with Greek and little or none with Greek philosophy and patristic literature. His Greek studies would, therefore, have taken place during the succeeding seven years. As against this it may be urged that the words of the Vatican librarian quoted above are more naturally interpreted to imply that Eriugena had learned his Greek in his own distant land. Furthermore it must be noted that Sedulius and Eriugena are only two amongst several Irishmen who displayed a knowledge of Greek at this period, a fact acknowledged by Esposito.[48] There is preserved at Laon, for instance, a curious collection of glossaries, paradigms etc., made about the middle of the ninth century, by one Martinus Hiberniensis and two companions for the benefit of students of Greek,[49] and a considerable number of Irish glosses on Greek manuscripts of the eighth and ninth centuries have engaged the attention of continental scholars.[50]

Indeed, the German scholar, Traube, goes so far as to say that 'whoever on the continent in the days of Charles the Bald knew Greek was an Irishman, or at least his knowledge was transmitted to him through an Irishman.'[51] The same view is supported by at least one modern authority, Dr. Nora K. Chadwick, who writes: 'All knowledge of Greek under the Franks seems to have been an Irish monopoly.'[52] In view of the decay of Greek studies in Europe at the time, it does seem more likely that these Irish scholars were already equipped with at least some knowledge of the language before their arrival on the continent than that they should simultaneously develop an interest in it, living as they did amidst circles in which it had almost died out.

Another German scholar, Heinrich Zimmer, was amongst those who held that Greek was studied, at least to some extent, in the Irish schools from the fifth to the ninth century. In this connection he stressed two important points. Firstly, Latin was never an official language in Ireland, as it was in Britain and the other Roman provinces. Secondly, there was at that period no Latin version of the scriptures generally accepted by the western Church. Irish students, therefore, were more likely to be attracted to the study of the original text of the scriptures.[53] This contention has some weight, but it must be remembered that, though Latin was never the official civil language in Ireland, it was, from the beginning, the official language of the Church, in the sense of being the medium of a large part of its teaching and liturgy.

CHAPTER 8

THE MONASTIC SCHOOLS (continued)

GLOSSES

The only textbooks used in the early Irish monastic schools were copies of standard authors, christian or pagan. As an aid to their pupils or themselves, teachers frequently wrote between the lines or in the margins translations of Latin or Greek words into Irish, or free translations of phrases or sentences. Such notes, which of course are not peculiar to ancient Irish documents, are known as glosses, from the Greek *glossa,* a (foreign) tongue. The modern Irish form of the word is *gluais.*

Large numbers of these Irish glosses are found in manuscripts of the seventh, eighth and ninth centuries, preserved in libraries all over Europe. Older Irish authorities believed that many of these manuscripts were brought to the continent by refugee monks during the Norse invasions. This, however, seems hardly likely, in view of the bulk of these manuscripts and the perils of the journey, and the modern view is that at least the vast majority of the glosses came from the pens of Irish exiles working on manuscripts written by themselves or others on the continent.[1]

The first scholar to study the glosses systematically was the Bavarian Johann Kaspar Zeuss (1806–1856). His studies included all the Celtic languages and resulted in the great work of his life, *Grammatica Celtica.*

Hyde gives a full account of the continental scholars who had studied the glosses up to the publication of his *Literary History* in 1899, Zeuss, Zimmer, Ascoli, Nigra, and details of the glossed manuscripts they had discovered in Milan, St. Gall, Würzburg, Carlsruhe, Turin, Vienna, Berne, Leyden, Nancy.[2]

But the most complete collection of glosses was made by the two scholars, Whitley Stokes and John Strachan. Having devoted years to this work and published a few lesser collections, they issued the results of their own researches and those of others in two large volumes, *Thesaurus Palaeohibernicus,* 1901 and 1903. The first volume contains glosses on biblical texts, the psalms, the gospels of St. Matthew and St. Mark, the epistles of St. Paul and St. Peter, with translations of the glosses and notes, chiefly textual and grammatical. The second volume has glosses on non-biblical texts, Augustine, Bede, Priscian, Propertius and others, and a large number of miscellaneous writings, poems and hymns, almost all of which date from before the ninth century.

This immense work, in spite of errors into which pioneers in such a field must inevitably fall, still remains a standard source for the study of Old Irish. What makes it more remarkable is that the study of Celtic languages was for both authors only a secondary occupation. Stokes, Dublin born, was an Indian civil servant, and did most of his writing in India or England, and Strachan, a Scot, was professor of Greek and Comparative Philology in the University of Manchester.

The glosses have been drawn on by all Celtic scholars, and are one of the recognized sources for the study of the most ancient forms of the Irish language. Thus their original purpose has been inverted. They were intended to explain the classical languages in the current vernacular. Now the Latin or Greek text is the key to the understanding of the archaic Irish notes.

It may be noted also, that, in addition to providing the key to the earliest form of written Irish, the glosses are a testimony to the familiarity of these monk scholars with a wide range of classical writings.

GLOSSARIES

The glosses date from as early as the seventh century. Of a later date are the glossaries, explanations of unusual or obsolete words, made to help scholars in the deciphering of ancient writings. These, however, were not intended for the use of ordinary students, so deserve here only a passing reference.

The most noteworthy is *Sanas Chormaic,* Cormac's Glossary, commonly attributed to bishop Cormac mac Cuilennáin, King of Cashel (d.908).[3] The attribution to Cormac is accepted by many authorities, but in varying degrees of certainty. O'Curry holds that 'there is every reason to believe that the Glossary was part of a lost work of Cormac, the *Saltair of Cashel'.*[4] Stokes summarizes the reasons, historical and philological, for acceptance of the attribution.[5] Hyde holds that the glossary may have been enlarged by later authors but that 'much of the matter remains Cormac's'.[6] Eleanor Hull expresses the view that 'whether actually written by or

for Cormac or not, it seems to date from near his time; and a
universal and ancient tradition ascribes it to him.'[7] Kenney simply
refers to it as the 'glossary of Cormac mac Cuilennáin'.[8]

Cormac's Glossary is described by Hyde as the 'oldest attempt at
a comparative vernacular dictionary in any language in modern
Europe'.[9] It provides explanations of over a thousand words or
phrases, the meaning of which had already in the ninth century
become obscure. It does this by tracing them back to their derivations, or by comparing them with words in the Hebrew, Greek,
Latin, British and Norse languages. The explations are almost all
in Irish, but an occasional Latin word or phrase is used. Dr. Healy
points out that the value of the glossary consists not so much in its
philological content as in the evidence it gives of the wide scholarship
which prevailed in the Irish schools even in the troubled times of
the ninth century.[10]

Together with Cormac's Glossary, Stokes published two other
glossaries, the Glossary to the *Félire,* Calendar or Martyrology, of
Oengus the Culdee, and a much later work, a glossary of Donal
O'Davoren, who conducted a famous law school in the Burren, Co.
Clare, in the sixteenth century.[11]

Oengus Céli Dé (servant of God, commonly anglicized Culdee)
lived in the latter half of the eighth century. He studied at the
monastery of Clonenagh in Laois, founded by St. Fintan, lived the
life of a recluse for many years, and later joined the monastery of
Tallaght. The earliest manuscript of the glossary belongs to the
fourteenth or fifteenth century, but the *Félire* itself is generally
accepted to be of about the date 800. It consists of quatrains
descriptive of the life and virtues of the saint of each day of the year.[12]

The title *Céli Dé* was probably given to Oengus in recognition
of his personal sanctity, but in the first half of the eighth century it
began to be given to groups of men, either within a monastery or in
association with it, who combined the strict life of a recluse with
community life under a superior.[13]

Another notable glossary is that of Brother Michael O'Cleary.[14]
It was published in 1643 at Louvain, where the great Franciscan
annalist had returned after the completion of the labours in Ireland
which resulted in the memorable *Annals of the Four Masters.* In his
dedication to Baothghalach Mac Egan, bishop of Elphin, who had
assisted him in his work, O'Clery describes it as 'a small gleaning of
hard words of our native tongue, collected from some of the old
books of our country, and explained according to the knowledge
and interpretation of the chief authors who have been in our country
of late, who have devoted themselves to the interpretation of the
ancient Gaelic.'

GRAMMARS

It is clear that the monastic scholars, as might be expected, were familiar with the standard Latin grammatical treatises of the time, especially with the *Institutiones Grammaticae* of Priscian, who flourished at Constantinople about 500 A.D., and the *Ars Grammatica* of the Roman Donatus, a slightly earlier writer, the tutor of St. Jerome. Kenney gives an account of the various copies of Latin grammatical texts found in continental libraries, which were obviously made by Irish monks and heavily glossed, both in Latin and Irish.[15] The most notable of these is the St. Gall Priscian, which Kenney holds to have been certainly written in Ireland, and whose glosses show a wide knowledge of other Latin writers. We have, however, no evidence as to whether, or how far, the monastic teachers used these grammars in their classes.

AN ANCIENT IRISH GRAMMAR

A treatise on the grammar of the Irish language can be traced back, at least in its original form, to the middle of the second half of the seventh century. In some of the tracts dealing with the studies of the *filid*, mention is made of the *Auraicept*, with which they were required to be familiar at an early stage. The full name of this work is *Auraicept na nÉces*, the Scholar's Primer.[16] In the fourteenth-century compilations, the *Book of Ballymote* and the *Book of Lecan*, are to be found Middle Irish versions of this very ancient tract on the Ogam alphabet and Irish grammar.

Various parts of the text are allegedly the work of four scholars, Ferchertne and Amergin, whom we have already met, Fenius Farsaid, ancestor of Milesius, and Cenn Faeled, of whom we shall hear later. Of these, the only reliable attribution is to Cenn Faeled, a well authenticated person who died in 679. However, the passages attributed to other poets may well be by anonymous writers of about the same time. The whole tract seems to have been compiled over a long period, from the middle of the seventh to the tenth or even eleventh century.[17]

The various sections of the *Auraicept* are as follows. Attributed to Cenn Faeled: The origin of Gaelic, divisions of the Latin and Irish alphabets, Latin and Irish treatment of the semi-vowels contrasted, genders in Irish, degrees of comparison in Latin, and qualitative distinctions in Irish. Attributed to Ferchertne: The seven elements of speech in Irish, the formation and powers of Ogam letters. Attributed to Amergin: A lengthy treatise on the origin of Gaelic. Attributed to Fenius: the alphabets of Hebrew, Greek and Latin, syllabic content of Irish words, consonant changes, the five kinds of Irish, the twenty-five inflections, the meaning of *alt*.

The grammatical portion of the *Auraicept* is largely identified with that treated by Latin grammarians, the alphabet, classification of letters, sounds and syllables, gender and declensions of nouns, comparative of adjectives, prepositions governing the dative and accusative cases, etc. Notable omissions, however, are the treatment of pronouns and accidence of the verb.

Bergin has pointed out the difficulties into which the author or redactor of the *Auraicept* runs. He 'tries to distinguish seventeen cases of nouns, giving a special name to each occurrence of the dative or accusative according to the preposition that precedes it. But for the verbs he had no models. In marked contrast to Latin, in which the Indo-European system has been utterly transformed, and the verbs fall into a few clear and definitive conjugations, the Old Irish verbal scheme is, as Kuno Meyer has said, "perhaps the most complicated of all languages". Latin analogies were of no help.'[18]

THE AUTHORSHIP OF THE AURAICEPT

Who was the author, or who were the authors of this ancient grammar? There are many indications that go to show that it was the work of native lay scholars. We have seen that at least the original form of one section may be fairly attributed to the late seventh century Cenn Faeled. Elsewhere there are passing references to tenth century lay grammarians, Ua Bruic, Ua Coindi, Ua Coirill and Ua Finn.[19] We have seen that knowledge of the *Auraicept* appears to have been a required portion of the studies of the *filid*. It is, perhaps, also of some slight significance that the fourteenth century compilations in which it is preserved were the work of lay scholars, the *Book of Ballymote* compiled mainly by Solomon Ó Droma and Manus Ó Duigennán, and the *Yellow Book of Lecan* by Gilla Ísa MacFirbis and a number of collaborators.[20]

On the other hand, the familiarity with Latin grammar displayed in the *Auraicept* suggests a monastic provenance. Professor Ó Cuív has pointed out that the very title of the work displays an intermingling of native and foreign learning. It is most probably based on the native prefix *a(i)r*, 'a beginning' and the Latin *acceptum* or *accepta*, 'that which is received', whilst *Éces* is one of the native names given to the *filid*. It is plausibly suggested by Professor Ó Cuív and also by Professor Binchy, that the solution of the question is that the author was a poet turned monk.[21] In any case, the *Auraicept* would have been known to monastic scholars from the time of its composition, since by then the fusion of the christian and native culture was complete. But whether, over its long history, it was ever in common use by them, must remain a matter of conjecture.

It is remarkable that, with the exception of the *Auraicept,* there is no trace of formal grammatical tracts in the Old and Early Middle Irish periods. Such tracts are not found until early in the sixteenth century, though they are based on the standardization of the literary language which began in the thirteenth century – a point to which we shall recur later. It has been pointed out by Bergin that the ancient Irish, like so many other nations, knew nothing of formal grammar. Latin influence, indeed, gave rise to an interest in etymology, which in Ireland led to a craze for far-fetched derivations. Furthermore, through the medium of Latin grammar, some fragments of grammatical knowledge came in, such as distinctions of genders and cases of nouns. The *Auraicept* was an unsuccessful attempt to construct an Irish grammar on the Latin model, and, as far as we know, had no successor.[22]

COPYING OF BOOKS

We have seen that Patrick and his followers brought with them the books necessary for their apostolate. It was an obvious step that these should be multiplied, and we find, in fact, that early in the sixth century the transcription of manuscripts flourished everywhere. We recall the importance attributed in the *Annals* to the office of scribe. There are also numerous incidents in the lives of the saints and other documents in which this activity plays a prominent part. We need not accept these anecdotes as being historical in every detail, but, taken cumulatively, they establish beyond doubt that writing was one of the common occupations of the monastic life.

There is, for instance, in Adamnán's Life of St. Columba the lively story of how Columba was in his *tugurium,* a little hut to which he used to retire in order to work undisturbed. The voice of a man was heard coming from the mainland, asking to be ferried across to Iona. 'This man is a blunderer', exclaimed the saint. 'He will surely upset my inkhorn'. To avoid this mishap, Diormitius, the saint's assistant, posted himself at the door of the hut, but was called away just at the crucial moment. The eager visitor arrived. He rushed to embrace the saint and the edge of his cloak caught the inkhorn, with the dire result which Colum Cille had foreseen,

When Colum Cille felt that his death was approaching, seated in his little hut, he was copying the Psalter. Coming to the words in the 33rd psalm 'Those who seek the Lord lack no good thing', he dropped his pen and said: 'Let Baithenus continue this', thereby, it was believed, indicating his successor. After his death, there were recorded the miraculous preservation of his manuscripts from destruction and their use in imparting blessings.[23]

There is a pleasant story told in the *Life of St. Comgall* of a boy pupil in the monastery of Bangor whom nobody could teach to write, for what he wrote was so illegible that 'one could hardly tell whether it was the work of a man's hand or of a bird's claw.' The boy, in despair, betook himself to Comgall, who blessed his eyes and hands. The miracle that followed was a generous one. Not only did the boy's writing so improve that he excelled all others, but in after life he became 'a teacher in that art'.[24]

WRITING MATERIALS

The most common form of writing material was parchment or vellum, the skins of sheep, goats, or calves.[25] Chemical analysis has shown that the ink was made from charcoal. Quill pens were used, as is evidenced in the earliest pictures, for example that of St. John in the Book of Kells. There are many allusions to quill pens in the ancient writings. In the Life of St. Molasius of Devenish there is the legend which relates how the saint was once at a loss for a pen, but was helped out by a passing flock of birds, one of which obligingly dropped a quill.[26] There is a delightfully human allusion to a pen in Adamnán's Life of St. Colum Cille when a monk named Molua asked the saint to bless a knife. Columba was busy writing, and gave the blessing with the pen still in his hand *'extensa manu sancta cum calamo signans benedixit'*.[27]

The vellum leaves were held together by some sort of binding. Jonas, the near contemporary of St. Columbanus, tells us in his *Life* of the saint that Athala, the second abbot of Bobbio, when setting everything in order in preparation for his death, arranged for the preservation of the monastery's manuscripts. One precaution was to have them bound. (*Libros ligaminibus firmat*).[28]

Notes not intended to be preserved were made on long thin wooden tablets, usually of beech or birch. Most commonly these were covered with wax and the writing was done with an iron style. A passage in the Life of St. Brendan relates how the 'holy father, taking his tablet and style, by the revelation of God, wrote on the wax'.[29] We find reference to both the temporary and permanent forms of writing in the introduction to Adamnán's *De Locis Sanctis*. Adamnán relates how he obtained from the Gaulish bishop, Ainulfus, a visitor to Iona, much information about Jerusalem, which he first took down *'in tabulas'* and then wrote *'in membranis'*[30]. The writing tablet in Latin documents is *tabula,* and also, from its coating, *cera* or *ceraculum*. There are various Irish equivalents of *tabula: taibhle, tabhall,* etc.[31] The style in Latin is *graphium,* the Irish form of which is *graib* or *graif*. When St. Patrick was in conflict with the idol Crom Cruach, his *graif* fell out of his mantle into the heather around him.[32] Again, in the *Book of Lecan* is found the legend of the death of King Brandubh. Demons were carrying his soul away, and Maedhog, abbot of Ferns, pursued them through the skies. As they passed over Iona, St. Colum Cille heard the tumult. He was writing at the time, and, sticking his *graib* into his cloak, he went to the rescue of the king.[33]

The ink was kept in a little vessel usually made out of part of an animal's horn. We have already come across the incident of a clumsy visitor knocking over the ink-horn of St. Colum Cille. In Adamnán's *Life* the word used is *corniculum,* a little horn. We find the exact equivalent *adircín* in a Middle Irish version of the same legend.[34]

BOOK SATCHELS

We find constant reference to the keeping of books in satchels, *tiaga* (from Latin *theca*). Apparently in the monastic libraries these satchels hung upon the walls. In the notes in the *Lebor Brecc* version of the *Félire* (Calendar or Martyrology) of Oengus Céli Dé there is an obituary of Longarad 'The White-legged' of Sliabh Mairge, in Laois, a sixth-century 'sage of learning and history and jurisprudence and poetry'. We are told that 'when Longarad was dead, men of lore say this that the book-satchels of Ireland (*tiaga lebar erenn*) fell down on that night. Or (according to another version), is it that the satchels wherein were books of every science in the cell where Columcille was that fell then, and Columcille and everyone in that house marvel and all are silent at the noisy shaking of the books.'[35] Satchels were also used for carrying books about. In Adamnán's Life of Columba we are told of a youth who, some years after the saint's death was carrying one of his books 'contained in a leather case'. The youth was drowned in a river, and when the body was recovered, this one book was found undamaged by the water.[36] More elaborate cases of leather or metal were used to preserve particularly valuable manuscripts. In the *Tripartite Life of St. Patrick* it is stated that 'the holy bishop Assicus was Patrick's copper-smith, and he made altars and quadrangular tables and quadrangular book-covers in honour of Patrick'.[37]

Fer Leiginn

The title *fer léiginn* (lit. man of reading, i.e. to others), translated by the editors of the Annals as *lector,* is found very frequently in the Annals, for example in the *Annals of Ulster* some twenty times from 894 to 1118. It obviously meant the head-professor or director of studies in an ecclesiastical school. Now and again the title *árd fer léiginn* (chief man of reading) occurs, but this does not imply any special distinction. It is obvious that any *fer léiginn* who was distinguished enough to deserve a place in the Annals must have been the head-professor in his establishment. Furthermore, an entry in the *Annals of Ulster* for 1220, which records a dispute between the monks of Derry and the Cenél Eogain, the sept in whose territory the monastery stood, about the succession to the position of *fer léiginn,* makes it clear that the holder of it was not one among several teachers, but was the supreme authority.

THE SCRIBE

The title *fer léiginn* is first found at the close of the eighth century. It occurs occasionally in the ninth and becomes common in the tenth.[38] Up to the ninth century we find frequent mention of the *scriba* (scribe), the expert copyist of manuscripts.[39] Gwynn points out that this title was evidently considered to be a most honourable one. 'It is often used to enhance the dignity of the Abbot or Bishop: nay we sometimes find, in the recital of honours the "accomplished scribe" commemorated, with the dignity of Bishop or Abbot or both attached as an accident of office'.

The same writer goes on to say: 'When in the process of time, the duty of theological instruction was added to the practice and teaching of penmanship, the more honourable title of Ferleghen... was adopted'.[40] We need not, of course, assume that the office of scribe was always merged with that of the *fer léiginn.* Doubtless it continued to be carried on by many monks who were not qualified theologians. Nor need we assume that the office of *fer léiginn* appeared suddenly in the ninth century. There must have been, from the beginning, some person in each monastery who directed the young monks in their studies. What is clear, however, is that from the ninth century on the office of *fer léiginn* assumes special importance. MacNeill, dealing with this matter says: 'This points to a new development in the schools of Ireland at that time.'[41] An interesting evidence of the high status of the *fer léiginn* is found in the entry in the Annals for 1049 where it is recorded that on the death of Amalghaidh, Abbot of Armagh, Dubhdaleithe 'assumed the abbotship from his lectorship (*as a firus léiginn*), on the same day on which Amalghaidh died.'[42] This development would have been a natural one according as the monasteries increased in size, but it may also have been partially due to the fact that about the tenth century many of the abbots had assumed the role of extensive landlords and would have left the intellectual activity of the monastery to the director of studies, who thus acquired a special dignity.

Kenney makes the point that the adoption of the title *fer léiginn* in place of *scriba* is an indication of the 'shifting of emphasis from

Latin to Irish'. He finds that the ordinary use of *scriba* 'seems to end in 932 with the obit of Fer-domnach mac Flannacán, scribe of Clonard.'[43]

A detailed study of the activity of the early Irish monastic scribes has been made by Dr. Kathleen Hughes.[44] She agrees with Gwynn as to the high position held by the scribes and the essential difference between him and the *fer léiginn*. She draws attention to some further interesting points. The regularly occurring obituaries in the Annals imply a comparatively organized *scriptorium,* but the fact that they are spaced often at intervals of a generation seems to indicate that only the master of the *scriptorium* was commemorated, with occasionally one of his assistants.[45]

As has been seen, after the middle of the tenth century, emphasis ceases to be laid on transcription. We find, indeed, both scribes and *lectores* mentioned, but only Armagh and Clonmacnois maintained both. The frequency of the obituaries of both scribe and *fer léiginn* at the close of the century is confirmation of the distinction between the two offices.

A minor, but interesting question discussed by Dr. Hughes is whether there was any connection between the rich period of the scribes and the anchoretic movement which took place in the eighth century under the influence of Duiblitir, abbot of Finglas and Mael Ruain, abbot of Tallaght. Of 96 scribes attached to specific houses, 22 are called anchorites by the annalists, and 21 come from houses which have no anchorite attached to them. Dr. Hughes concludes: 'The evidence suggests that the anchorites became scribes through their association with the great *scriptoria* of the period, and that the majority of the anchoretic settlements developed no distinguished scribal tradition.'[46]

PERSONALITY OF THE SCRIBE

The ancient Irish scribe had the engaging habit of occasionally jotting down in the margin and at the end of his manuscript personal observations (as distinct from his glosses). This practice, which was common to the monastic and to the later lay scribes, has the merit of revealing to us much of the personality of the copyist.

In 1926, Plummer published a detailed examination of a number of these marginal notes and colophons, ranging over many centuries.[47] They cover a wide and varied field of topics. The scribe records at times his gratitude to his patron: 'A year and a half have I been stopping in this place, and long and lasting life to the family, to wit Brian MacEgan and his children, and Gormlaith and all of them.' But at other times, he airs his grievances: 'May God forgive the owner of this book for compelling me to work on the eve of Sunday'. He alludes to historical events and also to trifling occurrences of daily life: 'My cat has gone astray', 'the robin is singing gloriously', 'O God of heaven, reveal the theft that was committed in the church last night'. We hear much of his discomforts: 'Twenty weeks from today until Easter Monday, and I am cold and weary without fire or covering.' 'Let me not be blamed for the script, for the ink is bad, and the vellum defective, and the day is dark.' 'Upon my word, it is a great torment to be keeping the Friday of the Passion in water, with the excellent wine which there is in the house with us.' He makes shrewd comments on the matter he is copying. Opposite the dictum of Priscian 'Virgil was a great poet' he writes, 'and he isn't easy either.' Of the venerable tale *Táin Bó Cuailnge* he remarks that it contains 'some diabolical wonders, some poetical figments and some matter to delight fools'. He gives expression to his anxieties and sorrows: 'I am between coming and going (strangely modern sounding, this), may God give me the right counsel.' 'I am grieved for the tidings which I hear even now, that my mother and sister have died in Spain.' He asks for prayers for himself, his relations and friends, and expresses his trust in God. 'It is Christmas Eve this night, and under the protection of the King of heaven and earth am I on this eve tonight. May the end of my life be holy, and may this great plague pass by me and my friends, and restore us once more to joy and gladness, Amen'.

PASSING OF THE *Fer Leiginn*

According to MacNeill: 'The Norman invasion brought ruin to all these schools. The last notice of the school or rather university of Armagh is in 1188'.[48] With the passing of the older monastic schools the title of *fer léiginn* disappears. In documents connected with the post-Norman monasteries or convents we find the title *lector,* which seems to apply to any professor, though perhaps in some cases to a director of studies, the equivalent of the *fer léiginn.*

THE *Scriptorium*

We have seen that at least a good number of the early monasteries could boast of a *scriptorium* in the sense of a centre or school of penmanship. It is a reasonable assumption that, when the monastic buildings became more spacious and permanent, a *scriptorium,* in the sense of a special building, should have been provided for the scribe, where materials for copying would be kept and the finished books stored; gospels, psalters, liturgical works, commentaries, homilies, extracts from the Fathers of the Church, canon law texts.

Reeves holds that 'there was most likely a Chamber for the

preservation of books and other literary apparatus'.[49] Joyce is more definite. 'It is plain that in all the important Irish monasteries there must have been good general libraries.'[50] Ryan surmises that 'special cells (or at least special facilities within their own cells) must have been provided for the monastic artists who copied and bound books'.[51] Professor Brian Ó Cuív, speaking of the great manuscript collections of the twelfth century, says: 'As we turn the pages of these manuscripts we can picture a monk sitting in the writing room copying pagan epic tales of the Ulster heroes such as *Táin Bó Cuailgne,* or the poem composed in praise of Colum Cille by the leader of the poetic profession at the end of the sixth century'.[52] According to Dr. Hughes, by the eighth century the more important monasteries had well established *scriptoria,* with a special official in charge.[53] It is clear, however, that here, as elsewhere,[54] she speaks of the *scriptorium* merely in the sense of a centre of penmanship.

The actual evidence for the existence of the *scriptorium* as a specially appointed building is sparse. The *Annals of the Four Masters* record at 1020 the burning of Armagh 'without the saving of any house within it, except the library *(teach screaptra)* only'. Under the date 1136 the same Annals tell us that there was at Armagh an official librarian *(leabhar-coimhédaigh),* the post being held by Mac Maelcoluim, who was also 'chief keeper' of the calendar of Ard-Macha and its 'chief antiquary'. Reeves remarks that 'these are the only references in our Annals to the existence of a monastic library.'[55] Dr. Hughes draws attention to a passage in the Salamancan *Acta Sanctorum,* where mention is made of a *monasteriolum,* adjoining the monastery at Devenish 'quod scola dicitur', which she takes to be a *scriptorium.*[56] But she also cites, as evidence that the scribe sometimes worked in his cell, the story from the Calendar of Oengus of how St. Colum Cille asked St. Ciarán to share with him the book he was writing. The conversation between the two saints is said to take place in Ciarán's hut or cell *(boith).*[57] Joyce cites a somewhat obscure passage from the *Book of Leinster* in which reference is made to 'a huge sea-fish, such as is called a *rosualt'.* Concerning this monster a line is attributed to the sixth-century poet Dallán Forgaill, 'Among the schools with libraries *(etir scolaib screptra)* thou has read the mysteries of the *Rosualt'.*[58]

Though the foregoing evidence is slight in itself, it goes to confirm the presumption that a building fulfilling the functions of *scriptorium* and library was provided at an early date in at least the larger monasteries. That it was a regular feature of the medieval monasteries is obvious from the extant evidence of their considerable collections of books.

The production of manuscript works lasted right up to the nineteenth century. In the seventeenth century paper began to supersede vellum. O'Grady lists one paper manuscript as early as 1592.[59] It is a collection of medical tracts, and O'Grady remarks that, being in several hands, it affords 'good examples of the semi-cursive and cursive styles which accompanied the substitution of paper for vellum.' The last well-known professional scribe, Joseph O'Longan, died only in 1880. The later manuscripts are, however, mostly mere transcriptions. The last noteworthy book which circulated in manuscript in Ireland – indeed the last to circulate in others during the many troubled epochs of Irish history.

And it must be recalled that what has been preserved must be only a fraction of the works composed by the native scholars. O'Curry lists some twenty-seven books which are referred to in twelfth-century manuscripts, another six stated by Keating in his History of Ireland to have been extant in his own time, the early seventeenth century, and four books drawn on by the O'Clerys in the *Lebor Gabála* or Book of the Invasions, all of which are now lost. He also points out that of the nine books drawn on by the Four Masters for their great Annals, completed in 1631, only one, the *Annals of Ulster,* is still in existence.[61] And it is obvious that, in addition to these known losses, there must have been numerous others during the many troubled epochs of Irish history.

THE BATTLE OF A BOOK

The practice of copying books was, according to Keating[62] and the Four Masters,[63] the cause of momentous events towards the end of the sixth century. St. Colum Cille, when on a visit to St. Finnian of Moville, secretly made a copy of a volume of the psalms brought back by his host from Rome, possibly the first copy of St. Jerome's Vulgate to reach Ireland.[64] Colum Cille's manuscript was claimed by Finnian, and the matter was referred to the High King, Diarmait. He gave the memorable, if not wholly logical decision: 'To every cow her calf, to every book its copy'. Colum Cille rejected this decision, and the quarrel was intensified when Diarmait executed the son of the king of Connacht, who had been placed under the saint's protection. Colum Cille's northern kinsmen then took up arms, and what had begun as a dispute about copyright ended in a great battle at Cul Dremne in Co. Sligo, between Benbulbin and the sea. Colum Cille's cousins were victorious, killing three thousand of the High King's men.[65]

Two years later, in 563, Colum Cille left Ireland, and crossing to Scotland, received from Conall, king of the Dal Riada, the island of Iona, where he founded the monastery which for almost three centuries was to be a centre of holiness and learning. The common tradition is that this exile was a penance, imposed by himself or his spiritual guide, for the bloodshed he had caused. This tradition is, however, rejected by several authorities. Amongst them are Reeves, who points out that Adamnán gives the desire 'to go on pilgrimage for Christ' as the sole reason for Colum Cille's departure,[66] and Lanigan, who, whilst admitting the historicity of the battle, describes the other incidents as 'a silly story...quite unbecoming the conduct of holy men and even the gravity of common history.'[67] But in any event, whether history or poetic fiction, the incident as related is of great significance, as showing the traditional value ascribed to manuscripts at the time.

GRADES OF RELIGIOUS LEARNING

In the Brehon Laws[68] we find enumerated seven degrees of religious learning, with the statement that 'so it is alike the degrees of wisdom and of the church correspond with the degrees of the poets.' However, the courses of the religious degrees are outlined in a much more general fashion than those of the *filid*.

We do not find any reference to specific elementary grades in the religious schools, corresponding to the *Ollaire, Taman* and *Drisac* in the secular schools. The grades enumerated are:

1. *Fealmac,* son of learning, 'a boy after reading his psalms.'

2. *Freisneidhed,* 'an interrogator, i.e. he interrogates his tutor with the sense of an ollamh (acting like a teacher rather than a pupil)... and he (the tutor) gives him the sense of everything which is difficult to him.'

3. *Fursaintid,* an illustrator. 'He answers his tutor with the sense of an ollamh...and he gives the sense of every difficulty on account of the clearness of his judgment, and the nobleness of his intellect.'

4. *Sruth do Aill,* a stream from a cliff. 'The practice of that cliff is that it drowns every little light, weak thing; it carries off loose rocks, so that they acquire the appearance of the strand by reason of the heat of the weather. The same doth the man who is likened unto it; he drowns bad scholars whom he confounds with rocks of testament (evidence) and intellect; and he is able to modify his instructions to the complexion of *simple* information, in mercy to the people of little learning...who ebb in the presence of a noble stream (*anruth,* the 6th grade).'

5. *Sai,* (professor) 'i.e. a man who professes a fourth part of the scientific course...A comely professor of the Canon [of Scripture] with his noble, good wealth [of knowledge].

6. *Anruth,* a noble stream; 'for four reasons he is so called, i.e., for the nobleness of his teaching; for the number of his intellectual

qualities; for the eloquence of his language; because he composes in every department, both poetry and literature and synchronism; but he does not reach to the top [of scholarship]'.

7. *Rosaí,* great professor. He is also called *ollamh,* chief doctor and su*í* littre, professor of written history.' The 'ollamh' sits in the banqueting house, because it is he that resides in his house with a king on that occasion. A great professor does not fail in any question in the four departments of knowledge'.

We have already remarked that it is not necessary to believe that the grades of the *filid* and their respective courses were exactly adhered to. The same may be said of these monastic grades. It may, indeed, be asked whether they were observed at all. There is no reference to them in any ecclesiastical writing. The purpose of the *Crith Gabhlach,* the treatise of the Brehon Laws in which they are set forth, is to establish the honour-price of the various grades of society.[69] It may be suggested that these grades were invented merely so that an honour-price could be fixed for ecclesiastical scholars at different stages, as it was fixed for the very definite grades of secular scholars. It may be noted that only in the first and fifth degrees is there any reference to specifically church learning. The one evidence that they were actually observed is that in the Annals many learned ecclesiastics are referred to as *Suí Littre.*

THE SEVEN GRADES OR ORDERS OF WISDOM

O'Curry, in the appendix to his *Manuscript Materials of Irish History,*[70] published and translated a passage explaining the 'Seven Orders of Wisdom', which is found in an ancient Law Glossary, compiled by Dubhaltach Mac Firbhisigh, one of the last of the legal ollamhs (d. 1660). In this is found a scheme of ecclesiastical studies which is almost completely different from that contained in the Brehon Laws, and is somewhat more definite about the content of the various courses. It appears to refer to teachers rather than to students, but the three lower grades were evidently also learners.

1. *Caogdach,* Fifty-man 'because that he chants [i.e., knows] the three times fifty Psalms.'

2. *Foghlaintidh,* learner, 'a man who has knowledge of ten books of the Fochoiré'.[71]

3. *Desgibal,* disciple, 'who has knowledge of the twelve books of Fochoiré'.

4. *Staruidhe,* historian, 'who has thirty holy lessons [of divinity] in his course of learning.'

5. *Foirceadlaidhe,* lecturer, 'who has [professes] grammar, criticism and orthography and enumeration and the courses of the year and the courses of the sun and moon.'

6. *Saoi Canóine,* doctor of the canons, 'who has knowledge of the canon [of scripture] and who relates the gospel of Jesus i.e., the word of God in the pure place in which it is found [the bible], i.e., catholic canonical wisdom.'

7. *Druimcli* [lit. ridge-pole)[72] 'i.e., a man who has perfect knowledge of Wisdom, from the greatest book, which is called Cuilmen[73] to the smallest book, which is called Ten Words, in which are well arranged the good Testament which God made unto Moses.'[74]

COMBINED RELIGIOUS AND SECULAR LEARNING

O'Curry makes the point that in the last mentioned scheme of grades of ecclesiastical teachers, we find it implied that their curriculum included Gaelic as well as Latin culture.[75] The *Foglaintidh* and the *Desgibal* were to be well versed in the Fochoiré, evidently a branch of Gaelic learning, whilst the lost Cuilmen, mentioned as part of the course of the Drumchli, is referred to in the *Book of Leinster* and the *Lebor Brecc* as one of the most ancient Gaelic writings.[76]

EDUCATION OF SECULAR CLERGY

We have seen that, even before the great growth of the monasteries, the priests of many of the larger ecclesiastical establishments lived in a semi-monastic state, grouped around their bishop, Armagh being the most notable example. It is also evident that provision was made by them of a college for the training of church candidates. But in the documents available there is no information concerning the training of such candidates elsewhere. Presumably they began, as did most of the young monks, by being put under the care of some individual priest or hermit, and either remained with him until ordination, or possibly studied for a while in an episcopal college or monastic school.

BISHOPS AND EDUCATION

We have earlier made reference to the document known as *Riagail Pátraic,* The Rule of Patrick, a miscellaneous collection of directions for ecclesiastical government. It has no connection with St. Patrick, the name being given to it merely in his honour. There are several versions. That from which we now quote is included as part of a treatise from the *Lebor Brecc,* known as the *Rule of the Céli Dé,*[77] which claims to be a prose paraphrase of a verse composition of Mael Ruain of Tallaght, chief apostle of the eighth century reform. Reeves assigned it to the thirteenth century, but Strachan considered that, in substance, it dates back as far as the ninth century. That part of it which is elsewhere known as the *Riagail Pátraic* contains the following passage:

'From this it comes that the names of the men of Erin are in the Testament of Patrick, that there should be a chief bishop in each chief territory in Erin, for ordaining men to holy orders and for consecrating churches, for the soul-friendship of princes and of erenachs, and of people in orders; for sanctifying and blessing their children after baptism, for ordering souls in every church, and training boys and girls to reading and piety (*ocas mac ocas ingean fria legend ocas crabud*); for if the boys do not read at all times, every church will die.'[78] In later passages the boys who are to be taught to read are spoken of as being 'offered to God and St. Patrick,' intimating that they are church candidates.

The passage is of interest as indicating that at an early date the education of all clergy was regarded as matter for episcopal care. It is reasonable presumption that it also reflects, at least to some degree, a general practice. It does not, however, throw any light on the actual education of the secular clergy, nor on another problem with which we are about to deal, the education of the laity.

The allusion to the education of girls, in spite of its vagueness, is of special value, since for this early period so little information is available on this point. Indeed, in the documents which have been searched in the compilation of this book, only four other allusions have been found to the mental equipment of women. The first is in the legend of the daughters of Loegaire converted by St. Patrick, one of whom had been fostered, so presumably educated by a druid. Then there is the unsupported statement in the Life of St. Brigid by Cogitosus, a monk or cleric, probably of Kildare, that the saint was well educated. '*A sua pueritia litterarum studiis inolevit.*'[79] In the *Annals of the Four Masters* in 933 we find a laconic mention of 'Uallach, daughter of Muineacan, chief poetess of Ireland', about whom no further information can be discovered. Lastly, there is the attribution of a number of poems to Gormlaith or Gormflaith, daughter of the high-king Flann Sinna (d. 916). She was in succession the wife of three kings, Cormac, king-bishop of Cashel, his foster-brother and conqueror Cerball mac Muirecán (d. 917), and Niall Glúndub, who fell in battle against the Norse in 919. She was a tragic figure. The *Annals of Clonmacnois* (905) record that by Niall Glúndub she had a son, Domhnall, who was drowned, 'upon whose death she made many pittiful and learned dittyes in Irish.' In her old age, she was reduced to begging 'from doore to doore, forsaken of all her friends and allies.' But the attribution of the poems to her is extremely doubtful. Bergin says that if any are her work, they are 'greatly changed in transmission.'[80]

CHAPTER 9

MONASTIC SCHOOLS (continued)

i. Lay and Foreign Students

ii. Schoolmasters of Europe

i. LAY AND FOREIGN STUDENTS

LAY STUDENTS IN THE MONASTERIES

It is confidently asserted by several writers that the monasteries, from the earliest times, provided education for lay students. This opinion is of weight when coming from such an authority as O'Curry. 'Some may imagine, from much that has been said of our great ecclesiastical establishments in early times, that their course of instruction was merely classical, ecclesiastical, and biblical or theological; and that no secular sources of education then existed in the country. That such, however, was not the case, we have ample evidence in our old writings.'[1] Joyce states that 'a large proportion of the students in these monasteries were young men – amongst them the sons of kings or chiefs – intended, not for the church, but for ordinary civil or military life, who attended to get a good education.'[2] Eleanor Hull is even more emphatic. 'The monastic schools sought to provide a general secular and religious instruction which, though it was primarily intended to fit men for the clerical and monastic life, included for some period of their lives almost the whole Christian population.'[3]

It is a curious fact that the only proof of their assertions given by these writers is a solitary incident quoted by both O'Curry and Joyce. It may be noted also that a much more cautious note is struck by Hyde. 'It is very difficult to say what was exactly the curriculum of the early Irish colleges and how far they were patronized by laymen.'[4]

The incident referred to by O'Curry and Joyce is as follows.[5] In the *Annals of the Four Masters,* at the date 645, there is recorded the death of Raghallach, 'the wicked', king of Connacht, who was murdered by one Maelbrighde, the son of Mothlacar. O'Curry states that he has in his possession a copy (unfortunately he omits all reference to the original) of a poem written by the king's poet, Fionntain, which relates how Cathal, the king's second son was studying at the school of Clonard when he heard of the murder. He at once set out with 'seven-and-twenty students of his own people', and took revenge on Maelbrighde by decapitating him.

In view of the warlike character of many of the monks of those early days, one cannot be as confident as O'Curry that all the followers of Cathal were laymen. However, the story does suggest that, at least at times, the children of great chiefs were accepted as pupils in the monasteries. But more than this isolated incident would be required to justify the statement that the practice was widespread. It is, of course, antecedently probable that a certain number of laymen of an enquiring mind would seek to acquire from neighbouring monks something of the newly imported skills of reading and writing. But, with all due deference to the authority of the writers quoted, it must be recorded that diligent research has revealed no positive evidence of this until well after the Norman invasion.

However, whether or not laymen, as such, sought for education in these early days, there must have been, in fact, a considerable educated laity, made up of church candidates who had spent some years in the cloister and then returned to the world. Possibly this is what O'Curry, Joyce and Eleanor Hull had in mind when writing as they did. In this connection, it must be borne in mind that the numbers of the monasteries and of their inhabitants were very large. There are definite records of about two hundred founded at various dates before 1200, apart from many hundreds of others of which there are only vague traces.[6] And, whilst we need not accept literally the figures given in some of the medieval Lives of the numbers in these monastic communities – Bangor and Clonard three thousand each, Mungret fifteen hundred, Rahan eight hundred[7] – there is reliable evidence that they actually were large. Jonas, for instance, gives us a vivid little picture of St. Columban arriving one day at one of his monasteries and finding sixty of the monks hard at work hoeing their land in preparation for the next season's crops.[8] We have also seen that boys entered the monastery at a very early age, a practice that would obviously tend to increase the number who did not persevere.

SONS OF MONASTIC TENANTS

Actually a regular system developed under which quite a number of boys must have been constantly found in the monastic schools. We have previously referred to the document, probably of the ninth century, known as *Riagail Pátraic*. In it there is constant mention of the *manaig,* layfolk who were tenants of monastery lands, and were possibly also under some fairly strict spiritual direction by the monks. The *manach* is urged to give his eldest son, and every tenth son after that ('the tithe of [the fruit] of his body') 'for the purpose of study' and ultimately 'to take ecclesiastical orders.' He is assured that this 'will be the same as if he renovated the churches of Erin and restored its belief after it had vanished.[9] Having regard to the number of the monasteries and the extent of their possessions, the number of eldest sons of their tenants must have been considerable. On this point, Dr. Kathleen Hughes remarks: 'In eighth-century Ireland, the proportion of literate laymen must have been abnormally large when compared with the rest of Europe. It is no coincidence that the Irish church was extraordinarily tolerant in her attitude to native secular learning, for the number of boys from the world being educated in the monastery, and of adults in the world who had received a clerical education, would tend to narrow the gap between the church and lay society. Each would sympathize with the other.'[10]

In connection with this question of the education of the laity, there are two other facts which must be taken into consideration. They combine to warn us that the distinction between lay and clerical students in the early monasteries is not absolutely clear cut. The first fact is that, from at least the eighth century on, it is difficult to distinguish between the strictly monastic members of the greater monasteries and their lay associates, the *manaig* mentioned above or others more loosely associated. We have to picture these establishments rather as monastic towns than as mere monastic houses. The second fact is that, by the eleventh century, the monastic writers were devoting themselves largely to the composition of verses of an historical nature, thus rendering it difficult to distinguish them from lay scholars who were in some way associated with the monasteries. We shall meet later with a notable example of this, Flann Mainistrech, who devoted himself largely to the secular history of the Uí Néill dynasty. Authors differ as to whether he was the abbot of Monasterboice, or, as seems more likely, a lay director of studies in the monastery.

STUDENTS FROM ABROAD

The high level of the education provided by the Irish monastic schools is attested by the numbers of students whom they attracted from other countries. The majority of these appear to have been from Britain. There is a letter extant from Aldhelm, Abbot of Malmesbury and bishop of Sherborne at the beginning of the eighth century, addressed to a certain Ehtfridus, whose identity is uncertain, but whom some believe to have been Eadfrid, bishop of Lindisfarne, others Aldfrid, king of Northumbria. Aldhelm congratulates his friend on the learning he had acquired during a stay of six years in Ireland. He goes on to assert that 'there is now no need for youths from Britain to go to Ireland for their studies', since the level of learning at Canterbury is now so high. Aldhelm was evidently somewhat touchy on this point, for he complains that the young Britons had been going to Ireland 'in fleet-loads.'[11]

Whether or not this Ehtfridus was identified with Aldfrid, we know from another source that the latter did study in Ireland. William of Malmesbury, the twelfth-century monk-historian, tells us that when Egfrid, the younger but legitimate son of King Oswiu, succeeded to his father, Aldfrid 'although the elder, having been thought unworthy of the throne, betook himself to Ireland, either through compulsion or indignation. There, safe from the hatred of his brother, in great peace he became absorbed in study and enriched his mind with every sort of knowledge.'[12]

There is extant a very ancient poem allegedly written by Aldfrid on leaving Ireland. It begins

> 'I found in Inisfail the fair
> In Ireland, while in exile there,
> Women of worth, both grave and gay men,
> Learned clerics, heroic laymen'[13]

That Aldfrid actually lived in Ireland for a considerable time is confirmed by the fact that in the Annals he is given an Irish name. Thus the *Annals of Tigernach* recording his death at the date 704, say: 'Alfrith mac Ossu (he was called Flann Fina by the Irish) rex Saxon fuit.'[14]

It has been held by some authorities that Alcuin, the monk of York who became Charlemagne's master of the palace school, studied for a while in the monastery of Clonmacnois. It is beyond doubt that he was in communication with Colgu Ua Duineachda, fer léiginn of the abbey (d. 794, *Annals of the Four Masters*). In a letter Alcuin announces that he is sending the monks a hundred sicles of silver from the emperor and himself, and a quantity of olive oil for sacramental purposes. That he was a former pupil of Clonmacnois has been argued from the fact that he addresses Colgu as 'blessed Master and Pious Father.'[16] This, however, may have been merely a title of honour. But the gifts, and more especially the intimate tone of the letter clearly indicate that Alcuin, whether past pupil or not, was a close friend of the director of studies of this far-off Irish monastery. He commences his letter, for instance, with the words 'I thought you would like to hear something about my journey and about recent world events.'

However, we are on completely safe ground with the various allusions made by such a reliable authority as Bede to British scholars who had studied in Ireland about the middle of the seventh century. Two of them were Ethelhun and Egbert, 'youths of great capacity of the English nobility.' The former was brother to Ethelwin, 'who also...went over to Ireland to study, and, having been well instructed, returned into his own country and became a bishop in the province of Lindsay.'[17] The two young friends fell ill of the plague. Ethelhun died, but Egbert, having made a vow that if he were spared he would remain an exile from his native Northumbria, recovered and spent a saintly life in Ireland, dying eventually in Iona. Another fellow-student of Egbert was Ceadda (better known as St. Chad), bishop of Lichfield and York. On his death in 672, Egbert recalled how he had 'long and zealously led a monastic life with the same Ceadda, when both were youths in Ireland, in prayer and self-denial and meditation on the Holy Scripture.'[18] Then there was St. Willibrord, apostle of the Frisians and archbishop of Utrecht. His early studies were made in the school of St. Wilfrid at York, but he used recall his stay 'in Ireland when, being only a priest, he led the life of a stranger and pilgrim for the love of the eternal country'.[19]

That these were not merely isolated instances is evident from a passage in which Bede recalls the pestilence which ravaged England about the year 644, and 'prevailed no less disastrously in the island of Ireland.' He tells how 'many of the nobility and of the lower ranks of the English nation were there at the time, who in the days of the bishops Finan and Colman, forsaking their native island, retired thither either for the sake of divine studies or of a more ascetic life; and some of them presently devoted themselves faithfully to a monastic life, others chose rather to apply themselves to study, going about from one master's cell to another. The Scots [i.e. Irish] willingly received them all, and took care to supply them with daily food without cost, as also to furnish them with books for their studies, and teaching them free of charge.'[20]

So constant was this flow of students from England that they appear to have had at times their own special quarters in the monastic schools. Petrie, in his essay on the Round Towers of Ireland, cites from a manuscript in the Bodleian library an episode in which the poet Rumann Mac Colmáin came on a pilgrimage to the monastery of Rahan in Offaly. He visited a neighbouring settlement, Cell Belaigh (Kilbally), which 'had seven streets of Galls in it', and 'gave the third of his wealth to it because of its extent, and a third to schools.'[21] As this was well before the Norse invasion (Rumann died in 747 according to the *Annals of Tigernach*) these Galls were presumably Saxons from England. And we hear of the burning in Armagh in 1092 of 'a street of the Third of the Saxons (*Triun Saxan*).'[22]

The evidence for the presence in Irish monastic schools of students from countries other than Britain is less reliable, but cannot be easily dismissed. In the various lives of the saints there are many references to the arrival of such students. The details are often obviously legendary, but the frequency of these stories is evidence that there was a strong tradition on the subject. Thus in the life of St. Senan we read: 'Then came a ship's crew from the lands of Latium on a pilgrimage into Ireland. Five decades were their number.'[23]

Again, in the *Litany of Oengus Céli Dé*[24] we find, together with the invocations of native saints, those of holy men from abroad who had settled in Ireland, 'The Romans in Acudh Galma, in Hy-Echach', 'seven Egyptian monks in Desert Uiligh', 'the Gauls in Magh Salad', 'the Saxons in Cluan Mucceda' and, among twenty saints in Glendalough 'Affinus (a Franc).'

Several authors state that Dagobert II, who became king of the Austrasian Franks in 674, studied in Ireland during his youth. All give much the same account as Archdall in his *Monasticon Hibernicum,* who states that in the year 653, on the death of his father, Sigebert III, Dagobert, then seven years of age, was by the direction of Grimoald, mayor of the palace, tonsured as a monk and banished into Ireland, whence after twenty years, he was recalled to the throne of France. Archdall gives this information in connection with the abbey of Slane, and adds, 'from oral information we learn that he was received into this abbey, where he obtained an education proper for the enjoyment of a throne', but gives no hint of the source of this information.[25]

It is interesting to trace the details added to this story by various writers. Mabillon merely states that Dagobert was 'banished into Ireland.'[26] Mezeray adds that we may surmise that he was 'confined in some remote monastery.'[27] Archdall gives us the local tradition that this monastery was that of Slane.

Here again we have the reliable testimony of Bede that Agilbert, a native of Gaul, had 'lived a long time in Ireland for the purpose of reading the Scriptures.' He came to Wessex in 643, and the king

Coinwalch 'observing his learning and industry, desired him to accept an episcopal see there'. Having ruled over the see of Dorchester for many years, Agilbert became, in the second half of the century, bishop of Paris.[28]

ii. SCHOOLMASTERS OF EUROPE

We have earlier drawn attention to the fact that the high standard of education aimed at from the first by St. Patrick was one of the causes of the success of the Irish monks in the evangelization of Europe during the seventh, eighth and ninth centuries. This extra-ordinary episode belongs properly to ecclesiastical history, but it may be mentioned here as evidence of the fact that the aim of Patrick was maintained by his successors. It is true that the success of religious apostles depends far more on their holiness and their personality than on their intellectual gifts. But it is also obvious that the Irish saints could not so easily have taken their place on the continent as great religious founders and promoters of intellectual as well as religious activity, unless their own early intellectual training had been of a high order.

It is enough here to make the briefest mention of the greatest figures in this spiritual and cultural conquest of Europe. Colum Cille's foundation on the little island of Iona in 563 was the centre from which christianity spread over Scotland and the remote islands, the Orkneys, the Shetlands, the Faroes. From Iona went Aidan in 635 to another island, Lindisfarne, from which the monks made settlements all over Northumbria, later over the midlands of England, and finally in the territory of the East Saxons. Columbanus, with twelve companions, arrived in Gaul probably in 591, spent some years evangelizing the half-christian towns and villages, then, having won the favour of Gontron, king of Burgundy, founded the monastery of Luxeuil at the foot of the Vosges. Later, having lost royal favour, he and his monks were expelled, and, after long wanderings and hardship, settled in 614 in Bobbio, thirty miles north east of Genoa, shortly before the saint's death in 615. The monastery prospered, and soon housed the most famous library in Italy, some of whose treasures have happily survived, though dispersed throughout the centuries.

Then there are lesser but great figures. St. Gall (Ceallach was possibly the Irish form of his name), was one of the companions of Columbanus, but after his exile from Luxeuil, settled as a hermit at Brigenz, east of Lake Constance, and died with such a reputation for holiness that his name and patronage were given to the Benedictine monastery which for centuries was one of the greatest centres of learning in Europe. St. Fursa, son of a prince of south Munster, having founded monasteries in Ireland and East Anglia, crossed to Normandy with his brothers and other monks, secured at Péronne the favour of the Mayor of the Palace to Clovis II, and between 640 and 650 founded near Paris the great abbey of Lagny. St. Killian (Cillène) in 684 founded a monastery at Würzburg and evangelized Franconia and Thuringia. St. Fergal (known on the continent by the latinized form of his name, Virgilius or Virgil), had been abbot of Aghad-bó in Offaly, but set out for France about 741, and was received at the court of Pepin the Short, who recommended him to Ottilo, duke of Bavaria. Early in the second half of the eighth century he became archbishop of Salzburg, and was a zealous apostle, especially of the heathen Carinthians. He was evidently a man of considerable learning – the *Annals of the Four Masters* describe him as 'the Geometer'[29]– and he engaged victoriously in two notable controversies with the great apostle of Germany, St. Boniface, one concerning the formula of baptism and the other the question of the existence of the antipodes.[30]

Owing to the fact that their work was perpetuated by their successors, the founders of monasteries undoubtedly made the largest contribution to the spread of christian culture in Europe. There were, however, other Irish scholars who achieved a high individual reputation for learning. Mention has already been made of Sedulius Scottus and Johannes Scottus Eriugena, both of the ninth century. To these two more may be added. Of the life of Dicuil we know very little except that he was an exile from Ireland and was attached to the court of Charlemagne, most probably as a teacher in the palace school. But three of his works have come down to us, verses *De Arte Grammatica,* a *Treatise on Astronomy* (814–816) and a treatise on geography – the earliest composed in the Frankish Empire – *Liber de Mensura Orbis Terrae,* completed in 825.[31] The last mentioned, Dicuil's most important work, is notable not so much for its scientific value as for the knowledge it displays of the then known works on the subject, which were a report of commissioners sent by the emperor Theodosius to survey the provinces of the Roman empire, Pliny's *Natural History* and a number of now forgotten treatises of the first to fifth centuries. In the eighth section there is a significant reference to 'our own island Hibernia'.

Another Irish name which appears in Frankish ecclesiastical history in the late eighth and early ninth centuries is Dungal. Scholars are divided as to whether it stands for one man or several.

We hear of a poor monk living as a recluse, attached to the monastery of St. Denis, who was learned enough to be consulted by Charlemagne as to the explanation of two eclipses of the sun which were alleged to have taken place in the year 810. Then there is Dungal who, in 825 is requested by Lothair, Charlemagne's grandson, recently crowned king of Lombardy, to open a school at Pavia, to which scholars flocked from the neighbouring cities. Two years later there appears from the pen of Dungal a theological treatise refuting the iconoclastic views of Claudius, bishop of Turin. Finally there are a few poems attributed to a certain Dungal.[32]

But, besides these more outstanding figures, a whole host of Irish monks have left their traces all over Europe. The traveller will find their names, even in the most remote places, given to churches, monasteries, towns and children. Some modern French writers[33] have accepted as substantially correct the figures given by the seventeenth century Jesuit scholar, Fr. Stephen White, in his *Apologia pro Hibernia adversus Cambri calumnias,*[34] for the sixth and seventh centuries alone, 115 missionaries in Germany, 45 in France, 44 in England, 36 in Belgium, 25 in Scotland and 13 in Italy. And indeed one has only to glance through the pages of the book in which these figures are cited or the better known works of Dom Louis Gougaud on the same subject, to see that these figures are not exaggerated.[35]

A modern Italian writer, Fra Anselmo Tommasini, discovered in his country no less than 220 parochial churches dedicated to Irish saints, besides numerous minor churches, chapels and shrines.[36] His book records the enduring memory in Italy of many Irish saints who are hardly known in their native country, such as St. Emilian of Faenza, St. Fridian of Lucca, St. Donatus of Fiesole. The last mentioned was a competent Latinist, and some of his works have survived, notably a poem on Ireland in which one detects a nostalgic longing for that 'best of lands, whose name is written in ancient books...whose air and soil are grateful to the body of man, whose fields flow with milk and honey.'[37]

There may also be recalled the often quoted testimony of that great German pioneer in Celtic studies, Heinrich Zimmer.

'Let us not forget that the Irish, from the seventh to the tenth century, were the schoolmasters of Europe, that they taught Latin grammar in Paris, Lüttich, St. Gallen, Pavia, Bobbio; that not less than four manuscripts of Priscian, written in Ireland at the beginning of the ninth century, were brought to the Continent, where, in spite of the fortunes of a thousand years, they are preserved – at Leyden, Carlsruhe (from Reichenau), St. Gallen, Milan (from Bobbio)'.[38]

CHAPTER 10

FUSION OF CHRISTIAN AND NATIVE CULTURES

Fusion of Christian and Native Cultures
As has been seen, the band of missionaries who landed in Ireland with St. Patrick did not find there a savage and uncultured race. The Irish were pagans, but they possessed a native culture of quite a high order. At first the missionaries regarded this with suspicion, in view of its pagan associations, but during the sixth century this suspicion was gradually allayed and a remarkable fusion of the two cultures took place.

This fusion was intimately connected with and helped by the emergence of the written form of the Irish language. There seems to be no doubt that the originators of this were the christian clergy. According to Ryan: 'Taking Latin as their model, the monks studied the sounds and structures of the spoken tongue and evolved a system of orthography which made the writing of Irish as easy as the writing of Latin.'[1] Kenney says: 'At an early date...they (the *filid*) took over from the Irish ecclesiastics the method of writing the Irish language which these latter had evolved.'[2] We shall deal presently with the part traditionally assigned to the Ulster warrior, Cenn Faelad, later a lawyer, poet and grammarian, in the general adoption of writing by the native learned classes. Of him MacNeill writes: 'Cenn Faelad did not originate the written literature of Irish. That honour belongs to the "Latinists", the churchmen who wrote Irish hymns and homilies, and from whom Irish had received a settled and peculiar orthography before Cenn Faelad learned to write.'[3]

Some authorities are slightly less definite about the origin of Irish writing. Dr. Kathleen Hughes holds that 'some seventh century Irish scholars applied the foreign methods of Latin scholarship to their own, and were sufficiently proud of Irish learning to want a permanent record of it.'[4] And Professor F. J. Byrne says of the native learned classes that 'they adapted the Latin alphabet to produce a native Irish literature'.[5] But both these scholars may be merely referring to the rapid adoption of writing by the *filid*.

That it was the christian clerics who devised the system of Irish writing is borne out by the fact that the earliest Irish writings we have are undoubtedly of monastic origin.[6] It was a natural, indeed inevitable development. By the beginning of the seventh century many of the monastic scholars were Irish-born, and all were Irish-speaking. Some of them had been pupils of the *filid* from their youth and knew the high status of their former teachers. It was only to be expected that men who were accustomed to studying Latin in a written form should think of preserving their native culture in a similar form.

Professor Binchy thus summarizes the stages of this development.

'At what stage Irish became the language of instruction in these [monastic] schools it is hard to say. We have Irish glosses on Latin grammatical texts, on the Epistles of St. Paul, on certain commentaries on the Psalms; but whether these were used in class by the teacher or whether they were simply notes taken by him for his own enlightenment is not an easy question to answer. We also get, at a comparatively early stage, Irish poems on religious subjects, hymns in honour of St. Patrick and some of the earlier saints. Finally in the second half of the eighth century, we get the vernacular used for the first time in longer devotional works in prose and verse.'[7]

From writing on religious topics, the monks naturally went on to write down the native lore, old sagas and poems, which received, as Professor Binchy points out, a certain 'dressing up' from their clerical scribes or redactors. This last mentioned point has also been stressed by Professor Mac Cana, who concludes that it is 'not unreasonable to suppose that the monastic redactors did in fact suppress elements of druidic teaching and practice which they could not record without seeming to compromise the doctrines of the universal Church.'[8]

It was inevitable also that within a comparatively short time the *filid* should adopt with eagerness this new method of communicating and preserving the wealth of traditional history, poetry, topography and genealogy which they possessed. Professor Binchy, dealing particularly with the transmission of the Brehon Laws, believes that towards the end of the sixth century 'writing in the Latin alphabet seeped into the native secular schools from the monastic schools.' Then came the writing down of the ancient laws, so that 'by the beginning of the eighth century the law-tracts had received the final canonical form which was henceforth regarded as authoritative and immutable'.[9]

The example of the lawyers was followed by the poets, historians and genealogists. According to MacNeill it was 'in the middle of the seventh century or thereabouts that the Filidh in general adopted the apparatus of the Latin schools, including the Latin alphabet and the use of reading and writing to transmit and record their various teachings'.[10]

It was natural also that this fusion of cultures should be more operative on one side than on the other. The monastic scholars not only took to writing in Irish, but as we shall see, from the tenth century on, began to draw much of their inspiration from ancient native traditions. The *filid,* though their writings took on a certain christian tone, had no reason to adopt Latin as a vehicle of expression for the legal, historical and genealogical lore which was their peculiar heritage. Some of them, no doubt, took up the study of the Latin language and literature, but there are only scattered evidences of this. The poet and historian Giolla Caímhghin, who flourished in the eleventh century, is by some writers credited with being the author of the Irish translation of the *Historia Britannica* of Nennius.[11] The Irish physicians who translated numerous Latin medical treatises from the twelfth century on, evidently knew the language reasonably well.

In one particular respect, however, the Latin culture had a marked influence on that of the *filid.* 'The majority of scholars,' Kenney tells us, 'agree that the classical system of Irish versification, which prevailed from the eighth to the seventeenth century, was in its origin based on the Latin versification of the later Roman Empire.'[12] This subject has been dealt with fully by the late Professor Myles Dillon,[13] who held that the views of Thurneysen, published in 1884, have not been superseded,[14] though much additional work has been done on this subject by scholars such as Kuno Meyer and Bergin.

Summarizing the views of these authorities, it appears that the earliest surviving poems are mere alliterative groups without rhyme or rhythm. They date from the sixth century. Towards the end of that century, under the influence of the Latin hymns, verse appears, but there is still no definite number of stresses or syllables. In the seventh century, there is both rhyme and regular rhythm. The final stage is in the eighth century when according to Professor Dillon, 'the syllable count becomes dominant, and there is no regular ictus, the word-accent serving only for alliteration and rhyme.' This system exemplified in various metres, was to prevail into the seventeenth century.

We have seen that the invention of Irish writing must most probably be credited to the monastic scholars, mainly for the reason that they were already familiar with the system of writing Latin.

Similarly, it must be granted that the adaptation of the Latin system of versification to the composition of Irish verse must be credited to the monks who were daily chanting according to that system. The point, however, is of little significance, since the *filid* took over the system so rapidly and completely.

It must here be noted that recently it has been established that early Irish poetic forms were not so completely derived from Latin models as had been previously held. In a very able and recondite article by Professor Calvert Watkins, of Harvard University, the view is held that 'we can now add Irish to the list of languages, Greek, Vedic and Slavonic, which have preserved the metrical form of Indo-European poetry'. This fact is 'yet another instance of the extraordinary archaism of the Irish tradition.'[15] Yet it would appear that Professor Watkins would not altogether exclude the influence of Latin verse forms on Irish. 'However,' he says, 'I cannot whole-heartedly agree with Murphy's conclusion that "the general line of Thurneysen's suggestions are almost certainly to be accepted as indicating how Irish syllabic metres were more or less consciously developed by Irish poets from sources traceable ultimately to a Latin origin." I think the purely native component in these new metrical poems has been underrated.'[16]

THE EARLIEST WRITINGS

When we come to consider the earliest surviving writings, whether in Latin or in Irish, we must make a distinction between those of which we have the actual manuscripts, and those which we have only in later copies, mainly of the eleventh and twelfth centuries, but whose linguistic characteristics demonstrate an earlier original composition.

Of the first class, actually written about the year 600, we have only a handful. One is the fragmentary copy of the psalms known as the *Cathach,* possibly that which led to the battle of Cúl Dremne, and the exile of St. Colmcille. It clearly shows the Irish style of writing before it became subject to seventh century continental influence. Another is a copy of the four gospels from the monastery of Bobbio, the *Codex Usserianus* I, preserved in the library of Trinity College, Dublin. There are two other manuscripts from Bobbio in the Ambrosian library at Milan, and a fourth at Turin, which, it is believed, may have belonged to St. Columbanus himself.[17]

Kenney gives a list of ten manuscripts of older date than A.D. 1,000, which have survived on Irish soil. They are all Latin biblical texts, and comprise, in addition to the *Cathach* and *Codex Usserianus* I, the *Book of Durrow; Book of Mulling* (embodying at least two distinct Mss.); *Book of Dimma* (in which a prayer after the gospel of St. Luke is in mixed Latin and Irish); *Domnach Airgid* (so-called for the silver case in which it was formerly enclosed); *Book of Kells; Book of Armagh; Garland of Howth* or *Codex Usserianus II.* These are all preserved in the library of Trinity College, Dublin, with the exception of the *Domnach Airgid,* which is in the Royal Irish Academy.[18]

Kenney adds that there are also at least fifty other books dating from before A.D. 1000, which were brought to the continent, probably mainly at the time of the Norse invasions, by Irish emigrants.

But today the number of early Latin texts of Irish origin would be reckoned as greater than when Kenny wrote forty years ago. For one thing, modern scholarship has tended to assign to many texts an earlier date than was formerly accepted. For another, there has been discovered in the libraries of Europe a considerable additional number of manuscripts with unmistakable Irish characteristics. It would be outside the scope of this book to deal in detail with these works.[19] We may just emphasize in passing the fact that to the seventh or early eighth century belong some of the more important documents to which we have made or shall make allusion, the *Confession* of St. Patrick and his epistle to Coroticus, the lives of St. Patrick by Tírechán and Muirchu, Adamnán's life of St. Columba, the writings of St. Columbanus and the paschal letter of Cummian to Ségéne of Iona and the hermit Béccán.

The number of texts in Irish dating from the seventh century is notably smaller than of those in Latin, as might be expected from what has been said about the evolution of Irish writing from the Latin script. The *Amra Coluim Cille,* a eulogy on St. Columba, to which we shall refer later, is now accepted as having been written as early as the end of the sixth century. Possibly to that date also belong certain archaic poetical fragments embodied in the legal tracts, the text of which, as distinct from gloss and commentary, belongs mostly to the early eighth century. Internal evidence seems to assign to the seventh-century *Baile Chuind* or 'Ecstasy of Conn', purporting to be a prophecy made by Conn Cétchathach (Conn of the Hundred Battles) of the kings who were to rule in Tara.[20] The *Cáin Adamnáin* is a text dealing with the law protecting those who did not bear arms in self-defence, 'clerics, women and innocent children', and in particular exempting women from war service. This law was, according to the Annals, brought about by Adamnán in 697. Before that time 'women were in bondage and slavery'. The text gives a highly imaginative description of the circumstances leading up to the law, and the kernel of it is a declaration, in Old

Irish legal language, of the rights of non-combatants in war.[21] The oldest parts of this document are to be assigned to the late seventh century.[22]

THE CAMBRAI HOMILY

In tracing the evolution of written Irish the document generally referred to as the 'Cambrai Homily' is of particular interest. In the public library of Cambrai is preserved an eighth century manuscript containing the text of part of the Irish Canons. It had been copied by a continental scribe from a manuscript in the Irish character. By chance a leaf had been inserted in the original manuscript containing a fragment, some ninety lines, of an Irish homily, two-thirds in Irish, one-third in Latin. The continental scribe had transcribed this fragment with many errors owing to his inacquaintance with the Irish script.[23]

The homily deals with the duty of the christian to renounce sin and practise self-denial. It closes with the well-known distinction of the three kinds of martyrdom:

'This is the white martyrdom to man, when he separates for sake of God from everything he loves, although he suffer fasting or labour thereat.

'This is the green martyrdom to him, when by means of them (fasting and labour) he separates from his desires, or suffers toil in penance and repentance.

'This is the red martyrdom to him, endurance of a cross or destruction for Christ's sake, as has happened to the apostles in the persecution of the wicked and in teaching the law of God.'

The Irish of this homily is very archaic and dates, at latest, from the beginning of the eighth century, possibly from the late seventh century. It is evident that by this time the orthography was definitely fixed, and it does not change for centuries. This gives good ground for the belief that writing in Irish began about the beginning of the seventh century. Hence, from this date for the first time, we can speak of Irish literature in the strict sense.

CENN FAELED

The fusion of the two cultures and the part played in it by the invention of Irish writing is all exemplified by the story of Cenn Faeled 'The Learned'. This is found in the introductory passage of one of the ancient law tracts, the *Book of Aicill,* a code of criminal law. As we have seen earlier, it is claimed in this introduction that the treatise is in part the work of Cormac Mac Airt. But with him

is linked as part author 'Cenn Faeled, son of Oilell', and the following
incident is related as having led to the latter becoming the writer
of a 'number of well-composed books which he left after him in Erin'.

Cenn Faeled was a young Ulster warrior, who sustained a severe
head wound in the battle fought in 637 at Magh Rath (Moira, Co.
Down) between the king of Tara, Domnall II (of Cenél Conaill in
Co. Donegal) and his rebel foster-son Congal Cloen, son of the
king of Dál Araide (E. Derry, W. Down and most of Antrim) and
his allies, the kings of Scottish Dál Araide (Argyllshire) and Ulster
(the modern diocese of Down). The wounded youth was brought
to the monastery of Tuaim Drecain (Toomregan, Co. Cavan),
whose abbot, St. Bricin, was apparently skilled in medicine. In
Tuaim Drecain there were three schools 'at the meeting of three
streets, between the houses of the three professors', a school of
Latin learning attached to the monastery, a school of *filidecht,* Irish
learning in general, and a school of Irish law. During his con-
valescence, Cenn Faeled attended all three schools, primarily no
doubt as a law student, to judge by his later career, and it is recorded
that 'whatever he used to hear rehearsed in these three schools
every day, he had by heart every night, and wrote them on slates
and tablets (*a lecaib ocus i tuiblib*) and transcribed them into a
paper (vellum) book (*ocus ro cuir seic a cairtliubair*)'.[24]
This incident was the subject of a detailed study by MacNeill,[25]
who concluded that Cenn Faeled, having learned at the Latin school
to read and write, invented for himself the method of committing
to writing the teachings of the schools of Irish law and *filidecht.*
'The point of the narrative, when it was originally written, was
this, that Cenn Faeled did what had never been done before.'
His argument is that otherwise the writer, whose date was probably
some centuries later, would not have thought the incident worth
recording. In a later work, however, MacNeill grants the possibility
that 'Cenn Faeled was only one of a school of innovators'.[26] In
any case, the story is of great interest, as being the first recorded
instance not only of Irish writing, but also of an institution in which
the Latin and Irish cultures flourished side by side.
There is constant testimony that Cenn Faeled was indeed a man
of learning. The *Annals of the Four Masters* (677) give him the title
saí in eccna, which O'Donovan renders 'a paragon of wisdom'. In
the *Annals of Ulster* he is described as *Sapiens* (678). In addition to
the *Book of Aicill* he is credited with the authority of another law
tract, of which only the title remains, *Dúil Roscad,* and we have seen
earlier that there is good reason to accept him as at least part-author
of the grammatical tract *Auraicept na n-Éces*. In the *Lebor Gabála*

there appears under his name a long poem on the journey of Mileadh from Scythia to Spain and the subsequent emigration of his descendants into Ireland.[27] Petrie cites from the *Book of Glendalough* a poem of Cenn Faeled on the tradition that Cú Chulainn's head and right hand were buried at Tara.

> Cuchullin, the beauteous tower fell...
> There is a monument for his head
> On the ridge at the upper part of Tara.[28]

And in the Annals and elsewhere, numerous historical quatrains are quoted, 'as Cenn Faeled sang'.[29]

The story of Cenn Faelad has been accepted as historical by many authorities, and even those who doubt its historicity accept it as evidence that the method of writing Irish had been adopted by at least some of the native scholars as early as the seventh century.[30] Yet it is an undoubted fact that the surviving Irish manuscripts which we possess are, up to the twelfth century, all products of the monastic schools. It is impossible to determine with certainty whether this was due to a certain time-lag in the adoption of writing by the *filid,* or, more probably, to the fact that manuscripts had a better chance of surviving in the more stable conditions of monastic life.

Flower, who deals with great ability with this interesting topic, divides the manuscripts into three groups.[31] The first comprises the theological and grammatical texts, with Irish glosses, already referred to, which were written on the continent or, less probably, brought thither by exiles in the eighth and ninth centuries. The second group, belonging to the eleventh and twelfth centuries, consists of religious writings like the two *Books of Hymns,*[32] or writings of a mixed character, with both sacred and secular texts, such as the *Lebor na hUidre,* the *Book of Leinster* and the manuscript known as Rawlinson B. 502, which is in the Bodleian library, Oxford. The third group contains the majority of Irish manuscripts written on vellum before the seventeenth century, and the notable paper manuscripts of that century. With few exceptions, the scribes of this last period are no longer clerics, but members of the great hereditary scholar families attached to the noble families, either of the old Gaels or of the assimilated Anglo-Norman lords. How this change came about will be seen later.

The Convention of Druim Ceat

We have traced what might be called the internal assimilation of the christian and native cultures, the process by which each came to borrow from the other, and we have seen that this began to make itself clearly evident at the beginning of the seventh century. It was, however, accelerated by an incident of the late sixth century which brought about an external assimilation of the two cultures by the establishment of the status of the native schools within the new christian framework. The incident was the Convention of Druim Ceat, and the significant figure in it was St. Colum Cille.

Born in 521, Colum Cille received his early schooling in or near his native Donegal, but, when he was already a deacon, he travelled to Leinster and there put himself under the guidance of an aged scholar named Gemman. Adamnán introduces the latter in a vivid scene in which teacher and pupil vainly endeavour to save a young girl from the pursuit of a murderous scoundrel.[33] All the details of this incident go to show that Gemman was one of the native scholars, whose store of ancient tradition must have enriched the mind of his young pupil from the north.

Colum Cille, therefore, as a result of his early education, was well qualified to play a sympathetic and decisive part in stabilizing the position of the *filid,* which had become gravely endangered by their excessive numbers and overweening behaviour. This was accomplished at an historic meeting with Aed, son of Ainmire, King of Ireland, at Druim Ceat, near Limavady, Co. Derry. There are indirect references to this event in Adamnán's *Life of Columba,*[34] and it is recorded in the *Annals of Ulster* under the date 575. The details of it are found in the Preface to the *Amra Coluim Cille,* to be described presently, and in later writings, *Betha Colaim Chille,*[35] compiled in 1532 by Manus O'Donnell, King of Tír Conaill with the help of various scholars, and Keating's History of Ireland (*Foras Feasa ar Éirinn*) composed between 1629 and 1634.[36]

According to O'Donnell, Colum Cille came over from Iona to secure from the king three concessions:

1. To save the native poets from expulsion from Ireland, which was threatened 'by reason of their multitude and their sharpness and their complaining and for their evil words.' They had dared to satirize King Aed himself.

2. 'To make peace between the men of Erin and the men of Alba concerning Dál Riada' (the kingdom in Argyll set up by the Dál Riada of Antrim).

3. 'To release Scannlán Mór, son of Cennfaeladh, the son of the king of Ossory, that his father had given as a hostage to Aed, son of Ainmire'.[37]

The saint was accompanied by an impressive retinue, twenty bishops, forty priests, thirty deacons and fifty clerical students. He persuaded Aed not to banish the poets in view of the lasting fame they could give him. But 'from their poetry he did take out the venom', and he ordered that their numbers and privileges were to be restricted.

Each *tuath* was to have its own chief bard 'to keep its lineage and its ancestry'.

No bard should go into another *tuath* to seek reward, nor undertake a poem for the chief of another *tuath* unless he had that prince's permission. 'And if he (the prince) should suffer him to make the poem for him, he should send forth his own bard to the border of his land to meet him. And if his own bard praised the poem, he should buy it from the other, and if he praised it not, the other should go back to his land.'

Colum Cille then gave the poets his blessing, on condition that they observed these conditions and sent them forth over Erin.[38]

Keating adds another regulation not mentioned by O'Donnell. 'It was also ordained that a common estate should be set apart for the ollamhs where they could give public instruction after the manner of a University, such as Raith Cheannait and Masruidhe Mhuige Sleacht in Breithine, where they gave free instruction in the sciences to the men of Ireland, as many as desired to become learned in *seanchus* (traditional lore) and in the other sciences that were in vogue in Ireland at that time.'[39]

Amra Coluim Cille

Each *fili* and *ollam* present at the meeting expressed his gratitude in verses in honour of Colum Cille. The best of these poems was held to be the *Amra Coluim Cille,* the eulogy of Colum Cille, composed by Dallán Forgaill, the chief poet of Ireland. There is a Preface to the *Amra* which is of later date than the text. Its main events, however, may go back to sources of the sixth century. This gives much the same account of the Convention as O'Donnell, but adds the detail that the retinue of the *ollam* was to be reduced from thirty to twenty-four, and that of the *anruth* (a lower grade *fili*) from fifteen to twelve.[40]

The proceedings ended with somewhat of an anti-climax. 'Afterwards came the poets to Columba, having songs of praise and many lays, and they made for him a mighty music. Now *aidbse* is the name of the music.' The saint was human enough to display his pleasure openly, whereupon he was rebuked by a certain holy man of his following named Baithin. 'It were more fitting' he said 'for him to give heed to the judgment of God than to worldly praise.' The saint took the rebuke like a saint. 'Then Columcille covered his head and wept sore. And he had sharp sorrow for his sin'.[41]

We have said that this intervention of the greatest monastic figure of the day hastened the assimilation of the christian and native cultures. Indeed, if the accounts of the event are accepted as substantially true, it may be held to have saved the native schools from near extinction. Furthermore, it is an indication that at least the majority of the *filid* had by that time embraced christianity. The saint would hardly have intervened on behalf of a purely pagan culture.[42]

Hisperica Famina

In certain manuscripts of the ninth and tenth centuries there are found fragments of a strange composition, or series of compositions, written in loosely rhythmic lines, and dating probably from as early as the fifth or sixth century.[43] It occupies a unique position, since it is the product of neither the monastic or bardic schools. Its title, *Hisperica Famina,* means literally 'the western words', but, having regard to the character of its contents, scholars have rendered it by some such form as 'the elegant sayings' or 'the urbane utterances.'

The language is basically Latin, but is obscured by the use of specialized or recondite words, artificial word-twisting, ordinary words used in exceptional senses, or having exceptional suffixes, words derived from Greek and Hebrew. Scholars have devoted much time to the study of this obviously artificial diction. Their views have differed, but the main modern consensus of opinion is that certain literary circles in Ireland and part of Britain conceived the plan of creating a specialized form of Latin which could be used for secular literature.

The main Hisperic composition with which we are concerned has undoubted marks of Irish origin. Its preface begins with the arrival of a group of scholars, 'rhetores', in some region where they must ask to be excused because they cannot 'utter good Irish speech'. Later one of them speaks of enjoying 'crusts of bread...for which there abounded a delicious smearing of Irish oil.' Irish origin seems also to be indicated by certain linguistic peculiarities.[44]

This curious jargon has left its traces in various writings of the period, but it died out suddenly within a space of about twenty years. It was obviously an artificial product, and it had no effect on the development either of Latin or of the Romance languages. It has, however, a certain significance in the history of education. The main specimen of it which we possess is probably one of the earliest Irish writings in Latin; it gives confirmatory evidence of some features of the activities of the learned classes in early christian Ireland which are known to us from other sources, and at least part of it appears to have had a definite pedagogical purpose.

Though the *Hisperica Famina* has a definitely christian character, it bears no marks of monastic origin. It has been suggested by

Kenney and others that it originated in a group of christians who were not clerics, but fugitive scholars from the barbarian invasions of Gaul and Britain, and who preserved for a time the cultural traditions of the Roman world. Kenney also makes the surmise that some of these scholars were the 'rhetores' referred to by St. Patrick in his *Confession,* who criticized the saint's latinity.

No clear plan can be discerned in this composition. The opening section describes the meeting of this band of wandering 'rhetores' with some native scholars who wish to know from whence they come. One of the latter proposes a contest: 'I challenge the adroit wrangler to a verbal duel', and then proceeds to deride his rival as being no scholar, but a mere peasant who has deserted his farm. He is advised to go home, 'for all your fences have broken gates, your herds of cattle are grazing on the sprouting crops.'

There follows a dissertation, 'On the Twelve Faults of Ausonian Diction.' The faults enumerated are of orthography rather than style, and it is not clear whether this passage is a continuation of the native scholar's invective or a separate composition. Finally, there are a number of miscellaneous pieces, which are generally taken to be model exercises, composed either by teachers or by pupils, as aids to acquiring a difficult vocabulary.

The most interesting of these, entitled 'The Rule of the Day', enumerates various features of student life. They are aroused from slumber by the 'noisy clatter' of their rustic neighbours. They remove 'the speckled volumes from the curved satchel', and devote themselves to their 'rhetoric assignment'. At noon they seek in an adjoining inn 'sweet food to the famished'. It is here that the foreign student encounters his language difficulties', his own tongue being bound with 'an Ausonian chain'. Night comes. The students assume 'coarse nightclothes' and seek the 'soft pillow.' Yet even in bed there are some who 'heed their learned reading with a keen mind.'

The succeeding pieces, 'On the Sky', 'On the Sea', 'Concerning the Fire', 'About the Field', 'About the Wind', 'About Many Things', deal conventionally with conventional subjects. Two of them describe literary apparatus with which we have already met, 'The Book Container', made of dried sheepskin 'in the form of a square'...'bound by twelve cords' and 'closed with a choice strap', and 'The Writing Tablet' carried in the right hand of the scholar' and made from 'choice pieces of wood, covered with 'rubbing wax from another region'. The document closes with two pieces which indicate a christian origin, 'About the Chapel' and 'On Prayer', and a third 'An Attack' robustly secular, an episode in which brigands slay, roast and devour a boar, whose enraged owners fall on the thieves, decapitate them and strip the corpses.

CHAPTER 11

NORSE INTERLUDE

THE NORSE INVASION 800–1014

At the close of the eighth century numerous hordes of freebooters from Norway and Denmark began to sail south in search of plunder. Early historians commonly described the men who invaded Ireland as Danes, but modern research shows that they were preponderantly Norse, the Danes turning their attention to England and Normandy.

Both sets of these marauders are referred to as Vikings. It was the name they would have applied to themselves, for 'viking' in the Norse language meant one who went trading or plundering across the seas (its original sense appears to have been 'a man of the camps' or 'a man of the creeks'). They were primarily buccaneers, but in time established themselves as colonists.[1]

The first indication to the Irish of the Norse peril was when the long low Viking ships with their high brows carved into fantastic animal shapes, some of them carrying up to 120 men, appeared off the coast of Iona. The monastic settlement of Colum Cille was twice raided and burned, and in 806 Abbot Cellach and the surviving monks fled to Ireland, bearing with them their founder's relics, and settled at Kells. In 837 came the real invasion. In that year there was 'a fleet of three score ships of Norsemen on the Boinn: another fleet of three score ships on the river Liffe'.[2] Turgesius (in Norse Thorgest) sailed with his fleet up the Shannon and Bann, thus dominating the kingdoms of Ulster, Connacht and Munster. In 852 Olaf the White and Ivar 'Beinlaus' sailed into Dublin Bay and fortified the rising ground above the Liffey. Here they established the fortified settlement which was to be the centre point of Norse power. The Irish gave to these settlements the name *'longphort'*, 'ship-fort', since they began with the hasty running up of a stockade to protect the anchored ship.

The next forty years was a confused period, Irish kings at times opposing the invaders, at times enlisting them as allies in their internal feuds and intermarrying with them. But early in the tenth century came a rapid spread of Norse power. Two grandsons of Ivar, Ragnall and Sitric, sailed into Waterford harbour and built a fortress there. Dublin, which had been for a time recovered by the Irish, was retaken by Sitric after a fierce combat in which he defeated the High King, Niall Glúndubh and the united forces of Ulster, Meath and Connacht. Limerick was occupied by the Norse in 920, and rapidly they established a line of fortresses along the east and south coasts from Dublin to Wexford, Waterford, Cork and Limerick. Dublin became a Norse kingdom, extending down to Arklow and inland as far as Leixlip (one of the few surviving Norse place-names 'the salmon's leap'). In the second half of the tenth century, Meath was subjugated by the Norse of Dublin, Munster was overrun through the control of its rivers by the Norse of Waterford, Cork and Limerick, and the invaders established themselves in the ancient capital of Cashel.

NORSE POWER BROKEN

The Norse were now at the height of their power, but it was shortly to be broken. In 968 Ivar was defeated at the battle of Sulcóit in Tipperary by Mahon and Brian Bóraimhe (Boru) 'of the cattle-tributes', the two sons of Cennédig, chief of the Dál gCais, one of the royal tribes of Munster, Limerick was regained by the Irish and Munster freed. In 980 Malachy, king of Meath and High King, became master of Dublin, though he was content to let it be ruled by the Norse Sitric 'Silkbeard', as his vassal.

Malachy and Brian now agreed to rule Ireland, the former in the north, the latter in the south, but in 1002 Brian forced his rival to yield to him the High Kingship of the entire country. The final destruction of the Norse power came at Clontarf in 1014, when the forces of Brian and Malachy defeated those of Sitric and his allies, Norsemen from Scotland and Man, and the men of Leinster under Maelmora, king of Leinster, Brian's brother-in-law. This victory by no means meant the expulsion of the Norse from the country. They remained in possession of their territory north and south of Dublin and of their fortress towns elsewhere, and were allowed to retain their citizen rights. But they gradually became christian, and finally in speech and customs assimilated to the Irish around them, though never completely absorbed.[3]

CULTURAL SETBACK

The Norse invasion was undoubtedly a grave setback to the progress of culture in Ireland. It was the commencement of a century and a half of fierce, if intermittent, conflict. Again and again we find in the Annals records of how the 'foreigners' 'burned', 'spoiled', 'slaughtered', 'plundered', 'levelled to the ground'.

Nor was the devastation entirely due to the invaders. Older historians tended to represent the struggle as a clear-cut one between them and the Gaelic inhabitants. This is the impression given by one of the chief sources of our knowledge of the period, *Cogadh Gaedhel re Gallaibh, The War of the Gaedhil with the Gaill* (strangers), written probably shortly after the battle of Clontarf with the aim of extolling the virtues of King Brian.[4] But it is clear from the Annals that the conflict was really a most confused one, the native princes sometimes combining to resist the Norse, sometimes enlisting the aid of the invaders in their hereditary feuds, whilst the Norse at times fought amongst themselves. The total result was for the mass of the people a time of unrest, with intermittent massacres, burnings and destruction.

PLUNDERING OF MONASTERIES

Apart from this general turmoil, the invasions brought a special menace to culture. The Norse, at least on their first arrival, came as mere freebooters looking for plunder. It was natural that they should fall upon the monasteries with their rich store of jewelled sacred vessels and ornaments. The sacking of Iona was the beginning of a long series of such plunderings. In 839 'Ard Macha was plundered three times in the same month by them, and Turgesius himself usurped the abbacy of Ard Macha.'[5] A little later 'the place where Ota, the wife of Turgeis, used to give her audience was upon the altar of Cluain Mic Nois.'[6]

There is extant a vivid contemporary piece of evidence showing the fear of the Norse invaders always present in the minds of the Irish learned folk. Probably about the ninth century, a copy was made in Ireland of the *Institutiones Grammaticae,* a treatise of the Latin grammarian Priscian (fl. c. 500). As well as the text there are a considerable number of glosses in Old Irish and also marginal notes of a personal character. The manuscript was brought to the continent by one of the wandering scholars, and found its way to the library of the monastery of St. Gall in Switzerland.

Among the marginal entries is a quatrain evidently written by the scribe on a stormy night. It may be thus translated.

> Bitter is the wind tonight;
> It tosses the sea's white mane.
> I do not fear the crossing of the Irish Sea
> By the fierce warriors from Norway.[7]

'DROWNING OF BOOKS'

A special menace to culture was the destruction of manuscripts by the Norse invader. There is frequent mention of the pitching of books, with other unwanted articles, into the nearest lake or river. Thus in 922 'there came after that a fleet on Lough Dergderch, and they plundered Inis Celtra, and they drowned its shrines, and its relicks and its books.'[8] This destruction of books may have been in some cases motivated by hatred for the religious character of most of them, but probably more often it was due to simple contempt for what appeared to be useless lumber. These Norse pirates were not indeed mere uncultured savages. When the Irish forces retook Limerick after the victory of Sulcóit, the booty they found included 'saddles beautiful and foreign', 'gold and silver', 'beautifully woven cloth of all colours and kinds'.[9] In the Norse cemetery opened up a hundred years ago when the railway cutting was being made at Islandbridge, Dublin, were found weapons and ornaments which display skilled workmanship in iron, silver and bronze, and the use of well-wrought tools, knives, hammers, tongs and sickles.[10] But the Norse were illiterate. They left in Ireland no trace of writing beyond a few rough inscriptions on stone, and, though they had their own store of legends and poems, there is no mention of any written record of them. To the Norse invaders of Ireland, therefore, books would be useless plunder, fit only for destruction, or perhaps in some instances objects of supersititious fear.

The Norse invaders had, indeed a notable influence in the development of Irish civilization, though not in the realm of letters. From them the Irish learned the use of ships and horsemen. Their styles of ornament were to some extent adopted. They introduced silver coinage. They set the pattern of town life, hitherto unknown. They opened up sea traffic with the continent. By the influence of their coastal towns they transferred social and political influence from the midlands to the eastern coast.

CULTURAL SURVIVAL

It would, however, be a mistake to picture this period as one in which intellectual activity was brought to a complete halt. It is true that in the material at our disposal there is little detailed information about such activity in either the monastic or lay schools. But there are clear indications that in many parts of the country these centres of learning continued their work. It must be realized that the Norse invasion was by no means a complete conquest of Ireland. As has been seen, the invaders' permanent settlements were restricted to the area around Dublin and Wicklow, and to the towns of the south and east coasts. Other areas they raided and devastated, but these might then be left in peace for years. There were large areas of the north and west coasts to which the Norse never penetrated.

CONTINUANCE OF RELIGIOUS LIFE

It is, therefore, not surprising to find in the Annals clear, if laconic, indications that ecclesiastical and monastic life continued undisturbed to a large extent during this period. Again and again we find the records of the deaths of bishops, abbots, lectors, etc. The number of these entries and their continuance over such long periods indicate that the episcopal sees or monasteries in question had preserved their existence in spite of frequent and violent interruptions. Not infrequently these obituaries show that their subjects had exercised their routine functions over considerable periods. And there are other brief indications of the continuance of the course of religious life.

Thus in 824 'the law of Patrick [a system of collecting tribute] (was promulgated) throughout the three divisions of Connaught by Airtri, son of Conchobhar, i.e. Bishop of Ard-Macha.'[11] In 834 we read of 'a change of abbots at Ard-Macha, i.e. Forannan of Rath-mic-Malais in place of Diarmaid Ua Tighearnaigh'.[12] In 848 'Indrechtach, abbot of Ia, came to Ireland with the reliquaries of Colum Cille.'[13] In 926 'Celedabhaill, son of Scannal, went to Rome on his pilgrimage from the abbacy of Beannchoir.' At his departure he composed a poem in quatrains several of which indicate that his monastic life had been, at least on the whole, undisturbed. One runs thus:

> Time for me to prepare to pass from the shelter of a
>   habitation
> To journey as a pilgrim over the surface of the noble,
>   lively sea.
> But only a part of one year is wanting of my three score,
> To remain under a holy rule in one place it is time.[14]

In 988 is recorded the death of Dunchadh Ua Braein, abbot of Cluain-mic-Nois, who had spent thirteen years at Ard-Macha. He made many attempts to return to his own monastery, 'but different parties of the church [of Ard-Macha] used to come at the end of each year to detain him.'[15] In 992 'Muireagan of Both-Domhnaigh, successor of Patrick, went upon his visitation in Tír-Eoghain; and he conferred the degree of king upon Aedh, son of Domhnall, in the presence of Patrick's congregation, and he afterwards made a great visitation of the north of Ireland.'[16] In 1004 'St. Aedh, lector of Frefoit, bishop, wise man and pilgrim, died after a good life at Ard-Macha, with great honour and veneration.'[17] In 1011 'Adamnán, a learned man, bishop and virgin, lector of Ard-Macha, and intended successor of Patrick... was buried with great honour and veneration in the great church of Ard-Macha, before the altar.'[18]

It may be noted also how frequently these ecclesiastical or monastic figures are praised, not only for their virtue, but for their intellectual worth. Such descriptions are constantly found as 'wise man and learned doctor', 'doctor in divinity and spiritual wisdom', 'most learned and most wise in all Europe', 'the best historian that was in Ireland', 'adept in the Latin language and the Scottish [Gaelic] language.' It may be granted that there is a certain amount of conventional exaggeration in these appellations, but their constant recurrence seems to indicate that they cannot have been wholly undeserved.

MAINTENANCE OF *Scriptoria*

Dr. Kathleen Hughes makes the interesting point that, throughout this period, there is constant mention of *scriptoria* in connection with the monasteries, showing that they were able, to some extent, to pursue their work of copying and preserving manuscripts.[19] The smaller monasteries appear to have suffered most. Thus Finglas and Kildalkey had *scriptoria* in the eighth or early ninth centuries, but no mention of their activities is found for many centuries afterwards. Exposed as they were to the attentions of the Norse of Dublin, they seem to have suffered temporary extinction. On the other hand, Armagh, Clonmacnois and Clonard, though often attacked, managed to preserve or replace their cherished *scriptoria*.

A GEOGRAPHICAL POEM, TENTH CENTURY

In the *Book of Leinster* there is a curious poem, the composer of which is stated to have been Mac Coise, *fer léiginn* of the monastery of Ros Ailithir in Corcu Loigde (now Rosscarbery, Co. Cork).[20] In the *Annals of Inisfallen* we are told that when the monastery was sacked by the Norse of Waterford in 990, Mac Coise Dobráin, the *fer léiginn,* was carried off, and had to be ransomed by King Brian Bóraimhe. And in the *Annals of Ulster* the death is recorded in 1016 of Airbhertach Mac Coisi Dobráin, *airchinnech* of Ros Ailithir. It is reasonable to assume that the Mac Coisi commemorated in the Annals is identical with the author of the poem,[21] which would therefore have been composed towards the end of the tenth century. It is a brief survey of the geography of the world, and the manner in which as much information as possible is packed into the 136 lines seems to indicate that it was intended to be learned by heart by students. Since so little is known of the actual methods of the early schools, the poem has considerable interest.

First there are enumerated the five traditional zones of temperature, two frigid, two temperate, one fiery. There follows a description of the three parts of the world, Asia, Africa, Europe. In Asia, amongst other places are noted 'Chaldea and Babylonia the strong', 'Palestina the glorious; there are the sons of Jacob', and 'Alaunia a burning fire', a clear reference to the oil wells of Baku. Coming to Africa we hear of the river Nile (*Nuchul*) which 'flows in the east unchanged for a space among the learned Egyptians'. This is a 'land of chattering black men.' In Europe, the poet passes rapidly over 'Germania west by the stream of lofty Rhine', 'Thracia, Moesia, smooth Pannonia...side by side south of the Danube, from Constantinople and the Pontic Sea.' Greece comprises Attica 'the great country which contains Attica', Achaia 'to which belongs the city of Corinth' and Arcadia which produces 'the stone called Asbestos (*Asbest*) since fire affects not its mass.' From the Alps are said to rise three streams, the Rhine, the Loire, the Rhone. Between the Loire and the Rhine in the east lies Gallia Narbonensis (*Narbónein*) and in the west are Lugdunum and Belgica (*Lugdon, Belgeic*). Finally the poet gives a glance at Britain 'victorious land', and ends on a patriotic note with a eulogy of *Ériu* 'land pleasant, joyous, full of wealth...land the most fruitful that is known.' For its time, the poem is remarkably accurate as to the situation of over a hundred countries and towns, their fauna and natural products.

Religious Writing in Norse Period

The most tangible proof of the continuance of the cultural life of the monasteries during the period of the Norse invasions is found in the numerous religious writings which were then produced. The *Tripartite Life of St. Patrick* is so called because it contains three sections, the early life of the saint, his journeys to Connacht, his journeys to Leinster and Munster and his death at Armagh. It is written almost entirely in Irish, interspersed with a few passages in Latin. The manuscripts we possess – the most important being in the Bodleian and British Museum libraries – are of the fifteenth century, but the date of composition is most probably the end of the ninth century.[22]

Saltair na Rann is a collection of one hundred and sixty-two poems, amounting to about nine thousand lines, written entirely in Irish and mostly in the metre called *deibide*. The poems deal mainly with the history of the Old Testament, but extend to the birth of Christ.[23] O'Curry attributed this work to Aengus Céli Dé, who flourished about 800, but internal evidence shows that it cannot belong to a period earlier than the late tenth century. Modern scholars have dated it 987 or 988. Dr. Gearóid Mac Eoin has recently argued very convincingly that its author was Aibertach Mac Coise Dobráin,[24] whose geographical poem, mentioned above, has great similarities of style and matter with the first 337 lines of *Saltair na Rann,* devoted to a description of the universe. In this the writer is sometimes remarkably accurate. He accepts the sphericity of the earth, 'like a perfect truly rounded apple', and gives a good estimate of the size of the moon as one-sixth of that of the earth. He names as the planets *'Satuirn, Ioib, Mercuir, Mars, Sol, Uenir, Luna'*. He touches on many other topics less correctly, as, for instance, the distance from the earth to the moon, the lunar month, the height of the tides, the signs of the zodiac.

Navigatio Brendani, the Voyage of St. Brendan, composed in the tenth century certainly by an Irishman, though possibly living on the continent, is perhaps the last great Hiberno-Latin writing. It is a curious mixture of religious teaching with myth and poetical imagination. Kenney describes it as 'the epic – shall we say the Odyssey – of the old Irish church'.[25] The Brendan legend rapidly became popular all over Europe, and translations of the *Navigatio* were made into many of the vernacular languages, Norman-French, Old French, Middle English, Flemish, Dutch, German, Provencal, Italian, Norse.

Brendan, the fifth-century Kerry-born abbot of Clonfert, is represented as setting sail with his monks and other followers for 'the land of promise of the saints' of which he had heard from a certain abbot Berinthus. Many are their adventures. They find one island with an abbot and twenty-four monks living a full religious life and having a square church with altars, candlesticks, chalices and patens of crystal. In another island three choirs of youths, one dressed in white vestments, another in blue, another in purple, sing psalms in alternation. In a third lives a hermit Paul 'like a bird on a rock'. These scenes represent the religious and ascetical ideal, but there are others interspersed which are inspired by poetic fancy and exuberant humour. The monks land on an island (the saint cannily remaining on the ship) and kindle a fire. To their horror, the island shakes beneath them and proves to be a whale. They meet with other more ordinary marvels, 'columns of clearest crystal' and a mountain 'thick with smoke at its summit' and casting up flames. Finally they reach their goal, a spacious land full of fruit-bearing trees and rich with jewels where there is never night, for 'Christ is its light'. A mysterious youth tells them that God had prevented them from finding it sooner, so that He might show them 'various wonders of the great ocean'. They return to Ireland where death soon comes to Brendan.[26]

Dillon says of the *Navigatio* that it 'had a great influence in the Middle Ages, and is supposed to have supplied an impulse to the voyages of discovery, which led to India and the New World'.[27]

THE 'VISION'

The 'Vision' type of literary composition, in which the writer or some other person visits the other world, is found in every age and nation, reaching its highest level in the *Divina Commedia*. It was natural that in the fervent early years of Christianity in Ireland the religious homily should sometimes be cast in this form. As early as the seventh century, the *Vision of St. Fursa,* founder of monasteries on Lough Corrib, in Suffolk and Lagny near Paris, was widely known. Bede, in the following century, speaks of 'a little book' he had seen describing how the saint 'not only saw the greater joys of the blessed, but also fierce conflicts of evil spirits'.[28]

There is a suggestion of the 'Vision' in *Navigatio Brendani,* but the earliest clear example of this type of composition is *Fis Adamnáin,* the *Vision of Adamnán,* written in Irish in the late tenth century. Its theme is thus enunciated. 'These, then are the tidings which Patrick, son of Calpurn, was wont to use [to wit], Heaven's rewards and Hell's pains'.[29] The central figure is Adamnán, the seventh-century abbot of Iona, whose soul, on his death, is conducted by his guardian angel 'to Paradise with the angels of heaven, and to hell with its rabble host.'[30] Heaven is portrayed as the dwelling-place of Christ in His glory. 'Vaster a thousand times the splendour that is a plain of Heaven's family around the throne of God Himself.'[31] Hell is depicted in all its horrors, 'a fiery furnace likewise, flaming continuously, is there',[32] but may be escaped by penance, martyrdom and acts of charity.

Another vision homily, written in Irish in either the tenth or eleventh century, is *Tenga Bithnua, The Evernew Tongue.*[33] It is probably based on a Latin original, and purports to be a dialogue between the Hebrew sages, assembled on Mount Zion, and the spirit of the apostle Philip, who thus explains his title of the Evernew Tongue. 'The Lord sent me to the tribes of the heathen to convert them. Nine times hath my tongue been cut out of my head by the heathen, and nine times I continued to preach again'. The picture given in this work of the Creation, Heaven and Hell, whilst conveying a spiritual message, is interspersed with apocrypha₁ legend and sheer poetic invention. The creation is depicted at great length, the universe, the seas, wells, rivers, precious stones and trees of the earth, the sun, stars, birds, men and beasts.

The Incarnation is briefly recorded: 'The Infant sleeping between the Virgin's arms, whilst the elements, and even the angels trembled, and the heavens and earth with its inhabitants and the monsters in the seas, and the dwellers in hell'.[34] Hell and Doomsday are depicted in dark colours, but the apostle concludes with an ecstatic portrayal of Heaven, 'where will be health and calm of seas, and great peace and unconquerable charity; where life is eternal; where old age will not appear...where there is a paradise sweet and abundant, and splendour of angels and brightness of justice; and a royal palm, and golden rivers, and melodious praise of angels, and meetings of all the saints.'[35]

FURTHER ASSIMILIATION OF CULTURES

It is apparent that during these centuries of the Viking incursions the process of assimilation of the two streams of culture continued. 'As we know from many sources', writes Mr. Liam de Paor, 'the process of fusion of the native and Latin traditions of literature and learning was carried on vigorously in the ninth and tenth centuries.'[36] And Dr. Hughes points out that the *Vision* homilies and other writings of the tenth and eleventh centuries show 'a much clearer combination of interest between the lay world and the clerics than did the ecclesiastical literature of the pre-Viking period'.[37] The monastic writers are now frequently writing in the vernacular, and, whereas they formerly drew their inspiration from the Bible, the Fathers and other religious writings, they now show the typically Irish trend towards the play of imagination and fancy.

CORMAC MAC CUILENNÁIN

One of the most outstanding figures of the period of the Norse invasions was Cormac Mac Cuilennáin. He illustrated in his own person the intellectual and political independence which survived in spite of the partial domination of the invaders. He was of the royal family of the Eoghanachta, who for generations at Cashel had ruled south Munster as bishop-kings.

The *Annals of the Four Masters,* under the date 855, state that Cormac received his early education from Sneidhius, a wise man, probably a monk, of Disert Diarmady, Castle Dermot, in Co. Kildare. Little more is known of him until 900, when, at the age of 65, he was elected to the kingship of Cashel, being apparently then already a bishop. He was not only an able monarch, but also a man of learning. An old chronicle thus describes him.

'The complete master of Gaelic and Latin, the archbishop most pure, miraculous in charity and prayer, a proficient in law, in every wisdom, knowledge and science; a paragon in poetry and learning, head of charity and every virtue and head [read 'sage'] of education, supreme king of the two provinces of Munster.'[38]

Cormac is generally held to have been the author of one of the famous 'lost books', *The Saltair of Cashel,* of which, portions have survived. When this work was lost is unknown. O'Curry alludes to the existence in the Bodleian library of such parts as still existed in 1454,[39] but Hyde found in the Royal Irish Academy a poem written between the Cromwellian and Williamite wars by one David Condon, in which he states that he had seen and read the *Saltair.*[40] From references to it in the Books of Lecan, Ballymote and others, the *Saltair* appears to have been a historical and genealogical work of great extent.

Of the portions which survive, that known as *Cormac's Glossary* has already been considered. Older authors held that the work known as *The Book of Rights* was part of the *Saltair of Cashel,* though rewritten at a later date.[41] In this document the tributes due from the tribal kings in each province to the provincial king, and the stipends due from the king of Ireland to the provincial kings and from them to the tribal kings, are set out in what appears to be a highly stylized fashion, intended to flatter the monarchs concerned. The payments are to be made by an allotment of the most varied objects of value, 'wounding swords', shields, 'splendid cloaks', horses, hounds, 'cows with rich milk', beeves, slaves, ships, sets of chess, bridles 'with splendid ornament of precious stones' and so on. As in the *Lebor Gabála,* the matter is presented mainly in verse, but each section is preceded by a prose summary of the contents. Those who trace the derivation of the *Book of Rights* to an older work by Cormac mac Cuilennáin rely on a passage in which it is stated that anyone memorizing this treatise 'will be a sage or a venerable ollam', with the added assurance 'Mac Cuilennáin has promised it.'[42] Modern scholars consider this passing reference insufficient to prove that the *Book of Rights* is an actual recension of a work of Mac Cuilennáin. However, it can hardly be denied that the introduction of his name shows the existence in the eleventh century of a well-recognized tradition that he was the author of, or at least helped in the compilation of a similar treatise. The last supposition appears to be that of MacNeill, who holds it to be 'almost certain that the *Psalter of Cashel* was composed in Cormac's time, and that additions were afterwards made to it.' He points out that the fact that different metres appear in the various poetical sections suggests diversity of authorship, and concludes that 'we may assume that the official poets of the chief kingdoms were invited to draw up on a uniform plan a statement of the rights of the over-kings, and that these statements, put together in the *Psalter of Cashel,* formed the original *Book of Rights,* the date of which would be about 900.'[44]

This great scholar, king and bishop came to an unhappy end. Urged on by his evil genius, Flaighbeartach, abbot of Inis Cathaig, afterwards king of Cashel, he unwillingly invaded Leinster. At the battle of Ballaghmoon, in south Co. Kildare, Cormac and his ally, Ceallach, king of Ossory, met the combined forces of Flann Sionna, king of Leinster and High King of Ireland, and Cathal, son of Conor, king of Connacht. The *Annals of the Four Masters* give the date as 903, other annals as 908. Cormac's forces were routed, and he himself was killed by a fall from his horse and beheaded by his enemies. He was buried not far from the battle at Disert Diarmada where he had studied as a youth. The *Annals of the Four Masters* record an elegy, composed by Dallán, son of Mor, which ends:

> The bishop, the soul's director, the renowned illustrious doctor,
> King of Cashel, King of Iarmumha; O God, alas for Cormac.

NATIVE SCHOOLS IN NORSE PERIOD

There is ample evidence also of the continued activity of the native schools during the Norse period. Hyde remarks: 'Strange to say, despite the troubled condition of Ireland during these two or three centuries, she produced a large number of poets and scholars, the impulse given by the enthusiasm of the seventh and eighth centuries being still strong upon her'.[45]

Flann Mac Lonáin, whose death is recorded in the *Annals of Ulster* in 895 and in the *Annals of the Four Masters* in 891, is described in the latter as 'the Virgil of the race of Scots, chief poet of all the Gaedhil, the best poet that was in Ireland in his time'. A native of Slieve Echtge (Aughty) in south Connacht, he was chief poet of Ireland in the early years of the reign of Flann Sionna.

Eight of his poems survive, comprising about a thousand lines. He evidently had no mean opinion of his own talents. One of his poems describes how Ilbrechtach the harper was travelling over the mountains with the poet Mac Liag. The poet remarked that it would be a great thing to be acquainted with all the lakes and fastnesses in the area. The harper replied: 'If Mac Lonáin were here, he could name them all.' Stirred apparently by professional jealousy, Mac Liag cried: 'Let this fellow be taken and hanged'. The harper begged a respite until the next day, when Mac Lonáin opportunely came on the scene and saved him by reciting a poem of one hundred and thirty-two lines on the beauties of Slieve Echtge.

Two of Mac Lonáin's poems extol the virtues of Lorcán, king of Thomond, grandfather of Brian Bóraimhe, who was apparently one of his patrons. One of eighty-eight verses celebrate Lorcán's victory over Glann, king of Erin. Another describes Lorcán's residence of Kincora, situated on the banks of the Shannon and rich in wealth and harvest fruits. Flann Mac Lonáin was a contemporary of Cormac Mac Cuilennáin to whose virtues he pays tribute.

The tenth century produced many famous poet-historians. Cinaedh O'Hartigan (died 975) was of noble birth, son of Cernach the Haughty, who was grandson of Aedh Sláine, High King of Tara. He is described by Tighearnach as 'chief poet of *Leth Cuinn* [the northern half of Ireland]', and by the *Annals of Ulster* as 'chief poet of Ireland.' Being sprung from the southern Hy-Niall, he naturally gave much place in his poems to singing the vanished glories of Tara and the heroes and heroines of its court, chief among them Cormac Mac Airt.

Some nine or ten of his poems are preserved, some in the *Dinnseanchas* in the *Book of Ballymote,* on the the *Lebor na hUidre* and two in the *Book of Leinster.* One of the last-mentioned is a short poem recording the well-known legend of the death of King Conor mac Nessa, when the 'brain-ball' of Mesgedhra, lodged in his head for seven years, burst out on the day of the Crucifixion.

An even greater figure than O'Hartigan was Eochaidh Ó Floinn (died 984). Copies of his poems are found in many of the great collections, the *Dinnseanchas,* the *Book of the Invasions,*[46] the *Book of Lecan,* the *Book of Ballymote.* O'Reilly lists fourteen of Ó Floinn's poems amounting to some 1,800 lines.[47] One valuable chronological poem found in the *Book of Leinster* and the *Book of Lecan,* gives a chronology of the kings of Ulster. In other poems Ó Floinn gives an account of the mythological races who first peopled Ireland, the Parthalonians, Fomorians, Tuatha Dé Danaan, Milesians.

Dr. Healy makes the point that these legends were not the mere fruit of the poet's imagination, but were the recording of bardic traditions which, whatever their original source, were of great antiquity. The essential function of the bardic chronicler was to preserve the relics of the past. It is also possible that poet-historians of the type of Ó Floinn may have drawn on earlier written sources lost during the Norse invasions.[48]

Towards the end of the tenth century flourished Mac Liag. He was a native of south Connacht, and was at first poet to Tadhg O'Kelly, Prince of Uí Maine. Later he was chosen by Brian Bóraimhe as his *Ard-Ollamh* (chief poet) and took up residence at the palace of Kincora. Some 1,200 lines of his poetry have survived, giving a vivid picture of life in Ireland under Brian's rule. One of the most beautiful of these is his lament for Kincora bereft of Brian and the other chiefs who fell at Clontarf. James Clarence Mangan's translation of this poem is familiar:

'Oh where, Kincora, is Brian the great'

but cannot equal the pathetic tone of the original.

Several scholars, O'Conor, Healy, Hyde, have attributed to Mac Liag the work entitled *Cogadh Gaedhel re Gallaibh, The War of the Gaedhil with the Gaill,* which records the struggle against the Norse. However, Dr. Todd, who edited and published this work in 1867 does not consider that there is sufficient evidence of Mac Liag's authorship, and neither Colgan, nor Keating nor the *Annals of the Four Masters* attribute it to him. All, however, are agreed that the author was either an eyewitness of the Battle of Clontarf or gathered his information from eyewitnesses. It is clear also from Mac Liag's poems that, though he was not present at the battle, he was given a vivid account of it by his fellow-poet, Erard Mac Coise, who was in the company of Malachy, king of Meath, and that he also visited the battlefield before the dead had been buried and was able to note the position in which they lay.

Another poet-chronicler who may be considered as belonging to the Norse period though he survived until 1024, is Cuán Ó Locháin, 'chief poet of Ireland', according to the *Annals of Ulster.* He was born on the borders of Meath and Longford, where his family were chieftains of Morgallion (Gailenga Mór). O'Curry lists six of his historical poems. The most important of these gives an account of the deeds and virtues of Cormac Mac Airt, and describes the former glories of Tara. In it is found the oldest reference to the lost *Saltair of Tara,* which Ó Locháin ascribes to King Cormac. The oldest copy of this poem was found by O'Curry in the manuscript of the *Dinnseanchas* contained in the *Book of Ballymote.* It is printed in Petrie's *Antiquities of Tara Hill.* Others of the poems attributed to Ó Locháin are found in the *Wars of the Gaedhil with the Gaill.* One details the *geasa* (prohibitions) and prerogatives of the High King and sub-kings. It was prohibited, for instance, to 'launch a ship on the Monday after May-day'. But, on the other hand, the royal personages were entitled to 'the salmon of the Boyne...the cresses of the river Brosnach'. Yet another poem gives a fanciful account of the origin of the river Shannon. The lady Sinan, granddaughter of Lir, the great sea-king of the Tuatha Dé Danann, ventured near a mysterious well of Connla in order to steal the 'nuts of knowledge' growing on the overhanding hazel-trees. The waters of the well swelled up, drowned the hapless lady and carried her corpse down to the river which is named after her.

In the *Annals of Clonmacnois* the following entry is found under the date 1022. 'After the death of king Moylseaghlin (Maelseachlinn or Malachy II) this kingdom was without a king for the space of twenty yeares. Dureing which time the Realme was governed by two learned men, the one called Cwan O' Lochan, a well-learned temporall man and cheefe poet of Ireland, the other Corcrann Cleireagh a devout & Holy man, that was anchorite of all Ireland, whose most abideing was at Lismore. The land was Governed like a free state, and not like a monarchy by them.' This tradition is not found in the other Annals, but is mentioned in the *Book of Leinster*. If true, it is a remarkable proof of the high standing of the poet-historian. Ó Locháin's regency came to a violent end when in 1024 he was murdered by the men of Tethfa [Teffia] in Co. Longford on the borders of his native territory. The *Annals of Loch Cé* record the fate of his murderers. 'God performed a "poet's miracle" manifestly on the party that killed him, for they died an evil death and their bodies were not buried until wolves and birds preyed upon them'. His fellow-regent survived him and ruled until 1040.

We may suitably here recall that during the tenth century the flow of Irish monks to the continent continued and even increased. Kenney, however, makes the observation that 'towards the close of the ninth century the character and direction of Irish emigration changed. Men whose chief interest was in scholarship disappeared from the movement, and the religious became again the dominating impulse.' This view is confirmed by the sparse literary remains of this period which are even remotely connected with the Irish monks abroad.[49]

KING BRIAN BÓRAIMHE, PATRON OF LEARNING

It is generally accepted by historians that, in the period between his assumption of the high kingship (1002) and the final breaking of the Norse power at Clontarf (1014), King Brian Bóraimhe not only brought about a large, if temporary, measure of political unity, but also gave to Ireland 'a new impetus of art, literature and culture not unworthy of her former Golden Age.'[50]

The classical testimony to Brian's patronage of learning is found in *Cogadh Gaedhel re Gallaibh*. 'By him [Brian] were erected also noble churches in Erinn and their sanctuaries. He sent professors and masters (*saoithe ocus maighestreacha*) to teach wisdom and knowledge; and to buy books beyond the seas and the great ocean; because their writings and their books in every church and in every sanctuary where they were, were burned and thrown into the water by the plunderers, from the beginning to the end; and Brian himself gave the price of learning and the price of books to every one separately who went on this service.'[51]

The author of *Cogadh Gaedhel re Gallaibh* was obviously an enthusiastic partisan, but the claims he makes for King Brian are to some extent substantiated from other sources. The well-known work on the rights and duties of kings, *Lebor na Cert,* to which we have earlier made reference, was obviously composed by lawyers of Brian's entourage. This is evidenced by the fact that the section on Cashel is the first and longest and makes claims for that kingship far greater than those of any other. 'It is prescribed here that the King of Cashel shall be head over all for ever, by sentence of the blessing of God Almighty...'[52]

It is also likely that at least some of the commentaries on the great collection of ancient Irish law tracts known as *Senchus Mór* were the work of lawyers of Brian's day. These, however, though they are evidences of interest in and study of the old law, do not indicate any high degree of legal learning, since they betray a considerable ignorance of the language of the ancient text and of the rules and institutions enshrined in it. Nor is there any evidence for the supposition that Brian himself had any direct hand in the composition of the commentaries.[53]

Various other instances are cited of the revival of culture during the reign of King Brian. The Munster *Annals of Innisfallen,* which, up to the end of the ninth century give a bare outline of dates and facts, become fuller and richer from the period of Brian's accession. The ninth-century codification of the rules of poetry was revised and systematized by poets of his court.[54] There are numerous testimonies to the liberality of Brian as a patron of the *filid.* One of them, Mac Giolla Caoimh describes a visit to the high king when the poet boasted how at the court of O'Neill he had received 'twenty steeds, ten ounces of gold, and ten score cows of cattle.' The hint was taken, and the poet could conclude: 'By the King of Heaven, who has brought me into silence this night, and who has darkened my brightness, I got two times as much as that at the banquet before Brian lay down'.[55]

Flower, who deals at length with this topic, compares the influence of Brian Bóraimhe on Irish culture to that exercised by Charlemagne on Frankish and Alfred on English culture. He also considers the claim made by the later bardic families that they dated from the time of Brian's rule. The seventeenth-century scholar, Dubhaltach MacFirbhisigh, in his great *Book of Genealogies,* declares that 'about that time [the reign of Brian] was settled the greater number of the family names of Erinn; and certain families chose or were ordered to be professors of history and other arts at that time, some of them before and some of them after that time. So that they remain in the countries of Erinn, with all the chiefs all round, for the purpose of writing their genealogies and history and annals: and to compose noble poems on these histories also; and also to preserve and to teach every instruction that is difficult or obscure in Gaedhlic, that is to teach the reading of the ancient writings.' MacFirbhisigh then enumerates the most famous of these families and their patrons.[56] Flower points out that there is no contemporary record of such an origin of the learned families, and that they first appear in the Annals about 1200. He admits, however, that there may be some slight foundation for the claim. 'It is, perhaps, safest to conclude that the institution was of gradual growth, but that it finally consolidated and established a tendency which had begun to manifest itself in his [Brian's] day and under his influence.'[57] We shall later consider the growth of the learned families and the influences which favoured it.

Finally, it may be fairly argued that the beneficent influence of Brian's rule was not confined to his own lifetime, but laid the foundation for the development of art and literature which marked the century and a half between his death and the Norman invasion.

CHAPTER 12

NORSE TO NORMAN

The century and a half which elapsed between the defeat of the Norse at Clontarf and the Norman invasion was a period of comparative peace in Ireland. The final blow had been given to the Vikings' hopes of establishing dominion over Ireland, and they contented themselves with developing the towns they had founded: Dublin, Wexford, Waterford, Cork, Limerick. They accepted christianity and finally became in speech and dress almost identical with the native Irish.

This period witnessed a notable revival of art and literature. Metal work and architecture reached a high level. The great processional Cross of Cong, to be seen today in the National Museum, Dublin, was commissioned about 1123 by Toirdelbach Ua Conchobhair, king of Connacht, and in 1134 Cormac's Chapel in Cashel, built by Cormac Mac Cárthaigh, king of Munster, was consecrated in presence of a great throng of ecclesiastical and royal personages. From this period also date three of the most valuable collections of ancient Irish literature, *Lebor na hUidre* (c. 1100), the *Book of Leinster*[1] (c. 1160) and the two eleventh-century codices which are commonly spoken of as *Liber Hymnorum,* and contain sacred poems and hymns in Latin and Irish.[2]

Lebor na hUidre, which is preserved in the library of the Royal Irish Academy, consists of one hundred and thirty-seven folios, evidently a mere fragment of the original, and contains sixty-five pieces, including the *Amra Coluim Cille* and an imperfect copy of *Táin Bó Cuailgne.* The title it bears, *The Book of the Dun Cow,* (*odhar,* brown; gen. *uidhre*), enshrines the tradition that the original manuscript, now lost, was written on vellum made from the hide of St. Ciarán's favourite cow at Clonmacnois.[3] In a note on the manuscript, made in 1345, we read: 'A prayer for Mael Muire son of Celechar, son of Conn na mBocht, who copied and searched out this book from various books.' Mael Muire, a monk of

Clonmacnois, was a member of a family distinguished in ecclesiastical circles. According to the *Annals of the Four Masters,* he was slain in the great church of his monastery in 1106. The manuscript of *Lebor na hUidre* has many interlinear glosses, showing the antiquity of the pieces, the language of which was already archaic in the twelfth century.

The *Book of Leinster* is preserved in the library of Trinity College, Dublin. The text was published in 1880 in a facsimile of a transcript made by O'Longan, with introduction by Atkinson. In 1965–67 the entire text was published in five volumes edited by Best, Bergin and O'Brien. The passages to be cited are Best's translation. (Vol. I, xv-xvii). The text of *Táin Bó Cuailgne* from the *Book of Leinster* has been published, with translation by Joseph Dunn (1914) and Cecile O'Rahilly (1967), both with valuable introductions.

The authorship of the *Book of Leinster* is established by two notes on the manuscript. The first runs: 'Aed Hua Crimthaind wrote this book and collected it from many books'. Aed, abbot of Tír dá Glas – the modern Terryglass on the banks of Lough Derg, Co. Tipperary – was evidently commissioned to compile the book by Find Ua Gormáin, bishop of Kildare (died 1160, *Annals of Ulster*), to whom it was sent in an unfinished state for approval. The second entry is a message from the bishop, returning the manuscript.

'Life and health from Finn, bishop (i.e. of Kildare) to Aed Mac Crimthainn, lector of the high king of Leth Moga (i.e. Nuadat), [Dermot Mac Murrough], and coarb [successor] of Colum, son of Crimthann [former abbot of Tír dá Glas, d. 548], and prime historian of Leinster in wisdom and knowledge and book lore and science and learning. And let the conclusion of this little tale[4] be written for me
accurately by thee, O acute Aed,
O man of stately form,
Whether I be a long or short while away from thee
my desire is that thou shouldst be with me.

Let the duanaire [song-book] of Mac Lonáin [the Connacht poet who died 891 or 895] be brought me that we may discover the meaning of the poems that are in it. Et uale in Christo.'

This message, with its authentic personal note, is unique in being the only private letter in Irish which has come down to us from the pre-Norman period. It also illustrates a point to which we shall recur later, namely that a certain number of the Irish chiefs appear to have received education from individual priests or monks. Aed Mac Crimthainn is described by bishop Finn Ua Gormáin as *fir leigind ardrig Leithi Moga. Fir leigind* is translated by Best as 'lector', but Todd and Dunn who render it as 'tutor' seem correct in assuming that, in the context, *fir leigind* is not used in the usual sense of head of studies in a monastic school, but as expressing some sort of personal educational relation to Dermot Mac Murrough.

The Annals give ample evidence that learning flourished during this period among both clergy and laity. Thus in the pages of the *Four Masters* we find the constant mention of bishops, abbots, priests and *filid* who are described in various terms as learned men, 'distinguished scribe', 'a learned historian', 'a doctor and learned senior', 'head of the west of Europe for piety and wisdom', 'chief doctor of the Irish in literature, history and poetry and in every kind of science known to man in his day'. As has been previously said, these titles need not be accepted literally, but on the other hand their total significance cannot be ignored.

The best known to us of these clerical scholars is Tighearnach Ua Braein, abbot of Clonmacnois (d. 1088), described in the *Annals of the Four Masters* as the 'chief successor of Ciaran and Coman... a paragon of learning and history'. His *Annals* are the earliest historical source we possess. They are partly in Latin, partly in Irish, and the many quotations found in them from Greek and Latin authors manifest the wide culture of the author.[5] Another clerical author whose writings have survived is Gilla-na-naemh Ua Duinn (d. 1160). O'Reilly describes him as 'chief bard to the king of Leinster', but according to the *Annals of the Four Masters* and the *Annals of Tighearnach,* he was 'lector of Inis-Clothrann,' and therefore most probably a monk. Six long poems of his are cited by O'Reilly, on the tribes sprung from the Milesians and on the christian kings of Leinster and Connacht. There had been an earlier annalist than Tighearnach, Dub-dá-leithe, *fer léiginn* of Armagh 1046–49 and head of that monastery 1049–60, but his 'Book', referred to in the *Annals of Ulster* under the date 962 and 1021, has been lost.[6]

A figure who occupies a unique place is Flann Mainistreach, Flann of the Monastery (d. 1056), lector of *Mainistir-Buithe* (Monasterboice). The *Annals of the Four Masters* describe him as 'the paragon of the Gaeidhil in wisdom, literature, history, poetry and science', and quote a quatrain in his honour:

> Flann of the chief church of melodious Buithe,
> Slow the bright eye of his fine head;
> Contemplative sage is he who sits with us,
> Last sage of the three lands is fair Flann.

Though O'Reilly speaks of him as 'abbot', it seems certain that he was a lay professor attached to the monastery. He thus exemplified in his person the fusion which took place so rapidly between the christian and the native cultures. O'Curry deals in detail with fourteen long poems attributed to Flann, almost all found in the *Book of Leinster*. They are mainly synchronisms of the kings of the Assyrians, Medes, Persians, Greeks and the emperors of Rome with the kings of Ireland, but there are also more valuable synchronisms of Irish monarchs with provincial kings and kings of Scotland. Hyde finds poems of this type 'anything but creative and imaginative'.[7] They are merely 'annals or history versified'. O'Curry, however, points out the value of such compositions, which give life to 'many a name lying dead in our genealogical tracts,' illustrate 'many an obscure historical allusion' and identify 'many an historical spot'.[8]

SURVIVAL OF THE MONASTERIES

Many of the older monasteries had perished during the Viking wars, but many had survived or risen again from destruction: Armagh, Clonard, Clonmacnois, Derry, Glendalough, Lismore, Monasterboice, Tallaght, to mention only a few of the most famous.[9] Up to 1148, there were as many as fifty abbeys of monks and seven of nuns. The numbers declined during the century, but after 1171 there were still twenty-four abbeys of monks living according to the old Irish rule.[10]

CHURCH REFORM, TWELFTH CENTURY

During the first three-quarters of the twelfth century a movement of reform took place throughout the Irish Church. One of its earlier initiators was Gilla Easpaic (Gilbert), bishop of Limerick from 1105. His tract *De Statu Ecclesiae*[11] aimed at the freeing of the Church from lay influence, the reviving of clerical celibacy, the creation of a hierarchy, the appointment of bishops by Rome and the establishment of territorial dioceses. Another vigorous reformer was Cellach Ua Sínaig (Celsus), bishop of Armagh, who together with the High King, Muirchertach Ua Briain, presided as primate of Ireland at the Synod of Ráith Breasail, near Cashel, at which Ireland was divided into twenty-four territorial sees. The Munster *Annals of Inisfallen* record this great local event with enthusiasm; 'They enacted discipline and law better than any made in Ireland before their time.

> The number of the pure clerical order
> In the synod of Ráith Breasail;
> Three hundred priests – a perfect festival –
> And a fair fifty bishops.'[12]

ST. MALACHY

But the greatest champion of reform was Mael Maedóc Ua Morgair, known in history as Malachy, bishop of Connor and for a period of Armagh, and described by the *Annals of the Four Masters* as 'a brilliant lamp which illumined territories and churches by preaching and good works, faithful shepherd of the Church in general'. Born about 1094 in Armagh, he died in 1148 whilst on his way to Rome, in the abbey of Clairvaux, surrounded by St. Bernard and his monks.[13] In his *Life* by St. Bernard,[14] the dark side of the spiritual and moral state of Ireland at the time is perhaps overemphasized in order to enhance Malachy's achievement. Yet it cannot be denied that there was grave need for reform by both the abolition of abuses and the regularizing of ecclesiastical organization.

Before his death in 1148, Malachy had induced the southern bishops to submit to the supremacy of Armagh. The completion of the work of reform was secured at the Synod of Kells in 1152, under Gilla mac Liag (also known as Gelasius, a latinized form of Giolla Íosa, the servant of Jesus) Malachy's successor, when three hundred clerics declared their acceptance of the whole reform programme. The number of sees was fixed at thirty-six and of archbishoprics at four. The *pallium,* token of Roman approval, was bestowed on the archbishops of Armagh, Cashel, Tuam and Dublin.

New Monastic Foundations

Malachy also brought a new spirit into the monastic life by the introduction, about 1140, of the Augustinian canons and canonesses and the Cistercians. Mellifont, founded in 1142, became the mother-house of the Cistercians in Ireland, and from it the Order spread rapidly throughout the country. After Malachy's death, his policy was continued by St. Laurence O'Toole, who became abbot of Glendalough in 1153 and archbishop of Dublin in 1162, and who introduced Augustinian canons into many places in Leinster. By the time of the Norman invasion, there were in all about sixty-two houses of Augustinian canons, twenty-four of canonesses, fifteen monasteries of Cistercians and two of Benedictines. These new foundations outnumbered and supplanted the older monasteries, which almost completely disappeared during the thirteenth century.[15]

Side by side with this spiritual reform went a revival of culture in the schools of Ireland, fostered by both bishops and temporal rulers. Gilla Mac Liag ruled the see of Armagh from 1137 to 1172, his declining years being overshadowed by the Norman invasion. He vigorously asserted the spiritual primacy of Armagh, and also maintained the cultural ascendancy of its school, thus securing theological orthodoxy. The *Annals of the Four Masters* record, under the date 1162:

'A synod of the clergy of Ireland, with the successor of Patrick, Gillamacliag, son of Ruaidhri, was convened at Claenadh [Clane] where there were present twenty-six bishops and many abbots, to establish rules and morality amongst the men of Ireland, both laity and clergy. On this occasion, the clergy of Ireland determined that no one should be a lector [*fer léiginn*] in any church in Ireland who was not an alumnus [*dalta*] of Ard-Macha before'.[16]

Seven year later, the Annals record how the cultural authority of Armagh was recognized by royal favour.

'1169. This was the year in which Ruaidhri Ua Conchobhair, King of Ireland, granted ten cows every year from himself, and from every king that should succeed him, forever, to the lector of Ard-Macha, in honour of St. Patrick, to instruct the youths of Ireland and Alba [Scotland] in literature'.[17]

Right up to the time of the Norman invasion, the monastic schools were producing scholars of high calibre. Such a one is commemorated by the *Annals of the Four Masters* at the date 1174.

'Flann (i.e. Florentius) O'Gorman, chief Lecturer (*airdfer lecchin*) of Armagh, and of all Ireland, a learned sage, and versed in sacred and profane philosophy, after having spent twenty-one years of study in France and England, and twenty other years in directing and governing the schools of Ireland, died happily on the Wednesday before Easter, in the seventieth year of his age.'[18]

Their fame, too, had never ceased to attract scholars from abroad. In 1088 died Sulien, bishop of St. David's, 'the wisest and most praiseworthy of all the bishops in Wales'. In his obituary, written in verse, we read that in his youth 'moved by the example of his forebears to love learning, he betook himself to the Irish famous for admirable wisdom'.

> *Exemplo patrum commotus amore legendi*
> *Ivit ad hibernos sophia mirabili claros.*

Later, possibly when already a bishop, he again 'sought the fields of Ireland' (*Scotorum visitat arva*).[19]

This pre-Norman period saw also the continuation of that cultural activity which the native scholars had managed to keep alive during the troubled era of the Norse invasion. Professor Ó Cuív has well emphasized the indignation with which these learned men must have repudiated the claim made by Henry II in his appeal to Pope Adrian IV for permission 'to enter the island of Ireland...to proclaim the truths of the Christian religion to a rude and barbarous people.' He points out that 'in the very century in which Henry came to Ireland, the leaders of their profession had reorganized their craft and had laid the basis for a prescriptive grammar of Irish, the first such grammar of a western European language.' In these two centuries, in addition to religious writings, there was produced a great quantity of new literature, 'tales and historical poems...the "Vision of Mac Con Glinne" which is a wild goliardic satire on the monks of the time; and the Irish version of the stories of Troy and Thebes, and the Civil War of the Romans; and we recall that there, too, Irishmen were innovators, for not even the oldest French version of the Troy story is as old as ours.'[20]

TWELFTH CENTURY LANGUAGE MOVEMENT

Professor Ó Cuív's allusion in the foregoing paragraph to the formation of Irish grammar has reference to a phenomenon remarked on by numerous scholars.[21] Towards the end of the twelfth century and in the beginning of the thirteenth there is observable in the poetry of the *filid* (to a lesser extent in prose) a definite uniformity of grammar and metrics which continues up to the end of the sixteenth century. This uniformity receives permanent expression in a number of grammatical tracts, which go back to 1500 or possibly even earlier. We will deal with these later. At this point it is enough to note that this process of standardization is so marked as to be ascribable only to some deliberate, possibly organized movement. Professor Ó Cuív holds that there must have been 'a normative or prescriptive grammar of Irish which was the product of an examination of the language by scholars',[22] whilst Bergin goes so far as to conclude that 'there must have been conferences of the *literati.'* Otherwise it is impossible to account for the 'many hundreds of poems in the standard dialect.'[23] The effects of this training were not merely narrowly linguistic. Professor Ó Cuív points out that 'the consolidation of the literary language... proved to be of immense importance in the confrontation between native and alien cultures which took place after the Anglo-Norman invasion.'[24]

PRE-NORMAN *Filid*

In the various Annals between 1014 and 1160 we find the records of between twenty or thirty of the most notable scholars, described in the usual way 'chief poet of Ireland', 'the most learned of Ireland in history', 'the most distinguished wise man of Ireland'.

We have already mentioned Erard Mac Coise and Cuán Ó Locháin, who lived on after the battle of Clontarf. Giolla Caoimhghin (died 1072) was a poet and historian from whose pen we have five long chronological poems on the mythological ancestors of the Gaedhil and the pagan and christian kings of Ireland. They consist largely of lists of names, and it has been suggested that they were aids to memory for use in the bardic schools. There is some evidence for the fact that Giolla Caoimhghin was the author of the translation into Irish of the *Historia Britonum* of Nennius. The origin of this curious work is obscure, but it seems to have been originally compiled about 822 by one Marcus the Anachoret who, British born, was educated in Ireland where he became a bishop, and then settled in France. His book was republished with additions about 858 by a British monk named Nennius. The connection of the original author with Ireland explains why the book contains a good deal of matter pertaining to Irish history. Copies of the Irish version are found in the *Books of Ballymote, Lecan,* and *Hy-Many*.[25] A lesser figure is Tanaidh Ó Mulconaire (died 1136) of whose poems two have survived, one on the Firbolg and one on the seven kings of the Tuatha Dé Danaan and the arrival of the Milesians in Ireland.

The Scholar Families

This is a suitable point at which to consider more fully the learned families to whom we have already frequently referred. We have seen that the tradition that they originated under the rule of Brian Bóraimhe cannot be fully substantiated, but may contain a grain of truth. What is certain is that in the course of the eleventh century their position became clearly recognized.

Flower thus summarizes the evidence. 'The Annals begin to record the deaths of members of these families early in the twelfth century. Cú Chonnacht na scoile Ua Dálaigh, of Bunbrosna in Westmeath, died at the monastery of Clonfert, the house of St. Brendan, in 1139. From his grandson Aengus are descended all the O'Dalys of Ireland. A Tanaidhe Ua Maelchonaire died in 1136, and in the Gospel of Maelbhrighde Ua Maelunaigh, written in Armagh in 1138, there is a poem by Néidhe Ua Maelchonaire, a member of the same family, who were historians and poets to the O'Conors and MacDermots and other related families of Connacht. In the same year died Amlaibh Mór mac Firbhisigh, whose family were the literary men of the other great people of Connacht, the Hy Fiachrach of counties Mayo and Sligo. Later in the century we find such names as Mael Íosa Ó Dálaigh, *ollave* of Ireland and Scotland, who died in 1185 and Rathnall Ó Dálaigh, dead in 1161. From about 1200 the literary families are firmly in the saddle, and in describing that unique phenomenon, the bardic order, one is at liberty to select from five centuries, for their constitution and outlook remained substantially the same throughout the Middle Ages, although it will appear that certain modifications of subject-matter were introduced from external sources in the course of that period.'[26]

How is the rise of these families to be explained? It may, of course, be held that the continuity of their possessions arose from the Irish social system, in which dignities, offices and trades were transmitted down through the family, owing to the fact that in each *tuath* special lands were appointed as possessions of these positions or callings, and were handed on, not by primogeniture, but in virtue of merit.[27]

But to explain the establishment of the intellectual ascendancy of these families is a more complex task. The theory advanced by Flower is as follows. Up to the twelfth century, the manuscripts which we possess are all of monastic origin. The greatest of these were written in monasteries in central Ireland, such as Clonmacnois and Terryglass. It was in this area that the most important bardic families appeared, the O'Mulconrys, O'Clerys and O'Duigenans, historians and genealogists; the MacEgans, lawyers; the O'Dalys, poets. Flower surmises that these learned men in some way took over the literary heritage of the monks, but does not discuss in detail how this came about.[28]

This problem has recently been studied in great detail by Professor Proinsias MacCana.[29] He accepts 'the broad outline of Flower's argument', but points out that it needs deeper examination and more exact qualification. To begin with, it seems likely that the rise of the scholar families was connected with the decline of the old Irish monasteries during the eleventh and twelfth centuries. During that period, the monastic possessions had become excessively extended, and were administered by lay tenants, who bore the title of *comarb* (co-heir) or *airchinnech* (one in a position of authority). These men had great influence in the life of the monastery, and at times even exercised the functions of abbot.[30] Now it is remarkable that many of them were also men of learning. Professor MacCana gives a long list of such families as that of Ua Breisleáin, *brethemain* to Maguire and *airchinnigh* of Derryvullan (Doire Mhaoláin) on the Erne, Ua Duibhgeannáin, *airchinnigh* of Cill Ronáin in Roscommon and historians to Clann Mhaolruanaidh, Ua Cianáin, *airchinnigh* of Claoinis in Loch Erne and historians and poets in Fermanagh and Airghialla.[31]

When the old monasteries declined, and finally disappeared by about 1200, their possessions met with different fates. Some passed into the hands of the Augustinian canons, many became parish churches, but retained their hereditary *comarbada*.[32] It seems a reasonable conjecture that at least some of the learned families developed out of the laicized personnel of the ancient monastic schools.

Professor MacCana suggests that this conjecture is strengthened by two considerations. The first is the curious fact that one of the main functions of the late *airchinnigh* was to dispense hospitality, and that this was also regarded as a feature of the late *ollamhain* of poetry and secular literature.[33] It seems probable that this is not a mere coincidence, but that the duty devolved on these families together with the temporal possessions which they had inherited from the original monastic owners. The second consideration is that in a late legal commentary on the privileges of the *ollamh* it is laid down that the inferior grades of poet had to perform certain services for him, the *cano* to feed his dogs, the *dos* his servants, the *driseach* to foster his children and the *airchinnech* to maintain his horses.[34] This seems to imply that the church tenant was in some way connected with the poetic hierarchy.

However, in spite of these various considerations which go to demonstrate at least the partial truth of Flower's theory, it would be an over-simplification to imagine that all the ancient Irish tradition was recorded by the monks, and by them handed on to the bardic families. For one thing, the monastic scholars were mostly concerned with *senchas,* national history and, in particular, synthetic world history. They did, indeed, to some extent devote themselves to other branches of literature, poetry, genealogy, topography, but these were in a far greater degree the province of the *filid*. Again, there is ample evidence that much of the learning later committed to writing by the learned families was handed on direct to them by oral tradition from earlier *filid*. In the opinion of Professor MacCana, the whole process of the transmission of the literary heritage is 'so complicated indeed that one can never hope to recover the manifold changes of the period except in their broadest outlines.'[35]

And finally, even if we agree in general with Flower's theory, it must be noted that, though a remarkable number of learned families stemmed from the midlands, the phenomenon was by no means confined to that area. There were, for instance, the Uí Chlumhain of Mayo and Sligo, poets to O'Hara, the Uí Eochasa, originally of Cinél Tighernaigh in Ulster, who became poets to the Maguires of Fermanagh, and the Uí Gnímh, the Uí Eachaidhéin and the Uí Uid of Trian Conghail or Clann Aodha Buidhe.[36]

CHAPTER 13

NORMAN IMPACT

THE NORMAN INVASION

In 1169, bands of adventuring Welsh-Norman and Flemish-Norman knights, with their auxiliary foot-soldiers and crossbowmen, invaded the south coast of Wexford, and towards the end of 1170 their leader, Richard Fitzgilbert de Clare, Earl of Pembroke, 'Strongbow',[1] disembarked with a formidable army near Waterford. The Anglo-Normans, aided by their superior military equipment and organization, and by the absence of political unity among the Irish chiefs, speedily over-ran the country. Within a few months, they had occupied Dublin. When Henry II arrived in October 1171 with another larger army, he received the homage not only of the Anglo-Norman invaders, but also of most of the Irish chiefs and their Norse allies. The conquest proceeded rapidly, though unsystematically, according as the Irish resistance was greater or less. Meath was soon studded with the castles of Hugh de Lacy, north-east Ulster fell to John de Courcy in 1172, and most of Munster was parcelled out among other knights.

In 1235 Connacht was invaded and held by a series of walled towns, such as Galway and Athenry. Thus, by the year 1250, three-quarters of the country had been over-run by the Normans. The conquest, however, was by no means entire. In the main, the invaders kept to the plains, the coasts, the rivers. Nor did they aim at the expulsion of the native population. Rather, these were encouraged to remain and cultivate the land as before. It was the Gaelic aristocracy which was dispossessed, and even it continued to rule undisturbed in certain large areas in Munster, Connacht and Ulster.

THE TURN OF THE TIDE

As the thirteenth century went by, the flow of the invaders

lessened, and the Irish chiefs began to strike back with increasing vigour. According to MacNeill, there were two main causes for this reversal of fortune. The first was 'national sentiment, intensified and supplied with a more definite political form under a sense of national oppression.' The second was the emergence of a 'well-organised, well-armed and well-trained permanent field force', supplied at first by bodies of men from Argyll and the Hebrides, the *Gallóglaich* 'foreign soldiers', Englished as 'gallowglasses', later by native Irish troops on the same model, the *buannachta,* 'buonies', men on permanent service.[2]

In Munster at Callann, near Kenmare (1261) and in Ulster at Athankip (1270) the Normans were heavily defeated and lost most of their conquests. During this century, too, there was a vigorous revival of Gaelic culture, and that remarkable process of assimilation began, by which the Anglo-Irish, as they are now more properly described, became 'more Irish than the Irish themselves.'[3] The statutes of the Kilkenny parliament in 1366, which will be discussed later, give evidence of the Dublin government's awareness of this phenomenon.

THE FOURTEENTH CENTURY

In 1315 Edward, brother of King Robert Bruce of Scotland, was invited by some of the Irish chiefs to assume the High Kingship of Ireland as a step towards the re-establishment of native sovereignty. For three years he and his allies harassed the English settlers and defeated them constantly in battle, but he was finally defeated and slain at Faughart near Dundalk. The Bruce invasion, though it caused havoc throughout the colony, was too brief and inconclusive to be reckoned as a major factor in the decline of English power. But this decline continued all through the century as a result of the evergrowing military power of the Irish chiefs.

In 1394, Richard II made a decisive effort to secure the Anglo-Irish hold on the country. He seemed to have succeeded when he forced the great Leinster chief, Art Mac Murrough, to come to terms, and secured the outward submission of the other Irish leaders. But his own troubles forced him to return to England, and the situation was left as it had been before.

THE FIFTEENTH CENTURY

In the fifteenth century the lessening of the territories under English control, the attacks on the colony by the native Irish, and the assimilation of the Anglo-Irish continued steadily. The area under formal English rule was now confined to the so-called 'Pale' comprising roughly the counties of Meath, Louth, Dublin and

Kildare. Outside of it, the Gaelic lords ruled according to their own laws and traditions, whilst the Anglo-Irish lords owed allegiance to the Crown in varying degrees. The three greatest, the Butlers of Ormond and the Fitzgeralds of Desmond and of Kildare, became constantly more and more assimilated to their Gaelic neighbours and more and more assertive of their independence.

During the Wars of the Roses, most of the Irish chiefs, both Gaelic and Anglo-Irish, supported the Yorkist cause, and in 1463 Thomas Fitzgerald, seventh Earl of Desmond, was appointed chief governor of Ireland by Edward IV. Three years later, he was executed on a charge of treason, and the ascendancy passed to the house of Kildare. In 1478 Garrett Mór Fitzgerald 'the great earl', succeeded to the governorship. By marriage he was connected with many of the Gaelic chiefs, notably with the O'Neills of Ulster. He was a man of culture, well versed in the native language and literature, and exercised ascendancy over the whole country. He did not, however, aim at establishing himself as an independent ruler, but remained faithful, at first to the house of York and later to the Tudors. After a temporary eclipse, he was restored to the chief governorship by Henry VII in 1496, and remained in office until his death in 1513.

A New Era

The accession of Henry VIII in 1509 opened a new era in the relations between England and Ireland, an era of more determined intervention in both the political and religious spheres. It also saw the first attempt on the part of the English government to utilize education as an instrument of that intervention. It thus marked the end of the centuries-old epoch with which this book is concerned, during which education was in the undisputed care of the family and the schools, lay and clerical.[4]

Old and New Cultures

The Anglo-Norman invasion had a profound effect on the political, social and cultural life of Ireland. A modern historian has said that 'no other event except the preaching of the gospel by Saint Patrick and his companions, has so changed the destinies of Ireland'.[5] It has, however, already been pointed out that the conquest was far from being complete. As the centuries went on, intermarriage and military alliances created close bonds between the invaders and the invaded. It is not surprising, therefore, to find that the intellectual life of the country presents a complicated pattern, in which the new and the old cultures appear at times clearly distinct, at times blended together.

RIVAL LANGUAGES

The invaders who landed in Ireland in 1169 spoke various languages, the rank and file mostly Welsh and Flemish, the leaders Norman French.[6] It was only in the reign of Edward I (1272–1307) that Anglo-Saxon became a second language among the aristocracy in England, and it was not accepted as an official language until about 1400. Of the three languages, only French prevailed in Ireland, and that to a limited degree. It was spread by the Norman aristocracy, churchmen and lawyers over south and east Ireland, but it was almost entirely confined to the towns, where for two centuries it was the language of polite society, of commerce and civil government. It is first used in Acts of Parliament in 1310, in the language of the Statutes of Kilkenny in 1366, and alternates with Latin until 1472 when it is replaced by English.

The statutes and ordinances also of Dublin, Waterford, Limerick and Galway up to 1365 are in French or Latin, but thereafter in Latin or English. French flourished particularly, under the patronage of the Earls of Ormond, in Kilkenny.[7] In the *Red Book of Ossory,* a collection of documents relating to the city and diocese, we find a complaint of Richard Ledrede, bishop of Ossory, (1318–64), that his clergy were given to the singing on feast-days of secular and even improper songs. He quotes the opening lines of some of these popular ditties, which are either in French or English. Thus we have:

> harrow, ieo su trahy
> par fol amor de mal amy

and

> alas, hou shold y syng yloren is my playing
> hou shold y with that olde man
> to leven and (forget) my leman
> swettist of al thinge.[8]

From this early Norman period some examples have survived of French vernacular literature. We shall have occasion shortly to refer to *The Song of Dermot and the Earl,* a verse history of the invasion written in the first half of the thirteenth century. Another poem by an anonymous author gives a lively description of the building of the walls of New Ross in the thirteenth century. The townspeople had 'cause of dread' owing to a feud between two barons, Sir Maurice and Sir Walter, and decided to fortify the city.

> Candlemas it was the day
> They began to delve in clay.

At first a hundred, then a thousand workmen 'went to the goodly work each day.' But these proving insufficient, all the citizens took a hand, vintners, drapers, merchants, tailors, butchers, fishermen, blacksmiths, carpenters. The clergy, too, were not behindhand.

> And the priests, when mass was chanted,
> In the foss they dug and planted.

And finally:

> Then on Sunday there cam down
> All the dames of that brave town

.   .   .   .   .   .

> In all the lands where I have been
> such fair dames working I've not seen.[9]

LATER LANGUAGE TRENDS

It is convenient here to outline in anticipation the varying fortunes of the competing languages in the period we are examining. Within a couple of centuries from the invasion, French died out completely. English, though it appeared less obviously, became the real rival of Irish. In the fourteenth and fifteenth centuries, the records of urban communities such as Cashel, Cloyne, Athenry, Ardee, show that they comprised large English-speaking communities, though blended with a large mass of Irish speakers. Of English prose or verse composition, however, there are few traces. From the fourteenth century there have survived a short poem on the death of Sir Piers de Bermingham in 1308, and a lengthy one satirizing both the religious orders and the various classes of the laity, which is attributed to one Friar Michael of Kildare.[10]

Then, in the fourteenth century, the tide began to run in favour of the native language. Irish advanced from the hills and plains up to the very walls of the towns. These, however, still clung to English. The archives of the city of Waterford, begun in 1390, are in English, as are also those of Galway, begun in 1485.[11] There are extant a number of legal documents drawn up by the Blake family, one of the 'twelve tribes' of Galway city, the earliest of which is dated 1430.[12] These are all in English. Kilkenny, under the protection of the pro-English Ormonds, held firmly to English. One curious evidence of this is the fact that in the famous prosecution for witchcraft in 1325 of Dame Alice Ketyl, a native of Kilkenny, a conjuration which she was alleged to have used was in English:

> To the house of William my sonne
> Hie all the welth of Kilkenie towne.

Furthermore, the bishop's demand that she and her accomplices should be put on trial was repeated three times in English and French so that it might be understood by all.[13]

But outside the towns, in the rural parts of the colonies, and in the territories of Kildare, Desmond, Ormond and Connacht, the Gaelic speech prevailed. The great lords had accepted their Irish tenants and adopted their language. As late as 1579 MacWilliam, head of the Clanrickard Burkes, knew no English, and from the middle of the fourteenth century the de Burgos of the west had abandoned the English language and renounced all communication with the English government.[14]

Nevertheless, English survived to some extent, even outside the Pale. The Desmonds and Kildares, and even more the Butlers, from 1400 on, began to be acquainted with the language which at that date was becoming the common language of the aristocracy in England. The Leinster Fitzgeralds were often Justiciars (the title given to the chief governors from the close of the 12th century)[15] and so had to deal with the English-speaking officials of Dublin. In the two great rentals of the Kildare family, the *Red Book* and the *Rental,* we find illustrated the varying use of language. The *Red Book,* begun in 1503, but embodying documents going back to 1302, is almost entirely in Latin, but a few later entries are in English.[16] The *Rental,* written between 1510 and 1560, is entirely in English, but an accompanying covenant of 1512 between Garret Mór, the 8th Earl, and Mageoghegan, is in Irish, as is also another covenant of 1530 between the 9th Earl and Mac Ranall of Muinter Eolais, Co. Leitrim.[17]

There were three main causes of the decline in the use of English in the fourteenth century, the resurgence of the native race, the cultural absorption of the original Norman aristocracy and the opposition of the Gaelic-speaking clergy to the foreign tongue. The second of these causes is intimated in an Anglo-Irish poem 'in a hand as ancient as the time of Edward III,' which laments the decline in English influence.

> By graunting charters of peas
> To false English, withouten leas,
> This land shall be mich undoo
> But gossipred and alterage
> And leesing of our language
> Have mickly holp theretoo.[18]

We shall see later that members of the Fitzgerald family were noted in the fourteenth, fifteenth and sixteenth centuries for their knowledge and patronage of the Irish language. And as late as 1541 when the Dublin parliament gave its 'liberal consentes' to the Act declaring Henry VIII king of Ireland, it is recorded that the speech of the Speaker 'after being answered by your graces chancellour in englishe and by therle of Ormond declared in yrish mooche contented the sayde lords and commons.'[19]

Clerical opposition to English is well illustrated in an episode in 1224, when the Pope, Honorius III, appointed to the see of Cashel, contrary to the votes of the canons, no less a person than the English or Scottish priest, Michael Scot, mathematician, physician and scholar, whose vast erudition gained him a fictitious reputation as a magician. Michael felt himself obliged to refuse the see, 'since he was ignorant of the language of that region', and it went to Marianus O'Brien, a Cistercian, bishop of Cork.[20]

Apart from external pressures, there was one intrinsic cause of this decay of English. The English dialect spoken by the colonists was that of the south-west, from which their forefathers came, but by Tudor times, the north-midland form of the language had been generally accepted throughout Ireland. Thus the Irish-English colonists found that their speech was barely intelligible to newly arrived English officials or immigrants. In this connection, Stanihurst has a pleasant anecdote.

'There was of late daies one of the péeres of England sent to Weisford as commissioner to decide the controversies of that countrie: and hearing in affable wise the rude complaints of the countrie clowns, he conceived here and there sometimes a word, some whiles a sentence. The noble man being very glad that upon his first comming to Ireland, he understood so many words, told one of his familiar friends that he stood in verie great hope to become shortlie a well-spoken man in the Irish, supposing that the blunt people had prattled Irish, all the while they iangled English'.[21]

It may thus be held that if the Tudor plantations had not taken place, Irish might have become the universal language. From 1200 to 1500 English had an uncertain hold. It produced no literature worth mentioning, whereas the Gaelic language, with its rich vocabulary, was the vehicle of expression of a long line of poets and scholars.

THE STATUTES OF KILKENNY

The strength of the Irish language was clearly evidenced by the fruitless effort to limit it made by the parliament of Kilkenny summoned in 1366 by the Lord Deputy, Lionel Duke of Clarence, second son of Edward III. The statutes there enacted – thirty-five in number – were an acknowledgement of the failure of the conquest to submit the whole country to English law and Norman lordship. They did not aim at anglicizing the whole country, but at preserving and strengthening the English tradition in those parts of it most amenable to the Crown – about one-third of the whole.

The statutes proscribed marriage or fosterage with the Irish, recourse to the Brehon law, the admission of Irishmen to benefices among the English, the use of the Irish language or other Irish usages, even the Irish way of riding a horse. Many of them proved ineffective, such as those against marriage and fosterage, but they had one most decisive result, that henceforth rights under English law were confined to the English or those Irish who had lived among them. There was thus created for the first time a definitive division between the settlers and the 'Irish enemy', as they are described in the preamble, which was later to have far-reaching effects in the matter of establishing titles to lands.

The statutes of Kilkenny were, therefore, in the main, important in their bearing on the social and political life of the country. The only ones which bore directly on its cultural life, and which are therefore of import in the history of education, were those prescribing that 'every Englishman do use the English language and be named by an English name, leaving off entirely the manner of naming used by the Irish, and that every Englishman use the English custom, fashion, mode of riding and apparel according to his station'.[22] These prohibitions were nominally in force for over a hundred years, but their failure was so obvious that they were silently dropped when in 1495 the Statutes as a whole were re-enacted in Poynings' parliament.[23]

By the beginning of the reign of Henry VIII, English was practically confined to the larger towns and the Pale. Stanihurst could say in 1587: 'As all the cities and towns in Ireland, with Fingall, the king his land, Meth, the counties of Kildare, Louth, Weisford, speake to this day English...even so in all other places their native language is Irish.'[24]

It may be noted also, though this brings us beyond the period with which this book is concerned, that during the second half of the sixteenth century even the town-dwellers became alienated from the English ways and tongue, by the attacks on religion and the confiscation of the property of the old Norman families. Fynes Moryson, writing at the beginning of the reign of James I, could say: 'The English Irish and the very cittizens, (excepting those of Dublin where the Lord Deputy resides) though they could speake Englishe as well as wee, yet Commonly speake Irish among themselves, and were hardly induced by our familiar Conversation to speake English with us.'[25]

Yet, at the very time when the Irish language appeared to have triumphed over the speech of Norse, Norman and Saxon, inexorable external forces were at work to bring about its decline. Their final effect, however, belongs to later centuries.

THE NORMAN MONASTERIES

Everywhere within their conquered territories the Normans established monasteries. Some of these were of the orders already established by Malachy in Ireland. Harvey de Montmorency, Strongbow's uncle, in 1182 gave land in south-west Wexford to the Cistercian monks of Buildevea in Shropshire for the foundation of Dunbrody. Other new foundations of the existing orders were the Cistercian Abbey of Tintern in Co. Wexford, and the Priories of Canons Regular of St Augustine at Kells, Co. Kilkenny and Killagh, Co. Kerry.[26]

The warlike de Courcy, having conquered Ulster in his blitzkrieg of 1177, studded it not merely with stone castles, but also with stately monasteries, of Benedictines at Downpatrick, Ards, and the island of Nendrum (now Mahee island) in Strangford Lough, Cistercians at Inishcourci (now Inch Abbey) near Downpatrick, where he also installed the *Cruciferi* or Crutched Friars; whilst his wife Affreca in 1193 founded the Grey Abbey of Cistercians in Lower Ards. All these monasteries were at first peopled by Anglo-Norman monks from England, and the Normans endeavoured to gain control in all the abbeys in districts occupied by them.[27]

Side by side with this extension of the monastic life in the Norman territories, there went a similar extension in those which remained under native rule. At the time of the invasion there were fifteen Cistercian abbeys. The Normans founded seven more, colonized from England and Wales, two others colonized from Dublin and one from France.[28] But during the twelfth and early thirteenth centuries fifteen new abbeys were colonized from the older Irish Cistercian houses. At the same period there were founded in the native Irish territories twenty-one houses of Augustinian canons and fifteen of Augustinian canonesses.[29]

THE FRIARS

The Normans also gave welcome during the thirteenth century to the newly-founded orders of friars. Side by side with the Norman castles there sprang up churches and friaries. Dominican monasteries numbered twenty-four by the end of the thirteenth century, and by 1507 thirty-eight. About 1229 came the Franciscans (Friars Minor), who by the end of the thirteenth century had thirty-one friaries, and by 1508 had fifty-eight. In 1270 came the Carmelites, whose houses numbered nine by 1300 and twenty-seven by 1539. The last to arrive were the Augustinian Friars, or Order of Hermits of St.

Augustine (to be distinguished from the Canons of St. Augustine). Their first foundation was about 1282. By 1300 they had four, and by 1539 twenty-two.[30]

The friars also penetrated into the Gaelic territories, and were welcomed by those of the chiefs who were still in possession of their lands. Thus in 1539 one-half of the Dominican and Franciscan and one-third of the Carmelite and Augustinian monasteries were of Gaelic Irish foundation.[31]

THE MONASTERY OF DONEGAL

One of the most famous of these Irish foundations was the monastery (or, more accurately, friary) of Donegal. Its foundation is thus recorded in the *Annals of the Four Masters:*

'1474. The monastery of Donegal was commenced by the O'Donnell, i.e., by Hugh Roe, son of Niall Garve O'Donnell, and his wife Finola, the daughter of O'Brien (Conor-na-srona), and was granted by them to God and the friars of St. Francis for the prosperity of their own souls, and that the monastery might be a burial-place for themselves and their descendants; and they not only granted this, but also conferred many other gifts upon them.'

Actually, it appears that the lady who was primarily responsible for the foundation was another Finola or Nuala O'Connor, the mother of Hugh Roe, who presented herself to the Franciscan chapter being held at Ross friary, near Headford in Co. Galway, and took the good friars aback by warning them of their responsibility before God if they did not come to the aid of the people of Donegal. Later, her daughter in law, the second Finola, joined with her husband in supporting the monastery, and thus merited the name of foundress given to her in the Annals.

Husband and wife were buried, as they wished, in the monastic burial-ground, Hugh in 1505 ('it were fitting' said the Annals, 'to name him the Augustus of the whole north-west of Europe'), and Finola in 1528, having spent twenty-two years as a Franciscan tertiary 'the woman who was the best that was in Ireland at one time with herself as regards God and the world.'[32]

The monastery of Donegal rapidly developed as a centre of religion and culture. It passed through many vicissitudes, particularly in the reign of Elizabeth, being pillaged by English forces in 1588 and again in 1600, when the friars were forced to scatter and go into hiding. After the flight of the Earls in 1607, all hope of recovering the monastery was lost, but during the following century community life was preserved and even flourished in various remote places of refuge. It was one of these that Brother Michael O'Clery and his assistants took as their headquarters when from

1627 to 1636 they laboriously collected and collated the material for their great Annals. The friars' library, in spite of repeated pillage, had still one of the finest collections of manuscripts in the country. When Sir James Ware was writing his *Antiquities and History of Ireland,* which was published first in Latin in 1654, he was able to say that 'this Convent was heretofore famous for a well-stored library'.[33]

The final blow to the monastery of Donegal came in 1687, when a royal proclamation ordered all religious out of the country, and from that date the Franciscans lived a precarious and hidden life until about the middle of the eighteenth century, when the last survivors ended their days acting as parish clergy.[34]

CHAPTER 14

STUDIES IN MEDIEVAL MONASTERIES

In the medieval monasteries the primary educational activity was, of course, the training of their own members in theology. In contrast to the wealth of information available concerning the foundation and organization of the Irish monasteries, our knowledge of the studies in them is sparse enough. We can, however, from what we know of studies in other countries, make certain general suppositions with regard to the Irish monastic schools. These we can confirm or supplement by whatever positive information can be gleaned from the sources at present available.

CONVENTUAL SCHOOLS

The Norman invasion preceded by only a few decades the foundation of the great new mendicant orders, the Dominicans, Franciscans, Carmelites and Augustinian Friars, and we have seen how, in the century which followed, they established themselves throughout Ireland. These religious, especially the Dominicans, had, at a very early stage, adopted the system of conventual schools, which served both as noviciates for the order and seminaries for the secular clergy. It was a fundamental principle with the Dominicans that in every monastery there must be a professor or 'lector', who expounded the Scripture and used it as a basis for his theological teaching. He might also use secondary texts, such as the Sentences of Peter Lombard or collections of cases of conscience. In larger monasteries he would be assisted by a sub-lector.

In the course of the thirteenth century, introductory studies were added, logic, natural science and the ethics, politics and economics of Aristotle. Promising students might be sent from smaller to larger monastic schools, or to one of the newly-founded universities, Oxford, Paris, Bologna, Montpellier, where each order had its own convent and not infrequently held some of the university chairs.

Owing to the fact that the decree of the Fourth Lateran Council (1215), requiring the appointment of a master of theology for each cathedral school, had not been generally implemented, many of the bishops were glad to avail themselves of these conventual schools for the education of their clergy.[1]

It is reasonable to presume that such conventual schools were established in Ireland by the newly-introduced Orders. Archbishop Healy says that 'there is no doubt that this system [of conventual schools] was in operation in Ireland, at least to some extent, during the Anglo-Norman period, in the convents of the Dominican Order especially, both within and without the Pale.'[2] Father M. H. McInerney agrees with Dr. Healy 'with some reservations', but points out that confirmation of this view can only be gathered with difficulty here and there, since 'the documents illustrating the literary history of the period are few and meagre.'[3] They are, however, sufficient to show that Dr. Healy's carefully qualified contention is correct.

THEOLOGICAL SCHOOLS: DOMINICAN

The two most important Dominican friaries were those of St. Saviour, Dublin and Saints Peter and Paul, Athenry. The former was founded in 1224, when the Cistercians of St. Mary's Abbey gave to the Dominicans a site at Oxmantown on the north side of the Liffey. In 1304 this part of Dublin was destroyed by fire, but the friary was shortly rebuilt. The eighteenth-century Dominican historian, Thomas de Burgo, gives us a good deal of information about the patrons of St. Saviour's, the privileges of the friars and the important persons buried within the monastery precincts, but little about the intellectual life of the friars.[4] However, the school of theology evidently enjoyed a high reputation. We shall see later that when in the fourteenth century an attempt was made to establish a university in Dublin, at least one of these Dominicans was appointed as professor, and also that in the early fifteenth century some sort of ancillary school or college was opened by the Dominicans on the south side of the river to relieve the strain on the professors of St. Saviour's, whose classes were evidently much frequented.

There is extant, though only in a seventeenth-century transcript, a document compiled in the fourteenth and fifteenth centuries, *Regestum Monasterii Fratrum Praedicatorum de Athenry,* Register or Chronicle of the Monastery of Friars Preachers at Athenry.[5] It is valuable as being the only medieval Register of its kind which has survived in its complete form. It deals largely with the benefactions of the Bermingham and de Burgo families, but throws indirectly much light on the way of life of an Irish medieval abbey.

There are only a few entries in the document which deal with the intellectual life of the monastery. One of these states that Florence O'Flin, archbishop of Tuam from 1250 to 1256 was 'a great benefactor of the friars' and built for them 'a house for scholars'.[6] It is not clear whether this house was for the use of the friars, or, as seems more likely, for the bishop's own ecclesiastical students, but the provision of such a building indicates the existence, already at this early date, of a theological school. After the lapse of two centuries, we find the obituaries of William Reydeymer (1431) and Gilbert Bron (1451), both Masters of the faculty of theology. The latter died in London, but the register records that he entered the order and was professed in Athenry and 'did much good for the convent.'[7] Towards the end of the fifteenth century it is recorded that Thomas Bermingham and his wife Anabla de Burgo donated one mark 'for the repair of the chamber (*camera*) of the English bachelors'.[8] We do not know whether this chamber was in a separate wing, or merely a special place for study or recreation, or whether these bachelors were ecclesiastics or laymen (most probably the former). But the brief entry is evidence of two facts, the continued existence of a theological faculty of considerable size, and the necessity (which we learn from other sources also) of a certain degree of apartheid, even within the monastic fold, among the Irish, Anglo-Irish and English students.[9]

A NOTABLE DOMINICAN SCHOLAR

One of the earliest Dominican foundations, that of St. Saviour's, Waterford (1226), produced a scholar whose extant works are evidence of the level of learning in the monastery (and incidentally of the prevalence of the French language in the Anglo-Norman towns).

In the *Bibliothèque Nationale* in Paris are preserved three manuscripts in a fine thirteenth-century hand. They are translations into French of the *Book of the Trojan War* by the pseudonymous Dares the Phrygian, the *History of Europe* by Eutropius and the *Secretum Secretorum,* an apocryphal text of Aristotle. The last-mentioned has a dedication to some unknown nobleman, in which the author speaks of himself as *'Jofroi de Watreford de l'ordine az frères precheurs le mendre'*. Both Ware and de Burgo conclude that this Dominican friar was a native of Waterford. Orpen speaks of him as a 'distinguished alumnus' of the Waterford Priory.[10] It seems likely that he was both born and educated in Waterford, but all three of the authors mentioned hold that he must have spent a considerable time in Paris, presumably because his works were published there. He was evidently a man of considerable learning. From his own words we learn that he knew Greek and Arabic as well as Latin and French. What is of peculiar interest is the fact that he was so completely familiar with the French language, thus indicating that it was fairly commonly spoken in Waterford at that time, at least in certain clerical and official circles.

THW SONG OF DERMOT AND THE EARL

Another interesting evidence of the persisting use of French among some of the Anglo-Norman population in the 13th century is the lengthy poem (over three thousand lines) known as *The Song of Dermot and the Earl*.[11] The theme is the familiar one of the abduction by Dermot MacMurrough of Dervorgilla, his dealings with Strongbow and the subsequent invasion of Ireland. There is only one existing manuscript of this poem, which is among the Carew Mss. in Lambeth Palace. The author is unknown, but the opening lines give some information as to the origin and date of the poem.

> Par soen demeine latimer
> Que moi conta de lui lestorie,
> Dunt faz ici la memorie.
> Morice regan iert celui,
> Buche abuche parla alui
> Ki cest iest endita:
> Lestorie de lui me mostra.
> Icil morice iert latimer
> Al rei dermot, ke mult lout cher.
> Ici lirrai del bacheler,
> Del rei dermot voil conter.

> By his own interpreter
> Who told to me the history of him,
> Of which I here make record.
> This man was Morice Regan,
> Face to face he spoke to him
> Who related this geste:
> The history of him he showed to me.
> This Morice was interpreter
> To King Dermot, who loved him much.
> Here I shall leave off about the bachelor,
> About King Dermot I will tell you.

From this passage Orpen deduced that the author based his work on an older poem brought to his notice by one Morice Regan, an official and interpreter of MacMurrough. Orpen therefore held that the existing manuscript was a transcript of the early thirteenth century, but that the original poem was composed soon after the death of Strongbow in 1176. These conclusions were submitted to a detailed criticism by Professor J. F. O'Doherty, who concluded that the person who brought the older poem to the notice of the author was not Regan, but the 'unnamed secretary' of an 'unnamed bachelor', who was in possession of, or perhaps was the author of the original *chanson de geste*. For this and other reasons, he would place the poem not in the first, but in the second quarter of the thirteenth century, which would lessen its historical value.[12]

There are indications that Carew (who, as President of Munster 1599–1603, combined ruthlessness towards the people of Ireland with a keen interest in their history), acquired the manuscript, together with a number of documents confiscated from the Corporation of Waterford in 1617. Orpen, therefore, surmised that it had belonged to the Dominican priory of St. Saviour.[13] There is, however, no evidence that the poem was the work of Friar Jofroi, whose French is much more pure. But Orpen argues that there must have been others in the monastery who, like Jofroi, knew French well, and therefore would value such a work as *The Song of Dermot and the Earl,* and would cherish it until it was acquired by Carew with the other looted documents in 1617.

THEOLOGICAL SCHOOLS: FRANCISCAN

In the preface to *Materials for the history of the Franciscan Province of Ireland* (p. xxviii) Dr. A. G. Little states that in the period covered, 1230–1450, 'probably all the friaries had theological schools.' Presumably he bases this view on the fact that the documents he presents mention the existence of 'lectors' in so many places, Limerick, Nenagh, Ennis, Ardfert, Armagh and elsewhere. Some of these records are of special interest. Roderic O'Mulruonig (died 1353) was 'former guardian of Nenagh and chief lector (*lector solempnis*) in various friaries'.[14] 'Thomas O'Huolachain (died 1361 or 1362) was 'a young and able (*valens*) lector of Ardfert'.[15] In 1375 we hear of a prospective bishop, Thomas O'Colman 'of noble birth...who has studied theology at Paris, Oxford and Cambridge' and is lector in the friary of Armagh.[16] In 1441 there is the record of the appointment of Thomas Macgillacundain 'a man of learning' to be lector at Ennis, and of Matthew Machegan to hold the same office at Askeaton 'after his return from the University of Bologna.[17]' Later we shall see that Franciscan students of greater promise were frequently sent to study abroad, doubtless with a view to their holding the office of lector at home.

THE ANNALS OF NENAGH

One of the sources on which Dr. Little had drawn is the *Annals of Nenagh,* the only Irish Franciscan chronicle after the middle of the fourteenth century which has survived, and that only in later and incomplete transcripts. The Franciscan convent of Nenagh, founded probably in 1254, was one of the earliest and most important of the Franciscan foundations in Ireland. The *Annals* cover briefly the period from 1336 to 1528.[18] Their main interest is that they emanate from the head of the most purely Irish of the five *custodiae* into which the Irish province was divided. They also are the main source of our knowledge of the existence of lectors in the various convents.

CISTERCIAN STUDIES

In his recent study of the Cistercian Order in Ireland, Dr. Gearóid Mac Niocaill has an appendix which outlines the available information concerning the medieval monks' essential studies.[19] From the decrees of the General Chapter there can be traced the organization of studies in the Order as a whole. In 1245 the Chapter ordered that 'there should be a *studium* in each monastery where it was possible...so that there should be at least a *studium theologicum* in each Province.' In 1281 it was recommended that monasteries which had more than eighty monks should have a *lector,* and other masters if possible. This, apparently, was not effective, and in 1300 the Chapter advised each monastery of sixty to have a *lector,* and also any monastery where it was possible, thus avoiding the necessity of sending monks to other *studia.* No further step was taken until 1331, when it was decreed that in each monastery of forty monks there should be a *lector in grammaticalibus et logicalibus* to teach the young monks. Lesser monasteries could either have a *lector* or send their neophytes elsewhere. In 1335 Pope Benedict XII collected these decrees and added others in the Bull *Fulgens sicut stella matutina.* There were to be *studia* at Paris, Oxford, Toulouse, Montpellier, Salamanca, Boulogne, Metz. The Irish were to go to Oxford, the students of other nations to Paris. Monasteries with forty monks must send two to Paris, those with thirty to forty must send one.

These various measures were apparently not wholly effective in promoting the establishment of *studia* in the monasteries, and decrees with the same aim followed in 1432, 1460 and 1461. In 1494 it was ordered that there should be a master in each monastery to instruct *in grammaticalibus, logicalibus, physicis usque ad theologiam.*[20]

Presumably these decrees were, at least to some extent, operative

in Ireland, but Dr. Mac Niocaill has found little information on
the subject. The Dublin monastery sent a monk or two from time
to time to Oxford. Thus about 1468–9 one Edward Ysfele died at
Oxford, and the University authorities recorded that 'there has
been exhibited to us by Walter, Abbot of the House of the Blessed
Virgin in Ireland, a procuration of four to receive any goods which
Edward Ysfele might possess in Ireland.'[21]

It would seem that the Dublin abbot was at times unwilling to
send his subjects abroad. In 1460 the Chapter ordered him 'under
penalty of the divine displeasure and that of the Chapter' to send
a monk, Richard, bachelor, *ad examen et studium,* so that he might
be able to obtain a higher degree of master or doctor.[22] In the
same year, the Chapter granted 'to the Irish religious residing in
the *studium* of Oxford all the privileges and rights of English
students.'[23]

MONASTIC LIBRARIES AND WRITINGS

Dr. Mac Niocaill points out that, apart from direct testimony,
there are three sources from which information may be gathered
concerning the intellectual life of the monasteries, catalogues of
their libraries, surviving manuscripts of these libraries, and the
monks' own writings. There is no known catalogue of medieval
Cistercian libraries, and very few manuscripts survive from them.
In the Bodleian Library, Oxford, there is portion of a Missal which
belonged to the Abbey of Rosglas, de Rossa Valle or Monasterevan,
the scribe being Donatus O'Kelly, who, though a monk of Rosglas,
did his work at Mellifont in 1503.[24] The Bodleian and British
Museum have each a chartulary from St. Mary's Abbey, Dublin,
and in the former there is also a fragmentary *regestum* from Dun
Bróithe (Dunbrody).

Surviving manuscripts from Cistercian libraries are evidences of
the spiritual and intellectual interest of the monks. Dr. Mac Niocaill
has traced six of these preserved in various libraries. Those of their
contents which interest us most are the theological treatises, which
give some idea of the type of text used in the medieval Irish schools,
St. Augustine *In Genesim,* two tracts of William of Thierry O.Cist.,
De Amando et Contemplando Deo, a sermon of St. Bernard on the
text *'ductus est Jesus in desertum',* Honorius Augustodunensis
*De Cognicione Verae Vitae, Epistola Galteri ad Hugonem de S. Victor
de Anima Christi,* and *Ambrosius ad Gratianum de Filio.* There are
also practical treatises, such as that on visitation of the sick by
Bishop Baudry of Dol (†1130), and apocrypha as, for instance, the
Gospel of the Pseudo-Matthew, and numerous historical works,
among them the *Polychronicum* of Ranulfus Higden, *De Gestis*

Anglorum of Henry of Huntingdon and Cambrensis' *Expugnatio Hiberniae*.[25]

Further evidence of the historical interests of the Dublin Cistercians is to be found in the fragmentary Annals of St. Mary's which are preserved in the library of Trinity College, Dublin. These annals have been fully examined by Professor Aubrey Gwynn, who points out that they are not only 'our main source for early Irish Cistercian history, apart from St. Bernard's *Vita Malachiae*', but also that internal evidence reveals the sources on which the Dublin monks drew, such as the Annals of the Benedictine monastery of Winchcombe in Gloucestershire, Henry of Huntingdon's *Historia Anglorum,* the *Vita Malachiae,* and a twelfth-century *Vita Bernardi*.[26]

THE ANNALS OF BOYLE

Older writers, Ussher, Ware, O'Conor, attributed Cistercian authorship to the thirteenth-century manuscript, partly Latin, partly Irish, preserved in the British Museum, and commonly referred to as the *Annals of Boyle*. They believed it to have been composed in the Cistercian monastery founded in 1161 near the site of an ancient Irish monastery in the vicinity of Boyle, Co. Roscommon.[27] It is not, however, the chronicle of the monastery itself, but a general account of events ecclesiastical and secular, beginning with the Creation (but the early entries are most fragmentary) and ending at 1258. O'Curry rejected the view of his predecessors and held that the chronicle was that of Saints' Island in Loch Cé.[28] O'Grady, who published a few short extracts, questioned O'Curry's view, but offered no alternative.[29] However, in 1924–7, the *Annals* were published in full by A. Martin Freeman, with translation of the Irish passages and a note by Dr. Robin Flower in which he established the fact that they are the original chronicle of the Premonstratensian house of the Holy Trinity on Holy Island in Loch Cé (founded circa 1215).[30] Flower admits, however, that they appear to be founded on an earlier chronicle, perhaps that of Boyle. The entry for 1161 '*Abbatia Buellenensis hoc anno fundata est,*' with a list of the abbots, suggests some connection with the abbey of Boyle. All authors agree that this chronicle was subsequently used by the authors of the *Annals of Loch Cé*.

AN ENGLISH CRITIC OF IRISH MONASTIC STUDIES

A little light is thrown on the question of the initial studies of the medieval Irish monks by an incident which occurred early in the thirteenth century.[31] By this time the Norman-founded monasteries had swelled their ranks by recruits from among the native population. In 1227, Stephen of Lexington, a Cistercian monk who had taken his bachelor's degree in Paris and studied theology at Oxford, was sent to Ireland. His main purpose was to reform the abuse by which certain abbeys, notably that of Mellifont, were acting, at least in practice, independently of the Order. On his arrival he found that there was considerable friction between the Norman and Irish monks. He had both bad and good to say of the latter. They were 'barbarous people not altogether but in large part', and yet they were 'endowed with much goodness, as far as was possible in such rough and intractable material'.[32]

After a study of eight months he issued a schedule of instructions governing the entire conduct of the monasteries. With regard to studies, he decided that 'no one shall be admitted to be a monk, no matter what his nationality, unless he can confess his faults in French or Latin, in order that when the visitors and correctors of the order come, he can understand them and be understood by them.'[33] He also ordered that 'the rule shall in future be explained only in French and the monks' chapter conducted in either French or Latin so that in the future anyone who wishes to be received as a monk must first have attended such a school as would teach him to conduct himself less uncouthly'.[34] His impression was that such preliminary education could not be obtained in Ireland, and so he suggested that the prospective novices should first go to the grammar schools of Oxford or Paris, or other seats of learning.[35] In this he had the support of the English abbot of St. Mary's, Dublin, but was opposed by the archbishop of Cashel, Mauritius O'Brien, himself a Cistercian. The plan would have automatically excluded the majority of Irish candidates, who would not have had the means to travel abroad, and it was never carried out. The more obvious plan would have been for the Irish abbeys to establish grammar schools of their own, but this had never been the custom of the Cistercians in other countries, who had relied on existing schools for their supply of candidates.

What facts emerge from this incident? There is no need to go into the question whether this English monk, whose family had been distinguished in the service of the Crown, was unduly prejudiced in his judgment of the intellectual equipment of the Irish monks. Two points, however, seem clear. Firstly, there was no suggestion that these prospective Cistercians might seek preliminary education in other monastic schools. This points to the fact that these schools were mainly destined for their own novices, and that the reception of other students was, at most, a rare practice. Secondly, the proposal that these youths should seek education abroad seems to indicate that other grammar schools, parochial or cathedral, were at least very rare.

ADVANCED SCHOOLS OF THEOLOGY, 1438

In his *Annales,* the Franciscan historian, Luke Wadding, records that in 1438 Pope Eugene IV directed the Irish Provincial of the Franciscans, John While (*sic*) and the Fathers of the province to establish two schools of theology at Galway and Drogheda. 'These schools,' says Wadding, 'were distinct from the ordinary schools of theology, being destined solely for the education of advanced scholars and those who had completed a course of theology *cum laude,* and who were intended to take the degree of bachelor, doctor or master in some *studium generale* or university.' Wadding adds that there is frequent mention of such studies in the register of the order.[36]

SCIENTIFIC STUDIES: A COSMOGRAPHICAL TRACT

Most of our information about the studies in the Irish medieval schools deals with theology and philosophy. There is, however, evidence that there was knowledge of, and use made of standard European scientific writings of the time. We shall see later that during the fifteenth century there was considerable activity in the translation of medical texts from the Latin, but it is apparent that this activity was going on at an earlier date, and was extended to other branches of scientific knowledge.

There is extant, for example, a lengthy cosmographical tract, based partly on a Latin translation of an Arabic treatise by Messchala or Mascha Allah, a Jewish astronomer of Alexandria, who flourished about A.D. 800. This tract was translated into Latin by Gerard of Sabionetta near Cremona in the thirteenth century, and, edited by J. Stabius, was published at Nuremburg in 1504, entitled *De Scientia Motus Orbis.* Gerard's translation was again edited by Joachim Heller under the title *De Elementis et Orbibus Celestibus* and reprinted at Nuremburg in 1549. It is not, however, clear that the Irish translation was taken from that of Gerard, and it contains passages probably drawn from other Latin texts. It was the subject of a paper by Rev. Maxwell Close in 1901,[37] and was edited in 1914, with translation and glossary, by Miss Maura Power, from manuscripts in the Royal Irish Academy and Marsh's Library, Dublin.[38] For some reason, the title given to it by Miss Power is *An Irish Astronomical Tract,* but in her preface she correctly refers to it as 'an astronomical, or rather cosmographical treatise'. Both writers place the Irish version at the end of the fourteenth or beginning of the fifteenth century.

The tract contains forty chapters dealing with the nature and functions of the four elements, earth, air, fire and water; the characteristics of the earth, water, volcanoes and tides; the heavenly bodies and their movements; the winds, thunder, clouds; rain, lightning; the planets.

The meteorology of the tract is Aristotelian, the astronomy Ptolemaic. It is fully discussed from the scientific point of view in the paper of Close. He draws attention to one point of particular interest, the clear declaration of this Arabic treatise of the influence of the moon on the tides, (ch. xi), which was not generally accepted in Europe until some two centuries later. Notable also is a reference (ch. vii) to 'old people who. . . .use glass spectacles (*spechlai glaine*) to magnify the letters they read.' This, if not an interpolation, would give a superior date for the Latin text about the middle of the fourteenth century, when the use of spectacles became common.

It is the opinion of Miss Power that such medieval Latin texts were translated into Irish 'for use in the schools of the fourteenth and fifteenth centuries.'[39] This is a reasonable surmise. The Irish scholars would hardly have undertaken this laborious task for their own use, since Latin was their accustomed reading.

EDUCATION OF SECULAR CLERGY

It must be acknowledged that with regard to the education of the secular clergy, as in former periods, we must rely mainly on speculation. Speaking of the twelfth century and of the diocese of Killaloe, so thorough a researcher as Gleeson recognises the paucity of information, and sums up the possibilities. His remarks are equally applicable to any other diocese at the period.

'Whether the clergy were trained at such places as Killaloe, Lorrha, Monaincha, Roscrea and Iniscathaigh; whether each priest kept a student or two in his residence;[40] whether secular academies such as the famous school of the Mac Egans in Lower Ormond, or the equally notable school of the Maol Chonaire family at Ardkyle, near Broadford in Clare, contributed to clerical education, as they so notably did to secular studies, we just do not know.'[41]

In one diocese at least there is evidence that the secular clergy were educated in a monastic school. We recall that Florence O'Flin, archbishop of Tuam in the middle of the 13th century, was a great benefactor of the Dominican friars of Athenry and built 'a house for scholars' for them. Though it is possible that this establishment was for the sole benefit of the friars, it seems more likely that the bishop had also the purpose of providing for the education of his own students.

AN EPISCOPAL SEMINARY, FOURTEENTH CENTURY

It is curious that Gleeson, in enumerating the possible places of education for the secular clergy, does not envisage the possibility of provision being made for it at the episcopal sees. There is available at least one fragment of evidence to show that this was a recognized practice.

In 1368 a papal mandate was issued to Conor Mac Cormaic O'Donnell, bishop of Raphoe (1367–1398). He had granted to a student, as he was entitled to do, a dispensation from the impediment of illegitimacy to receive tonsure and minor orders, but papal dispensation was required for ordination to the priesthood.

'Granted to John O'Farrell, Bachelor of Canon Law, belonging to the diocese of Ardagh, and member of the fraternity of Cornelius, Bishop of Raphoe, a further dispensation to accept any order of dignity inferior to a bishop'.[42]

This mandate is cited in the *History of the Diocese of Raphoe* by Canon Maguire, who describes John O'Farrell as 'attending the Raphoe seminary'.[43] His presumption seems to be correct, that the 'fraternity' in which this young man, not yet a priest and belonging to another diocese, had qualified as a Bachelor of Canon Law, was a theological school under the aegis of the bishop of Raphoe.

It must be acknowledged, however, that all during the medieval period there is no further evidence of the existence of schools specifically devoted to the education of the diocesan clergy. Mgr. E. A. D'Alton, historian of the archdiocese of Tuam, notes that at the close of the fifteenth century there were many unworthy holders of ecclesiastical benefices. This he attributes to two causes, the patronage of the chieftains and lack of education. On the latter point he is even more explicit than Gleeson. 'There were, he writes, 'no seminaries where the priests could be properly educated. For the priest was educated either by the mendicant orders, by some member of the diocesan chapter, or by some other learned ecclesiastic, and this mode of training fell far short of what was required.'[44]

It should be noted that this lack of organized training for the clergy up to the middle ages was not peculiar to Ireland. All over Europe, the situation was much the same. The large majority of clerical students were privately taught by their local priests; a few had the opportunity to study at cathedral monastic schools, and an even smaller privileged number at the universities. It was only at the time of the Council of Trent that this state of affairs was remedied by the decree (twenty-third session, 1563) establishing diocesan seminaries.

SYNOD OF CASHEL 1453

A little light is thrown on the question of the education of the secular clergy by two decrees of the Provincial Synod of Cashel, held in 1453. Decree 53 prohibits masters, under pain of excommunication, from admitting noblemen or others to their lectures concerning whom 'there was no hope that they would advance in the Church of God'. A similar decree (No. 71) forbids clerics, under pain of a fine of forty shillings, to take the sons of noblemen into their houses for fosterage, without special licence from the bishop.[45]

Both of these decrees seem to have had the same purpose, to prevent ambitious young laymen from acquiring sufficient education to enable them to secure some benefice, without any intention of proceeding to major orders. What interests us is that the decrees imply that the education of candidates for the secular priesthood might be under the direction of a qualified master in a monastic or cathedral school, or else in the household of an individual cleric.

CHAPTER 15

IRISH SCHOLARS ABROAD

The Norman invasion of Ireland took place at the end of the twelfth century, and it was at this very time that the universities of Europe were gradually taking shape. It is, therefore, not surprising to find that, from the thirteenth century on, many both of the native Irish and of the Norman settlers were prompted to pursue their higher studies abroad in these newly-founded institutions.

Irish students of law had particular reason to frequent the universities of Oxford and Cambridge as well as the Inns of Court at Westminster. English law prevailed throughout the Pale, and even the Anglo-Irish and Irish living outside it had need of the knowledge of that law when there was question of making treaties or determining boundaries.

THE IRISH AT OXFORD

Oxford in particular, from the earliest days of its existence, saw an influx of Irish students. By 1252 their numbers were so considerable that a formal document could be drawn up settling disputes between them and the Northern British students. It arranged for the appointment of twelve arbitrators on each side, and the swearing in of thirty or forty 'rich men whether Regents or otherwise', to observe the conditions of peace.[1]

Mrs. Stopford Green gives a striking summary of the outward evidences of the presence of the Irish in Oxford.

'There was already (1252–55) an Yrysshmanstrete, an Ireland Meadow on the west of South Bridge, an Irishman's Mede belonging to Brasenose, an Irishman's Pool and Piscaria in Holywell.[2] Irish scholars gathered in "the ancient Patrikehall", "Aula Hibernorum";[3] there were halls set apart for law students – Aula Aquilae or Hyron hall, Vine hall, Aristotle hall, Coventry hall, and others were either Irish or enrolled Irish students – de la Schield hall, La Chymney hall, Dunstan and some of the old neighbouring halls,[4] while the ancient Bovina or Beef hall was inhabited by Irish clerks.'[5]

Mrs. Green gives a list of over a hundred Irish scholars studying at Oxford from 1285–1600. They are of all types. We find 'David de la Hyde, Probationer Fellow of Merton...an exquisite and profound clerk, very well seen in the Latin and Greek tongues, expert in the mathematicals', and also 'William Nangull, a poor Irishman with few friends'. [6] It may be noted that only some twenty-five of these entries occur in the period with which we are concerned, up to the beginning of the sixteenth century. Mrs. Green's list does not purport to be exhaustive, but other evidence confirms the impression that though the presence of Irish students at the English universities was constant, their numbers were never great.

For instance, in A. B. Emden's *Biographical Register of the University of Oxford to A.D. 1500*, under the letter O, where mention of students of Gaelic families would occur most frequently, we find some thirty entries, spread over three centuries. All are clerics and destined to hold ecclesiastical office. Thus at the beginning of the fourteenth century there is David O'Bugey, Prior Provincial of the Carmelites in Ireland. Then we have Thomas O'Colman, Archbishop of Armagh in 1381, Turlough O'Brien, bishop of Killaloe in 1483, John O'Leachluyer (O'Lalor), abbot of the Dominican Monastery of Baltinglass in 1453 and John O'Hedian, bishop of Ossory in 1479.

Evidently students in the Middle Ages, as today, were occasionally hard up. It is recorded that on 28th June, 1368, Roger O'Duvaill and John Offergaill (O'Ferrall) with other students from Ireland 'deposited a copy of *Lectura Hostiensis* in the Langton chest as caution for a loan.'

Under the heading 'Mac' there are only thirteen Irish entries, again all clerics and mostly destined for ecclesiastical distinction. Bernard McMurrough of the Ardagh diocese, and of noble birth 'had studied canon and civil law for nearly 10 years' by December, 1411, and became Rector of St. Andrew's, Multyfarnham. Dermot McCloskey 'had studied canon law at Oxford and in *studia particularia*' for several years by December, 1417. He became Dean of Derry in 1432. There are two Maguires. Peter studied canon and civil law for about three years at Oxford and for seven years in non-university schools (*particularia seu privata studia*) and was made bishop of Clogher in 1433. Nicholas Maguire 'studied in Oxford although it was but 2 years and three months, yet he profited so much in logik, philosophie, the seven liberal arts and divinitie that in his latter years he seemed to excel.' Nicholas Maguire became bishop of Leighlin in 1490, and was venerated for his learning and preaching.

Concerning Maguire, Emden is quoting from the Annals composed at the close of the sixteenth century by Thady Dowling, Chancellor of Leighlin, and published in 1869 by Richard Butler, Dean of Clonmacnois. (pp. 8, 14, 31, 32). It is obvious that Dowling relied a good deal on a *Chronicon Hiberniae* compiled by Bishop Maguire.[7]

It may be noted that together with the Dowling *Annals* Dean Butler published the *Annals* of John Clyn, the first guardian of the Franciscan monastery at Carrick-on-Suir, founded by James, 1st Earl of Ormond in 1336. These *Annals* run from 1315 to 1348, when the author probably died of the plague which he so vividly describes. Clyn is a reliable historian, a first-hand witness of the events which he chronicles.[8] Reference will be made again later to the *Annals* of both Clyn and Dowling, in connection with the foundation of the University of St. Patrick in the fourteenth century.

An Irish Chancellor of Oxford

It is curious to find little trace in these Oxford registers of Irishmen with distinctive Norman names. Thus there are only three names with the prefix 'Fitz'. One of these, however, is a most memorable one, Richard Fitzralph. He was born in Dundalk towards the close of the thirteenth century of a purely Anglo-Norman family. He possibly received his early education in the Franciscan monastery in his native town, but entered the university of Oxford about 1315, and, having taken his mastership in arts, became a bachelor of theology in 1329 and doctor in 1331. He must have displayed outstanding ability, as we find him chancellor of the university from 1332 to 1334. Circumstances then led him to abandon an academic for an ecclesiastical career. Appointed dean of Lichfield in 1335 and Archbishop of Armagh in 1346, he became famous as administrator, preacher and writer.[9]

Even more curious is it to find so few Irish names on the rolls of the Cambridge colleges. In the volumes of *Alumni Cantabrigienses* covering the Middle Ages, no entries appear under the prefixes Mac or Fitz, and under O but two of no importance.[10]

Papal Letters

Some of the entries found in Emden concerning Irishmen at Oxford are drawn from papal letters of the period. The fourteen volumes of these letters, covering the fourteenth and fifteenth centuries, provide some further general information as to how and where the medieval cleric or monk studied.[11] There are a number of documents addressed to bishops or other authorities in Ireland enabling them to admit a certain candidate to a benefice or to permit him to enter a monastery. In these, mention is uniformly made either that the candidate has studied for a number of years in a university outside Ireland or elsewhere, or else that he is granted leave of absence to complete such studies. It is intimated that seven years was a common period of study. A few typical examples may be cited.

1431. David Oduynd, clerk of the diocese of Kildare 'who has studied at universities for about seven years.'

1467. Philip Okerog, Canon of Ossory, who is to be free to 'study for at least seven years in some university or non-university place, according to the Irish custom'.

1473. Thady Omulhacha, clerk of the diocese of Ardfert 'not to be bound for seven years, while dwelling in any *studium* after the manner of the Irish'.

1484. William de Mewry to be free for seven years 'whilst residing in the Roman court or studying letters at a university'.

Among these entries is one worth recording for its human interest. It gives us a curious glimpse of the sorrows of a schoolboy of the Middle Ages. In 1469, faculties are granted to various religious superiors to absolve 'Patrick Occowlton, scholar of the diocese of Armagh, from the perjury which he incurred when a boy at school by denying under oath to the master that he had taken part of the binding of a book to the value of 1d.'

In 1400 we find an entry which gives further evidence that attendance at foreign universities was a normal, if not frequent event in the lives of Irish monks. It is the confirmation by Pope Boniface IX of various decrees issued by Berengarius de Landora, master-general of the Dominicans, giving a large measure of independence to the Irish vicariate of the English province. Amongst these is the permission 'that the friars of Ireland may have two students in the convent at Oxford, two in that of Cambridge, one at Paris, two at London and others in other universities; that in the *studia particularia* of philosophy in England some apt youths should be assigned.'[12]

Later in this document the wish is expressed that 'some suitable friars of your country should, by the judgment of your counsellors (*discretorum*), be promoted to the degree of bachelor and Master'.[13] This seems to imply two facts, firstly that the Dominicans had in Ireland at least one theological school which had the power to confer degrees, and secondly that during the first century of their existence in Ireland, they had not thought fit to exercise that power.

There is evidence that the Franciscans also constantly sent their more able students to study abroad. In 1364 a mandate was given by Urban V to Francis de Cardaillac, O.F.M., to grant the degree of master and the licence to teach in the faculty of theology to

Philip Torrington, O.F.M., (later archbishop of Cashel), 'who has toiled in the said faculty in the Universities of Oxford and Cambridge, and has been a lecturer in many convents of the Order,.[14] In 1375 Edward III granted permission to two friars of Ennis, Marianus Curydary and Laurence Omorth to travel to England and thence to Strasbourg to pursue their studies, 'provided that they bring with them nothing prejudicial to the king, the crown or the faithful people.[15] In 1376 Gregory XI issued a mandate to Philip Torrington, Archbishop of Cashel, 'to confer the degree of master on Hubert de Kalvesnaken O.F.M., S.T.B., who has studied in the theological faculty at Paris, Oxford, Cambridge and other universities and has been appointed by the general chapter to lecture on the sentences at Oxford in order to obtain the degree of master, if after examination by the archbishop, and at least four other masters in the faculty of theology in the University of Avignon, he be found suitable.'[16] The historian, Luke Wadding, records a number of scholastic appointments in 1441. 'In the friary of Askeaton Matthew Machegan was appointed professor and preacher on his return from his studies at Bologna. Some youths of promise and unusual talent, John Macharry, John Ochal and Gilbert O'Hallim, belonging to the Irish province, were sent to Cologne. Cornelius O'Mahony having taken his bachelor's degree, was sent to the convent of the University of Cambridge to study the Sentences in preparation for his mastership'.[17]

DISTINGUISHED IRISH SCHOLARS

That the level of learning in the Irish monasteries was at least as high as that in other countries is evident from the records of Irish monks who distinguished themselves abroad.

David Obuge (or Obugey), a Carmelite, was born in the town of Kildare and died there in 1320. But during his lifetime he travelled widely, and, according to Holinshed, 'for his learned lectures and subtle disputations openlie published in Oxford and in Treuers in Germany, he was taken for the gem and lanterne of his countrie... He was in philosophie an Aristotle, in eloquence a Tullie, in divinitie an Augustine, in the civil law a Justinian, in the Canon a Panormitane.'[18]

Sir James Ware also take note of Obugey. His praise is less exuberant, and therefore more convincing than that of Holinshed. 'He was an excellent Philosopher, Orator and Divine, and most knowing of any person in the laws, so that he was esteemed the Light, the Eye and the Honour of the Irish Nation'. His works included *Discourses to the Clergy, 32 Letters to Several Persons, Propositions Discussed* and *'Lectures which he made at Treuers'*.

He was brought back to Ireland to be Provincial of his Order, and died very old at Kildare, 'where he lies buried in a Convent of his own order.'[19]

St. Thomas's Irish Teacher

All the earliest biographers of St. Thomas Aquinas state that when at the University of Naples about 1236, not yet a Dominican, he studied natural science under one Master Peter of Ireland. No doubt has ever been cast on this statement. In the sober pages of the *Dictionary of National Biography* Peter Hibernicus or Peter de Hibernia is described without comment as 'the tutor of Thomas Aquinas'.

Until recently almost nothing was known of this Peter of Ireland.[20] From the eighteenth century on, identifications were made by various scholars, but all turned out to be mistaken. There was a Petrus, but of Ysernia (modern Calabria) not Hibernia, and a jurist, not a professor *in naturalibus*. There were a Magister P. of Naples, but he was a grammarian, and a Petrus whose only claim was a confusion between Alvernia (Auvergne) and Hibernia.

However, in modern times two important discoveries were made by German scholars. In 1920 C. Baeumker published a *determinatio magistralis* or master's decision of a scholastic disputation by Petrus de Hibernia which he had found in the state library of Erfurt,[21] and this was the subject of a learned commentary by M. Grabmann.[23] The two scholars drew from this work valuable conclusions as to the possible influence of Peter in the development of the thought of St. Thomas. It may be claimed that Peter was the first to introduce the young Aquinas to the teachings of Aristotle, and also that he may have been responsible for the not altogether unfavourable attitude displayed towards Averroes in the earlier works of St. Thomas. Again, in 1922, Mgr. Pelzer discovered in the Vatican library commentaries by Peter of Ireland on the *Isagoge* of Porphyry and various works of Aristotle.[23]

A good deal, therefore, is known of the thought of Peter of Ireland, but very little of the man himself. It may be taken as certain that he was an Irishman. The constant title *de Hibernia* can hardly be otherwise explained. Two reasons may be adduced for thinking that he was an Anglo-Norman. Firstly, the name Peter is common in Norman families and rare in Irish families of the time. Secondly, the link between Anglo-Normans and the Norman kingdom of Sicily would go to explain how Peter came to be teaching in Naples. Finally, it seems certain that he had studied in some continental university or universities before coming to Naples. As we shall see, there was no *studium generale* in Ireland before 1320, and the monastic schools would not have provided the training necessary for a professor *in naturalibus.*

A LEARNED FRANCISCAN

Towards the close of the period we are studying, we find another Irishman who distinguished himself abroad, Maurice de Portu or O'Fihely. Holinshed, drawing on the account given by Johannes Camertes, a Franciscan contemporary, describes O'Fihely as 'a greie frier profest, verie well seene in logike, deeply grounded in philosophie, learned in the metaphysickes, in divinitie peerless. When he had professed at Padua the liberall arts manie yeares with no small renowne, he was created by Julius the second. . . archbishop of Tuam.'[24]

Sir James Ware gives further details of the career of this learned Franciscan. He was, according to most authorities, 'born in the County of Cork, a town celebrated for its fine harbour [the antient seat of the O'Fihelys lying in that neighbourhood; from where he got the Name de Portu].' Anthony a Wood[25] states that he studied 'Grammaticals and Trivials'[26] for a time at Oxford before taking his doctorate at Padua. He was appointed archbishop of Tuam in 1506, and took part in the two first sessions of the Lateran Council in 1512. In the following year he returned to Ireland, but 'fell into a mortal distemper at Galway, where he landed.' He was buried in the church of the Franciscans in that city. His works include a *Dictionary to the Scriptures, Commentaries on Scotus, Book of Distinctions, Compendium of Truth in Rhyming Verse* and a book on Porphyry.

Ware adds the curious information that during O'Fihely's residence in Italy, a nobleman of the city of Mons, named Octavian Scott, set up in Venice a press for the publishing of learned works, and that O'Fihely, 'who was then called Maurice the Hibernian, was the Principal Corrector of his Press; an Office which the greatest and most learned Men of that Age thought worthy of their Employment.'[27]

But, whilst there is ample evidence of the presence of Irish students, destined both for the regular and secular clergy, in universities abroad, and of the high standard of their learning, it must be acknowledged that the numbers recorded are small compared with the great mass of the monks and secular priests. It must be concluded that these were educated in Ireland, either in the monasteries, or in schools attached to cathedral seats or other centres, or else by individual priests.

Confirmation of the fact that the sending of young clerics abroad for study was, though a regular practice, confined to a select few, is found in a sermon of Archbishop Richard Fitzralph addressed to the provincial Council of Armagh held at Drogheda in 1355. He urges that his clergy should make a general subscription to enable some of their number to go abroad and study at a university. He himself had already sent three or four, and he cites the example of Pope Benedict XII who had seen to it that some members of his own Cistercian order were sent to higher studies 'at the common expense'.[28]

IRISH EXCLUDED FROM OXFORD

When Irish students had been frequenting the English universities and the English Inns of Court for some two hundred years, there came an interruption, short but far-reaching in its effects. In 1410, during the reign of Henry IV, the parliament of the Pale decreed 'that no Irish men adhering to the enemies shall be suffered hence-forth to pass over the sea by colour of going to the schools of Oxford Cambridge or elsewhere.'[29] Students from the Pale, however, could continue to frequent the universities under royal licence.

In 1422 a more stringent law was passed, this time by the English parliament, in the preamble of which complaint was made of various crimes committed in Oxford and its vicinity' as well by divers persons resorting to the town of Oxford as by others dwelling there under jurisdiction of the University,' some of whom were 'enemies to him [the King] and his kingdom called "wylde Irishmen".' It was therefore enacted that 'all people born in Ireland shall depart out of the realm within a month after proclamation, saving graduates in the schools, men beneficed in Ireland, Irishwomen married to Englishmen and Irishmen to Englishwomen.' Irish graduates were not to have a hall of their own, and Irish scholars could enter the universities only by letters under the seal of the Lieutenant or Justiciar of Ireland.[30]

This legislation was allegedly due to the turbulence of the Irish, especially at Oxford. There is, however, no evidence that they were more lawless than the average run of students in the Middle Ages, and the true cause seems to have been the fear that Irishmen, unless firmly attached to English rule, would prove, if highly educated, more difficult to deal with. In point of fact, the law, though only partially exclusive, proved gravely harmful to the English colony in Ireland. Though it aimed only at the 'Irish enemies', in practice it proved to be so sweeping as to restrict the flow even of the Anglo-Irish students. This had two effects. The colony was deprived of a regular supply for its administration of men educated in the English tradition, and the exclusion from English education increased the alienation of the Anglo-Irish from

English rule. This state of affairs prevailed for some fifty years, but towards the close of the century the law seems to have fallen into abeyance, and Irish students began again to frequent the English universities and Inns of Court in considerable numbers.[31]

CHAPTER 16

EDUCATION OF THE LAITY IN THE MIDDLE AGES

i. In the Monasteries

When we come to consider the education of the laity in the middle ages in Ireland, we find that the information, though less sparse than in the earlier period, is nevertheless very scattered, and on some important points, bafflingly incomplete.

Elsewhere in Europe in the middle ages there was a well-established system of schools. The third Lateran Council (1179) directed the clergy to establish schools for the free education of all children, irrespective of the social condition of their parents. There were three main types of school. Parochial or 'little' schools, established under the direction of the parish priest, and supported by the local landlord or a group of parishioners, provided elementary education. A more advanced curriculum was offered by the monastic schools, but in the middle of the twelfth century advocates of reform began to view with disapproval the existence of lay schools side by side with those of religious novices, and lay education began to pass into the hands of the secular clergy. In their hands, the third type of school, the episcopal, capitular or cathedral school, enjoyed remarkable success. Early in the twelfth century there were some fifty in France alone, and the third Lateran Council obliged every diocese to open one.[1] Rashdall, who deals in some detail with this subject,[2] concludes that, at least in the later Middle Ages, 'except in very remote and thinly populated regions, [a boy] would never have had to go very far from home to find a regular grammar school.'

Turning to Ireland, we find at this period scattered yet sufficient evidence that at least some lay men and women received education in monastic schools. But there is extraordinarily little to be discovered about parish or other local schools, whilst the only cathedral school of which we have record is that of St. Patrick's, Dublin, and that not definitely until the middle of the sixteenth century. It is difficult to know whether or not this absence of information denotes that such schools were in fact very rare. The Normans, both clerical and lay, must have been conversant with the educational activity which was going on in England and on the continent, and could hardly have failed to imitate it in their new surroundings. Nor does it seem likely that the decree of the third Lateran Council as to the establishment of cathedral schools could have met with almost no response from the Irish bishops, whether Gaelic or Norman.

MacNeill held that the Norman invasion was 'a complete reversal of all the efforts towards reconstruction and progress...In the conquered parts, the Irish were excluded from education and ecclesiastical preferment. There was much building, and much writing of official documents, but no progress in learning or the arts, not one school of note, and in an age when universities were springing up over Christendom, there arose in Ireland only one university, which was stillborn'.[3]

But this consideration, though well founded, does not explain the apparent dearth of schools for the Normans' own children, and the sparse evidence for the existence in the unconquered territories of schools corresponding to the parish or cathedral schools in other countries. It is possible that further research may throw light on this puzzling problem, though unfortunately the explanation may be found in the great destruction of documents that has taken place in so many periods of our history.

We will deal first with the question of the education of the laity in monastic schools, and then consider whatever evidence can be found for the existence of other schools, either parochial or attached to a cathedral.

LAY PUPILS IN THE MONASTERIES

It is remarkable that so many historians confidently assume that in the medieval monasteries provision was made – and not as an exceptional measure, but as a regular system – for the education of lay pupils. It is equally remarkable that they give little or no evidence to justify their assumption. Thus Flower, enumerating the various types of literary men found in medieval Ireland, places first 'the *sapientes,* clerics or laymen, attached to the monastic schools'.[4] But nowhere does he give evidence of the presence of lay students. Reference has already been made to Joyce's confident assertion that 'the monastic schools had many lay pupils', and the tenuous evidence offered for it.[5] In such an authoritative work as Orpen's *Ireland under the Normans,* the sole reference to lay students in the monasteries is the unsupported statement that 'the nunneries were places where the daughters of the well-to-do classes could receive such education as was then deemed suitable'.[6]

Mrs. Stopford Green, speaking of the time before 'the commercial invasion under the Tudors', asserts that 'the knowledge of Latin spread through the commercial as well as the learned classes...the women were educated... Country schools of the old type were maintained in vigorous work, and town schools were added of a more modern sort, but of equal ardour, to which the Irish country gentry came to learn English and Latin with the townspeople.'[7]

If by 'country schools of the old type', Mrs. Green designates the native schools of poetry, history, law and medicine, her statement is quite correct, and we shall have ample proof of their continued activity. But, as we have seen, there is no evidence that they provided for any but their own professional class.

Mrs. Green goes on to give an account of the 'town schools' of which she speaks. Her statement that they existed before the time of the Tudors is somewhat confusing. Actually they sprang up at the very time of, and in opposition to the attempt of the Crown to use the schools as instruments of political and religious policies. They were grammar schools of the Renaissance type which were founded by the Anglo-Norman townsmen of Kilkenny, Galway, Clonmel, Limerick, Drogheda and New Ross. Two deserve particular note. That of Kilkenny was founded by Piers Roe Butler, 8th Earl of Ormond in 1538. It went through many vicissitudes and educated many famous men. The Galway school, founded in 1566 by Dominick Lynch, had a strongly Gaelic character which the others lacked, amongst its pupils being Dr. John Lynch, author of *Cambrensis Eversus,* Dubhaltach Mac Firbhisigh, the last of a famous scholar family, and Roderic O'Flaherty, the antiquarian, author of *Ogygia.*[8] These sixteenth-century schools, however, lie outside the scope of the present work, and in no other part of her book does Mrs. Green throw light on the education of the laity in the middle ages.

In the volume *Franciscan Donegal,* published in 1952, Fr. Canice Mooney, O.F.M., speaking of 'the beginning and middle of the sixteenth century', states that the friars of Donegal 'helped to educate the children of the district'.[9] It is remarkable that in an otherwise fully documented article by this reliable historian of his Order, no authority is given for this statement.

A contemporary historian, Professor Otway-Ruthven, states that 'such an education as was available in Ireland in the middle ages must have been provided by the church.[10] If we prescind from the specialist education given by the native schools, her statement is doubtless correct. But the evidence she offers in support of it is slight enough, two brief references to town schools and one to a chantry school. These references are certainly valuable, and we shall refer to them later. But none of the schools in question were connected with a monastery.

It is, of course, *a priori* most likely that lay pupils should, at least at times, have been found in the medieval monastic schools. The Norman monks would have naturally brought with them the system that was common throughout Europe. The actual evidence, however, for the presence of lay pupils in the monasteries must be gathered from various sources and over the whole medieval period.

THIRTEENTH CENTURY. A SCHOOL FOR GIRLS

Curiously enough, the earliest clear evidence of provision in the medieval monasteries for lay pupils has reference to what must have been comparatively rare, the education of girls. In 1297, on the order of the Justiciar, (the title then given to the governor of Ireland), an enquiry was held at Cork into a proposed grant of lands 'to Agnes de Hareford, formerly a recluse of Cork, for the sustenance of her and of the nuns who are to serve God in the house which she intends to build at Cleynboly (or Clonboly).' The empanelled jurors gave it as their opinion that 'it would be much for the convenience and utility of the country if the house should be founded for nuns, for there is no other house of nuns where knights and other free men in those parts may have their daughters brought up or maintained, nor in three counties adjoining'.[11]

THIRTEENTH-CENTURY ESTATE ACCOUNTS

There are preserved in the Public Record Office, London, a collection of thirteenth-century documents which are, from several points of view, of great interest.[12] They are the accounts rendered during the years 1279–1294 to Roger Bigod, Earl of Norfolk (the great-great-grandson of Strongbow and Eva), by the administrators of his vast estates in Carlow and Wexford. There was a whole hierarchy of these officials, Seneschal, treasurer, constables, provosts of burghs and manors. The accounts are rendered mostly by the last named.

These documents were brought to light in 1892 by James Mills, Deputy Keeper of the Records in Ireland, and were the subject of an article by him in the *Journal of the Royal Society of Antiquaries in Ireland*.[13] He brought them to the attention of Herbert F. Hore, the historian of Wexford, who transcribed and translated them almost in entirety. Selections from them appeared in the *History of the Town and County of Wexford* edited and published in 1900 by Philip Herbert Hore, son of Herbert F. Hore.[14]

The accounts throw a remarkable light on the economic and social life of the middle ages, since they give minute details of the sales of cattle and crops, leases of land, wages, costs of buildings and repairs, agricultural methods, and also bring before our eyes a procession of the innumerable personages employed on, or in any way connected with the estates, with their various functions and ways of life.

Most of the entries, though informative, are of an everyday nature. 'For the repair of 5,000 shingles and for roofing the Grange [of New Ross] with them 16s. 8d. For hired workmen perforating the said shingles and for roofing the Grange with them 12d.' 'For a man hired to get the sand from the seashore for 8 days 8d.' 'For a certain man hired to carry the flour from the mill [of New Ross] to the town for sale for 52 weeks 4s 4d for each week'. 'For the expenses of a boy snaring rabbits 4d'.

But many others conjure up a lively picture of more unusual events. 'Paid a certain sailor for the hire of his boat in which the dogs [of the Earl] were placed on one occasion 1 marck'. 'For a rope bought to hang a certain robber.' [No price given]. 'For bread and wine and 3 lampreys bought and 2 salmon bought to make a presentation to Sir R. de Ufford, justice of Ireland and the Treasurer of the same place 22s by the Seneschal'. 'For 4 iron headpieces made and sent for the use of the Earl into Wales 10s by command of the Seneschal.' 'For the expenses of Sir John Cas, Knight, who was assigned by the Seneschal, to take charge of the Manor of Ross for 15 days for fear of the robbers – as it is said, 16s 10d.' 'For one jar of wine bought and sent as a gift on the part of the Lord Earl to Lord Nicholas de Clere, Treasurer of Ireland, staying the night at Carlow the vigil of St. Nicholas 16d.' 'Paid for silk and satin and red cloth and for the making at Ross of two standards and banners for the proclamation of the King's Army at Kildare in the 16th year [of the reign of Edward I, 1288–89], 19s 7d.'[15]

What interests us particularly in these accounts is the fact that they are entirely in Latin. The language is naturally simple and repetitive, and the usual contractions are used, but the grammar and syntax are in the main correct. No great fault can be found, for instance, with such entries as: 'In vigilat[oribus] locatis per Nundin[as] per metum latronum 10s hoc anno,'[16] or 'In quodam carpentar[io] locato ad magnam aulam cooperiendam ubi necessarium fuit per 12 dies 8s qui capit per diem 4d per stipendium et potum.'[17] At times, but rarely, a French word intrudes. Thus we have 'In quodam garcone locato ad custodiendos agnos post separationem, 3s 8d.'[18]

We do not know who the men were who actually drew up these

accounts. Presumably they were not the officials themselves, but clerks in their employment. There are frequent references to clerks, their salaries and costumes. But the point is that the documents reveal the existence of a good number of laymen who were not only trained in rendering accounts, but were also capable of doing so in Latin. Why they did so is not clear. Possibly they still spoke an antiquated Norman French, which would not have easily been understood in England, and had not a sufficient grasp of the English which was gaining the upper hand in England at that time.[19] Or they may have been following the ordinary custom of the time of drawing up public documents in Latin. How and when they learned their Latin is a matter for conjecture, but it is at least possible that it was in local monastic schools.

A Fourteenth-Century Chantry School

Early in the fourteenth century we find mention of the education of lay pupils, not indeed by a monastic community, but by a group of secular priests. In 1305 the Justiciar submitted to a jury the request of Richard de Burgo for approval of a grant of lands for the establishment of a chantry at either Loughrea or Tipperbryde.[20] The decision was that such an establishment would be advantageous 'if for no other reason, for teaching the boys of these parts where learning is very scant'.[21] There is no suggestion that the teaching was to be confined to church candidates.

Fifteenth-Century Dominican 'Gymnasium' in Dublin

The Dominican historian, de Burgo, records that in the year 1428 the Dominicans of St. Saviour's Priory (situated in the vicinity of the present Four Courts) had 'a *gymnasium* dedicated to St. Thomas Aquinas in the suburb of the old city now called Usher's Island, to which youths used to flock for the study of philosophy and theology; and, since the professors, lecturers and religious, and also the youths of Ostmanstown[22] could not get to it conveniently across the river which occasionally was in flood, a stone bridge of four arches was constructed at the expense of the Friars Preachers and their benefactors.'[23]

What was the nature of this establishment? In eighteenth-century Europe the term 'gymnasium' was used, as it is in Germany still, to designate a secondary school, but it is obvious that de Burgo is using it in the classical sense of a school in general. Two things, however, are clear. Firstly, this 'gymnasium' was something quite distinct from the famous theological school of St. Saviour's, and presumably of a somewhat lower standard. Secondly, it was frequented by youths other than the Dominican students. Furthermore, the impression given by the whole passage is that the number of these youths was considerable. They 'used to flock' (*confluebant*) to Usher's Island, and it was thought worth while to build a bridge for the use of themselves and their teachers. Hence it is most likely that they included not merely clerics other than Dominicans, but also laymen.[24]

FIFTEENTH AND SIXTEENTH CENTURIES: FRANCISCAN SCHOOLMASTERS

A remarkable feature of the history of the Franciscans in Ireland is the large number of foundations in the fifteenth and early sixteenth centuries of houses of the Franciscan Third Order Regular. This order was a development from the Third Order Secular, composed of societies of lay men and women, which appeared in Italy in the early thirteenth century, mainly in places where there were friaries of the First Order, and whose members assisted the friars by their prayers and good works. In the late thirteenth century groups of fervent Tertiaries, priests and laymen, began to erect their own residential buildings so as to be withdrawn from the world, and later took the three vows of religion.

The first house of the Third Order Regular in Ireland was founded at Killeenbrenan, Co. Mayo, about 1426, and numerous others followed, some forty in all. They were all convents of men, though in other countries the Order admitted women. Their rapid growth was peculiar to Ireland. In England there were no such foundations, in Scotland only two for nuns. The explanation probably lay in the fact that in the fifteenth and sixteenth centuries there were founded in other countries numerous colleges of secular priests living in community, but in Ireland only three or four. Hence, the Third Order Regular provided for those who wished to lead a regular life, but were not attracted to the older Orders of which many at that time were in decline.[25]

What interests us is that these Franciscan Tertiaries appear to have devoted themselves in a special way to the education of youth. There is extant a document entitled *'Donatus Moneyus de Provincia Hiberniae S. Francisci'*. This Father Donagh Mooney was Provincial of the Irish Franciscan Province, and based this account of the Order on his official visitation in 1616.[26] He gives a list of some thirty-two monasteries, almost all of which had by that time been suppressed by the English government. He states that the Tertiaries were 'principally occupied in pastoral work in adjacent parishes, and in conducting schools for boys, and in each of their monasteries there was a building which even to the present day is called the schoolhouse.'[27]

This brief statement gives us a certain amount of valuable information. The fact that the Tertiaries undertook education as one of their chief works seems to corroborate the impression which we get from other sources that parish schools were not plentiful. Again, though doubtless many of the pupils were candidates for the Order, Father Mooney gives no indication of any limitation in this respect. Finally, the fact that teaching is given as one of the Tertiaries' chief works goes to show that it was undertaken from the earliest years of their foundation in the early fifteenth century.

FIFTEENTH-CENTURY TERMONERS.

In the *Annals of the Four Masters*, under the date 1496, is found the following entry:

Maguire (John) was set at liberty by Con O'Donnell, all the termoners of the province having flocked to him to request and demand his liberation.

On this passage O'Donovan has this note:

In a manuscript in the Lambeth library, quoted in the Ordnance Memoirs of the parish of Templemore—Townlands, the following account of Termoners occurs. "The tenants of the church lands are called Termoners, and are for the most part scholers and speake Latin; and anciently the chief tenants were the determiners of all civill questions and controversies among their neighbours".

This description of the 'termoners' is also cited by Maguire in his *History of the Diocese of Raphoe*,[28] who identifies the author of it as Bishop George Montgomery, who was appointed by James I in 1607 bishop of the united dioceses of Derry, Raphoe and Clogher. The passage occurs in a document preserved in the British Museum library, entitled 'The Ancient Estate of the Bishoppricks of Derry, Raphoe and Clogher.'[29]

Maguire also cites the explanation of the word 'termoner' given by O'Donovan. *Terminus* was the name of the classical deity who presided over landmarks or boundaries, and was represented by the upright boundary stone. The christians adopted the name. 'This work, *Terminus,* was afterwards used by the Latin Church to designate a *territorium ecclesiasticum,* the limits of which were pointed out by sacred landmarks.' The Irish form of the word was *tearmann,* and the tenant of such a church property was a *tearmannach.*[30]

It seems clear that these 'termoners' mentioned by Bishop Montgomery were the successors of the original *airchinnigh* or *comharbai* who inhabited these former monastic lands. In fact, the exact wording of the bishop's description is 'Eirenaci, Corbani or Termoners', and in another document he refers to these church tenants as 'herenaghs'.[31] Whence came the latinity which they possessed in 1607? The old monasteries had long passed away, the later ones had been suppressed. It must only be surmised that the knowledge of Latin, originally derived from some monastic source, had been handed down from generation to generation of these church tenants.

Confirmation of the existence of this class of tenants of monastery lands who were educated men is found in the *Annals of Ulster* at the date 1528.

MacCraith of the Termon of Dabeog (Termonmagrath, Co. Donegal), namely Ruaidhri, son of Diarmuid, son of Mark, son of Maurice MacCraigh died this year. And a noble termoner was that man...and he was a learned antiquarian (*agus dob' arsaigh ealadhanta....é*).

Ruaidhri MacCraith was evidently also a patron of the *filid,* as the fifteenth to sixteenth-century copy of the *Annals of Ulster* preserved in the Bodleian library adds that he was 'the one for whom this book was made.'[32]

SCHOOLS IN PERIL

There is, then, fairly conclusive, though sparse evidence that during the first three centuries after the Norman invasion there was at least some provision for the education of the laity in the monasteries. This evidence is strongly reinforced by a document of the early sixteenth century.

In 1539 a petition was addressed from the Lord Deputy and Council of Ireland to Thomas Cromwell, Lord Privy Seal, asking that six monasteries should be exempted from the measure which 'hath been openly bruted the Kinges Graces pleasure to be, that all the monasteries within this land should be suppressed, none to stand.' The six monasteries were 'Sainte Marie Abbaye adjoyning to Dublin, a house of White Monkes; Christes Churche, a house of Chanons, situate in the middis of the citie of Dublin; the Nunrie of Grace-Dewe in the countie of Dublin; Connell in the countie Kildare; Kenlys and Gerepont in the countie of Kilkenny'.

Amongst the reasons given for the preservation of these monasteries was that 'in them yonge men and childer, bothe gentilmen childer and other, bothe of man kynd and women kynd, be brought up in vertue, lernyng, and in the English tonge and behavior, to the grete charges of the said houses; that is to say, the women kynd of the hole Englishrie of this land for the more part, in the said nunrrie, and the men kynd in the other said houses.'[33]

It seems clear from the wording of this document that the young people spoken of were not merely future monks or nuns. This supposition is borne out by another petition addressed to Cromwell in 1565 for the preservation of St. Mary's Abbey in which it is urged that its occupants were 'but stywardes and purveyors to other mens uses, for the Kinges honour; keeping hospitalitie, and many pore men, scholars and orphans...'.[34]

It is true that this evidence is found towards the close of the period we are considering, but it is reasonable to conjecture that the education of lay pupils had been a normal function of these monasteries for a considerable time, indeed, when the other evidence is considered, that it had always been their practice.

EDUCATED CHIEFS

Some further light is thrown on the question of the extent of education among the laity in the middle ages, by the fact that in the Annals there is constant praise given to members of the great families, both Gaelic and Norman, for their learning. It may, perhaps, be held that these men were exceptional, but their number and their constant recurrence throughout the centuries are certainly significant. It may also be granted that the tributes paid to them are couched in the usual exaggerated style of the Annals, but it is inconceivable that these should have been paid at all unless the recipients were known to have been at least moderately well-educated.

Thus we have (1307) Domhnall Ua Conchobair, tanist of Connacht 'a general scholar,'[35] (1369) the son of Cu-Uladh Mac an Ghirr 'chief of his own tribe, who was a learned and illustrious Professor of Sciences in England',[36] (1400) John O'Farrell, Lord of Annaly, 'an intellectual, ingenious, erudite and learned man',[37] (1425) Brian Mac-Uí-Néill-buidhe, 'namely the one son of a king, that was best in hospitality and in knowledge of every science that was heard of',[38] (1426) O'Connor Roe (Turlough the son of Hugh the son of Felim) 'illustrious for his knowledge and skill in all the sciences',[39] (1476) Donnchadh Mag Uidhir 'a man who was eminent ...in knowledge of every science that was heard of, and one who was to be king of Fir Manach without opposition',[40] (1481) Toirdelbach Mag Uidhir...the son of a sub-king...that had the best knowledge of every science and was best in intelligence and most bought of bardic composition...and sad were the erudite and ollams of all Ireland after him',[41] (1507) 'Henry, son of Aodh O'Neill, an eminent leader and a person who had best knowledge of every science in his own time',[42] (1522) Domnall 'the clerk, son of John O'Cathain...a person intelligent, accomplished respecting Latin and Gaidhelic and one who was to be lord of Oirecht-Ui-

Cathain',[43] (1535) 'Maelsechlinn son of Cairbre O Birn, that chieftain's son...that scholar most widely skilled and accomplished in every art of all men living in the five Provinces of Ireland',[44] (1544) 'O'Neill's son, namely Niall son of Art Oc, he was of the seed of Niall of the Nine Hostages...a man full of knowledge and bounty and skill in art and music both of hand and voice',[45] (1563) O'Donnell (Manus son of Hugh Duv...Lord of Tirconnell etc.) 'a learned man, skilled in many arts, gifted with a profound intellect and the knowledge of every science',[46] (1584) 'Brian, son of Donnchadh Mag Uidhir, the son of a king that was...of best knowledge of every science'.[47]

THE ANGLO-IRISH

As has been previously mentioned, the Annals are mainly concerned with the Gaelic families. The fact, therefore, that there is little mention in them of learning among the Anglo-Irish chiefs is no proof that it did not exist. There are, indeed, clear indications here and there that it did. We find two of them in the fifteenth century described in much the same terms of eulogy, Walter de Burgh (1432), grandson of the Earl of Ulster, was 'the foreign youth who was the best that was in his time for hospitality and prowess and knowledge of every accomplishment',[48] and Nicholas Plunkett (1483) was 'the foreign youth who was best in humanity and knowledge and eloquence that was in his time'.[49]

The Fitzgerald family, in particular, produced at various times men of culture. John Fitzthomas Fitzgerald, Baron of Offaly, was in 1316 created by Edward II first Earl of Kildare. Nearly three centuries later, in 1601, the tradition of his learning was recorded by the poet Muireadach Ó Dálaigh:

> John the redoubtable
> Than who no poet was more learned
> The first Leinster Earl, without reproach.[50]

John's son, Thomas, the 2nd Earl, during his justiciary in 1326–7, was called on to quell a feud between the Geraldines (with the Butlers and Berminghams) and the le Poers and de Burghs, the ostensible cause of which (there were many others) was that Arnold le Poer had scornfully alluded to Maurice Fitzgerald, later 1st Earl of Desmond, as a 'rhymer', the title given by the English settlers to the native poets.[51]

GEARÓID IARLA, GERALD THE RHYMER

To what extent Maurice Fitzgerald merited the appellation of 'rhymer' we do not know, but his son, Gerald, 3rd, or according to some, 4th Earl of Desmond, known by the two titles Gearóid Iarla and Gerald the Rhymer, was undoubtedly a poet and a man of considerable education. He also illustrated in a remarkable way the manner in which the Anglo-Irish chiefs had become gaelicized, a process which seems to have commenced almost from the beginning of their settlement in Ireland.

Gerald ruled as Justiciar from 1367 to 1369 under Edward III, and in 1381 and 1386 in the reign of Richard II, as deputy of the Justiciar for Munster, then in a turbulent state. He is depicted in the records as the chief upholder of the king's cause in Munster, yet his general policy seems to have been to set the law at defiance and to adopt Irish ways and sympathies.

He is described in the *Annals of the Four Masters* (1398) as 'a cheerful and courteous man, who excelled all the English and many of the Irish in the knowledge of the Irish language, poetry and history', and in the *Annals of Clonmacnois* as 'a witty and ingenious composer of Irish poetry, and a learned and profound chronicler.'

A notable instance of his Irish sympathies is the fact that in 1388 he obtained the royal licence to allow his son James to be fostered among his old enemies, the O'Briens of Thomond, despite the Statute of Kilkenny. The perhaps over-trustful King Richard II granted this favour in view of the fact that 'he had learned of the good dispositions towards the King of Gerald Fitzmaurice, Earl of Desmond, within his Munster possessions.'[52]

A considerable number of Gerald's Irish poems have come down to us. In the *Dean of Lismore's Book*[53] there are nine poems attributed to him, with varying degrees of certainty, and some of these have been published in various journals.[54] But about 1927 the interesting discovery was made in the *Book of Fermoy* of *Duanaire Ghearóid Iarla,* the Earl's Verse-book, containing thirty poems. This has been published, with introduction and notes, by Dr. Gearóid Mac Niocaill.[55] There can be no reasonable doubt about the authorship of these poems, as the *Book of Fermoy* was written at latest within a few years of the Earl's death.

Some writers consider that Gearóid Iarla was the first to introduce the *dán grádha,* love-song, into Irish literature. It is certain that we have from his pen the oldest examples of this genre.[56] Dr. Mac Niocaill has been unable to find any information as to how or where Gearóid acquired his skill in Irish versification, but points out that he was evidently in touch with various *filid,* indeed on intimate terms with them. In one of his poems addressed to Tomás Mór Mág Craigh, a north Munster poet, he makes light of some unfavourable rumours he had heard about his friend. In another, he good-humouredly takes to task the same poet, or perhaps his father, Maolmhuire, a fellow scholar of Gofraidh Fionn Ó Dálaigh (d. 1387), for an uncomplimentary poem about himself.[57]

In the *Book of Ross or Waterford* (Harleian Mss. No. 913) there are two quatrains in Anglo-Norman French, entitled *'Proverbie Comitis Desmonie'*. Crofton Croker, who published them in *The Popular Songs of Ireland*,[58] says that the history or point of them 'is not very evident, beyond an ingenious play upon words'. Flower believes them to belong to a period earlier than that of Gearóid Iarla.[59]

This 3rd Earl of Desmond had in his lifetime a great reputation. After his death it became legendary. In the *Relation of the Fitzgeralds of Ireland* (1638) by Thomas Russell,[60] he is spoken of as 'a very powerful and wise man. And some would have it believed that he had some skill in magicke.' Gilbert, in his *History of the Viceroys of Ireland,* says: 'This Earl lived long in Irish legends, according to which he, once in seven years, revisited his castle in Lough Air or Gur near Limerick.'[61] The *Dictionary of National Biography* gives this tradition in an even more romantic form. 'The Munster peasantry' would have it that he did not die but 'only disappeared beneath the waters of Lough Air.'

THE GREAT EARL

The greatest political figure among the Fitzgeralds was Garret Mór, the Great Earl of Kildare, the real ruler of Ireland from 1478 to his death in 1513. By the marriages of his sister and daughters, he had links with the chief Anglo-Irish and Gaelic families. It is, therefore, not surprising to find that he showed a sympathetic interest in the two languages and cultures of Ireland.

It can hardly be doubted that he was himself a man of some education, though there is little positive evidence on the subject. It is true that in the sixteenth-century Book of Howth[62] he is described as 'half an innocent man without great knowledge or learning, but rudely brought up according to the usage of his country', but Gilbert takes this to be the biased statement of a Lancastrian supporter. In a modern study of the Great Earl, Donough Bryan is cautious in his estimate of his intellectual equipment. He holds that 'we do not know by whom the Earl was educated', but points out that he certainly spoke English, that his close relations with the Irish chiefs imply that he spoke Irish, and that the fact that he presided over parliaments in which Norman-French was still the official language makes it likely that he had some knowledge of that language. Various examples of his signature exist, but this can hardly be adduced as a proof of literacy.[63]

Bryan's final verdict is that 'there is no reason to believe that Gerald was artistic or that he had himself any scholarly inclination'. This, perhaps, is ultra-cautious. The Earl certainly displayed some interest in the history of his country and especially of his family. Gilbert and Bryan cite a long letter in English addressed by him to the Florentine family, the Gherardini, with whom he claimed kinship, asking them whether they have any knowledge of his ancestors.[64] It is to be noted, however, that neither Gilbert nor Bryan offer this letter as a proof of Garrett's literacy, presumably because there is no evidence that it comes from his own hand. The Earl also employed 'Philip Flattisburie, a worthie gentleman, and a diligent antiquerie', of Johnstown near Naas, to write 'in the Latine toong...diversas chronicas'.[65]

THE EARL'S LIBRARY

In the British Library are preserved two lists of 'Bokys remayning in the lyberary of Geralde Fitzgeralde, Erle of Kyldare, the XV day of Februarii, Anno Henrici VIIIi XVIIo.' [A.D. 1525–6]. Some hundred volumes are listed, Latin, French, English, Irish. Among the last-mentioned are *The Psalter of Cashel, The Beginning of the chronicles of Ireland, [Lebor Gabála]* and *The Death of the children of Ler.*[66]

At the date mentioned, the Earl of Kildare was the ill-fated Garret Og, son of Garret Mór and father of Silken Thomas. It may be surmised, however, that at least many of these books had been acquired by Garret Mór during his long tenure of the castle of Maynooth. This surmise is borne out by the fact that also in the British Museum there is a copy of *Lile na Heladhan Leighis* (an Irish translation of a famous medical treatise, *Lilium Medicinae,* written by Bernard de Gordon in 1303), which has a marginal note. 'A prayer for Earl Garrett that bought this book (Justice of Ireland) for a score of kine... This year in which I am is the year of grace, one thousand and five hundred years'.[67] In any case, the possession of what was in those days an extensive library is evidence of a tradition of education in the Kildare family.

Scattered references show that education was not confined to the menfolk of the noble families. The *Annals of Ulster* commemorate in 1490 the death of 'Margaret...wife of Thomas, son of Glaisne Ua Raighilligh, to wit, a woman that was learned in Latin and in English and in Irish.'

How these members of the aristocracy obtained their education is a matter of conjecture. Some may have attended a monastic school for a while, but it seems likely that the majority were taught by a private tutor, some neighbouring priest or monk. We have

already come across Aed Mac Crimthainn, abbot of Tír dá Glas
and compiler of the *Book of Leinster*, who appears to have been
tutor to Dermot Mac Murrough.[68] Further evidence is provided
by the memoranda written in a manuscript preserved in the Bodleian
library. (Laud Misc. 610.) The first testifies that this manuscript
was the 'Psalter' or Book of Sir Edmund Mac Richard Butler,
chief of a branch of the Butlers of Ormond. Being taken prisoner
in the battle of Pilltown in 1462, he was obliged to give as ransom
to his captor, Thomas, 8th Earl of Desmond, his treasured 'Psalter'
and another valuable manuscript, the *Book of Carrick*. The second
memorandum runs as follows:—

'A blessing on the soul of the Archbishop in Cashel, Richard
O'Hedigan, for by him the owner of this book was fostered, Edmund
son of Richard son of James. And today is the Sunday before
Christmas, and may everyone who shall read this say a prayer for
their souls.'

In the British Library are preserved two further memoranda.
Attention was drawn to this marginal entry by O'Donovan,
who refers to the Ms. as 'a fragment of the lost *Psalter of Cashel*.[69]
Detailed studies by the late Professor Myles Dillon[71] and by Anne
and William O'Sullivan,[71] show that the document comprises
historical, religious and miscellaneous pieces by various scribes,
the chief being Seán Buidhe Ó Cléirigh. There are, however, entries
which imply that the writer had the *Psalter of Cashel*, or some
document purporting to be the *Psalter*, before him, and copied
portions of it, but it is impossible to identify these. The translation
of the marginal note is that of Professor Dillon.[72]

What has been said above concerning Toirdelbach Mág Uidhir[73]
suggests that he owed his erudition to association with the *filid*.
We have also seen that the Earl of Desmond 'Gearóid Iarla', was
on intimate terms with some of them.[74] It is, therefore, possible
that some of these learned chieftains had been tutored in their
youth by neighbouring *filid*, though we recall that the tendency of
the latter was to confine their teaching to the members of their
own order.

CHAPTER 17

EDUCATION OF THE LAITY IN THE MIDDLE AGES

ii. Cathedral and Parochial Schools

THE CATHEDRAL SCHOOL OF ST. PATRICK'S

We have earlier mentioned the evidence for the existence in the fourteenth century of an episcopal seminary attached to the cathedral of Raphoe. It, however, appears to have been devoted solely to the education of church students. There are some grounds for holding that a grammar school open to students, both clerical and lay, was attached to the cathedral of St. Patrick's, Dublin.

St. Patrick's was originally founded as a collegiate church in 1191, though within a few years it attained the status of a cathedral. In the charter establishing it, John Comyn, the first English archbishop of Dublin, laid a certain stress on its educational character. He declared that he had found that learning (*studia litterarum*) did not flourish in Ireland as in the rest of the world, and had therefore determined to establish 'a prebendal church of St. Patrick, Dublin, and to place in it a college of clerics of proven life and learning, who may be to others an example of upright life, and may give instruction to the simple (*et pro litteratura sint simplicibus eruditioni*).'[1]

It is difficult to decide whether Archbishop Comyn envisaged a formal school attached to the church, or was merely thinking of the general religious instruction which the collegiate clerics should impart. However, the whole tenor of the passages cited would seem to justify the cautious statement of the former Dean of St. Patrick's, Dr. Hugh Jackson Lawlor, that 'we may perhaps assume that there was from the beginning a school in connection with the cathedral.'[2] Yet it must be acknowledged that there is no record of the activities of any such school until 1555, from which date there are extant records of the schoolmasters.[3] At about the same time we find a decree (1546) of Edward VI requiring the dean and chapter to appoint a 'schoolmaster and usher to teach grammar', and an almost exactly similar decree of Philip and Mary only eight years later (1554) suggesting that the former decree had not been complied with.[4]

GRAMMAR SCHOOLS, ARMAGH

The question of the existence of grammar schools in the medieval diocese of Armagh has been fully investigated by Professor A. Gwynn.[5] He concludes that 'the absence of any Acts Book of the dean and chapter of Armagh deprives us of information that would have been most welcome as to the reorganization of grammar schools in either section Irish and English-speaking of the diocese.' In England there are numerous entries in the medieval chapter-books of licences for approved schoolmasters issued by the chancellor, but no such information survives in the Armagh registers.

Father L. J. Murray, parish priest of Dunleer, who has made many contributions to the history of the province of Armagh, makes the suggestion that grammar schools were maintained in connection with the chantry foundations which were plentiful in the fifteenth century in Louth and Meath, at Dundalk, Ardee, Kilsaran, Drogheda and elsewhere.[6] It would be reasonable to presume that the chantries in Ireland, as in England, in addition to their primary duty of singing Masses for the repose of the souls of their founders and others, would undertake the task of education. We have, indeed, already referred to one such school near Roscrea.[7] But Fr. Murray's own detailed study of the Ardee chantry failed to produce any positive proof of the existence there of a grammar school.[8] He did, however, establish the fact that in 1487 the principal chaplain of the foundation, Walter Verdon, erected a collegiate building (of which the ruins survive) 'to the intent that certain chaplains engaged in the Church of St. Mary may be compelled to reside there in common.'[9] Commenting on this establishment, Professor Gwynn argues that no doubt similar provision for residence existed in other chantries (and, it may be added, long previous to that of Ardee). He concludes: 'We may conjecture, therefore, though proof is lacking, that some of the resident chaplains were expected to act as schoolmasters for boys who sang in the chantry-choir.'[10]

PAROCHIAL SCHOOLS

Although in the documents available the references to schools other than those attached to monasteries are tantalizingly few, there is one characteristic of them that seems to be of significance. They are all made in a passing way, implying that the occurrence of such a school was of ordinary occurrence.

We have already referred to the accounts rendered to Roger Bigod, Earl of Norfolk, by the managers of his estates in Carlow and Wexford. Mills draws attention, in his article on these documents, to the significance of one particular entry. It is in the account of Robert the Napper, Provost of Rospont (New Ross), from Easter to Michaelmas 1283. 'For loss of rent of the house where the School is held 1s, as the Earl's hay is placed therein.'[11] There is obviously question here of a school of lower grade, presumably under parochial care. The curious fact may be added that this practice of using the schoolhouse as a haybarn lasted for quite a while. In 1284, 1287 and 1288 the successive provosts, Raymond de Exomia, Laurent Brodheye and David May conscientiously noted the shilling due for the 'loss of rent of the school house in Beulen.'[12]

Under the date 1336, among the papers of the Dowdalls, minor landowners in Co. Louth, we find a deed stating that 'Thomas Abouthmille grants to Wm. Luchefeld an acre of meadow with appurtenances in the Newmede of Ballymacgles, which acre is called the scole akir, lying between the Blakewater S. and Adam the White's land N.....' In 1349 Wm. Luchefeld transferred the same property (now written 'scoleakir') to one John de Kerisley.[13] It can hardly be doubted that this little property was or had been the site or part of the endowment of a local school.

In the *Register* of Archbishop John Swayne we find in 1452 a reference to 'a mandate to the perpetual vicar of St. Peter's, Drogheda, to declare excommunicate those of unknown names and persons, who had committed damages to the fountain called St. Patrick's, near the house of scholars of the town of Drogheda, and washed skins near it, preventing the scholars from having refreshment thereof.'[14]

Here again, there is the tantalizing vagueness as to the type of 'scholar' concerned, yet it is obvious that there is question of some non-monastic institution.

THE INSCRIBED SLATES OF SMARMORE

In view of the scarcity of evidence as to the existence of parish schools in the medieval period, even the slightest vestige of such a school is of interest. This is to be found in the inscribed slates found near the ruins of the ancient church of Smarmore, in Co. Louth, forty-nine in 1959 and three more in 1962. They are now in the National Museum, Dublin. They are of irregular shape and vary in size from about eight inches by five to an inch square. The writing on them was engraved with a sharp point, and is in English and in Latin. There are indications that the slates had previously been used for roofing. The inscriptions are in various hands and have been placed by experts in the first half of the fifteenth century. The date is confirmed by the linguistic features of the English texts.

The majority of the English inscriptions consist of medical or veterinary prescriptions. The Latin inscriptions are mainly ecclesiastical. Four of the slates are inscribed with musical notation, the character of which, according to experts, confirms the date indicated by the English texts.[15]

SCHOOLBOYS' EXERCISES

The subject-matter of a number of the Latin inscriptions suggests that they were the exercises of schoolboys. One is a simple sentence written in alternate Latin and English phrases, the English being underlined, the Latin containing several obvious errors. Another is a list of useful Latin phrases and words, jotted down at random. A third is a list of clerical titles and functions, liturgical hours and other church offices, such as a young church candidate might be expected to learn.

Two very puzzling inscriptions are thus explained by Bliss. The first is a prayer for the repose of the soul of some departed person. This appears in almost identical form on the two sides of the slate, written in different hands. It may have been that a familiar prayer was used as a writing exercise. The second consists of a number of statements concerning the process of dyeing cloth. It is in very bad Latin, suggesting the work of a pupil, whilst it is most unlikely that the writer was himself a dyer. Hence it would seem that the slate contains the 'Latin composition' of a boy whose father was a dyer, or who had some other close connection with that art. One short passage may be given as a sample of this juvenile effusion. 'In rubis de madera libra tingitur pro tribus deneriis. Item in blodio libra pro VI deneriis.' (A pound [of cloth] can be dyed madder-red for 3d. Item, a pound [of cloth] can be dyed blue for 6d.).

WHAT KIND OF SCHOOL?

The nature of the school in which these slates were used must be a matter of conjecture. There is no evidence that there ever was a monastic school at Smarmore, the rectory of which was subject to the abbey of the Blessed Virgin at Navan. It is possible that the school was established for the preliminary education of the novices for the abbey at Navan. But a more likely explanation is that it was in some way connected with the chantry of Ardee, which has already been mentioned. Smarmore is only two miles south of Ardee. We have seen that it is likely that there was a chantry school at Ardee, and it could have been that some of the boys attending it brought their school slates home with them. This theory, however, does not explain why all these slates (written on in different hands) were found together, and why they were found in the vicinity of the church. A more probable supposition is that the abbot of Navan had appointed as curate in Smarmore one of the Ardee chantry-priests, who set up a village school for local boys, who might later go to the grammar school at Ardee.

THE MASTER'S JOTTINGS

The writers of these inscriptions were, therefore, probably school-boys. The remaining inscriptions, mainly medical and veterinary prescriptions, together with a few musical notations, are obviously the work of some more mature and better educated person. They appear to have been jotted down as memoranda, the medical ones possibly copied from some borrowed manuscript. It is a reasonable conjecture that they were the work of the master, who also may have acted as village doctor and veterinary surgeon, and that, when some repairs had been carried out on the roof of the church of Smarmore, he, being a thrifty man, made use of the discarded slates for the exercises of his pupils and his own notes.

THE NENDRUM INSCRIBED SLATES

Slates somewhat similar to those of Smarmore were discovered between 1922 and 1924 during excavations at Nendrum or Noendruim on Mahee Island in Strangford Lough. They are now in the Belfast Museum. About A.D. 445 a monastery was founded here by St. Mochaoi, who, according to the *Tripartite Life,* received the crozier from St. Patrick, and in 1179 a small Benedictine foundation was made, of which considerable ruins remain.[16]

The slates, thirty in number, were found in a building west of the church, which may have been a monastic school. Unlike those of Smarmore, the majority of the Nendrum slates are inscribed, not with writing but with decorative patterns of the characteristic Irish type, many embodying animals and birds. Only three bear some fragmentary lettering. The fact that four iron styles were found with the slates seems to indicate that the work was done on the spot, where there was some sort of school. It is difficult, however, to establish the nature of the school. The designs suggest some sort of craft teaching. The size of the styles indicates that they were for use by adults. Possibly the pupils were young monks. The main interest attached to these slates is that they provide further evidence of the use of such material for writing in the medieval monastic schools.

It is not without interest to note that the use of slates as writing material was to last in the schools for another five hundred years. In the Irish elementary schools they were discarded only in the twenties of the present century.

CHAPTER 18

UNBROKEN SUCCESSION OF NATIVE SCHOOLS

During the centuries after the Norman invasion the native schools of poetry, history, law and medicine continued to flourish in the regions outside English domination, supported mainly by the patronage of the Gaelic chiefs, but at times also by that of the Anglo-Norman families.

In the Annals we find constantly recurring mention of these learned men. A few of their obituaries, taken almost at random, give a glimpse of the intellectual activity which continued throughout all these troubled centuries. Thus in 1216 we have 'Giolla Arnain O Martan, chief Ollave [professor] of law in Ireland',[1] in 1231 'Duinnin O'Mulconry, Ollave [chief poet] of the race of...the Sil-Murray',[2] in 1301 'Gilleissa Mcffervessy, chief chronicler of Tirefiaghrach, wonderfully skilled in historie, poetry, compilation and many other sciences',[3] in 1342 'Flann Oge O'Donnell, Ollav of Connaught in poetry',[4] in 1350 'Aengus Ruad O Dalaig, master-poet of Ireland',[5] in 1357 'Fergal Ua Duibhgennain, ollam of the Breifni...a poet that was not bitter, a historian impartial and a bounteous person'.[6]

The year 1376 saw heavy mortality among the *literati,* 'Conor O'Began, a learned historian; Killach Mac Curtain, chief historian of Thomond; John O'Rooney, chief poet to Magennis; Melaghlin O'Mulvaney, ollav to O'Kane; Donogh Mac Firbis, a good historian; and Ruarcan O'Hamill, chief poet to O'Hanlon'.[7] Toward the end of the fourteenth century there occurs the name of a poet many of whose works have survived, Gofraidh Fionn O'Daly (1387),[8] also those of the 'Chief Physician of Tirconnell', Maurice son of Paul Ultach (1395)[9] and Matthew O'Luinín (1395)[10] 'a man of various professions and skilled in history, poetry, music and [general] literature'.

In the first half of the fifteenth century we find a numerous succession of 'learned historians', 'learned poets', 'ollavs' in history, poetry and law to various great families. In the second half we hear of 'Teige Oge, the son of Teige, son of Gilla-Colaim O'Higgin, Chief Preceptor of the poets of Ireland and Scotland' (1448),[11] of O Cassidy of Cuil (Teige son of Joseph) Ollav of Fermanagh in medicine (1450),[12] and of 'Aedh Mac Diarmata the Blind, to wit a small blind man that retained much poetry and a man of great memory for every thing he heard of and in particular for the ages and for the stories of the people.'[13] (1458) Owney, grandson of Cathal O'Conor, who died in 1474, is described as 'light of the wisdom of Ireland and Chief Master of the Sciences'.[14] And in 1495 'O Duigennan of Kilronan (Duffy, the son of Melaghlin, son of Matthew Glas) a learned historian, who kept a house of general hospitality, and the richest of the *literati* of Ireland in flocks and herds, died in his own house at Kilronan at a venerable old age'.[15]

The record of these scholars is quite as constant all during the sixteenth century down to the fatal date of the battle of Kinsale, when the power of the Irish chiefs was broken and their patronage was lost. It is enough for the scope of our study to cite a few of the more notable names that occur in the first half of the century, Domnall, son of Brian O hUiginn (1502) 'teacher of the schools of Ireland in poetry',[16] a second O Casaide of Cuil (1504) 'to wit the medical ollam of Mag Uidhir and a recognised master in literature and physic',[17] O Breslen (Owen Oge, son of Owen) ollav to Maguire in judicature (1525)[18] Cosnamaid, son of Fergal, son of Donnchad Dub Mac Aedacain (1529) 'a man pre-eminent in Brehon law and in Poetry',[19] Mac Ward (Conor Roe, the son of Farrell) (1541) Ollav to O'Donnell in poetry, a superintendent of schools (*oide scol*) and a man not excelled in poetry and other arts'.[20]

Dealing with the scholars from the thirteenth to the fifteenth century, Hyde expresses the opinion that, in spite of their prestige and influence, their writings are marked by a definite mediocrity. His chapter, indeed, is entitled 'Four centuries of decay'. He finds that the *filid* 'seem to have continued on the rather cut-and-dry lines of tribal genealogy, religious meditations, personal eulogium, clan history, and elegies for the dead. There reigns during this period a lack of imagination and of initiative in literature...There is great technical skill exhibited, but little robust originality'.[21]

This criticism of the bardic poetry of these centuries is, in the main, justified. We must, however, bear in mind the point already raised, that the function of the *file* was primarily to be what is called today the public relations officer of the chief or chiefs to whom he was attached, and that the necessity of constantly exercising this function was often not conducive to high poetical inspiration. It must also be noted that frequently, even in the most artificial

effusions, we find sudden bursts of real lyrical beauty and quite
moving expressions of deep religious faith.

THIRTEENTH CENTURY

In the thirteenth century there are about half a dozen poets of
note, amongst whom the most outstanding is Donnchadh Mór
Ó Dálaigh (d. 1244), described in the *Annals of the Four Masters*
as 'a poet who never was, and never will be surpassed'. He was the
greatest of the Ó Dálaigh family, the most important of all the
scholar families. He lived at Finnyvara in the north of the Burren,
Co. Clare, but died at Boyle and was buried in the great abbey there.
Owing to this fact and to the devotional character of his poems,
it has sometimes been thought that he was abbot of Boyle (O'Reilly
thus describes him), but other writers, among them O'Donovan
and O'Grady, think it more likely that he was a layman. O'Reilly
mentions over thirty extant poems of his, amounting to over four
thousand lines. About this number of poems was published in two
collections, *Dán Dé* (1922) and *Díoghluim Dána* (1938) by Fr. L.
McKenna, who, however, acknowledges that some of those
attributed to Donnchadh Mór may be the work of a lesser namesake,
who flourished in the fourteenth century.

FOURTEENTH CENTURY

In the fourteenth century the scholars are much more numerous.
Some twenty of them are known to us, of whom some have been
mentioned above. Perhaps the most important is Seaan Mór
Ó Dubhagáin (d. 1372) chief poet of the O'Kellys, not so much for
the quality of his poems as for the valuable information which one
of them gives concerning the tribes and territories of Meath, Ulster
and Connacht at the time of the Norman invasion. Ó Dubhagáin's
unfinished poem on Leinster was completed by his contemporary,
Giolla na naomh Ó hUidrin.[22] Another poet of note is Gofraidh
Fionn Ó Dalaigh (d. 1387) a Munster man, whom we have already
met as the chronicler of the famous Christmas banquet given to the
literati by O'Kelly of Uí Maine. His chief patrons, however, were
the MacCarthys. Over a dozen of his poems have been edited by
Fr. L. McKenna in *Dioghluim Dána* (1938) and *Aithdioghluim Dána*
(Part I, 1939, Part II, 1940).[23]

FIFTEENTH CENTURY

The number of poets known to us as having flourished in the
fifteenth century is about the same as in the fourteenth, but more
of their writings have survived, about ten thousand verses. Perhaps
the best known is Tadhg Og Ó hUiginn. The *Annals of the Four*

Masters record his death in 1448. 'Teige Og, the son of Teige, son of Gilla-Colaim O'Higgin, chief Preceptor of the poets of Ireland and Scotland, died after penance at Cill Connla Kilconly, [barony of Dunmore, Co. Galway] and was interred in the monastery of Ath-leathan'. His popularity as *ollamh* is shown from the list of princes to whom or about whom he composed poems: Ó Neill, Ó Domhnaill, Ó Conchobair Cairbre, Ó Ceallaigh, Ó Conchobair Ciarraidhe, Ó Cearbhaill, Mag Uidhir, Mac Domhnaill (Lord of Ile), Mac Diarmuida, the Earl of Ormond, the Earl of Desmond, MacUilliam Iochtar, MacUilliam Uachtar. Almost all of his poems will be found in the collections already referred to, his secular poems, twenty-six in number, in *Aithdioghluim Dána,* and his religious poems in *Dioghluim Dána* and *Dán Dé.*

During this century the *filid* were beginning to experience opposition and persecution from the English authorities, who recognized their power of kindling and fostering the national spirit. Thus in the *Annals of Connacht* under the year 1415 we read how the Deputy, Lord Furnival, 'plundered many of the poets of Ireland; Ó Dálaig of Meath, Diarmait that is, and Aed Oc Mac Raith and Dubthach Mac Eochada Eolach and Muirgius Ó Dálaig. And in the following summer he plundered Ó Dálaig of Corcumroe, Fergal son of Tadc son of Aengus Ruad, at Bruiden Da Corca in Machaire Cuircne.'[24]

GREAT 'BOOKS'

From the fourteenth and fifteenth centuries date some of the most famous surviving manuscripts. The *Yellow Book of Lecan* is a volume of some five hundred quarto pages containing some seventeen sections written by different scribes. The title belongs properly only to the first manuscript which appears to have belonged to the Mac Firbhisigh family. Another was written in 1380 by Filla-Íosa, son of Donnchadh Mór Mac Firbhisigh. This volume is preserved in the library of Trinity College, Dublin.

The *Book of Ballymote,* which has been dated about 1400, consists of five hundred and two folio pages, the work of various scribes, chief of whom are Solam O Droma and Manus O Duigenan, pupils of a certain Domhnal Mac Egan. It begins with an imperfect copy of the *Lebor Gabála,* which is followed by ancient chronological, historical and genealogical tracts in prose and verse, pedigrees of saints and great families, mythological legends, an ancient grammar and prosody, legal treatises, a copy of the great topographical tract, the *Dinnsenchus,* and many other writings.

At the end of the fourteenth or beginning of the fifteenth century there was compiled the *Lebor Brecc* (the Speckled Book). It is more properly known as *Lebor Mór Dúna Doighre,* from the name of a place on the Galway side of the Shannon below Athlone, where the Mac Egans long kept schools of poetry, law and literature. Most probably it was the work of one of the family. Compiled from many ancient books in the monasteries of Connacht, Munster and Ulster, its contents are almost entirely religious, scripture tracts, lives of saints, moral treatises. It is important as being the chief collection of ancient religious compositions in the Irish language. It is written in a beautiful hand on folio vellum.

The *Great Book of Lecan,* compiled in 1416 by Gilla Íosa Mór Mac Firbhisigh, runs to six hundred and four folio pages, and in general resembles in its contents the *Book of Ballymote.* All three of the last mentioned manuscripts are preserved in the library of the Royal Irish Academy.[25]

HISTORICAL WORKS, FOURTEENTH AND FIFTEENTH CENTURIES

Probably about the middle of the fourteenth century, though some authorities have placed it a century later, was composed a historical work, *Caithréim Thoirdhealbhaigh* (the warlike exploits of Turlough), by Seán Mac Ruaidhrí Mac Craith, hereditary historiographer of the Dalcassian race. It deals largely with the struggle of Turlough O'Brien against the usurping Thomas de Clare, to whom Edward I had granted in 1276 the lands of Thomond, but also gives an outline of 'all notable deeds that for two hundred years and more (being almost from the time when first the English prevailed in Ireland down to de Clare's death) were wrought in Thomond or North Munster'.[26] Though the style of this work has been correctly described by Flower as 'turgid, adjectival, alliterative', its historical value is generally recognized.

In the fifteenth century were composed two historical works of note. The *Annals of Ulster,* compiled from older annals now lost, by Cathal Maguire, Canon of Armagh and Dean of Clogher, who died in 1498, provide one of the most valuable sources for the early history of Ireland. The older title of this work was the *Annals of Senait Mac Maghnusa,* since the clan name of Maguire was Mac Maghnusa and his residence was on the island of Senait in Lough Erne. The Annals begin in 444 and continue to 1498, the date of Maguire's death. They were continued by Ruaidhrí Ó Caiside down to the year 1537 or 1541, and by other persons to 1604. The oldest copies of them are preserved in the Bodleian Library, and in the libraries of Trinity College, Dublin and the British Museum.[27]

Of lesser importance, but still worthy of note, are the *Annals of Clonmacnois,* extending from the earliest period to 1408. The original Irish version has been lost, but a translation in racy Elizabethan English was made in 1627 by Conell MaGeoghagan

(Conall Mag Eochagáin), of Lismoyne in Co. Westmeath. Several copies of this translation have been preserved, one being in Trinity College, Dublin, another in the Bodleian Library, Oxford. It was published in 1896 by Father Denis Murphy, S.J. There is no explanation of the traditional connection with Clonmacnois.[28]

GRAMMATICAL TRACTS

We have earlier considered the tract *Auraicept na nÉces,* an attempt to construct a grammar of the Irish language on the Latin model. We have seen that parts of it may go back as far as the seventh century, the rest having been added at intervals up to the tenth century or possibly the eleventh. We noted that, with this solitary exception, no grammatical tract has been discovered belonging to the Old and Middle Irish periods. Of recent years, however, a number of tracts have been published dating from about 1500, but possibly containing earlier matter. One group of four of these, edited by Professor Bergin, appeared in *Ériu* between 1915 and 1955, another group, edited by Fr. L. McKenna, in 1944.[29] These tracts, and the standardization of language which is reflected in them, have been the subject of discussion by various scholars.[30]

It would appear that, while their compilers were, to some extent, familiar with and influenced by Latin grammar, much of their systematizing and terminology was of their own devising, some of it possibly deriving from the basic text or the later commentaries of the *Auraicept.* 'The later bardic grammarian,' says Professor Ó Cuív, 'was, then, a traditionalist. His terms, whether of Latin or native origin, were, to a large extent, drawn from an earlier corpus of terminology. Though many of them are similar to what we find in the glosses or in Priscian, the others, as we have seen, show an independence of the Latin tradition.'[31]

It is impossible in a short space to give an adequate idea of the very full treatment of grammar and syntax given in these tracts. Bergin holds that the standard dialect 'is described with a wealth of detail unparalleled in any European language of the period.'[32] Those who are interested, if they are unable to read the original texts, will find numerous excerpts, with explanatory translations, in the papers by Professors Bergin and Ó Cuív. These indicate the wide scope of the tracts, which deal with sounds and letters, formation of compound words, declensional and conjugational forms, phonological changes, synthetic and analytic forms of verbs.[33]

Two short excerpts from Professor Bergin's paper will give an idea of the thoroughness with which these medieval grammarians applied themselves to their task.

'The declension (*ceart*) of nouns is treated with extraordinary fullness. The nominative is called *ainm* 'name', the oblique cases *réim* 'course', with subdivisions *taeibhréim* 'side course' for the genitive and *tuilréim* 'front course' for the dative. The accusative singular, differing as a rule from the nominative singular in feminine nouns and adjectives, is called simply *réim,* but scores of phrases are cited exemplifying its use, especially when it is found after certain prepositions with a different meaning from the dative. The accusative plural (*tothlughadh*) is carefully noted.

'The order is always the same – nominative singular, dative singular, genitive singular, nominative plural, dative plural, genitive plural, accusative plural. The paradigm is followed by a list, short or long, of nouns and adjectives similarly declined, with notes such as 'not used in the plural', occasional inflexions not found in the pattern, fluctuation in gender and so on. There is little or no theorizing. If a particular form is not recognized in the literary language, it is marked "wrong", occasionally "doubtful" (*lochtach más fíor*). Sometimes we find the admirable remark, too often forgotten by modern grammarians, *lochtach ó nach cantar* "incorrect because it is not used".' The tract on declension is followed by over 2,000 citations [34]

CHAPTER 19

LAWYERS, DOCTORS, PATRONS

THE LAW SCHOOLS

The great lawyer families continued to study and interpret the ancient laws of Ireland. The most outstanding among them was that of the Mac Egans, whose names recur again and again in the Annals. In 1317 we meet with Maelisa Mac Egan 'the best learned in Ireland in the brehon law'.[1] Then come Farrell (d. 1363), Teige (d. 1378)[2], Brian (d. 1390) 'ollav brehon of Breifne'[3], Baothgalach or Boethius (d. 1400), a man of two callings, 'extensively skilled in the Fenechus (Brehon) law and in music',[4] Gilla-na-Naev (d. 1400), Gilla Iosa (d. 1436) 'ollav to Mac Wattin (i.e., Fitzwatkin, a name assumed by the Barrets of Tirawley, Mayo), in law, a pious charitable and humane man', Conor (d. 1438), Gilla-na-Naev (d. 1443), Hugh (d. 1443) 'died in the springtime of his prosperity. He was the most fluent and eloquent of the Irish of his time'. In 1529 died two men of varied talents, Cosnamhach Mac Egan 'the most distinguished adept in the Fenechus, poetry and lay brehonship' (the meaning of this title is not clear), and Donnell Mac Egan 'head of the learned of Leath Mhogha (Southern Ireland) in Fenechus and poetry.' It is a most extraordinary record of hereditary professional skill, and we note, too, how widely the branches of this family were spread, in Connacht, Breifne (Leitrim–Cavan), Westmeath, Offaly, Munster and North Tipperary, where they kept a celebrated law school.[5]

Other noted lawyer families were the MacClancys (Mag Flannchadha) brehons in Thomond and Ossory, the O'Dorans (Ua Deoradháin) brehons in South Leinster and the O'Davorens (Ua Duibdábhoireann) in Corcomroe and Burren, Co. Clare.[6]

YOUNG LAW STUDENTS AT WORK

The law school of the O'Davorens in the Burren was founded about 1500 by Gilla na naomh Mór (son of Aodh, son of Maghnus).

A remarkable feature of it was that the buildings in which it was housed stood within an ancient ring-fort, Cahermacneachtain. A detailed description of this establishment is given in a deed of family agreement made in 1675 by the sons of Gilla na naomh Óg O'Davoren, where reference is made to 'the large house of the caher within,' 'the kitchen-house,' 'the house site between the front of the large house and the door of the caher' and 'the large house which is outside the door of the caher'.[7]

Some time in the sixteenth century some members of this legal family, Domhnall, son of Aodh, and his kinsmen, Maghnus and Muircheartach, left the Burren and set up school in a place called *Páirc,* probably identified with the townlands of Park East and West in the parish of Clonbern, Co. Galway, some eleven miles from Tuam.[8] In the British Library there is a manuscript (Egerton 88) written about 1564 by Donal O'Davoren and some of his pupils. A digest of this is given by O'Grady in his *Catalogue of Irish Manuscripts*. It contains tracts on law and grammar, and some historical tales in prose and verse. It was more probably composed in Donal's own school, after he had left the Burren.

Apart from its historical worth, this manuscript has a human value, as many of its pages are enlivened by the marginal comments of the budding lawyers, indulging in good-humoured grumbling at the expense of their master. 'Donall, this bit is no friendship's offering', [i.e. 'I write under compulsion']. 'You are well off, Donall, to be getting in the harvest and I slaving for you'. 'Holy Mary, Donall, bad luck to you that are driving me distracted (lit. 'all over the country') requiring a head-letter from me, and I not having so much as a drop of ink to help me out with the job. I am Aedh'. 'There's for you Donall, from Sémus mac Firbis's son, and there never was a more accomplished rogue than you'.

The master's table d'hôte, whether from poverty or stinginess, appears to have been meagre. 'A dinnerless Tuesday is a cold thing, Donall, and immediately before Christmas, too.' 'This is not a fair thing, Donall, you with the dinner all to yourself and I in grief'. And small commons was not the only affliction of these youths. 'My writing equipment is bad; a soft spiky pen; foxy thick ink; vellum stony and thin and [into the bargain] grief'. Yet now and then a more cheerful note is struck: 'I am well pleased with that quantity of the old book which I have this day finished off.'[9] These scribblings give a vivid picture of the life of these young men, undeterred in their studies by poverty, cold and hunger.

MEDICAL FAMILIES

The families of physicians were also numerous and held in high esteem. Some of the most famous may be mentioned, most of whom were attached to noble households. Mac Duinnshléibhe (Mac Dunlevy), physicians of Ulster; Mac Beatha (McBeth), who settled in Scotland; Ua Caiside (O'Cassidy), physicians to the Maguires of Fermanagh; Ua Callanáin (O'Callanan), physicians to the MacCarthys of South Munster; Ua Ferghussa (O'Fergus), physicians to the O'Malleys of Iar-Umhall in Co. Mayo; Ua Liagha or Ua Leagha (O'Lee), physicians to the O'Flahertys of Connacht; Ua hÍcidhe (O'Hickey), physicians to the O'Briens of Thomond, the O'Kennedys of Ormond and the MacNamaras of Clare; Ua Luinín (O'Luinin), poets and physicians of Fermanagh; Ua Siaghail (O'Shiel), physicians to the MacMahons of Oriel and the MacCoghlans of Delvin in Offaly. It is to be noted that two of these names, O'Hickey and O'Lee, signify the profession of the person designated (*ícidhe,* the healer, *liaigh,* the leech), showing that the families concerned must have been long associated with medicine, possibly from the tenth century when the assumption of family names became common.[10]

Amongst these medical families, the most prominent in the north was that of the Mac Dunlevys, physicians to the O'Donnells of Tirconnell. They were themselves of equally noble stock as their patrons. Formerly princes of Ulaidh, they had been dispossessed of their lands by de Courcy, but continued to bear the title of Ultach. Their names occur again and again in the Annals. In 1395 died 'Maurice, son of Paul Ultach, chief physician of Tirconnell'.[11] It was doubtless of him that an anonymous writer of the fourteenth century wrote: 'Mac Donlevy, physician of the schools: himself shall not exist, but his fame shall be.'[12] In the Bodleian library there is a translation of a Latin medical tract *'Gualterus de Dosibus'.* (The identity of 'Walter' is not known). There is a colophon to the tract which reads: 'Here ends Gualterus his book of the doses of medicine. Cormac Mac Donleavy it is that for Dermot MacDonall O'Lyne has put this summary into Irish: and to himself and his sons may so profitable a commentary render good service. On the fourth day of the kalends of April this lecture was finished at Cluain Umha [Cloyne, Co. Cork] in the year when the number of the Lord's annals was this: 1459.'[13] In 1526 died 'the physician O Donleavy (Donough son of Owen) a Doctor of Medicine and learned in other sciences, a man of great affluence and wealth, who kept a house of general hospitality'.[14] And in 1586 died Owen (the son of Donough) 'a doctor in legend of learning, for he excelled the medical doctors of Ireland in the times in which he lived.'[15]

A reputation equal to that of the Mac Dunlevys in the north was enjoyed by the O'Callanans in the south. It lived on into modern times in the popular saying: 'Even O'Callanan cannot cure him.'[16] In the Bodleian library there is a fragment of an Irish translation of a Latin medical treatise which concludes: 'And thus is cured quinsy by God's grace and the Art's. The Age of Christ when these Aphorisms were by Angus O'Callanan and Nicol O'Hickey put into Irish was 1403.'[17] And in the library of Trinity College Dublin, there is another fragment of a medical tract with a colophon stating that it was translated by the same Angus O'Callanan, with the help of his master, Piaras O'Huallacháin, for Mac Carthy Riach, Lord of Carbery, when the latter was dying in 1414 'and a blessing go with it to him.'[18]

A third medical family which figures frequently in the Annals is that of O'Cassidy. Thus we have in 1450 Teige O'Cassidy of Cuil, in 1490, Conla O'Cassidy and in 1495 William 'the Green'[19] O'Cassidy, all described as ollamhs to the Maguires of Fermanagh, the last mentioned being also 'a man truly learned in literature and medical science, who had kept a house of general hospitality.'[20]

MEDICAL EDUCATION

Of the training of these doctors we have little knowledge. However, we have earlier noted that there must always have existed some system of apprenticeship by which traditional lore was handed down from one generation to another. With regard to the Middle Ages, this presumption is strongly reinforced by the emergence of the hereditary physician families.

We have also noted that our knowledge of medical practice in the early ages is gathered almost entirely from surviving medico-legal treatises. These, however, indicate clearly that there was a considerable body of native medical lore. When we come to the Middle Ages, we are surprised to find that we have no direct information concerning native medical knowledge and practice. There are, indeed, extant many medieval medical treatises, but they are largely translations or compilations from the works of famous European physicians, and, though valuable from a linguistic standpoint, do not throw much light on the practices of the Irish doctors or the indigenous remedies which they used. They show, however, that the writers were well acquainted with the standard works of other nations. Standish O'Grady, in his *Catalogue of Irish Mss. in the British Museum,* has noted in the five medical treatises which he lists references to some thirty authorities European or Asian.[21] One of these treatises has already been mentioned as having belonged to Garret Mór, the Great Earl of Kildare, *Lile Na Heladhan Leighis,* the Irish translation made in 1482 of Bernard de Gordon's famous treatise *Lilium Medicinae.* From the

handwriting, O'Grady identifies the scribe as Domhnall Albanach
Ó Troighthigh, a physician of Co. Clare, from whose hand we
have a copy of the *Tripartite Life of St. Patrick,* also in the British
Museum Library.[22]

Only here and there do we get a suggestion that the Irish physician
is prescribing some native remedy. We have already referred to a
medical tract translated partly by Cormac Mac Duinnshléibhe. In
the latter part of this manuscript, which is the work of some unknown
scribe, probably another medical man, we find: 'Concerning the
treatment of fetid breath... Item; for nine days chew dilisk or the
inner bark of a willow.' Of this O'Grady remarks that 'it has all
the appearance of being a homespun recipe'. It does not appear in
the *Lilium Medicinae* or in another well-known treatise, *Rosa
Anglica.*[23]

ROSA ANGLICA

There is available an excellent edition of an Irish translation of
part of the last mentioned treatise.[24] The original, published about
1314 was the work of an English physician, John of Gaddesden,
(c. 1282–1361), who studied arts, theology and finally medicine at
Merton College, Oxford, acquired a great reputation in his profession – he is mentioned in the Prologue to the Canterbury Tales
as one of those whose writings the 'Doctour of Phisik... wel knew' –
and was Court Physician to Edward II, in addition to holding several
benefices. The name of the translator is not known, but the language
of the translation is early modern Irish, placing it somewhere
between 1300 and 1600. An inserted slip has the date 1460, which
the editor thinks roughly correct.

Some interesting information is to be found in the Introduction
to this edition. *Rosa Anglica* was apparently well known to the
physicians of Ireland. There are several translations of it in the
libraries of Trinity College, Dublin, the Royal Irish Academy,
and the British Museum, and in the National Library, Edinburgh.
Of Irish translations of other medical tracts, the editor traced
twenty-nine in Trinity College, Dublin, seven in the Royal Irish
Academy, three in the King's Inns Library, eleven in the National
Library of Scotland and eight in the Library of the British Museum.
The earliest of these dates from the late thirteenth century. The
rest belong to the fourteenth and fifteenth centuries.

In the Middle Ages, medicine was, all over the world, an amazing
conglomeration of charlatanry and superstition, enlightened here
and there by the lessons of experience. The care devoted to the
translation of the standard treatises of the day shows that, in this
respect, Ireland did not differ from other countries. It is hard for

us, for instance, to picture these Irish doctors laboriously translating and transmitting to their disciples such gems of wisdom as the many cures for epilepsy, which included – to select the least repulsive – the eating of raven's eggs, wolf's flesh or the ashes of a swallow, or the drinking of weasel's blood and vinegar.[25] As against this, some effective though primitive surgery seems to have been practised, such as the removal of stone or the treatment of abscesses.[26]

MEDICINE AND PHILOSOPHY

An interesting feature of the curriculum of the medieval Irish doctors is that it included philosophy. This was in accordance with the medical tradition throughout Europe, in which the physics and psychology of Aristotle were held to be an essential propaedeutic for the study of the pathology of both body and mind.

This point received special attention from Professor Francis Shaw, S.J., who traced and studied some twenty Irish translations of standard Latin philosophical treatises to be found in the libraries of Trinity College, Dublin, and the British Museum, the National Libraries of Ireland and Scotland and the Royal Irish Academy. They date almost all from the fifteenth century, and cover the fields of logic, cosmology or physics, and psychology.

Thus in logic there are translations of the standard textbooks, Aristotle's *Categories* with the Commentary of Boethius, Porphyry's *Isagoge* and a commentary on the *De Sex Principiis* of Gilbert de la Porrée; in cosmology or physics several treatises *de principiis naturae,* a *compendium de natura,* and three *opuscula* of St. Thomas dealing with questions related to physics; and in psychology treatises by Johannes de Rupella, or Jean de la Rochelle, who succeeded Alexander of Hales in the chair of the Franciscans at the University of Paris, and Walter Burley, who lectured at Oxford in the late thirteenth and early fourteenth century.

Apart from the fact that we know that such studies were considered elsewhere in Europe to belong to the domain of medicine, there is clear evidence that these Irish translations were the work of medical men. Thus, in the translation of St. Thomas's *De Operationibus Naturae* there is a colophon attributing it to Cormac Mac Duinnshléibhe, whom we have mentioned above. Another translation is that of a *Tractatus Medico-philosophicus de Potentiis Animae,* whose title speaks for itself, and which quotes as authorities Galen, Isaac and Constantine, in addition to Aristotle, Plato and Averroes.[27]

MEDIEVAL PATRONS OF LEARNING

The tradition of patronage of the native scholars continued

among the Gaelic chiefs right up to, and even beyond the Tudor period. All through the Annals, in addition to the records of scholars permanently attached to the heads of families as ollaves in history, poetry, law, medicine and music, we find mention in the obituaries of patrons who had extended their support not merely to their personal experts but also to the learned class in general.

Thus we have (1265) Felim son of Cathal Crovderg O'Conor, 'the exalter of the clerical orders and men of science',[28] (1338) Rory *an-einigh* (the hospitable) Maguire, Lord of Fermanagh 'a man who had bestowed more silver, apparel, steeds and cattle on the learned men and chief professors of Ireland than any other of the Sil Uidhir', [29] (1376) Hugh O'Farrell, 'like to a fountain had his generosity and bounty flowed on the *literati* of Ireland',[30] (1381) William O'Kelly, Lord of Hy-Many, 'who had given a general invitation of hospitality to the schools of Ireland' (we have earlier alluded to this Christmas festivity in 1351, when 'Poets, Brehons, Bards, Harpers...every one of them was well used'),[31] (1407) O'Carroll, Lord of Ely 'general patron of the *literati* in Ireland',[32] (1461) Felim O'Neill 'a protector of the learned...and a man who had purchased more poetry and had a larger collection of poems than any other man of his time',[33] (1468) Cathal Oc, son of Cathal Ruad Mag Ragnaill 'chieftain in full of the Muintir Eolais,' on whom the annalist invokes a blessing for 'his great heart and his free spending and his wealth; for he was wont to spend this great wealth on the poets and strangers of Ireland',[34] (1511) O Conchobair Failge, Cathaír son of Conn son of Cathal 'a joyous universal patron to the scholars and ollavs of Ireland'[35] (1531) 'Mac Cartaigh Riabhach i.e. Domhnall son of Finghin, son of Diarmuid, a young lord of Cairbre, and a man of general bounty to poets and men of learning...who had given a school invitation to the men of Erinn,'[36] (1537) O'Donnell (Hugh, the son of Hugh Roe, son of Niall Garv, son of Turlough of the Wine, Lord of Tirconnell, Inishowen, Kinel-Moen, Fermanagh and Lower Connacht) 'a man who duly protected their termon lands for the friars, churches, poets and ollavs',[37] (1583) Con, the son of Calvagh, son of Hugh Duv, son of Hugh Roe O'Donnell 'the supporting pillar of the *literati*...a man who had spent much of his wealth in the purchase of poems and panegyrics'.[38]

The Annals chronicle the patronage almost exclusively of the Gaelic aristocracy, but there are indications that at least some of the Anglo-Norman chiefs were also favourable to the learned class. In 1519 we find the obituary of Revelin Savage who 'died after having been hunted out of his kingdom through the power of the Earl of Kildare...Tis no wonder he died of pining for his land, to wit Tricha Cet na Soillse [the Cantred of Light, Lecale, Co. Down]. This man was the most bountiful and humane of all the Galls of Ireland: the blessing of poets and exiles on his soul'.[39] In the same year occurred the death of 'Mailin, son of Torna O Mailchonaire Ollav of the Sil Murray...who had been chosen by the Fitzgeralds and the Galls from all the Ollavs of Ireland; who used to get jewels and treasures from all of whom he sought them'.[40] In 1529 a tribute is paid to James, 6th Earl of Desmond 'who had the best reputation of all the sons of the Galls for bounty and nobility, who was...the best patron of poets.'[41]

WOMEN PATRONS

It is noteworthy that the women of the ruling class were not behindhand in the encouragement of learning. In 1433 'two general invitations were given...by Margaret, daughter of Ua Cerbaill, king of Offaly to the [bardic] bands of Ireland and to their retinues.'[42] In 1481 died 'Slaine, daughter of Ua Briain [Conor, king of Thomond, died 1498] namely wife of Mac William of Clann Ricaird – to wit a general protector of the [bardic] bands,'[43] in 1513 Mairgrec, daughter of Conchobar O Briain and wife of O'Ruairc, 'hearth of hospitality and maintenance, humanity and charitable entertainment for scholars and ollavs',[44] in 1524 Gormlaidh, the daughter of O'Donnell [Hugh Roe] and wife of Hugh, who had 'bestowed many gifts upon the orders and churches, and upon the literary men and ollavs (which indeed, was what might have been expected from her for she had a husband worthy of her),[45] in 1527 'Mor, daughter of Maelsechlainn Mac Caba, wife of O hAinlige, the best woman who ever lived in Cenel Dobtha, foster-mother to the poets and exiles of Ireland',[46] in 1580 'the daughter of Cu Connacht, son of another Cu Connacht [Maguire]...hospitable...to [bardic] bands and retinues.'[47]

THE SCHOLARS' ESTATES

When we speak of the chiefs as being patrons of the *filid*, we must dispel from our minds any picture of these latter as mere hangers-on at the court of their masters. They had their own residences, were sometimes endowed with extensive lands, and apparently often acquired considerable wealth.

One general indication of the social condition of the native scholars is the fact that throughout the centuries we find it constantly asserted of them that they 'kept a house of general hospitality'.[48] Some are singled out for special mention of their wealth, such as (1426) Magrath, the son of Flann Magrath, ollav of Thomond in poetry, 'a prosperous and wealthy man',[49] (1507) Mac Conmidh,

that is Solamh 'an eminent poet of great wealth'[50] (1527) O'Clery
(Gilla-Reagh, the son of Teige Cam) 'a scientific adept in history,
poetry and literature, and a man of consideration, wealth, prosperity
and great power',[51] (1542) Mac Conmidhe (Brian Donagh, the son
of Solomon (Mac Solaimh) 'a man skilled in poetry and literature,
a rich and affluent man'.[52] (1543) Maurice, the son of Paidin
O'Mulconry, 'a man learned in history and poetry, a man of wealth
and affluence, a learned scribe, by whom many books had been
transcribed, and by whom many poems and lays had been composed,
and who had kept many schools superintending and learning,
several of which he had constantly kept in his own house'.[53]

Gleeson gives an illuminating account of the lands held by the
brehon family of Mac Aodhagáin under various clans.[54] Speaking
of the territory then held in Lower Ormond by the O'Carrolls, he
says: 'The Civil Survey of 1654...finds the brehon family of
Mac Aodagáin holding their mensal demesne of Kilnahalagh with
its castle there. This famous family were brehons also to Ua
Cinnéide, and from them they held, also in Lower Ormond, Baile
Mac Aodagáin and Coillte Ruad (Ballymacegan and Redwood)...
in Upper Ormond they held Lisheen in Kilkeary parish from
Ua Cinnéide Donn. From Ua Mechair (Meagher) in Uí Cairin
(Ikerrin) they had Ballinamoe and its castle (the modern Honey-
mount). Here at Kilnahalagh ('Henceforth and forever to be called
Sopwith' as is stated in the patent issued by Charles II to the
Cromwellian Colonel Sadler) they had the "brehon's share" from
Ua Cerbaill'.

CHAPTER 20

INCHOATE UNIVERSITIES

THE UNIVERSITY OF ST. PATRICK

The twelfth and thirteenth centuries had seen the beginnings and rapid growth of universities all over Europe. It was, therefore, not surprising that, early in the fourteenth century, an attempt should be made to establish in Dublin a university which would give to the Anglo-Norman settlement a centre of culture.[1] A petition was made to Pope Clement V in 1312 by John de Lech, archbishop of Dublin, and in the bull which resulted the Pope enumerated the reasons which had been given for the establishment of a university in that city:

'...in the land of Ireland, though there are some doctors and bachelors, at least in the faculty of theology, and others who lecture on grammar, nevertheless there is not in Ireland nor in Scotland nor in Man nor in the parts of Norway any university of scholars or *studium generale*,[2] because there are few in the whole land who are adorned with the knowledge of letters.'

'since the aforesaid land of Ireland is surrounded by the Ocean, no access is possible to any *studium generale* save by crossing that sea at great risk.'

The petitioner begs that Dublin be chosen 'since it is suitable for such a *studium generale* owing to its convenient site and useful conditions.'

The bull proceeds: 'By our apostolic authority we decide that in that same city of Dublin...there should be a university of scholars and a *studium generale* in every lawful science and faculty...in which masters may have liberty to teach and students to hear lectures in the same faculties.'[3]

The action of the Pope was in keeping with the general policy of the Avignon popes. Between 1303 and 1365, universities of which they were the founders, or in whose foundation they participated, had sprung up at Rome, Avignon, Perugia, Cahors,

Grenoble, Prague, Vienna, Montpellier and Orange. Unfortunately Clement's zeal for higher education was not matched by his knowledge of conditions in Ireland. He clearly envisaged a university for the whole country, and did not see, as anyone on the spot could see, that such an establishment in the heart of the English Pale would be narrowly limited in its intake of students.

CONSTITUTION OF THE UNIVERSITY

Archbishop de Lech died in 1313, and owing to the disputed election to the see and the disturbed state of the country as a result of the Scottish invasion, no further step was taken until 1320. In that year the successful candidate for the archbishopric, Alexander de Bicknor, (his rival, Walter Thornbury, had been drowned in Dublin Bay on his way to urge his claim on the Pope at Avignon), obtained from John XXII confirmation of the bull of establishment, and drew up a constitution for the proposed university.

This was largely on the Oxford model, wide powers being given to the chancellor elected by the regent masters. He had the power to make statutes and had jurisdiction over masters, students and their servants. The licensing of bachelors was to be decided by the votes of the chancellor and regents. Yet, in contrast to Oxford, the chancellor was to a large extent subject to the Archbishop of Dublin. Statutes had to be submitted to him for approval, and the chancellor had to take an oath of fidelity to him.[4]

Curiously enough, there is in this *Ordinatio* of de Bicknor no mention of any faculty of arts, although this had been specifically mentioned in the bull. It was apparently thought well, for a start, to concentrate on the main subjects of philosophy and theology.

THE TEACHING STAFF

For his initial teaching staff de Bicknor drew upon the existing theological schools of the Dominicans and Franciscans in Dublin, appointing as masters William de Hardits, a Dominican, Henry Cogry, a Franciscan and Edmund de Kermerdyn, who belonged to one of the two orders. He took care, however, to put the whole establishment under the direction of his own Dean of St. Patrick's, William de Rodeyard, who was appointed both master and chancellor.

In the *Chartularies of St. Mary's Abbey*[5] it is stated of William de Hardits and William de Rodeyard that each 'solempniter incepit', the former in theology, the latter in canon law. Monck Mason translates this phrase 'were admitted to the degree.'[6] Ware says that the three friars 'were created Doctors of Divinity' and that de Rodeyard 'was promoted to the degree of Doctor of the Canon

Law.'[7] It is evident, therefore, that there was a formal conferring
of degrees on the incoming teachers and possibly on other students
who had been educated elsewhere. There is no evidence of further
graduations, but no positive proof that (as Rashdall assumes) they
did not take place.[8]

It is possible that some of the lectures were given in the Dominican
or Franciscan friaries, but there is some evidence that the university
had a local habitation of its own in the vicinity of St. Patrick's
cathedral. In a lease dated 14 Richard II (1390–91), the mayor and
commons of Dublin devise to one Thomas Mareward 'a messuage
with its pertinences without St. Patrick's Gate, extending in length
to the east from the corner of the stone wall outside the said gate
beside the king's way to the arches of the ancient schools there,
and in length (*sic*) from the aforesaid street beyond the stream of
water that flows to the Mill of the Poll as far as the land of the
aforesaid schools.'[9] What were ancient schools in 1390 may well
have been buildings erected or allotted in 1320 to house the
university.

'A UNIVERSITY IN NAME'

There is little evidence of activity by the inchoate university after
1320. It is evident that lectures were given for some time, but, as
has been said, there are no records of further graduations after the
first formal ones. Friar John Clyn, the Franciscan of Carrick-on-Suir,
whom we have met earlier, dryly remarks in his *Annals:* '1320. The
university of Dublin commenced, a university in name, but would
that it were such in fact and reality'. And two centuries later Chancellor Thady Dowling of Leighlin records: 'I do not find that this
academy was abolished, rather I believe that it collapsed through
negligence and want of support.'[10]

The failure of the University of St. Patrick was, as has been pointed
out, mainly due to the general situation which made impossible
the Pope's design for a *studium generale* to serve the whole country.
Curtis suggests that, in more favourable circumstances, the
University might have 'come into full flower as a centre of culture
and civilisation among the colonists, as a means for the diffusing
of European thought, and as the most effective agent for anglicising
the native race itself, so conservative but yet devoted to learning.[11]
But it may well be doubted that the lure of academic lore would
have prevailed against the independent spirit of either the Gaelic
clans or the Anglo-Norman families outside the Pale.

Whatever hopes might have been entertained for the success of
the University were sadly dimmed by the chequered career of its
founder, on whom it must have largely depended for financial

support. In 1324 de Bicknor was convicted of having made fraudulent returns whilst acting as treasurer of Ireland in 1307–13, and was also excommunicated by the Pope's financial agent in England, Robert Pinchbeck, for non-payment of a debt due to the see of Rome. He joined the English malcontents who were rallying around Queen Isabella in Aquitaine, and helped to bring about the overthrow of Edward II. But Edward III insisted that he should pay his debts. This he stubbornly refused to do, and he died in 1349 a broken old man.

STRUGGLE FOR EXISTENCE

In spite of the downfall of its founder and patron, there is evidence that the university continued for a while to function to some extent. In 1358 a supplication was made to Edward III by certain clergy and scholars of Ireland 'that through want of means and on account of the great Perils they sustained in passing the Seas for the sake of Learning, that they were terrified any longer to repair to foreign Parts upon that Score and therefore proposed to continue in the City of Dublin, both in reading and hearing Divinity, the Civil and Canon Laws, and other Clerical sciences, and to exercise all kinds of Studies there by the Favour of God.' They therefore asked the king's protection for this purpose, which he granted to 'them, their servants and Attendants, together with their Goods and Luggage, both in coming to the said University, their Abode in it and their Return from there'.[12]

Again in a document of 1364 reference is made to the university. It records the grant of land at Stackallen, Co. Meath, to the dean and chapter of St. Patrick's, Dublin, by the king's younger son, Lionel Duke of Clarence, then Deputy Governor in Ireland. (It was towards the close of his term of office in 1366 that the Statutes of Kilkenny were enacted). The grant was made on two conditions; firstly, masses were to be said for the king and his family, both in life and after death and for the repose of the souls of his forefathers, and secondly the services were to be secured 'of a fit friar of the order of Augustinian friars to read theology in the house of scholars of the said dean and chapter at Dublin forever.'[13]

The latter condition seems to have been due to a purely personal preference. The Austin friars in Ireland at this time had no special qualifications as theologians, but the Clarence title was taken from Stoke Clarence in Suffolk, where the English Augustinians had their first foundation, and where the Duke, by his own wish, was buried in the convent graveyard.[14]

But a document of 1363 shows that, even if the university continued to exist at that date, it was not regarded as a true *studium generale.* This is a petition from eighteen Irish priests of various dioceses, seeking for benefices and other favours, which begs the Pope to expedite the petitions for these persons 'inasmuch as this is the first roll he has received from them, and he must not be surprised that the persons have no scholastic degrees, inasmuch as in all Ireland there is no university or place of study'.[15] It will be seen that a century later the same statement was made by the Commons of Ireland when petitioning for the foundation of a university at Drogheda.[16]

PROPOSED UNIVERSITY AT DROGHEDA

In the second half of the fifteenth century another attempt was made to provide some form of higher education. Thomas, 8th Earl of Desmond, like most of the Irish chiefs, had during the Wars of the Roses, supported the Yorkist cause, and in 1462 he defeated at Pilltown, Co. Kilkenny, the forces of the Ormond Sir John Butler, who was endeavouring to revive Lancastrian sympathy. Thomas thus established himself as the most powerful leader in Ireland. In 1463 Edward IV appointed him Deputy to the king's brother, George Duke of Clarence, who was nominal Lord Lieutenant, warning him at the same time against his known favouring of the adoption of Gaelic laws and customs.[17]

Thomas was a man of culture and sincere faith. In 1464 he founded at Youghal, Co. Cork, which city formed part of his estates, a college consisting of a warden, eight fellows and eight singing men. This, however, was not primarily an educational establishment, but was intended as an endowment for choral service in St. Mary's, Youghal, which was then erected into a collegiate church.[18]

In 1465 a parliament was held at Drogheda, presided over by the deputy, Desmond. The corporation and townsmen drew his attention to the failure of the University of St. Patrick in Dublin, and urged him to set up such an institution in Drogheda. An Act was passed, of which the Norman-French text is thus translated by Ware:

'Because that the Land of Ireland has no University, nor general place of Study within it, a work of which Sort would cause a great increase of Knowledge, Riches and good Government, and would prevent Riot, evil Government and Extortion within the said Land; it is therefore ordained, established and granted by Authority of the Parliament, that there be a University in the town of Droghedah, in which may be made Batchelors, Masters and Doctors, in all Sciences and Faculties, as they are made in the University of Oxford;

and that they may also have, occupy and enjoy all manner of Liberties, Privileges, Laws and laudable Customs, which the said University of Oxford hath occupied and enjoyed.'[19]

Nothing, however, came of the project. Three years later Desmond was deposed on the charge of treasonable relations with the Gaelic Irish, and, instead of a University, the town of Drogheda was treated to the spectacle of the beheading of one of whom the *Annals of Ulster* recorded that 'the learned relate that there was not ever in Ireland a foreign youth that was better than he.' The *Annals of Connacht* add: 'And the hearts of the men of Ireland and of their wives were broken by these tidings.'

ANOTHER INCHOATE UNIVERSITY IN DUBLIN

By 1475 it had become so apparent that the University of St. Patrick was no longer a reality, that a fresh and independent effort was made to establish a *studium generale* in Dublin. In a bull of 27th April, Pope Sixtus IV referred to a petition lately made to him by 'the minister, prior and vicars and friars of the orders of Friars Preachers, Friars Minors, Austin friars and Carmelite friars...of Ireland', alleging that 'in the said island which is surrounded by the sea...there is no university in which masters and doctors can lecture and scholars study'. Many friars of these orders wished to pursue their studies in theology and arts, but saw their 'abilities daily diminish, because they have no safe access to any university except by crossing the said sea, with grave danger, many being frequently drowned; and that they cannot conveniently dwell in foreign *studia* or universities on account of the lack of means to pay, etc.' The petitioners, therefore, asked for the erection in the city of Dublin of an university of arts and theology, and the Pope replied with this bull by which he erected in that city 'a university of theology and the liberal arts necessary for the knowledge thereof', with indult to its doctors, scholars, etc., 'to enjoy all the privileges, etc., granted to the University of Oxford'.[20] Almost all that is known of this project is to be gathered from the Dominican eighteenth-century historian, de Burgo, who states that there is no evidence of the provision for it either of a building or of revenues.[21]

FINAL FAILURE

On the other hand, in spite of the allegations of the friars that there was 'no university' in Ireland, it seems that there remained what Sir James Ware calls 'some footsteps' of the University of St. Patrick in the reign of Henry VII. In 1496, in a provincial synod held in Christ Church, Dublin, presided over by Archbishop

Fitzsimon 'certain annual Pensions were granted for seven years to the Lecturers of the University by the Archbishop and his suffragans of the Province of Dublin'. Dublin gave £10, Ossory and Ferns each £5, Leighlin and Kildare each 5 marks.[22] This measure was, no doubt, part of the Tudor policy to strengthen the influence of the English colony. But the new policy of Henry VIII was to put an end to all hope of giving effect to the bull of Clement V.

Though it lies outside the scope of the present work, brief mention may be made of the final incident in the history of the University of St. Patrick. In 1568 the parliament in Dublin passed a motion to re-erect the University 'and to support it by voluntary contributions.' The Deputy, Sir Henry Sidney, and the Council recommended this step to the Lords of the Council in England, but, as Ware tersely remarks, 'this matter took no effect.'[23]

Earlier we have recorded the suggestion that Edmund Campion's visit to Ireland in 1570 was in some way connected with this scheme, and have shown that the facts do not support it. However, in his *History of Ireland* Campion shows that he was well acquainted with the history of the University of St. Patrick during the two hundred and fifty years that had elapsed since its foundation, and also with the recent effort to revive it.

He recalls the petition of Archbishop Alexander de Bicknor 'for priviledg of an universitye to be ordained in Devlin, which toke effecte.' The first three doctors 'kept their termes and commencements solemnely'. Campion's account continues: 'neyther was the same ever disfranchised, but only throwe varieties of tyme discontynued, and now since the subvercion of monastereyes utterly extincte; wherein the devines were cherished and open exercise maynteyned'.

It may be noted that in these words Campion seems to imply that the University actually functioned to some extent right up to the suppression of the monasteries by Henry VIII. He concludes: 'A motyon was made in this last parliament to erect it againe, contribucions layde together. Sir Henry Sydney, then Lord Deputye, proferred twentie pounde lands and one hundred and twenty poundes in money; others followed after their abilityes and devocions; the name desired Mr. Acworth Plantolinum of Plantageneth and Bulleyne. But while they disputed of a convenient plan for it and of other circumstances, they lett fall the principall.'[24]

In the course of this survey of education during the ancient and medieval periods in Ireland, we have often had occasion to regret the paucity of information at our disposal. Yet, fragmentary though it is, this survey gives an inspiring view of these remote scholars, labouring under conditions which a modern pedagogue would find intolerable, to hand on to the coming generation their accumulated store of knowledge.

The early sixteenth century seems to be a suitable point at which to come to a close. Up to this time, the pattern that emerges is a simple one, the native lay scholars and the monastic scholars each contributing their quota of learning, with a degree of collaboration which appears to be a unique feature of Irish cultural history. From now on, the pattern becomes much more complicated. Under Henry VIII, there was to appear the new concept of education as an instrument of government policy, in this case both civil and, later, religious. The monastic schools were to be destroyed, yet to revive in a different form three centuries later. The native schools were also to die – theirs a more lingering death – yet their tradition was to be carried on by the eighteenth-century poets and schoolmasters and by the nineteenth-century scholars. Numerous new influences were to come into play, differences of religious belief, political, social and economic theories and movements, increasing familiarity with the cultures of other peoples, the opening up of vast areas of knowledge in the domain of physical science, the complicated demands of modern technology.

Yet all along, the original cultures, christian and native, never ceased to form a part of that complicated pattern, indeed to give to it its peculiar character. In no spirit of narrow conservatism, but merely having regard to the acknowledged value of ancient tradition, it may be expected that they will continue to do so in any future system of education in Ireland.

APPENDIX

MUSIC

The study of ancient and medieval documents reveals two facts concerning music. The first is that it played a most remarkable part in the cultural life of the Irish people. The second is that we know regrettably little about the manner in which it was taught. The latter fact explains its relegation to an appendix.[1]

EARLY RECORDS

In the most remote ages of Irish history music finds constant mention. Thus, to take a few examples at random, we hear of Onnoi the 'fair all-beautiful harper of Eber', (one of the Milesian invaders), who filled the south of Ireland with 'string sweetness of music'.[2] In the *Colloquy of the Ancients,* it is related how Fionn Mac Cumhaill was one day on the slopes of Slievenamon when he saw 'a tiny man that, close to him on the green, played and performed on his harp'. On the arrival of the Fianna, the mysterious dwarf continued to play 'a superlatively sweet music', and he 'tarried with Fionn until he died.'[3]

According to the *Uraicecht Becc,* 'a harp is the one art of music which deserves nobility...it has the nobility of a *"bó-aire túise"* ' (one of the higher classes in the ancient Irish social scale).[4] The *Crith Gabhlach* tells us that the harper had a place of honour in the royal palace, next to the king's poets and personal guests.[5]

THE SAINTS AND MUSIC

In the lives of the early christian saints music also plays a large part. Thus in the life of St. Brigid attributed to St. Ultan it is related that on one occasion she visited the King of Munster to ask pardon for a prisoner. The king was absent, but was awaited by some friends. Brigid noticed some harps hanging on the walls and asked for music. One of the king's friends replied that all the court harpers were away, and then addressed his companions in a jocular tone (*iocoso verbo*) 'play to us on the harp and let Brigid bless your hands so that you may be able to do what she asks'. Brigid did in earnest what had been proposed as a joke, and the astonished guests found themselves able to play. There was a happy sequel. The king, on his return, was so moved by this wonder that he released the prisoner.[6] Again, St. Ciarán of Saigher was appealed to by Oengus Mac Nadfraoich, king of Munster (d.c. 490), whose harpers had been drowned in a lake by the king's enemies. At the prayer of the saint, the musicians arose from the lake, with their harps in their hands.[7]

There is a pleasant story told in the Life of St. Brendan of Clonfert contained in the *Book of Lismore*. One Easter day, when the monks were gathered for dinner, a young cleric entertained them on his harp. In high spirits, he went off to play also for the abbot, but, to his chagrin, at the first sound of the harp, Brendan filled his ears with wax. Asked for an explanation, he related how, seven years before, a bird had appeared to him (it was the Angel Michael in disguise) and had made for him such heavenly music that he could no longer listen to the melodies of the world. Graciously, however, the saint relented to the extent of allowing the cleric play 'three strains', gave him his blessing and assured him that 'thou shall have heaven for that playing.'[8]

MIDDLE AGES. THE HARP

In the middle ages, references to music are again constant. The Welsh priest, Gerald de Barry, (better known as Giraldus Cambrensis), who, in the train of Prince John, visited Ireland in 1184–6, and who had little good to say of that country, pays a generous tribute to the skill of the Irish harpers: 'They are incomparably more skilful than any other nation I have ever seen... It is astonishing that, in so complex and rapid a movement of the fingers, the musical proportion [the time] can be preserved; and that throughout the difficult modulations on their various instruments, the harmony is completed with such sweet rapidity...They enter into a movement and conclude it in so delicate a manner and tinkle the small strings so sportively under the deeper tones of the bass strings, they delight so delicately and soothe with such gentleness that the perfection of their art appears in the concealment of art.'[9]

In another passage, Cambrensis alludes to the employment by the clergy of music to arouse religious fervour. 'Bishops, abbots and holy men in Ireland are accustomed to carry harps about with them, and with their strains to fill their hearers with pious joy.'[10]

POETS ON THE HARP

There are extant two poems of Gilla Brighde Mac Conmaidh
(also called Gilla Brighde Albanach, d.c. 1260), in praise of the
Dalcassian chief, Donnchadh Cairbreach Ó Briain. In one, the
poet declares that 'strings so sweet as his conversation on a willow
harp no fingers have played.' The other poem is addressed to the
harp of the chief himself, indirectly flattering its owner:

> He to whom this music-tree belonged
> Was a noble youth of sweetest performance.
> Many an inspired song has he sweetly sung
> To that elegant, sweet-voiced instrument.[11]

A similar poem addressed to a harp is that of Gofraigh Fionn
Ó Dálaigh (d. 1387), again indirectly flattering the owner, who was
probably one of the family of Mac Eochagáin, lords of Cenél
Fiachad in Westmeath.

> O choice instrument of the smooth, gentle curve,
> Thou that criest under red fingers,
> Musician that has enchanted us,
> Red harp, high-souled, perfect in melody.[12]

THE *Timpan*

The harp was clearly the most valued of musical instruments,
but there were numerous others. The *timpan* was not, as modern
musicians would conclude, a form of drum, but a stringed instrument
smaller than the harp and with fewer strings. O'Curry cites a quaint
story from the *Book of Leinster* relating how Eoghan, son of Oilioll
Oluim, king of Munster, and Lugaidh Mac Con, his step-brother,
once heard music coming from the midst of a yew-tree. The player
proved to be 'a little man with three strings in his *timpan*', who
had such skill that he made the two princes by turns to cry, to laugh
and to fall into a deep sleep.[13] One derivation of *timpan* given in
Cormac's Glossary is 'Timpan. i. tim. i. sail [willow] agus ban. i.
umae bis inti [brass what is in it]'.[14] Whilst not endorsing the
etymology, O'Curry cautiously proposes this passage as evidence
that the frame of the *timpan* was of willow and the strings of bronze
or brass. He is more confident in his conclusion that the *timpan*
was played with a bow, which he draws from a passage in some
notes on musical instruments which he found in a manuscript in
the library of Trinity College, Dublin, dealing with the Ancient
Laws, 'The Timpanist has a wand and hair.'[15] The *timpan,* though
inferior to the harp, was evidently held in esteem. We shall see that
timpanists were not infrequently thought worthy of mention in
the Annals.

OTHER INSTRUMENTS

Numerous other musical instruments were used by the ancient Irish. There were simple wind instruments of the recorder type. Several of these are represented, some single, others double or treble, on the crosses at Monasterboice and Clonmacnois.[16] Bagpipes (*tinne*) were also in common use. In the tale *The Destruction of Da Derga's Hostel,* found in *Lebor na hUidre* and other manuscripts, there is a description of the nine pipers of King Conaire, who wore 'mantles speckled with colour' and carried 'nine bagpipes, four-tuned, ornamented.'[17] Bronze trumpets of various sizes and shapes were used in war and hunting, and for the greeting of distinguished guests. In the National Museum, Dublin, there are exhibited ten of these trumpets, dating from the late bronze age (about 800 B.C.), and two from the early iron age. Fragments of about a dozen others have been found. It is a curious fact that, over the long period with which we have been concerned, the only musical instruments which have survived belong to such a remote age. In a study of these bronze age trumpets, Dr. Eoin MacWhite made the interesting suggestion that, since they have frequently been found in pairs, tuned to different pitches, they may have been played in groups 'forming a sort of primitive orchestra'.[18]

There is no record of percussion instruments, with the exception of bells, if they can be reckoned as such. Poets are constantly described as carrying a *Craebh Ciuil,* or musical branch. This appears to have been a small branch or pole, on which was hung a cluster of bells, which rang in harmony. It was not a musical instrument in the strict sense, since no tune could be played on it. It merely served to enhance the poet's dignity and to call for silence before he began to recite.[19]

In addition to the harp, timpan, pipe, bagpipe and horn, O'Curry gives a list of some sixteen other instruments mentioned in ancient documents, and, with his usual painstaking diligence, cites the numerous passages in which they appear. However, it would seem that all were variations of the harp and the pipe.[20]

THE ORGAN

The organ, in some primitive form, was known to the Romans, and by them introduced certainly into Spain, and presumably to other European countries, but the art of organ-building seems to have been lost after the Roman withdrawal and appears again only in the eighth century. There was considerable activity in organ-building in England in the tenth century, but the first mention of the instrument in Irish records is much later. Michael Treguy, archbishop of Dublin, in his will dated December 10th, 1471, bequeathed 'a pair of organs' to St. Patrick's cathedral, to be used in St. Mary's chapel.[21] In the records of Kilkenny Corporation, December, 1476, there is an entry granting a ground-rent to one John Lawless 'organ-maker', on the condition that he was 'to practise his art within the said town of Kilkenny.'[22] The Annals of the Dominican Abbey, Athenry, record that in 1479 Thomas Bermingham, Baron of Athenry and his wife Anabla bestowed 'three silver marks towards the building of the abbey-church organ.'[23]

HARP ACCOMPANIMENT

Singing and also the recital of poetry were often accompanied by the harp. St. Colum Cille was visited, on the shores of Lough Key, by a poet named Cronan. When Cronan left, the saint was asked by his disciples why he had not asked his visitor for a poem 'sung, as was his wont, to a musical accompaniment'. Colum Cille replied that he could not bring himself to ask 'for a song of joy' of a man whose impending tragic death he had foreseen.[24] And O'Curry cites a most realistic scene found in the *Book of Lecan,* and probably taken from the lost *Psalter of Cashel.* 'On a certain day in the season of autumn, as Feidhlimidh Mac Crimthainn [d. 845], monarch of Erinn, was in Cashel of the kings, there came to him the abbot of a church of the Uí Cormaic, and he sat on the couch, and he took his little eight-stringed [instrument] (Ocht-Tedach) unto him from his girdle and he played sweet music and sang a poem to it.'[25] The *Annals of the Four Masters,* under the date 592, cite these lines from the *Amra* or eulogy of St. Colum Cille, composed by Dallan Forgaill.

> Like a song to a harp without a *ceis*
> Are we after being deprived of our noble.[26]

It was apparently a common custom for poets to recite their compositions to a harp accompaniment. Though this is going somewhat beyond the period which we are discussing, it may be noted that the lengthy poem 'The Image of Ireland' composed in 1578 by John Derricke, a follower of the Deputy Sir Henry Sidney, contains a particularly interesting passage alluding to this custom,

> Both Barde and Harper is preparde, which by their
>   cunning art,
> Doe strike and cheare up all the gestes with
>   comfort at the heart.

An accompanying woodcut shows the two performers at a feast, the harper seated on the ground with his harp on his knees, the poet standing with arms outstretched.[27]

TYPES OF MUSIC

The ancient Irish distinguished various types of music. There were three main types, the *Gentraige,* lively tunes of a cheerful nature, the *Goltraige* expressing sorrow and the *Suantraige* which produced slumber. O'Curry gives numerous passages in which allusion is made to these three main types and also to another dozen, whose nature, however, is obscure.[28]

Both O'Curry and Joyce believed that there was some knowledge of harmony, but the evidence they give is slight. O'Curry adduces the definition of *ceis* as a small harp which accompanies the large harp.[29] Joyce relies on the description of Irish harp-playing given by Giraldus Cambrensis, the small strings tinkling under the deeper tones of the bass strings, and on the number of Irish words which signify 'playing or singing together', *cómseinm, cóicetul, aidbse, cepóc* or *cepóg, clais, clais-cetul* and *foacanad.* He grants, however, that in some instances, these terms might signify merely playing in unison or in octaves.[30]

Musicians will find further interesting reading in the chapter in which O'Curry tentatively suggests that some of the airs which still survive may possibly be the original airs to which ancient poems were set,[31] and also in W. K. Sullivan's study of Irish music in connection with the history of the development of European music.[32]

HYMNS: PSALMODY

As elsewhere in Europe, the singing of hymns and chanting of psalms played, from the earliest ages, an important part in the religious life in Ireland. The eighth-century hymn attributed to St. Fiacc of Sletty tells us of St. Patrick that 'hymns and apocalypse, the three fifties, [i.e. the one hundred and fifty psalms], he used to sing them.'[33] On the death of St. Finbarr, for twelve days 'synods of the churches of Desmond were busied about the body of the master with hymns and psalms and recitation of hours.'[34] The hymn *Altus Prosator,* which is attributed to St. Columba, proclaims:

> By chanting of hymns continually resounding
> The Trinity is praised, with three eternal repetitions.[35]

In the *Martyrology of Donegal,* compiled by Michael O'Clery in the 17th century from ancient sources, we find these lines on St. Mochta (d. 534 or 536), who was probably the last survivor of St. Patrick's disciples.

> Three-score psalm-singing seniors
> Were his household, royal the number,
> Without tillage, reaping or kiln-drying,
> Without work, except reading.[36]

Adamnán relates how St. Colum Cille and his companions began to recite evening prayers near the fort of King Brudeus. The king's druids tried to prevent them, but the saint began to sing the 44th psalm in a voice which swelled 'like a terrible thunderstorm', and terrified both king and people.[37]

The numerous hymns contained in the *Liber Hymnorum* were, no doubt, for the most part intended to be sung. There is clear evidence of this regarding one of the most famous, which is found in the seventh-century Antiphonary of Bangor and begins, *'Sancti venite, corpus Christi sumite'*. In the preface to the hymn of St. Sechnall, it is related how the saints, Patrick and Sechnall, heard a choir of angels singing this hymn 'around the oblation in the church'. The preface continues: 'Hence this hymn is sung in Ireland when one goes to the body of Christ, from that time onward.'[38]

HARP ACCOMPANIMENT TO CHANT

There is some evidence that the harp provided accompaniment to the chant. An eighth-century treatise on the Psalter, adapting a text of Cassiodorus (the sixth-century Roman writer, statesman and monk), explains the word 'psalmus' as 'what was invented for the harp and is practised on it'; 'psalmus cantici', as 'what is taken from the harp to the choir'; and 'canticum psalmi' as 'what is taken from the choir to the harp' – in each case supplying the word 'harp' where Cassiodorus simply says 'musical instrument'.[39]

As to the nature of the chant used in the early Irish church, we must rely largely on surmise. It is probable that it was at the beginning closely allied to that of the Gallican liturgy, which St. Patrick, a disciple of Germanus, would have brought from Auxerre. Bede and other contemporary writers state that the chant of the Irish monks who settled in England differed from that brought from Rome by St. Augustine and his companions.[40]

It is just possible that, as a result of the Norse invasion, some knowledge of the Roman chant may have come to Ireland. Christianity in Scandinavia was under Anglo-Saxon influence, and the Roman liturgy had predominated in England since the Council of Clovesho, in 747. But, up to the Norman invasion, there is no definite evidence that the old Irish tradition was abandoned. There are no surviving Irish manuscripts of that period which contain musical notation. There is just one indication that, on the eve of the coming of the Normans, an effort had been made to introduce the Roman chant. In the Life of St. Malachy (d. 1148) by St. Bernard, we read:

'Moreover, in all churches he ordained the apostolic sanctions and the decrees of the holy fathers and especially the customs of the holy Roman church. Hence it is that in this day there is chanting and psalmody in them at the canonical hours after the fashion of the whole world.'[41]

St. Malachy had visited in 1140 the abbey of Arrouaise in the diocese of Arras, the original foundation of the Augustinian Canons, and had influenced the adoption of the Arroasian observance in many places in the north of Ireland.[42] It is a reasonable surmise that his support of the Roman chant stemmed from Arrouaise.

The Norman bishops, at the Council of Cashel, 1171, enjoined on their subjects the observance of the Sarum rite (that of Salisbury Cathedral).[43] It probably spread slowly in the Norman-controlled areas. Elsewhere, the Arroasian rite seems to have been for a time preserved, but to have gradually yielded to the influence of the particular liturgies of the new orders, in particular of the Benedictines and Augustinians.[44]

MUSICAL EDUCATION. 1. SECULAR

Whatever slight information we have with regard to the teaching of secular music comes mainly from the *Annals*. There we find, between the twelfth and early sixteenth centuries, the names of some thirty musicians. Most of them are described simply as musicians, usually with some laudatory addition. Thus we have: 1269, 'Hugh O fflyn, a good musitian',[45] 1364, 'Brian O Broyn, a good Tympanist',[46] 1469, 'Ruaidri, son of Donnchad son of Eogan oc O Dálaig, the most musical-handed harpist in Ireland',[47] 1495, 'Florence Ua Corcrain, namely an eminent harper and player of [other] stringed instruments', and a good vocalist and instrumentalist',[48] 1544, 'O'Neill's son, namely Niall son of Art oc . . . . a man full of knowledge and bounty and skill in art and music both of hand and voice.[49] One of the briefest of these entries has a peculiar significance: 1369, 'John MacEgan and Gilbert O Bardan, two accomplished young harpers of Conmaicne, died.' (It was a year of plague).[50] It is a striking evidence of the esteem in which music was held that these two obscure young musicians should find a place among kings, abbots and learned men.

It could be reasonably surmised that at least some of these eminent musicians would have had pupils. However, the supposition is much clearer in the case of others who evidently also belonged to the class of *filid,* and hence would be directors of schools in other subjects. Thus we have, 1396 'Matthew O'Luinin, Erenagh of Arda...skilled in history, poetry, music and literature,'[51] 1399, 'Boethius (Baothgalach) Mac Egan, a man extremely skilled in the Fenechus law and music.'[52] And to a few the title *saoí* or *ollam* is given, implying even more clearly the role of teacher. In 1177 we find 'the Timpanist – Ua Coinnecen, ard-ollam of the North of Ireland,'[53] 1226, Aedh, son of Donnsleibhe O'Sochlachain air-chinneach of Cunga, a professor (saí) of singing and harp-playing, who made, besides, an instrument for himself, the like of which had never been made before',[54] 1269 'Hugh O'Finghty, saoí timpánoig',[55] 1360, 'Gilla-na-naem O'Conmaidh, ollam of Thomond, namely in timpan-playing',[56] 1405, 'Gilla-Duibin Mac Cruitin, the ollam of Ua Briain, to wit one eminent (saoí) in music and in history'.[57]

The supposition that these musicians mentioned in the Annals had pupils or even formal schools, is borne out in one instance from other evidence. In 1328 the *Annals of the Four Masters* record the death of 'the blind O'Carroll [*recte* MacCarroll] i.e. Mulrony, chief of the minstrels of Ireland and Scotland in his time.' The *Annals of Ulster* describe him (The Blind Mac Cerbail, namely Maelruanaigh) as 'the most choice timpanist of Ireland and Scotland and of the whole world.' The fourteenth-century Franciscan Friar Clyn, whom we have already met more than once, gives in his *Annals* a full account of this musician and his death.

'1329. In that battle,[58] the battle in which the Louth men killed their new Earl, John Bermingham, fell Caech O'Kayrwill [O'Carroll] that famous tympanist and harper, and with him fell about twenty tympanists, who were his scholars. He was called Caech O'Kayrwill, because his eyes were not straight, but squinted: and if he was not the first inventor of stringed music, he was the corrector, the teacher ('doctor') and director.'[59]

Whilst, apart from the *Annals,* there are, as we have seen, references to musicians in numerous other ancient documents, the only passage in which the formal title of teacher of music is used occurs in the tale entitled *Imtheacht na Tromdháimhe,* 'the Proceedings of the great bardic Institution'. In this, Seanchán Torpéist, the newly appointed chief poet of Ireland, arrives at the court of King Guaire of Connacht, and, at the request of the king's brother, Marbhán, calls on some of his retinue to give specimens of their musical art. Marbhán being at first dissatisfied, one of Seanchán's poet musicians volunteers to perform, and introduces himself as *'ollamh timpanachta na tromdháimhe',* 'professor of timpanism to the great Bardic Institution'. There follows a curious disquisition on the origin of both the harp and the timpan.[60]

MUSICAL EDUCATION. 2. SACRED

Though no explicit mention is made of it, regular training of novice monks in psalmody must have been given in the early Irish monastic schools, as everywhere else in Europe. It is significant that

there were Irish monks whose musical reputation had spread
beyond the limits of their own country. In the seventh century,
Gertrude, the daughter of Pepin, mayor of the imperial palace,
and abbess of Nivelles in Brabant, invited St. Foillan and St. Ultan,
brothers of St. Fursa, to instruct her nuns in psalmody.[61] And in
841 we read of Moengal, an Irish monk 'learned in sacred and
human literature', and presumably also in music, since he was
invited to become master of the schools of St. Gall, and was
succeeded in that office by no less a person than the famous sacred
musician, Notker Balbulus.[62]

CHOIR SCHOOLS
We have seen that boys were received at an early age in the
ancient monasteries. These would have been trained in psalmody
as part of their religious formation. Thus the choir school must
have been in every period a regular feature of monastic or
ecclesiastical life. However, to find formal mention of it, we have
to turn to the late middle ages. In his will, dated March 26th, 1476,
Richard White, of Swords, making provision for his burial, included
'to 12 boys 12d.' In the same year on June 10th, Nicholas Delaber
named among the beneficiaries of his will a choir-boy, Robert
Plunket.[63] In 1497 the Mayor and Corporation of Galway enacted
that William Mollogan and Matthew Lurcan, clerks of the
collegiate church, should undertake the care of four boys 'to sing
daily at the choir', whom they must 'enforme and teache to singe
after the best facion.'[64] In the records of St. Patrick's Cathedral,
Dublin, the first mention of the 'master of the Boy Choristers'
(one John Russell) is in 1509, but the office had evidently existed
for long before that date.[65]

NOTES

PREFACE

1. Atkinson, Norman, *Irish Education,* 1969. Dowling, P. J., *A History of Irish Education,* 1971.
2. Work is proceeding on a third volume by Dr. Rolf Baumgarten, under the auspices of the Dublin Institute for Advanced Studies.

CHAPTER 1
THE EARLIEST TEACHERS

1. Macalister, *The Archaeology of Ireland,* 176, Westropp, *Ancient Forts of Ireland,* 9–10.
2. It is generally accepted by historians that the Celtic colonization of Ireland took place at the end of the bronze age, in the sixth century B.C. For criticism and modifications of this theory, see O'Rahilly, *Early Irish History and Mythology* Ch. XI, App. IX. Raftery, *Prehistoric Ireland,* 178–81. MacNeill, *Phases of Irish History,* 48–9.
3. In addition to the works cited in the previous note, the following have been drawn on in the compilation of the foregoing summary: Macalister, *The Archaeology of Ireland,* (embodying much of the material in the same author's earlier work, *Ireland in pre-Celtic Times*), Chs. I, II, III, Kenney, *Sources for the Early History of Ireland,* 110–18, Coffey, *The Bronze Age in Ireland,* O Riordáin, *Antiquities of the Irish Countryside,* Dillon and Chadwick, *The Celtic Realms,* 34–38, Mitchell, *Prehistoric Ireland* (in ed. Moody and Martin. *The Course of Irish History,* 30–42).
4. I wish to acknowledge my debt in compiling the foregoing section to Dr. Raftery's *Prehistoric Ireland.*
5. O'Curry, *Manuscript Materials of Ancient Irish History,* 168–73.
6. *Lebor Gabála Erenn.* Irish Texts Society, vols. XXIV, XXV, XXXIX, XLI. On the limitations of this edition see review by Professor D. A. Binchy, *Celtica,* II, 195–209.
7. Hyde, *A Literary History of Ireland,* 15–19. Macalister, *Archaeology of Ireland,* 17, 27. Mac Cana, *Celtic Mythology,* 64.
8. Joyce, *A Social History of Ancient Ireland,* 222. Hyde, *op. cit.* 89.
9. Ed. Macalister, *op. cit.,* III, 9–11, 26–27, 56–57.
10. *Ibid,* III, 151.
11. *Ibid,* III, 169, IV, 109.
12. *Ibid,* II, 21, 75, 101.
13. Hyde, *op.cit.,* 293–362. O'Curry, *op.cit.,* 32–40. De Blacam *Gaelic Literature Surveyed,* 31. Raftery, *Prehistoric Ireland* 212. Byrne, *Early Irish Society, The Course of Irish History,* 43. Mac Cana, *Celtic Mythology,* 97–106.
14. O'Curry, *op.cit.,* 250–95.
15. Hyde, *op.cit.,* 293–318, 341–362.
16. O'Curry, *op.cit.,* 243 and Appendix LXXXIX.
17. *Táin Bó Cúalnge,* from the Book of Leinster, ed. Cecile O'Rahilly, IX–XII.
18. This tale, *Tochmarc Etáine,* is found in various versions in *Lebor na hUidre,* in the Egerton Mss, British Museum, and in a section of the *Yellow Book of Lecan.* The first two Mss. were published by Windisch, *Irische Texte,* 1st series, Vol. I. The passage cited, which is from the Egerton Mss., is on p. 129.

The English translation given is that of A. H. Leahy, *Heroic Romances of Ireland*, I, 21. The *Yellow Book* Ms. was published with translation by Bergin and Best, *Eriu* XII, 137–196. It does not contain the passage. Cf. also Gwynn, L. 'The two versions of Tochmarc Etaine', *Zeitschrift für Celtische Philologie*, IX, 353–6.

19. Ed. O'Rahilly, *Táin Bo Cualgne from the Book of Leinster*, 163–64. Cf. O'Curry, *op.cit.*, 200, Hyde, *op.cit.*, 90, note 1.

20. O'Curry, *Atlantis* (a journal published under the aegis of the Catholic University of Ireland) July, 1858. *The Only Jealousy of Emer*. This tale is from the same Ms. as *The Sick-bed of Cú Chulainn*.

The tale *Tochmarc Emire, The Wooing of Emer*, was translated by Kuno Meyer, one version in the *Archaeological Review*, I, 68 ff., another in the *Revue Celtique*, XI, 442–43. Meyer does not include the tale of *The Only Jealousy*. These translations were drawn on by Eleanor Hull in *The Cuchullin Saga in Irish History*, 56–84 (*The Wooing of Emer*), and by Lady Gregory in *Cuchulain of Muirthemne*, 21–47 (*The Courting of Emer*) and 276–93 (*The Only Jealousy of Emer*).

21. This story was published with translation by O'Curry in *Atlantis*, July, 1858. *The sick-bed of Cuchulainn* etc. The quotations are from pp. 25–29. O'Curry found it in a 14th century Ms. in the Royal Irish Academy, in which a note stated that it was from the lost *Yellow Book of Slane*. cf. also O'Curry, *Manners and Customs of the Ancient Irish*, 198–20. The story does not appear in any other edition of the Ulster cycle.

22. Hyde, *op.cit.*, 153–54.
23. Ed. Stokes I, 33, 35.
24. *Ibid*. I, 45, 55, 57–59.
25. *Ibid*. II, 449–67.
26. *Ibid.*, I, 41, 43.

CHAPTER 2

THE EARLIEST TEACHERS (continued)

1. There were two chief districts inhabited by Celtic-speaking peoples which were known to the Romans as *Gallia. Gallia Cisalpina* or *Citerior* comprised Northern Italy between the Alps and the Apennines. The far more important *Gallia Transalpina* or *Ulterior* comprised modern France and Belgium and parts of Holland, Germany and Switzerland.

2. T. D. Kendrick, *The Druids*, 74–6. This book, published in 1927, was the first complete study of the Druids to appear in English. It is still regarded as a standard work. It is particularly useful for students in that in an appendix the original texts are given of all the classical authors quoted. The translations here given are taken from it.

3. O'Curry, *Manners and Customs of the Ancient Irish*, 184. 'The origin of Druids in Erinn is carried back by our ancient writings (and I am convinced with great probability) to the earliest colonizers of the country.' Joyce, *A Social History of Ancient Ireland*, 221. 'It is pretty certain, indeed that the druidic systems of Gaul, Britain and Ireland were originally one and the same.'

4. Nora K. Chadwick, *The Druids*, 84. In this work (xiii-xxii) will be found an exhaustive list of classical writers who deal directly or indirectly with the Druids, and of modern writers who have collected extracts from their writings. It also deals critically with practically all the passages cited by Kendrick.

5. *De Situ Orbis*, III, 2, Kendrick, 87.
6. *De Bello Gallico*, VI, 14. Kendrick, 78.
7. *Geographia*, IV, 4, c. 197, 4. Kendrick, 83.
8. *Histories* V, 31. Kendrick, 82.
9. *De Bello Gallico*, VI, 13. Kendrick, 77–78.
10. *Geographia*, IV, 4 c 197, 4, Kendrick, 83.
11. Camille Gullian, *Histoire des Gaulles*, vol. 2, ch. 4. 85 ff. Cited Chadwick *op.cit.*, 4–5, 97 with other supporters of this view. Kendrick, *op.cit.*, 79, 128,

133. Francoise le Roux, *Les Druides,* 5–6, suggests that a limited number were priests.
12. *De Bello Gallico,* VI, 13. Kendrick, 77.
13. *Ibid.* 16, Kendrick, 78.
14. Chadwick, *op.cit.,* VII, 246, 97.
15. e.g. Dillon in Dillon and Chadwick, *The Celtic Realms,* 10, 14.
16. In a lost work cited by Ammianus Marcellinus (4th century). Kendrick, 84. Chadwick, *op.cit.,* 18 note.
17. *De Divinatione,* I, XLI, 90. Kendrick, 80.
18. *Histories* IV, 54. Kendrick, 93.
19. Orations XLIX. Kendrick, *ibid.*
20. *De Bello Gallico* VI, 13. Kendrick, 78.
21. *Geographia,* IV, 4, Kendrick, 83.
22. *Histories,* V, 31. Kendrick, 82.
23. XV. 9. 8. Kendrick, 84.
24. *op.cit.,* 133. Chadwick, *op.cit.,* 18–19, 27, holds much the same view.
25. *Natural History,* XVI, 249. Kendrick, 89.
26. *ibid.,* XXIV, 103, 104. Kendrick, 89.
27. *ibid.,* XXIX, 52. Kendrick, 90.
28. *Philosophumena,* I, 92. Chadwick, *op.cit.,* 47 note K.
29. *De Bello Gallico* VI, 14. Kendrick, 78.
30. *De Situ Orbis* III, 2, 18, 19. Kendrick, 87.
31. *De Bello Gallico,* VI, 14. Kendrick, 78.
32. *Geographia,* IV, 4. Kendrick, 83.
33. *De situ Orbis* III, 2, 18 and 19. Kendrick, 87.
34. *Histories,* V, 28, 6. Kendrick, 82.
35. *Pharsalia* I, 450–8. Kendrick, 88.
36. Chadwick, *op.cit.,* 45.
37. *De Bello Gallico* VI, 14. Kendrick, 78.
38. O'Curry, *op.cit.,* 225.
39. O'Curry, *op.cit.,* 203–8. Joyce, *op.cit.,* 224–25.
40. O'Curry, *op.cit.,* 213–14.
41. O'Curry, *op.cit.,* 215–16.
42. Joyce, *op.cit.,* 229. O'Curry, *Manuscript Materials,* 285.
43. Joyce, *op.cit.,* 230, 232–33.
44. Ed. Stokes, *Lives of Saints from the Book of Lismore,* 265.
45. *Ibid.,* 183–6.
46. E.g. Healy, *Ireland's Ancient Schools and Scholars,* 1. Curtis, *A History of Ireland,* 2.
47. Hyde, *A Literary History of Ireland,* 83.
48. Joyce, *op.cit.,* 240.
49. O'Curry, *op.cit.,* 227.
50. MacNeill, *Early Irish Laws and Institutions,* 72.
51. *Op.cit.,* I, 222.
52. Hyde, *op.cit.,* 82.
53. Healy, *op.cit.,* 1.
54. MacNeill, *op.cit.,* 82, cf. also 72–76.
55. *Manners and Customs of the Ancient Irish,* 183.
56. O'Curry, *op.cit.,* 201.
57. Hyde, *op.cit.,* 92.
58. Ed. O'Rahilly, *Táin Bó Cualnge from the Book of Leinster,* 163–164. O'Curry, *op.cit.,* 200–01.
59. Ed. Stokes, *The Tripartite Life of St. Patrick,* 93, 99, 103, 105. O'Curry, *op.cit.,* 201–2.
60. ed. Stokes, *Lives of Saints from the Book of Lismore,* 178. Hyde, *op.cit.,* 91–92 points out that though the seer is entitled *'faidh',* a prophet, in the Lismore text, the whole proceeding suggests that he was a druid. O'Curry, *Manners and Customs of the Ancient Irish* refers to the Life in the *Leabhar Breac,* in which it is the saint's mother who seeks advice, and the druid actually becomes the boy's tutor.

CHAPTER 3
PRE-CHRISTIAN WRITING

1. Joyce, *A Social History of Ancient Ireland*, I, 239.
2. Hyde, *A Literary History of Ireland*, 105–107.
3. Hyde, *op.cit.*, 107. Ed. Stokes, *The Tripartite Life of St. Patrick*, 57. The same incident is related in the Memoir of St. Patrick by Muirchu Maccu Mactheni, Ed. Stokes, *op.cit.*, 284. Kendrick, *The Druids*, 119, regards this incident as 'a rather dubious hint'.
4. Ed. Stokes, *op.cit.*, II Appendix 562–5.
5. *Ancient Laws of Ireland*, I, 15, 17.
6. O'Curry, *Manuscript Materials of Ancient Irish History*, 463, 472.
7. *Ibid.*, 472.
8. *A Social History of Ancient Ireland* I, 396.
9. *Ibid.*, 397–98.
10. *Ibid.*, 401–03.
11. Joyce, *op.cit.* 403 quotes from a summary of this work made by a priest named Jerome, and published at Leipzig by Wuttke in 1854, p.14.
12. *Op.cit.*, 407.
13. Ed. George Atkinson. Brash, *The Ogham Inscribed Monuments of the Gaedhil in the British Islands*, 12.
14. Healy, *Ireland's Ancient Schools and Scholars*, 4.
15. Bury, *The Life of St. Patrick*, 184–86.
16. Curtis, *A History of Ireland*, 7.
17. Flower, *The Irish Tradition*, 73.
18. Ed. Moody and Martin, *The Course of Irish History*, 61.
19. A few authorities add q. The use of a sign for q does not, however, constitute evidence of Latin origin. The signs for c and q(u) are distinguished in Ogam because they represented different sounds in Goidelic, though these had united in the sign written C by the Old Irish period.
20. Ed. Calder, *Auraicept na n-Éces, The Scholar's Primer*, being the texts of the Ogham Tract from the *Book of Ballymote* and the *Yellow Book of Lecan*, and the text of the *Trefhocal* from the *Book of Leinster*. On the *Auraicept* see p. 85sq. The title *Trefhocal* is thus explained by Calder (xlviii). 'The whole scheme of correct versification would have been comprised under a set of mnemonics, each mnemonic consists of three hears, the name of the fault and the name of its two correctives. Hence a three-word scheme'.
21. Joyce, *op.cit.*, I, 398–99. Hyde, *op.cit.*, 107–21, de Paor, *Early Christian Ireland*, 61–62, Dillon and Chadwick, *The Celtic Realms*, 207–08. On Ogam in general, O'Donovan, *Grammar of the Irish Language*, Introduction xxvii-liv, MacNeill, *Phases of Irish History*, 170–74, Greene, *The Irish Language*, 8–10.
22. Joyce, *op.cit.*, 398, Brash, *op.cit.*, 5, Dillon and Chadwick, *op.cit.*, 207. ed. Calder, *Auraicept na n-Éces*, 273.
24. Hyde, *op. cit.*, 113–16.
25. MacNeill, *op.cit.*, 170–71.
26. *The Celtic Realms*, 207. (Dr. Chadwick, joint author of this book, discusses Ogmios on p. 141).
27. Joyce, *op.cit.*, 398. Hyde, *op.cit.*, 109. De Paor, *op.cit.*, 61.
28. Ferguson, *Ogham Inscriptions in Ireland, Wales and Scotland*. Brash, *op.cit.*, Graves, 'On an Ogam Monument recently found in County Kerry', *Proceedings* Royal Irish Academy, III, 374–79.
29. cf. also Macalister, *The Archaeology of Ireland*, Ch. IV.
30. Hyde, *op.cit.*, 109. On p. 120 he cites without comment the unusual view of Graves that Ogam belongs to a period as late as between the 5th and 7th centuries, A.D.
31. Hyde, *op.cit.*, 110, 'as late as 600'. De Paor, *op.cit.*, 61, 'until the 7th century'.
32. De Paor, *op.cit.*, 62.
33. O'Grady, *Silva Gadelica* 174–175 (text from *Book of Lismore* and translation). Also cited Brash, *op.cit.*, 31. Stokes, *Irische Texte, Vierte Serie*, 1 *Heft.* (1900), text from Mss. in Bodleian Library and Franciscan Library,

Dublin, and parts of Lismore text omitted by O'Grady, with English translation.

34. Joyce, *op.cit.*, I, 397. The story in which this passage appears is found in full in the Appendix to *The Voyage of Bran*, ed. Meyer and Nutt, 48–52.

35. O'Curry, *Manuscript Materials of Ancient Irish History*, 464–70. Hyde, *op.cit.*, 110–11.

36. Ed. O'Rahilly, *Táin Bó Cualnge*, from the *Book of Leinster*, 154–55.

37. O'Curry, *op. cit.*, 468–69. This story is found in Ms. H. 2.16. T.C.D.

38. O'Curry, *op.cit.*, 469, cites *Book of Leinster* fol. 206. Hyde, *op.cit.*, 111–112.

39. O'Curry, *op.cit.*, 468. Hyde, *op.cit.*, 110 (the translation is his). Ed. Stokes, *Three Irish Glossaries*, 21 (the entire Irish text).

40. O'Curry, *op.cit.*, 464–6, 470–71.

41. *Ibid.*, 472.

42. Hyde, *op.cit.*, 117.

43. Ibid., 116. O'Grady, *op.cit.*, 101 (Irish text) 108 (translation).

44. *Op.cit.*, 111.

45. Ed. Meyer and Nutt, *The Voyage of Bran*, I, xvi, 6, 34.

46. Ed. Moody and Martin, *The Course of Irish History*, 61.

47. Hyde, *op.cit.*, 121.

48. Dillon and Chadwick, *op.cit.*, 207.

49. Greene, *op.cit.*, 9.

50. Cited Calder, *op.cit.*, Introd., 50.

51. Binchy, 'The Background of Early Irish Literature', *Studia Hibernica*, I, 8.

52. O'Rahilly, *Early Irish History and Mythology*, 495.

53. Hyde, *op.cit.*, 121.

54. Macalister, *Studies in Irish Epigraphy*, I, 3.

55. MacNeill, *Early Irish Laws and Institutions*, 80–81.

CHAPTER 4
EVOLUTION OF LEARNED ORDERS

1. Hyde, *A Literary History of Ireland*, 562, Ch. XLII *passim*. Curtis, *A History of Ireland*, 222–3, 233.

2. As a result of a Government Commission in 1852, a large number of these law treatises were published in six volumes (one a glossary), in the Rolls series, the translation being the work of John O'Donovan and Eugene O'Curry. This edition, though held by experts to be in many ways defective, was a notable achievement, and is still the only one available.

3. Hyde, *op. cit.*, 586.

4. *Zeitschrift für Celtische Philologie* 16, 186.

5. *Ancient Laws* I, 19.

6. Bergin, 'Bardic Poetry', *Journal of the Ivernian Society*, V, 155–66, 203–16. Reprinted 1970 in *Irish Bardic Poetry*, Texts and Translations, together with an introductory lecture, by Osborn Bergin, foreword by D. A. Binchy, compiled and edited by David Greene and Fergus Kelly, 3–22.

Another notable article, published in the same year (1913), is Quiggin, 'Prolegomena to the study of the later Irish Bards', *Proceedings of the British Academy*, Vol. V. It contains an interesting comparison between Irish bardic poetry and that of Scandinavia and Wales.

7. Carney, 'Society and the Bardic Poet', *Studies*, 1973, 233–50.

8. *Ancient Laws of Ireland*, IV, 361.

9. Ed. Murphy, *Annals of Clonmacnoise*, 1315.

10. Ed. O'Donovan, *Annals of the Four Masters*, ed. MacCarthy *Annals of Ulster*, ed. Freeman, *Annals of Connacht*, ed. Hennessy, *Annals of Loch Cé*, ed. Murphy, *Annals of Clonmacnoise*.

11. Ed. O'Donovan, *The Tribes and Customs of Hy Many from the Book of Lecan and the genealogical MSS. of Dubhaltaigh Mac Firbisigh*, 104.

12. *Proceedings of the Royal Irish Academy*, VI, 51–54, text and translation of part of the poem by O'Curry. *Ériu V* 50–67, poem in full with notes and translations (from which quotations in text are taken) by Eleanor Knott.

13. *Annals of the Four Masters.*
14. Mac Neill, *Phases of Irish History*, 319–20.
15. O'Grady, *Silva Gadelica*, I, 255, II, 288.
16. Mac Neill, *op. cit.*, 317–18.
17. Healy, *Ireland's Ancient Schools and Scholars*, 6.
18. O'Curry, *Manners and Customs of the Ancient Irish*, II, 227.
19. MacNeill, 'Ancient Irish Law. The Law of Franchise'. *Proceedings of the Royal Irish Academy*, 1923, p. 268.
20. Hyde, *op. cit.*, 239.
21. *ibid*, 88.
22. Dillon. *Early Irish Literature*, xvi.
23. Ed. Moody and Martin. *The Course of Irish History*, 60.
24. Kenney, *Sources for the Early History of Ireland*, 13. Cf. also Ware, *Writers of Ireland* (1745 ed.), Chs. I to IV (up to A.D. 700), O'Reilly, *Irish Writers* (names in chronological order), O'Curry, *Manuscript Materials of Irish History*, (Chapters deal not with periods, but with various styles of writings; (references to particular *filid* can be assembled by means of the copious index), *On The Manners and Customs of the Ancient Irish*, II, Chs. I–V, Hyde, *op. cit.* Ch. XIX, Best, *Bibliography of Irish Philology and Literature*, I and II, Hull, *A Text Book of Irish Literature* (has a useful chronology), De Blacam, *A First Book of Irish Literature* (another useful outline). The same author's *Gaelic Literature Surveyed*, recently republished, gives an interesting survey, but few source references.

The work entitled *De Hibernia et Antiquitatibus ejus Disputationes* by Sir James Ware, was first published in London in 1654. An imperfect English translation was published in Dublin in 1705, the work of Ware's son, Robert and other writers. A fresh translation by Walter Harris (whose wife was a granddaughter of Ware) published in Dublin in three volumes entitled *The Whole Works of Sir J. Ware concerning Ireland*, Vol. I (Bishops of Ireland) 1739, Vol. II (Antiquities of Ireland) 1745, Vol. III (Writers of Ireland) 1746. Harris made many corrections and additions. The work will be entitled throughout 'Ware', but, unless intimated to the contrary, the references will be to Harris's edition of 1739–46.

25. Ed. Macalister, *Lebor Gabála Érenn*, V, 33, 111–15.
26. Hyde, *op. cit.*, 240.
27. Ed. Macalister, *op. cit.*, V. 455.
28. The poem in praise of Ollam Fodhla, of which we have cited the first verse, is attributed to Ferceirtne in *Lebor Gabála*, ed. Macalister, V, 241, 455–59. Cf. Best. *op. cit.*, I, 183, and II, No. 1476.
29. Ed. Stokes, *Immacallam In Da Thuarad. The Colloquy of the Two Sages.* Revue Celtique XXVI, 51. Cf. O'Curry, *Manuscript Materials of Ancient Irish History*, 383–85. *Manners and Customs of the Ancient Irish*, II 20, III 315. Hyde, *op. cit.*, 240.
30. Best, *op. cit.* II, Nos. 140, 1495, 1556, 1560, 1803. Most of these are edited by Meyer with German translations, but two with English translations and a good note on Torna are to be found in McKenna, *Iomarbhágh na bhFile, Contention of the Bards*, Irish Texts Society, XX, 2–11.
31. O'Curry, *Manuscript Materials of Ancient Irish History*, 482–94.
32. Ed. O'Donovan, 235–7, Ed. Dillon, 120–21.
33. Ed. O'Donovan, *Ancient Laws*, I, 10–15.
34. Best, *op. cit.* I, 135, 147, 241. *Amra Senáin*, ed. Whitley Stokes, *Zeitscbrift für Celtische Philologie*, III, 220–25.
35. Connellan, *Imtheacht na Tromdáimhe* or the *Proceedings of the Great Bardic Institution* (English translation). Transactions of the Ossianic Society 5, 1–129. Cf. also Hyde, *op. cit.* 263–66, Hull *op. cit.*, 4. De Blacam, *Gaelic Literature Surveyed.* 29–31.
36. Hardiman, *Irish Ministrelry* II, 192–3, Seanchán's Lament over the dead body of Dallán, text and verse translation. Other poems, Best, *op. cit.* I, 184, II Nos. 1340, 1647. Ed. Macalister, *Lebor Gabála*, V, 293, 479–80.

37. *Annals of the Four Masters*, A.D. 499, 507, 527, 668. Ed. Macalister, *Lebor Gabála*, Part II, 73, 107–117.

38. O'Curry, *Manners and Customs of the Ancient Irish*, II, 50–52 and chapters III to VII.

39. *Op. cit.*, 12.

40. *Op. cit.*, 189.

41. *Op. cit.*, I, 419.

42. *Ancient Laws*, III, 83.

43. Ed. Meyer, *The Instructions of King Cormac mac Airt* (*Tecosca Cormaic*). Hyde, *op. cit.*, 246–50, gives long extracts from this work.

44. O'Curry. *Manuscript Materials of Ancient Irish History*, 9–10. Cites other references to *Saltair* in *Book of Ballymote* and *Yellow Book of Lecan*. Keating points out that this title *Saltair* was given to various historical works because, like the psalms, they were written in verse. Ed. Comyn, *Foras Feasa ar Érinn* I, 90–94. Irish Texts Society, Vol. IV. The title does not necessarily assign the work to the christian era, as it might have been added later than the date of composition.

45. *Ogygia or a Chronological Account of Irish Events* (Latin version 1685). Hely, English translation 1793, Vol. II, 239.

46. O'Donovan. *Annals of the Four Masters*, Vol. I, p. 116, note r.

47. These are fully dealt with in O'Curry, *op. cit.*, 301–10. Cf. also Hyde, *op. cit.*, 275–386, Hull, *A Text Book of Irish Literature*, 226–7. There is a fine study of the Fenian cycle in De Blacam, *Gaelic Literature Surveyed*, 226–7.

48. *Ancient Laws of Ireland*, II, 153, 155, 157, 161.

CHAPTER 5
TRAINING AND STATUS OF SCHOLARS

1. O'Curry, *Manners and Customs of the Ancient Irish* I, 49–50.

2. *Ancient Laws and Institutions of Ireland*, Vol. I, 45–47, Vol. IV, 355–61, Vol. V, 27–29.
Crith Gabhlach has been edited recently for students with vocabulary and notes by Professor Binchy. *Medieval and Modern Irish Series*, Vol. XI. I, 171–73.

3. I, 171–73.

4. Ed. Stokes and Windisch, *Irische Texte, Dritte Serie, I Heft*, 31–36, 115–120.

5. *A Social History of Ancient Ireland*, 422–36. Cf. also Hyde, *A Literary History of Ireland*, 487–88, Hull, *A Text Book of Irish Literature*, 189–93.

6. *Op. cit.*, 173.

7. Cf. ed. Stokes, *Three Irish Glossaries. Sanas Chormaic, Cormac's Glossary*, translated and edited by John O'Donovan, both under the word *Anair*, the name of a poetical composition. The version in the text is O'Curry's, differing slightly from that of O'Donovan.

8. *Ancient Laws*, V, 29.

9. ed. Stokes, *Anruth*, 5, 6; *Cana*, 34; *Cli*, 34; *Dos*, 53, 58: *Fochlocon*, 72; *Mac Fuirmid*, 107; *Ollam*, 127.

10. *Proceedings of the Royal Irish Academy*, VI, 51.

11. Ed. Dineen, *Foras Feasa ar Éirinn*, III, 79.

12. O'Curry, *Manuscript Materials of Ancient Irish History*, 462.

13. *Ancient Laws*, I, 42–43.

14. O'Donovan *Leabhar na gCeart*, 7, cf. also 237.

15. Dillon, *Lebor na Cert*, Irish Texts Society, XLVI, 121.

16. Ed. Meyer, *Sanas Cormaic, Anecdota from Irish Manuscripts* IV. 85–6.

17. Ed. Stokes. *Three Irish Glossaries*, 33.

18. Ed. Connellan, *Transactions Ossianic Society*, V, 15, 109, 111.

19. O'Curry, *Manners and Customs of the Ancient Irish*, II, 129. On the visitation' cf. also *Ancient Laws* IV, 355. O'Grady, *Silva Gadelica*, II, 419–21.

20. Flower, *Catalogue of Irish Manuscripts in the British Museum*. Vol. III, 13–17.

21. 1722 ed., clviii, clix, clx, clxiii, clxvii.

22. Trans. Osborn Bergin. 'Unpublished Irish Poems XXV', *Studies*, March, 1924. Reprinted, *Irish Bardic Poetry Texts and Translations by Osborn Bergin*, ed. Greene and Kelly, 147–50 (text), 280–2 (trans.).

23. The definitive work on Campion's History is Dr. A. F. Vossen's *Two Bokes of the Histories of Ireland compiled by Edmund Campion*, ed. from MS. Jones 6. Bodleian Library, Oxford (1968). Sir James Ware published Campion's History together with others in *Ancient Irish Histories* 1809. Two well-known biographies of Campion are those of R. Simpson, 1867 and Evelyn Waugh, 1935.

24. Vossen, *op. cit.*, p. 24. It has been noted that the estimate of twenty years for the courses is probably exaggerated. Joyce, *op. cit.*, 419.

25. Edward Gwynn. *The Metrical Dindshenchas*, Part III, 110–11.

26. Osborn Bergin, 'Unpublished Irish Poems', No. XX, *Studies*, June, 1920, 261–3. Reprinted, *Irish Bardic Poems*, ed. Greene and Kelly, 118–9. Cf. also Eleanor Knott, *Irish Classical Poetry*, 44–66.

27. Bergin, *op. cit., loc. cit.*, Greene and Kelly, *op. cit., loc. cit.*

28. Bergin. 'Bardic Poetry', *Journal of the Ivernian Society*. V. 1913, 160–61. Reprinted, ed. Green and Kelly, *op. cit.*, 159–60, (text), 286 (trans.).

29. This summary is based on that of de Blacam, *Gaelic Literature Surveyed* 9.

30. Flower, *The Irish Tradition*, 73.

31. *Ibid.*, 79–85.

32. *Ibid.*, 100.

33. P. 38.

34. A detailed study of these two treatises by Professor Eoin MacNeill is to be found in the *Proceedings of the Royal Irish Academy*, December 17th, 1923. 'Ancient Irish Law. The Law of Status or Franchise'.

35. *Ancient Laws* V. *Uraicecht Becc*, 109.

36. *Ibid*, 107.

37. MacNeill, *op. cit.*, 268.

38. *Ibid.* 276.

39. *Ancient Laws*, V. 25.

40. MacNeill, *op. cit.*, 274.

41. *Lóg enech*, in earlier, *eneclann* or *enechlann* in later writings, sometimes also *díre* (off-payment), which strictly meant a fine imposed over and above restitution. MacNeill, 270–71.

42. *loc. cit.*, 274.

43. *Seoit*. The standard *sét*, the chattel which is the normal unit of value in the laws, was a *samaisc*, a young cow before her first calf, reckoned at half the value of a milch cow. MacNeill, *ibid*.

44. *Ancient Laws*, V, 44, 69.

45. *Ancient Laws*, V, 101. MacNeill, *op. cit.*, 279.

46. *Ancient Laws*, V. 112. MacNeill, *op. cit.*, 281.

47. *Ibid.*

48. We pass over the remote ages in which medicine was regarded as identical with magic. Many well-known episodes are recorded in Joyce, *A Social History of Ancient Ireland*, 598–99, and O'Curry, *Manuscript Materials of Ancient Irish History*, 637–643.

49. *Ancient Laws*, III, 321, 347–9, 477, 533, 535. IV, 301. V, 147, 149, 487, 489. These prescriptions will be found in great detail in Joyce, *op. cit.*, 600–04.

50. Dian Cecht, 'tutelary god of medicine, Irish Aesculapius' (Dinneen, Irish Dictionary). In the *Senchus Mór* (*Ancient Laws* I, 9) we hear of 'the judgments of Dian Cecht, the physician, which, indeed were first of all'. In the *Lebor Gabála* it is related that Dian Cecht 'the leech' fitted Nuada Airgetlam, king of the *Tuatha De Danaan* with a silver arm. (Ed. Macalister IV, 115. Cf. also 123, 125, 159, 183).

51. Ed. D. A. Binchy. *Bretha Crólige, Ériu* XII, *Bretha Déin Checht, Ibid.*, XX. The former is followed by an erudite essay by Professor Binchy on the subject of *othrus*. Both articles have valuable introductions.

52. Binchy, *op. cit.*, 15, 19, 21, 23, 25, 37, 39, 41, 49, 51, 105, 112, 119.

53. Shaw, *Irish Medical Men and Philosophers*, 76, No. VI in *Seven Centuries of Irish Learning*, ed. Ó Cuív.

54. *Ériu*, Vol. XX, 1–66.

55. *Ancient Laws*, V, 15, 91–95.

56. *Nemeth*, later *nemed*, meant 'having free status'. There were two kinds of *nemeth*, free *nemeth* (*soírnemeth*) and subject *nemeth* (*doírnemeth*). The free *nemeth* persons were churchmen, rulers, *filid*, Féni. The subject *nemeth* persons were the practitioners of the arts and crafts, including medicine. They were so called because they served the free *nemeth* persons, but they themselves were *nemeth* persons. On this subject cf., MacNeill, *op. cit.*, 273–4.

57. Shaw, *op. cit.*, *ibid.*

58. Joyce, *op. cit.*, 597.

59. Joyce, *op. cit.*, 597, 602. He refers to an article in the Irish Census 1851, Part V. Table of Deaths, Vol. I, 22–23. This gives an interesting history of medicine in Ireland, but is not more explicit on the subject of medical pupils.

60. *Ancient Laws*, V, 95.

CHAPTER 6
THE CHRISTIAN SCHOLARS. PATRICK AND HIS SUCCESSORS

1. On this name cf. ed. Stokes, *The Tripartite Life of St. Patrick and other documents relating to that saint*, I, 17, II, 413, Bieler, *The Works of St. Patrick*, 3.

In 1943 the theory was propounded by Professor T. F. O'Rahilly that there were actually two apostles of Ireland bearing the same name. Discussion of this question is outside the scope of this work. What concerns us is the impact of Christianity on Irish culture, irrespective of the identity of those who imparted it. A bibliography of the controversy on the two St. Patricks and other aspects of the life and work of the saint, by Professor F. X. Martin, O.S.A., is to be found in *Saint Patrick*, by Professor Eoin MacNeill, edited by Professor John Ryan, S.J., 221–24. A very full discussion of the various views on this subject is in an article by Professor D. A. Binchy, 'Patrick and his Biographers', *Studia Hibernica*, No. 2, 1962, 7–173.

2. Healy, *Ireland's Ancient Schools and Scholars*, 43–50. Bury, *Life of St. Patrick*, 37–41, 48–54, 59. Ryan, *Irish Monasticism*, 60–66. MacNeill, (ed. Ryan), *op. cit.*, 60–61. Hughes, *The Church in Early Irish Society*, 33. ed. Moody and Martin, *The Course of Irish History*, 62.

3. Bieler, *The Works of St. Patrick*, 23, 24, 36, 41.

4. Bieler, *op. cit.*, 23.

5. *Ibid.* 15–16.

6. *Ancient Laws of Ireland, Rolls Series*, I, XXVII. O'Curry, *Manuscript Materials of Ancient Irish History*, 16–17.

7. *Ancient Laws of Ireland*, I, 17.

8. *Ibid.*

9. *Ancient Laws*, III, 27–29, V, 477–79. Cited Stopford Green, *History of the Irish State to 1014*, 107–111, with comments by MacNeill.

10. MacNeill, *op. cit.*, 101.

11. Stokes, *op. cit.*, II, 303.

12. This point is fully dealt with in MacNeill, *op. cit.*, 75–6, 99.

13. Healy, *Ireland's Ancient Schools and Scholars*, 62.

14. Stokes, *op. cit.*, 282–83.

15. *Ibid.*, 328. The Oingae can be identified with the Nanny river, near Duleek, Co. Meath. The Saele may have been a tributary of it. The various passages in Tírechán and Muirchu in which reference is made to *pueri Patricii* are noted in the index to *The Book of Armagh*, ed. J. Gwynn.

16. Ed. Stokes, *Lives of the Saints from the Book of Lismore*, 156. The same story appears in Tírechán's *Collections*. Ed. Stokes, *The Tripartite Life of St. Patrick and other documents*, II, 303. On Benen as successor of Patrick, cf. Bury, *Life of St. Patrick*, 206, 319, 332.

17. Stokes, *op. cit.*, I, 36–37.

18. MacNeill, *op. cit.*, 51–52.

19. Kenney, *Sources for the early History of Ireland*, 339–40, gives a full account of the editions of this poem.

20. ed. Stokes, *Tripartite Life,* II, 421.

21. *Ibid.,* 105.

22. *Ibid.,* 326.

23. *Ibid.,* 300.

24. *Ibid.,* 75.

25. Healy, *op. cit.,* 64. Joyce, *Social History of Ancient Ireland,* I, 383. Hyde, *A Literary History of Ireland,* 135. Occasionally the word is used in the usual sense. Ryan, *op. cit.,* 379.

26. Ed. Stokes, *Tripartite Life,* I, 189–91.

27. *Ibid.,* 191. Healy, *op. cit.,* 83–85. Ryan, *op. cit.,* 75, 86, 95.

28. Ryan, *op. cit.,* 77–81, gives details, taken mainly from Tírechán, and from other passages in the *Book of Armagh,* of some forty of these entrusted to bishops, ten to priests, and another half dozen of a somewhat monastic character. Bury, *op. cit.,* 127–148, 162, describes a number of these personal foundations of Patrick, mainly in the north and west of Ireland. MacNeill, *op. cit.* Ch. VII. *The Building of the Church,* Ch. XI, *Bishoprics in Western Ireland.*

29. Ryan, *op. cit.,* 88, gives various references from the early Patrician documents. Cf. also, Hughes, *The Church in Early Irish History,* 33.

30. Bury, *op. cit.,* 154.

31. Ed. Stokes, *op. cit.,* II, 290–91. *Book of Armagh,* ff. 2–8. *The Tripartite Life* has a more elaborate version, *op. cit.,* 229–231.

32. Duleek in Co. Meath is *Daimhliag Chianáin.* Petrie, *Of the Round Towers of Ireland* I, 139–56 gives a full account of the *daimhliag.* He also notes (150) that the Irish also used for a church the names *cill, tempull, regles, eclais,* all derived from Latin.

33. *Annals of the Four Masters.*

34. Petrie, *op. cit.,* 432–8, Reeves, *Life of St. Columba by Adamnán,* 224, note.

35. The case against St. Patrick's Armagh bishopric may be found in O'Rahilly, *The Two Patricks,* 37, 50–51, 67. (O'Rahilly, however, grants that Patrick was the founder of Armagh [67] and made it his headquarters [37], Professor J. Carney, *Studies in Irish Literature and History,* 391–98. For an assessment of the evidence cf. Professor T. O'Fiaich, 'St. Patrick and Armagh', *Irish Ecclesiastical Record,* 1958, LXXIX, 153–70.

36. A full discussion will be found in Hughes, *op. cit.,* Ch. 11, *Armagh's claims to Archiepiscopal Authority,* 111–120.

37. Healy, *op. cit.,* 114, 116–17.

38. Ed. Stevenson, *Gildas de Excidio Britanniae,* preceded by a Life of Gildas, XXIV–XXV. There is doubt about the identiry of Caradoc, but the text seems authentic. Cf. Ussher, *Britannicarum Ecclesiarum Antiquitates* (1639 ed.) 859.

39. The second two obituaries are from the *Annals of Ulster,* the others from the *Annals of the Four Masters.*

40. For the history of the *Book of Armagh,* see Kenney, *Sources for the Early History of Ireland,* 337–38, where it is said to be 'the most important historical document of Ireland prior to the twelfth century.' The entire text is to be found in *Liber Armachanus, The Book of Armagh,* edited by John Gwynn with an introduction and appendices, correctly described by Kenney as 'one of the monuments of contemporary Irish scholarship'.

CHAPTER 7

THE MONASTIC SCHOOLS

1. On this title see Gougaud, 'The Isle of Saints', *Studies* XIII, 363–80. The earliest written attribution of it is in the *Chronicon* of Marianus Scottus, who died at Mayence in 1082 or 1083, *'Hibernia, insula sanctorum, sanctis mirabilibus perplurimis sublimiter plena habetur'.* (Migne, *Patrologia Latina,* CLXXIV, 1220). The earliest non-Irish user of the title is the Cistercian, Jocelin of Furness, between 1180 and 1186 (*Vita Patricii,* Boll. *Acta Sanctorum,* Vol. VIII, March 17th, 572). The additional 'and scholars' seems to be of modern origin. Ware, *Antiquities of Ireland* II, p. 11 gives the title merely 'Island of Saints'.

2. There is some variety in these dates as given by various authors. Those in the text are taken from Butler's *Lives of the Saints*, revised by Thurston and Attwater (12 vols. 1925–38). They agree substantially with those given by older authors such as O'Hanlon (*Lives of the Irish Saints*) and Healy (*Ireland's Ancient Schools and Scholars*).

3. Ryan, *Irish Monasticism*, Section 2, Chs. III, V, Hughes, *The Church in Early Irish History*, Chs. 6, 7, 8, Curtis, *A History of Ireland*, 11–12, ed. Moody and Martin, *The Course of Irish History*, 64–8.

4. *Ancient Laws*, V, 411–413.

5. Cf p.

6. This topic is fully dealt with in the Introduction (vi) to the 1972 reprint of Ryan, *Irish Monasticism*, first published in 1931.

7. Plummer, *Vitae Sanctorum Hiberniae* II, 37.

8. *Ibid.*, I, 99. Stokes, *Lives of the Irish Saints from the Book of Lismore*, 247–49.

9. Plummer, *op. cit.*, I, 258–59.

10. *Ibid.*, 268–69.

11. Stokes, *op. cit.*, 282.

12. O'Grady, *Silva Gadelica* II, 20.

13. *Ibid.*, 15. cf. Ryan, *op. cit.*, 208–09 for several other instances of the reception of young children into monasteries. There was, indeed, in the rule of St. Columban, provision for this.

14. Stokes, *op. cit.*, 249.

15. Plummer, *Lives of the Irish Saints*, II, 46. Cf. Stokes, *op. cit.*, 249–50.

16. Plummer, *Vitae Sanctorum Hiberniae* II, 19.

17. Plummer, *Lives of Irish Saints*, II, 12–14.

18. ed. Krusch, *Ionae, Vitae Sancotum Columbani, Vedastis, Johannis*, Liber I, 3a, pp. 155–6.

19. Ryan, *op. cit.*, 372–5.

20. Ed. G. S. M. Walker, *Sancti Columbani Opera*, lxvi–lxxvii, 190. Before the publication of this scholarly work, the chief editions of the works of St. Columban were those of the prose and poetic epistles by W. Gundlach, in *Monumenta Germaniae Historica* Epistolae iii, and of the third and eleventh sermons by O. Seebass.

21. Reference will be made again later to this work. Published in 1857, it is still regarded as a classic (cf. Dillon and Chadwick, *The Celtic Realms*, 187). A new translation published in 1961 by A. O. and M. O. Anderson, is, in the opinion of Professor D. A. Binchy, 'a welcome supplement' to Reeves, but does not supersede it. (*Studia Hibernica*, No. 3, 1963, 193–5).

22. *op. cit.*, 103.

23. *op. cit.*, 216–19.

24. *op. cit.*, 410.

25. *Proceedings of the Royal Irish Academy*, May, 1892.

26. *Studies*, December, 1912. Esposito, son of Commendatore Esposito, well-known in Dublin musical circles, was an independent scholar. Several of his articles are listed in Best, *Bibliography of Irish Philology and Manuscript Literature*, II.

27. *Op. cit.*, 382. cf. also MacNeill, *Phases of Irish History*, 244.

28. *The Making of Ireland and its Undoing*, 247.

29. *History of the Irish State to 1014*, 165.

30. Plummer, *Vitae Sanctorum Hiberniae* I, 141.

31. Ryan, *op. cit., loc. cit.* The text is to be found in *Monumenta Germaniae Historica*, Ep. iii, 170. Stokes, *op. cit.*, 194. Hyde, *op. cit.*, 217.

32. Hyde, *op. cit.*, 292–93. Joyce, *op. cit.*, 410. Healy, *op. cit.*, 237–40(Stokes, *op. cit.*, 194. The text is given in Archbishop Ussher's *Veterum Epistolarum Hibernicarum Sylloge*, (1632) 24–35.

33. Stokes, *op. cit.*, 195. Hyde, *op. cit., loc. cit.*, Text in *Migne, P. L.*, t. *lxxx*, col. 328.

34. Esposito, *op. cit.*, 671. This author cites a number of fragmentary passages in other works.

35. Ryan, *op. cit., loc. cit.*, where detailed references are given.

36. *op. cit.*, 187.

37. Stokes, *op. cit.*, 197. MacNeill, *op. cit.*, 244. Stopford Green, *History of the Irish State to 1014*, 165.

38. *op. cit.*, 674.

39. Hyde, *op. cit.*, 106–07, Healy, *op. cit.*, 29–35. Dillon and Chadwick, *The Celtic Realms*, 231.

40. Kenny, *Sources for the Early History of Ireland*, 135.

41. Kenney, *op. cit.*, 553–69 gives a full account of the works of Sedulius and his circle. The same is given by Dillon and Chadwick, *op. cit.*, 192–5, together with an appreciation of his poetry. The poems have been published in Traube, *Monumenta Germaniae Historica*, Poetae Aevi Carolini, 151–237. Cf. also Stopford Green, *History of the Irish State to 1014*, 184–6, *Catholic Encyclopedia*, 1912 ed., *Sedulius Scotus*.

42. Kenney, *op. cit.*, 571.

43. Daniel-Rops, *The Church in the Middle Ages*, 465.

44. There has been controversy in the past concerning the nationality of Eriugena, but it has finally been settled in the monumental work of Dom M. Cappuyns, O.S.B., *Jean Scot Erigène,* cf. Nerney, 'Johannes Scottus Eriugena', *Studies,* September, 1935, 415–32.

45. Migne, *Patrologia Latina*, 115, 1012.

46. Healy, *op. cit.*, 576–88, Hyde, *op. cit.*, 218, Stokes, *op. cit.*, 199, Kenney, *op. cit.*, 578–82. Gougaud, *Gaelic Pioneers of Christianity*, 51. Text in Migne, *Patrologia Latina*, CXXIX, 739 and Ussher, *op. cit.*, (1665 ed.) 45.

47. *op. cit.*, 681.

48. *Ibid.*

49. Kenney, *op. cit.*, 589.

50. Stokes, *op. cit.*, 201, cites amongst others D'Arbois de Jubainville and Wetstein.

51. *O Roma Nobilis*, 354, cited Kenney, *op. cit.*, 572, who, however, seems to hold that the arguments for either view are evenly balanced.

52. Dillon and Chadwick, *op. cit.*, 195.

53. Zimmer, *Pelagius in Ireland. Texte und Untersuchungen zur patristischen Literatur*, 7 note.

CHAPTER 8
THE MONASTIC SCHOOLS (continued)

1. Dillon and Chadwick, *The Celtic Realms*, 132.

2. Hyde, *A Literary History of Ireland*, 267–8.

3. Ed. Stokes, *Three Irish Glossaries* (of which the first is the Irish text of Cormac's Glossary). *Sanas Chormaic* Cormac's Glossary, translated and edited by John O'Donovan. (This does not give the Irish text of the explanation). Meyer, *Sanas Cormaic,* Anecdota from Irish Manuscripts IV, On Cormac, see p. 129sq.

4. *Manuscript Materials of Irish History*, 19–20.

5. *Op. cit.* XII–XVIII.

6. *Op. cit.*, 420.

7. *A Text Book of Irish Literature*, I, 178.

8. *Sources for the Early History of Ireland*, 149.

9. *Op. cit.*, loc. cit.

10. *Ireland's Ancient Schools and Scholars*, 612.

11. Stokes later published another edition of O'Davoren's Glossary, with an English translation. *Archiv für Celtische Lexikographie*, II Band, 3 Heft. 1904.

12. Ed. Stokes, Henry Bradshaw Society, Vol. XXIV.

13. Reeves, *On the Céli-dé, commonly called Culdees*. Proceedings of the Royal Irish Academy, Vol. 24 (1864) 119–263. Kenney, *op. cit.*, 470.

14. Ed. with English translation and notes by Arthur W. K. Miller, *Revue Celtique,* Vol. IV, 349–428, Vol. V, 1–69.

15. Kenney, *op. cit.*, 674–81.

16. Ed. Calder, *Auraicept na n-Éces, The Scholar's Primer*. The forms

Uraicept, Eraicept, Uraicecht and *Eraicecht* are also found. Profuse information regarding the derivation of this title is to be found in a sixteenth-century tract from the hand of Donal O'Davoren, the Co. Clare jurist, or of one of his students. (Egerton 88). O'Grady, *Catalogue of Irish Mss. in the British Museum*, I, 102. Also in O'Grady's note *ibid.*

17. Calder, *op. cit.*, xxvii–xxxi. O'Curry, *Manners and Customs of the Ancient Irish*, 53–54, writing before Calder, places the *Auraicept* in the 9th century.
18. Bergin, 'The Native Irish Grammarian'. *Proceedings of the British Academy*, 1938, 4.
19. Calder, *op. cit.*, xxxi.
20. Kenney, *op. cit.*, 24. O'Curry, *Manuscript Materials of Ancient Irish History*, 188–92.
21. Ó Cuív, 'Linguistic Terminology in the Medieval Irish Bardic Tracts', *Transactions of the Philological Society*, 1965, pp. 158–9.
22. Bergin, *op. cit.*, 3, 4.
23. ed. Reeves, Adamnán, *The Life of St. Columba*, I, 25 p. 54; III, 23, p. 233; II, 8, p. 115–16, 9, p. 116–17, 44, p. 175. Cited Ryan, *Irish Monasticism*, 380, where many other references are given.
24. Plummer, *Vitae Sanctorum Hiberniae*, Vol. II, 13.
25. In the 10th century Cormac's Glossary the word *cairt*, derived from the Latin charta, is equiparated with *memrum* from the Latin *membrana*. 'Carta enim in qua nondum scribtor quisque scripsit iss e (ainm) do memrum'. In Irish christian documents both names signify parchment. Cf. ed. Meyer *Sanas Cormaic* (from *Yellow Book of Lecan*) p. 27, No. 31, ed. Stokes, *Sanas Cormaic* (from Ms. in R.I.A.), included in *Three Irish Glossaries*, 13.
26. O'Grady, *Silva Gadelica*, II, 23.
27. Ed. Reeves, *op. cit.*, 143.
28. Ed. Krusch, *Ionae Vitae Sanctorum Columbani, Vedastis, Johannis*, 5a, 237.
29. Reeves, *op. cit.* 358, cites *Vita Brendani* c. 17 (Cod. Marsh, fol. 58 b.a.).
30. Ibid. lviii. Reeves cites Mabillon, *Acta SS. Ord. Bened. saec. iii*, p. 456 (Venet. 1734).
31. Many examples of the use of these terms are to be found in Reeves *op. cit.* 358–359. Joyce, *A Social History of Ancient Ireland* 478–85 (gives a detailed account of the various tablets used by both monks and *filid*). Ryan, *op. cit.*, 292, 380.
32. Ed. Stokes, *Tripartite Life of St. Patrick*, I, 92, cliii (where *graif* is translated 'writing style').
33. Reeves, *op. cit.*, 205. Note.
34. Ed. Stokes, *Three Middle Irish Homilies* (from *Lebor Brecc*) *on the Lives of Saints Patrick, Brigit and Columba*, 121.
35. Ed. Stokes, *On the Calendar of Oengus*. Transactions of the Royal Irish Academy, Vol. I, Part i, cxli.
36. Reeves, *op. cit.*, 114–115. A detailed note is added on various types of satchel. cf. also Joyce, *op. cit.* 486–9.
37. Ed. Stokes, 97.
38. *Annals of the Four Masters*, 789 (recte 794). Colgu Ua Duineachda of Clonmacnois; *Annals of Ulster*, 878, Mochta of Armagh; *Annals of the Four Masters*, 894. Breasal of Armagh.
39. In the Index to the *Annals of Ulster* will be found a list of 65 scribes from 697 to 1098. Only six are found in the 10th century and two in the 11th. It is to be noted that the Latin form *scriba* is used throughout the Annals.
40. *Liber Armachanus*, xvi.
41. MacNeill, *Phases of Irish History*, 258.
42. *Annals of Ulster, Annals of the Four Masters*.
43. Kenney, *op. cit.*, 11.
44. *The Distribution of Irish Scriptoria and Centres of Learning from 730 to 1111*. Section V in *Studies in the Early British Church*, ed. Chadwick, 243 sqq.
45. Dr. Hughes cites Finglas 796, 812, 838, 867, Duleek 872, 907, 920, 929, 961 (p. 247).
46. *Op. cit.*, 265.

47. Plummer, 'On the colophons and marginalia of Irish scribes', *British Academy Proceedings*, XII, 11–44.

48. MacNeill, *op. cit.*, 285. *Annals of Ulster*, 1189 'Ard Macha was pillaged by John de Courcy and by the Foreigners of Ireland'. The *Annals of the Four Masters* add: 'Armagh was burned from St. Bridget's Crosses to St. Bridget's Church, including the Rath, the Trian and the churches'.

49. Reeves, *op. cit.*, 358.

50. Joyce, *A Social History of Ancient Ireland*, I, 485.

51. Ryan, *op. cit.*, 291.

52. Ed. Moody and Martin, *The Course of Irish History*, 108.

53. *The Church in Early Irish History*, 154.

54. *The Distribution of Irish Scriptoria and Centres of Learning from* 730 to 1111. Section V in *Studies in the early British Church*, ed. Chadwick, 243 sqq.

55. *Op. cit.*, 359. Note M.

56. *Op. cit.*, 243, *Acta Sanctorum ex Codice Salmanticensi*, ed. de Smedt and De Backer, vol. 894.

57. *Ibid*, cf. Ed. Stokes, *Féilire Oengusso Céli Dé*, 203–05.

58. O'Grady, *Silva Gadelica*, 480, 527. O'Grady's translation of *etir scolaib screptra* is 'among the library-provided schools'.

59. *Catalogue of Irish Manuscripts in the British Museum*, I, 280. (Egerton 159).

60. Dillon, *Early Irish Literature*, xvi–xix.

61. O'Curry, *Manuscript Materials of Irish History*, 20–23.

62. *Foras Feasa ar Éirinn. The History of Ireland*. Book II, Irish Texts Society, Vol. IX, ed. Dinneen, 87–89.

63. *Annals of the Four Masters*, A.D. 555.

64. An ancient copy of the psalms, believed to be that made by Colum Cille, was for centuries an heirloom of the O'Donnells, his descendants. It was carried by them into battle and hence known as the *Cathach* ('Battler'). A large portion of this manuscript is preserved in the library of the Royal Irish Academy. It is undoubtedly a copy of St. Jerome's second edition of the Vulgate, and scholars hold that the writing assigns it to before the seventh century. Hyde, *op. cit.* 1975–76. *The Course of Irish History*, 71.

65. Healy, *op. cit.*, 310–16, Hyde, *op. cit.*, 175–7, Stopford Green, *History of the Irish State* to 1014, 137–8, Curtis, *History of Ireland*, 13, ed. Moody and Martin, *The Course of Irish History*, 71.

66. Ed. Reeves, *The Life of St. Columba by Adamnán*, lxxiv–lxxv, 9.

67. Lanigan, *An Ecclesiastical History of Ireland*, I, 144, 148–9.

68. *Ancient Laws of Ireland*, IV, Sequel to *Crith Gabhlach*, 355–57, Joyce, *op. cit.*, (whose order is followed), I, 430–34.

69. See p. 59-60.

70. 494–95. cf. O'Curry, *Manners and Customs of the Ancient Irish*, 84. Joyce, *op. cit.*, I, 435–36. The Ms. of this glossary is in the library of Trinity College, Dublin.

71. This obscure term is translated by O'Curry (*Manuscript Materials*, 495) 'books of science', and (*Manners and Customs*, 84) 'native education'. It evidently designated some recognized branch of learning.

72. So called because the scholar in this grade had 'climbed up the pillar or tree of learning to its very ridge or top'. O'Curry, *Manuscript Materials of Ancient Ireland*, 9, Note (8).

73. One of the 'lost books' of Ancient Ireland. O'Curry, *op. cit.* 29–32.

74. According to O'Curry, the Ten Words, i.e., The Ten Commandments was a name given to the Pentateuch, *loc. cit.*

75. *Manners and Customs of the Ancient Irish*, 84.

76. *Manuscript Materials of Ancient Irish History*, 29–32.

77. Ed. O'Donovan, in Reeves, 'On the Céli-dé, commonly called Culdees', *Royal Irish Academy Transactions*, XXIV. Kenny, *Sources for the Early History of Ireland*, 472–73. Other versions, O'Keefe, 'The Rule of Patrick', *Eriu* I, 216–24, Stokes, *Lives of the Saints from the Book of Lismore*, 133 (fragments), 359 (note), E. Gwynn, *Hermathena* XLIV, Second Supplementasy Volume, 78–82, gives a new translation of the text from the *Lebor Brecc*.

78. Ed. O'Donovan, *op. cit.*, 213.

79. Colgan, *Triadis Thaumaturgae seu Divorum Patricii, Columbae et Brigidae...Acta*, 522 (*recte* 519). Cf. Lanigan, *An Ecclesiastical History*, I, 385.

80. *Texts and Translations together with an introductory lecture by Osborn Bergin*, with a foreword by D. A. Binchy, compiled and edited by David Greene and Fergus Kelly, 204–15 (text), 308–315 (trans), 202–3, history of Gormlaith.

CHAPTER 9
THE MONASTIC SCHOOLS (continued)

1. *Manners and Customs of the Ancient Irish*, 83–4.

2. Joyce, *A Social History of Ireland*, I, 409–10, 417.

3. Hull, *A Text Book of Irish Literature*, I, 189.

4. Hyde, *A Literary History of Ireland*, 215.

5. O'Curry, *op. cit.*, 83–84.

6. Gwynn and Hadcock, *Medieval Religious Houses, Ireland*, 27–44, 372–409.

7. Archdall, *Monasticon Hibernicum*, I, 222, 435, Petrie, *Of the Round Towers of Ireland*, 422, ed. Moody and Martin, *The Course of Irish History*, 72.

8. Ed. Krusch, *Ionae Vitae sanctorum Columbani, Vedastis, Johannis*, 183.

9. *Hermathena*, No. XLIV, *Second Supplementary Volume, The Rule of Tallaght*, ed. Edward Gwynn, 83–85. Cf. ed. Reeves, *Prose Rule of the Céli Dé*, *Royal Irish Academy Transactions*, XXIV, 213.

10. Hughes, *The Church in Early Irish History*, 154. Cf. also the same author's contribution to *The Course of Irish History*, 79.

11. *Monumenta Germaniae Historica. Auctorum Antiquissimorum Tomus*, XV. Ed. Ehwald, *Aldhelmi Opera*. Epistle 5. P. 484, 492. *'Quo catervatim istinc lectitantes classibus advecti confluunt.'*

12. *Gesta Regum* Lib. I c. 3. Cited Lanigan, *Ecclesiastical History of Ireland*, III, 96.

13. The original is preserved in Trinity College, Dublin, (H. 2, 16). It has been printed and translated in various versions, cf. Reeves, *Life of St. Columba* by Adamnán, 185, note 1. Hyde, *op. cit.*, 220–21. The version given of the first strophe is that of Mangan, amended by Hyde.

14. Cf. *Annals of Inisfallen*, 705, Reeves, *loc. cit.*

15. Healy, *Ireland's Ancient Schools and Scholars*, 272–3, Joyce, *op. cit.*, 416, Hyde, *op. cit.*, 206.

16. 'Benedicto Magistro et Pio Patri Colcuo Alcuine humilis levita salutem'. Cited, Healy, *loc. cit.* Migne, *Patrologia Latina*, Vol. 100, pp. 142–3.

17. Bede, *Ecclesiastical History of England*, III, xxvii, trans. A. M. Sellar, 204–06.

18. *Ibid.* IV, iii, *trans.* 223.

19. *Ibid.* III, xiii, *trans.* 161.

20. *Ibid.* III, xxvii, trans. 203–04.

21. Petrie, *Of the Round Towers of Ireland*, 348–50. Cf. O'Curry, *Manners and Customs of the Ancient Irish*, III, 38. Joyce, *op. cit.*, I, 415.

22. *Annals of Ulster*, 1092.

23. Stokes, *Lives of the Saints from the Book of Lismore*, 209.

24. Though older authorities, such as O'Curry and Petrie, believed this Litany to be the work of the eighth-century anchorite and monk Oengus, it is generally held to belong to the tenth or eleventh century. (Kenney, *Sources for the early history of Ireland*, 728). The quotations are from the translation by Rev. B. McCarthy, *Irish Ecclesiastical Record*, 1867, 385–97, 468–77. The litany was also edited and translated by Plummer, Henry Bradshaw Society, Vol. LXII, *Irish Litanies*, xx, 61–75.

25. Archdall, *Monasticon Hibernicum*, 570–71, Lanigan, *The Ecclesiastical History of Ireland*, III, 100–02, Healy *op. cit.*, 590, Joyce, *op. cit.*, 413. Cogan, *History of the Diocese of Meath*, I, 61–62, Smith and Ware, *Dictionary of Christian Biography and Literature*, art, Dagobert II.

26. Mabillon, *Acta Sanctorum Ordinis Benedictini*, II, 427, Note.

27. *A General Chronological History of France*, by the Sieur de Mezeray, Historiographer of France, translated by John Bulteel (1683) 60, 66.

28. Bede, *op. cit.*, III, vii, *trans.* 148–50.
29. *Annals of the Four Masters*, 784 [recte 789].
30. Kenney, *op. cit.*, 523–6.
31. A recent edition is Ed. J. J. Tierney, with contributions by L. Bieler, *Dicuili de Mensura Orbis Terrae, Scriptores Latini Hiberniae*, pub. *Dublin Institute for Advanced Studies*, text, translation, valuable introduction and notes. On the life and works of Dicuil cf. Kenney, *op. cit.*, 545–48.
32. On the identity or non-identity of the various Dungals cf. Kenney, *op. cit.*, 538–42, Tierney, *op. cit.*, introduction 5–6.
33. Georges Cerbelaud-Salagnac and Bernard Guillemain, professor of the faculty of letters at Bordeaux, in *The Miracle of Ireland*, ed. Daniel-Rops, 46, 70. Cf. also ibid., 127–137, *The Contribution of Ireland to Medieval Christian Thought*, by René Aigrain.
34. Printed 1849 by Rev. Matthew Kelly, from Ms. preserved in Brussels, 14–16, 21–26, 36–45, 63–79.
35. *Les Chrétientés Celtiques* (*Christianity in Celtic Lands*), *Gaelic Pioneers of Christianity*.
36. Tommasini, *Irish Saints in Italy*, trans. J. F. Scanlan, 7.
37. *Ibid.*, 391.
38. *Zeitschrift für Vergleichende Sprachforschung* (containing Zimmer's *Keltische Studien*) 30, 256. Cited Henderson, *Bricriu's Feast*. Irish Texts Society, Vol. II, p. xix.

CHAPTER 10
FUSION OF CHRISTIAN AND NATIVE CULTURES

1. Ryan, *Irish Monasticism*, 377.
2. Kenney, *Sources for the Early History of Ireland*, 3.
3. MacNeill, 'A Pioneer of Nations', *Studies*, March, September, 1922, 446.
4. Ed. Moody and Martin, *The Course of Irish History*, 77.
5. *Op. cit.*, 60.
6. MacNeill, *Phases of Irish History*, 175. Hull, *A Text Book of Irish Literature*, I, 187. Flower, *The Irish Tradition*, 73.
7. Binchy, 'The Background of Early Irish Literature', *Studia Hibernica*, No. 1. 1961.
8. Mac Cana, *Celtic Mythology*, 134.
9. Ed. Ó Cuív, *Seven Centuries of Irish Learning*, 50. Cf. also Hughes, *The Golden Age of Early Christian Ireland*, in ed., Moody and Martin, *The Course of Irish History*, 78.
10. MacNeill, *St. Patrick*, 76.
11. See p. 144.
12. Kenney, *Sources for the Early History of Ireland*, 7.
13. Dillon, *Early Irish Literature*, 151–53.
14. Thurneysen, *Zur Irischen Accent- und Verslehre, Revue Celtique*, Tome VI, 326–47. Other writings of Thurneysen are cited by Dillon, *op. cit.*, 151. The same view is held by the late Professor Gerard Murphy, (*Early Irish Metrics*, 12, 25) and Dr. Eleanor Knott (*Irish Classical Poetry*, 25, in Knott and Murphy, *Early Irish Literature*).
15. Watkins, *Indo-European Metrics and Archaic Irish Verse, Celtica*, VI, 249. This view is cited with approval by Professor James Carney, *Medieval Irish Lyrics*, Introd. viii–x.
16. Ibid. 247. For Murphy, see note supra.
17. Ed. Moody and Martin, *The Course of Irish History*. O'Fiaich, *The Beginnings of Christianity*, 71–72.
18. Kenney, *op. cit.*, 9.
19. A full account of these Mss. will be found in an article by Professor F. J. Byrne, 'Seventh-Century Documents'. *Irish Ecclesiastical Record*, September, 1967, 164–82.
20. Ed. Murphy, *Ériu*, XVI (1952) 145–61.
21. Ed. Meyer, *Cáin Adamnáin, An Old Irish Treatise on the Law of Adamnán*.

From Mss. in the Bodleian Library and Bibliotheque Royale, Brussels. Thurneysen, *Studies in Early Irish Law*, VIII, 269, 76, Ryan. 'The Cáin Adomnáin'.

22. Kenney, *op. cit.*, 244. Byrne, *op. cit.*, 169.

23. Ed. Stokes and Strachan, *Thesaurus Palaeohibernicus*, II, text, 244–47; cf. also *ibid.* I, xxvi.

24. *Ancient Irish Laws*, III, 89. Cf. O'Curry, *Manuscript Materials of Ancient Irish History*, 48–49. Joyce, *op. cit.* 483, Healy, *op. cit.*, 602–03, Hyde, *op. cit.*, 412, MacNeill, *Early Irish Laws and Institutions*, 84–6.

25. MacNeill, 'A Pioneer of Nations, *Studies*', 1922, March and September.

26. MacNeill, *Early Irish Laws and Institutions*, 86.

27. Ed. Macalister, *Lebor Gabála*, Part II, 73, 106–117.

28. Petrie, *On the History and Antiquities of Tara*, Transactions, Royal Irish Academy, XVIII, 226.

29. *Annals of the Four Masters*, A.D. 499, 507, 527, 668. Ed. Hennessy, *Chronicum Scotorum* A.D. 497, 512, 530, 563. Best, *Bibliography of Irish Literature and Philology*, I, 141, 166, 178.

30. E.g. Dr. Kathleen Hughes, in *The Course of Irish History*, 77–78.

31. Flower, *The Irish Tradition*, 73–79, 116.

32. Two codices, one of the eleventh century (Trinity College, Dublin), the other a little later (Franciscan Library, Dublin). They contain largely identical matter, and are usually alluded to jointly as the Irish *Liber Hymnorum*. The prefaces to the hymns are in a mixture of Latin and Irish. Of the hymns, rather more than half are in Irish, the rest in Latin. Todd, in 1855 and 1869 published the first eighteen poems of the Trinity College Ms., but the complete poems, with notes and translations of the Irish texts, were published in 1898 by Bernard and Atkinson. Most of the Irish hymns were also published by Stokes and Strachan, *Thesaurus Palaeohibernicus*, II, 298–359. Cf. also Kenney, *op. cit.*, 716–18.

33. Ed. Reeves, *Vita Sancti Columbae*, 137.

34. Ed. Reeves, 17, 32, 37–39, 91–2, 436.

35. Ed. O'Kelleher and Schoepperle, 341–55.

36. Ed. Dinneen, Irish Texts Society, IX (Book 2 of Keating) 78–93.

37. Ed. O'Kelleher and Schoepperle, *op. cit.*, 341–43. Cf. ed. Dinneen, *op. cit.*, 93.

38. Ed. O'Kelleher and Schoepperle, *op. cit.*, 355.

39. Ed. Dinneen, *op. cit.*, 95.

40. Ed. Bernard and Atkinson, *Liber Hymnorum*, I, 162–83 (Text), II, 53–80 (Translation), 223–35 (Notes). Ed. Stokes, *The Bodleian Amra Choluimb Chille*, *Revue Celtique*, XX–XXI. Refs to retinues XX, 39, 45. Kenney, *op. cit.*, holds that Stokes's edition of the *Amra*, 'a composition of extraordinary obscurity', is 'the best but far from final'. Stokes (32) assigns the text of the *Amra* to the ninth century, but it is now generally accepted to be of the late sixth century. Cf. Byrne, 'Seventh-century Documents', *Irish Ecclesiastical Record*, September, 1967, 165, Dillon and Chadwick, *The Celtic Realms*, 183.

41. Ed. Stokes, *op. cit.*, XX, 41, 43. Ed. O'Kelleher and Schoepperle, *op. cit.*, 357.

42. A fully documented and critical account of this event is given in 'The Convention of Druim Ceat', by Professor John Ryan, S.J. *Journal of Royal Society of Antiquaries of Ireland*, April 1946. Whilst questioning some of the details, Professor Ryan accepts the historicity of the main details of the story. Cf. also Joyce, *op. cit.*, 456–7, Hyde, *op. cit.*, 489–90, Curtis, *A History of Ireland*, 13–14, MacNeill, *Phases of Irish History*, 176.

43. Kenney, *op. cit.*, 255–8. The most recent and authoritative edition of the text is that of Herren, M. W. (1974). In both these works will be found full bibliographies and discussions of the theories put forward by earlier scholars on the origin and purpose of *Hisperica Famina*. The most valuable recent article is that of Grosjean, P. *Celtica*, III, 35–85. *Confusio Caliga. Remarques sur les Hisperica Famina*.

44. Grosjean, *op. cit.*, 59–64.

CHAPTER 11
NORSE INTERLUDE

1. Kendrick, *A History of the Vikings*, i, v. Keary, *The Vikings in Western Christendom*, 140, 141, 153.

2. Ed. Hennessy, *Chronicum Scotorum*, 141.

3. In addition to the works of Kendrick (274–79) and Keary (72–85) already cited, the following have been drawn on for the foregoing historical survey: Curtis, *A History of Ireland*, 22–30, MacNeill, *Phases of Irish History*, 249–73, De Paor, *The Age of the Viking Wars*, in ed. Moody and Martin, *The Course of Irish History*, 91–106, Ó Corráin, *Ireland Before the Normans*, 80–113.

4. Ed. Todd, *Cogadh Gaedhel re Gallaibh. The War of the Gaedhil with the Gaill.*

5. Todd, *op. cit.*, 9.

6. *Ibid.* 13.

7. Stokes and Strachan, *Thesaurus Palaeohibernicus*, II, 290.

8. Todd, *op. cit.*, 39, cf. also 41, 139.

9. *Ibid.*, 79.

10. Ed. Moody and Martin, *op. cit.*, 96–7. Kendrick, *op. cit.*, 23.

11. *Annals of the Four Masters.*

12. *Ibid.*

13. *Annals of Ulster.*

14. *Annals of the Four Masters.*

15. *Ibid.*

16. *Annals of Ulster.*

17. *Annals of the Four Masters.*

18. *Ibid.*

19. *The Church in Early Irish History*, 207–08. See also the same author's *The Distribution of Irish Scriptoria and Centres of Learning from 730 to 1111*, section V in *Studies in the early British Church*, ed. Chadwick, 250.

20. Olden, 'On the Geography of Ros Ailithir', *Proceedings of the Royal Irish Academy*, 1884, 219–49, commentary, text and translation. Healy, *op. cit.*, 493–5. This poem together with *Saltair na Rann* (to be considered presently), has recently been dealt with in detail by G. Fahy, 'Geography in the Early Irish Monastic Schools', *Geographical Viewpoint*, Vol. 3, 1974, 31–43.

21. Olden rejects this identity because of the different titles given to Mac Coise in the two annals, *fer léiginn* and *airchinnech*. But there is no reason why the two offices should not have been held, at least successively, by the same man. The title *airchinnech* (anglicized erenagh), 'head', 'superior', is sometimes given to the lay administrator of church lands, but in post-Viking times is commonly applied to the head of a lesser monastic church, and is equivalent to the Latin *abbas*. Cf. MacNeill, *op. cit.*, 351–2, Kenney, *Sources for the Early History of Ireland*, 12, Barry, 'Erenagh in the Monastic Irish Church', *Irish Ecclesiastical Record*, LXXXIX, 424–32, Hughes, *The Church in Early Irish History*, 223, Ryan, *Clonmacnois*, 19–20.

22. Ed. Stokes, *The Tripartite Life of St. Patrick*, mainly based on Rawlinson B. 25, British Museum. Cf. O'Curry, *Manuscript Materials of Ancient Irish History*, 345–50. Kenney, *op. cit.*, 342–5, Mulchrone, *Betha Phátraic*, I, Text and Sources, (II, Translation, not published).

23. Ed. Stokes, *Saltair na Rann, A Collection of early Irish Poems*, O'Curry, *Manuscript Materials of Ancient Irish History*, 21, 360–61, Hyde, *A Literary History of Ireland*, 414–8, Hull, *A Text-book of Irish Literature*, 161–3, Hughes, *op. cit.*, 232–3, Fahy, *op. cit.*, 35–6.

24. Mac Eoin, 'The Date and Authorship of Saltair na Rann', *Zeitschrift für Celtische Philologie* XXVIII (1960–61), 51–67.

25. Kenney, *op. cit.*, 408–12, 414–17. Cf. by the same author, 'The Legend of St. Brendan' (*Transactions of the Royal Society of Canada* Sect. II, 51–71). Well-known texts of the *Navigatio* are those edited by Jubinal (*La Légende Latine de S. Brandaines*) and Schröder (*Sankt Brandan*) both with vernacular versions. The most recent is that edited by Selmer (University of Notre Dame, *Publications in Medieval Studies*, Vol. XVI), to which references are given.

26. Selmer, *op. cit.*, 6, 20–21, 33–35, 50, 55, 70, 73, 79, 81–82.

27. Dillon, *Early Irish Literature*, 124.

28. *Bede's Ecclesiastical History of England*. Book III, c. 19. Trans. A. M. Sellar, 173. On Vision of St. Fursa, cf. Stokes, *Life of Fursa, Revue Celtique* XXV, 385–401. O'Hanlon, *Lives of the Irish Saints* I, 222–286. Kenney, *op. cit.*, 500–503.

29. Stokes, *Adamnán's Vision*, transcribed and translated from the *Book of the Dun Cow, Lebor na hUidre*, line 284. Another translation is that of C. S. Boswell, *An Irish Precursor of Dante*, 28–47. Windisch, *Irische Texte, Erste Serie, Heft 1*, 165–196, from *Lebor Brecc* and *Lebor na hUidre*, text only. Cf. Dillon, *op. cit.*, 133–9, Hughes, *op. cit.*, 232.

30. Stokes, *op. cit.*, 3.

31. *Ibid.*, 4–5.

32. *Ibid.*, 10–11.

33. Ed. Stokes. *Tenga Bithnua, The Evernew Tongue* (from the Book of Lismore). *Ériu*, Vol. II, 1905, 96–162.

34. *Ibid.*, 143.

35. *Ibid.*, 145. On this vision cf. also Hughes, *op. cit.*, 231–2, Dillon, *op. cit.*, 139–43, *Celtica* 9, 1971, 1–59, (a translation by Una Nic Enri and Dr. G. Mac Niocaill, based on the recension preserved in the library of Trinity College, Dublin).

36. Ed. Moody and Martin, *The Course of Irish History*, 102.

37. Hughes, *op. cit.*, 230–32.

38. Ed. Stokes, *Three Irish Glossaries*, XI, cites a fragment in Burgundian Library, ed. O'Donovan, *Three Fragments*, 208.

39. O'Curry, *op. cit.*, 19. A detailed study of this Ms. (Laud Misc. 610) by Professor Myles Dillon appears in *Celtica* V, 64–76.

40. Hyde, *op. cit.*, 266. This poem was edited, with notes, by Cecile O'Rahilly in *Five Seventeenth-century Political Poems*. Line 163 (p. 42) runs: '*Saltair Chaisil is dearbh gur leir dham*.

41. There are two editions of this work, with a century between them, Ed. O'Donovan, *Leabhar na gCeart*, 1847, and Ed. Dillon, *Lebor na Cert, The Book of Rights*, 1962.

42. Ed. O'Donovan, x, 87. In the text is given the rendering of Dillon, 43. O'Donovan's is: 'He has the support of Mac Cuilennáin'.

43. Dillon, *Celtica* IV, 'On the Date and Authorship of the *Book of Rights*' (cites other authorities), *Lebor na Cert*, ix–x. But he admits the possibility that Cormac may have been the compiler of the rest of the *Saltair of Cashel, Celtica*, V, 66.

44. MacNeill, *Celtic Ireland*, 85–6.

45. *Op. cit.*, 419.

46. Ed. Macalister, *Lebor Gabála Érenn*, III, 27, 55–61, IV, 125, 183, 212–19.

47. O'Reilly, *Irish Writers*, LXVI.

48. Healy, *Ireland's Ancient Schools and Scholars*, 619–20.

49. Kenney, *op. cit.*, 605–13.

50. Curtis, *A History of Ireland*, 31. Cf. also Hyde, *op. cit.*, 443–44, Flower, *The Irish Tradition*, 88–93, Dillon, *Lebor na Cert*, xx.

51. Ed. Todd, 139.

52. Dillon, *op. cit.*, 19. Cf. also ed. O'Donovan, *Leabhar na gCeart*, xxiii–xxv, MacNeill, *op. cit.*, 73, 76, 84.

53. E. G .Hyde, *op. cit.*, 587.

54. Flower, *op. cit.*, 89.

55. Hyde, *op. cit.*, 432–43, cited from Hardiman, *Irish Minstrelsy*, ii, 202. It does not seem fanciful to detect in these lines a reference to the custom of the *filid* of composing in the dark.

56. Cited O'Curry, *op. cit.*, 219. The Irish text and a more modern translation of the passage cited will be found in Ó Raithbheartaigh, *Irish Manuscripts Commission, Genealogical Tracts* I, A. p. 8.

57. Flower, *op. cit.*, 89–90. Cf. de Blacam, *A First Book of Irish Literature*, 55.

While this book was going through the press, the important Viking discoveries were in progress at Wood Quay in Dublin. Until these have been completed and evaluated by experts, it would be premature to attempt to decide what further light they throw on the influence of Viking culture on that of Ireland.

CHAPTER 12
NORSE TO NORMAN

1. This Ms. has borne this title for over a hundred years, but it was originally known as *Leabhar na Nuachongbala, the Book of Noughaval* (a townland in the parish and barony of Stradbally, Laoighis). Cf. Best, Bergin and Ryan, *The Book of Leinster* Vol. I, introd. xi–xv.

2. Ed. Bernard and Atkinson, *The Irish Liber Hymnorum.* An earlier volume, ed. Todd, contains only a limited number of the hymns.

3. For further history of this tradition cf. O Curry, *Manuscript Materials of Ancient Irish History,* 30, Walsh, *Irish Men of Learning,* 133–4.

4. 'The page to which the foregoing note is appended contains the story of the progress of Tadhg, son of Cian, son of Oilill Olum, into Meath, or the battle of Crinna,. Todd, *Cogadh Gaedhel re Gallaibh. The War of the Gaedhil with the Gaill Introd.* X. The story is on pp. 1252–61 of *The Book of Leinster* ed. Best, Bergin and O'Brien, Vol. V.

5. Ed. with translation, Stokes. *Revue Celtique,* XVI–XVIII, 1895–97.

6. Kenney, *Sources for the Early History of Ireland,* 12. O'Curry, *op. cit.,* 19.

7. Hyde, *A Literary History of Ireland,* 445.

8. O'Curry, *Manners and Customs of the Ancient Irish* II, 157.

9. Curtis, *A History of Medieval Ireland,* 3–4, Gwynn and Gleeson, *History of the diocese of Killaloe,* 503. Kenney, *op. cit.,* 9.

10. Gwynn and Hadcock, *Medieval Religious Houses in Ireland,* 3.

11. Kenney, *op. cit.,* 763–4.

12. Ed. Mac Airt, *Annals of Inisfallen,* 269. Curtis, *A History of Medieval Ireland,* 5–6, Hughes, *The Church in Early Irish Society,* 257–58, 267 ff., ed. Moody and Martin, *The Course of Irish History,* 118–20.

13. A scholarly account of the life of St. Malachy will be found in three articles 'St. Malachy of Armagh', by Professor A. Gwynn, S.J., *Irish Ecclesiastical Record,* LXX, 1948, 961–78, LXXI, 1949, 134–48, 317–331.

14. Trans. H. J. Lawlor, *St. Bernard of Clairvaux's Life of St. Malachy of Armagh.*

15. Gwynn and Hadcock, *op. cit.,* 3–4, 121–44, 146–200.

16. An almost identical entry occurs in the *Annals of Ulster.* Cf. MacNeill, *Phases of Irish History,* 285. Curtis, *op. cit.,* 26.

17. *Annals of the Four Masters.* The entry in the *Annals of Ulster* is almost identical.

18. An almost identical obituary is found in the *Annals of Ulster.*

19. Haddan and Stubbs. *Councils and Ecclesiastical Documents relating to Great Britain and Ireland,* Vol. I, 298, 665.

20. Ed. Moody and Martin, *The Course of Irish History,* 108–11.

21. Bergin, 'The Native Irish Grammarian', *Proceedings of the British Academy* 1938, 5–6. Murphy, *Duanaire Finn* III, 190, *Eigse* VI, 353. Ó Cuív, 'Linguistic Terminology in the Medieval Irish Bardic Tracts', *Transactions of the Philological Society* 1965, 142. 'The Linguistic Training of the Medieval Irish Poet', *Celtica* X, 1971, 114–40.

22. Ó Cuív, *op. cit.,* 'Linguistic Terminology', *loc. cit.*

23. Bergin, *op. cit.,* 6.

24. Ó Cuív, *op. cit.,* (*Linguistic Training*), 117.

25. ed. Todd. *Leabhar Breathnach Annso Sis. The Irish Version* of the *Historia Britonum of Nennius,* Introduction, v–xiv. The evidence for Giolla Caoimhghin's authorship of the translation will be found on pp. xi, 21.

26. Flower, *op. cit,.* 94. A list of some forty of these families and their patrons will be found in Kenney, *op. cit.,* 20–21. Numerous examples of long succession are given in Stopford Green, *The Making of Ireland and its Undoing,* 313–4. Walsh, *Irish Men of Learning,* gives detailed accounts of the families of

Ó Duigenan (Ó Duibhgennáin), Ó Maelconaire, Mac Firbhisigh, Ó Cuirnín, Mac an Bhaird, and the physicians Mac an Leagha.

27. Kenney, *op. cit.*, 20.
28. Flower, *op. cit.*, 84–5, 88–90.
29. MacCana, 'The Rise of the Later Schools of Filidheacht', *Ériu,*Vol. 25, 126–46.
30. Ryan, *Irish Monasticism* (1972 *ed.*) introd. viii.
31. MacCana, *op. cit.*, 129, 131.
32. Ibid. 130, Gwynn and Gleeson, *op. cit.*, 323–4.
33. Many examples of the exercise of hospitality by both classes are given in MacCana, *op. cit.*, 131–32.
34. O'Curry, *Law Transcripts*. Trinity College, Dublin, Ms. H. 3.18.
35. MacCana, *op. cit.*, 136.
36. *Ibid.*, 137. The points emphasized are only the chief ones in Professor MacCana's essay concerned with the rise of the scholar families. He deals also with many other topics, such as the character of the later schools of *filidecht*, what they assimilated from the monastic scholars, and how far they preserved their own particular tradition.

CHAPTER 13
NORMAN IMPACT

1. This sobriquet appears to have been first bestowed on Richard's father, Gilbert. The earliest mention of it as applied to Richard is in a Tintern Abbey Charter, May 22, 1223. (Orpen, *Ireland under the Normans*, I, 88).
2. MacNeill, *Phases of Irish History*, XII, *The Irish Rally*, 125–26.
3. This often quoted description of the Anglo-Irish is of comparatively recent origin. The substance of it, though not the exact wording, is found in Spenser's *View of the Present State of Ireland*, 1596 (ed. Renwick, 1970, p. 63), 'The English that were are now much more lawless and licentious than the very wild Irish'. (cf. also 63, 66). Dr. Lynch evidently refers to these passages in *Cambrensis Eversus*, 1662 (ed. Kelly, 1851, p. 176). '*Et Spenserus vehementer queritur, Hibernos Anglicae originis majori quam puros putos Hibernos novorum Anglorum odio teneri*'. The earliest author known to use the exact form of the saying in English is Sylvester O'Halloran in *An Introduction to the Study of the History and Antiquities of Ireland*, 1772, p. 251, 'more Irish than the mere Irish'. The earliest to give the Latin form is Plowden in *An Historical Review of the State of Ireland*, 1803, Vol. I, p. 245. '*Ipsis Hybernis Hyberniores*'. (I am indebted for the foregoing information to Mr. Art Cosgrove).
4. Standard works on the Norman period are: Orpen, *Ireland under the Normans 1169 to 1333*, 4 vols. (recently republished), MacNeill, *op. cit.*, Chs. XI–XII (contains useful criticisms of some of Orpen's views), Curtis, *A History of Medieval Ireland* and *A History of Ireland* Chs. IV to X, both long recognized as reliable sources. Recent works are: Ed. Moody and Martin, *The Course of Irish History*, Chs. 8 and 9, *The Gill History of Ireland*, Vols. 3–6, Edwards, *A New History of Ireland*, pp. 55–63.
5. Professor F. X. Martin, in *The Course of Irish History*, 123, *The Anglo-Norman Invasion*.
6. For much of the matter and sources of the succeeding paragraphs I am indebted to a lengthy and erudite article by the late Professor Edmund Curtis, 'The Spoken Languages of Medieval Ireland, *Studies*, VIII, 234–54.
7. In the *Chain Book* of the city of Dublin, 14th century, the Regulations for city and citizens are in Latin, but there is a considerable section in French *'Les Leys et les usages de la cyte de Divilene'*. The oldest record of the Corporation of Kilkenny, 1350, is mainly in Latin, but contains acts in French concerning the election of city officials. Gilbert, *Facsimiles of the National Manuscripts of Ireland*, III, vii and Facsimile X, xv and Facsimile XLIII.
8. *Red Book of Ossory*. *Historical Manuscripts Commission*, 10th Report, Appendix, Part V, 244.
9. Gilbert, *op. cit.*, III, iii, iv (English translation by Letitia Elizabeth Landon). Appendix II, French text.

10. Gilbert, *op. cit.*, III, iii and Facsimile IV, iii and Facsimile V. Hoogland. *1000 Years of Irish Poetry*, 313.

11. *Historical Manuscripts Commission*, 10th Report, Appendix, Part V. Waterford, 265, 291, sqq., Galway, 380 sqq.

12. O'Flaherty, *Chorographical Description of West or Iar Connacht*, 203–4, 211–2, 228–9.

13. *Annals of Thady Dowling, Chancellor of Leighlin*, 1325. Ed. Gilbert. *Chartularies of St. Mary's Abbey, Dublin...and Annals of Ireland*, 1325.

14. Curtis, *op. cit.*, 243.

15. Gilbert, *History of the Viceroys of Ireland*, 64.

16. Mac Niocaill; *The Red Book of the Earls of Kildare. Historical Manuscripts Commission*, Appendix to Part II of 9th Report, 263.

17. *Histlrical Manuscripts Commission*, 9th Report, Appendix 264–5, Hore, *The Rental Book of Gerald Fitzgerald, ninth Earl of Kildare, Kilkenny Archaeological Society Journal*, 1858–9, 1862, 1866, O'Grady, *Catalogue of Irish Manuscripts in the British Museum*, I, 149–50.

18. *Discovery of the true causes why Ireland was never entirely subdued*, etc., by Sir John Davies, Attorney General under James the First. Cited Morley, *Ireland under Elizabeth and James the First*, 298.

19. *State Papers, Record Commission*, St. Leger to Henry, June 26th, Lord Deputy and Council to Henry, June 28th. Cited Wilson, *The Beginnings of Modern Ireland*, 247. Gilbert, *Facsimiles of the National Manuscripts of Ireland*, introd. xx, Facsimiles LXXI–LXXIII.

20. Ed. Sheehy, *Pontificia Hibernica, Medieval Papal Chancery Documents concerning Ireland* 640–1261, I, pp. 249–50, 253–5.

21. Holinshed, *Chronicles of England, Scotland and Ireland*, Vol. VI, Ireland (1808 ed.), *Description of Ireland by Richard Stanihurst*, 6.

22. The original Anglo-French text has been lost, but there are transcripts in the British Museum and Lambeth Palace Libraries. The text has been published with translation by Hardiman, *Tracts relating to Ireland*, Irish Archaeological Society, Vol. I, and by Berry, *Irish Statutes* Vol. I. The passage quoted is Hardiman's translation of the British Museum transcript (pp. 11–13).

23. Curtis, *A History of Ireland*, 152–3, Ed. Moody and Martin, *The Course of Irish History*, 168.

24. Holinshed, *Chronicles of England, Ireland and Scotland*, Vol. VI, Ireland (1808 ed.). *Description of Ireland*, by Richard Stanihurst, 6.

25. *Of the Commonwealth of Ireland*, in Hughes, ed., *Shakespeare's Europe, Unpublished Chapters of Fynes Moryson's Itinerary*, 213. Cf. also *ibid.*, 201–2, 214, for similar remarkable testimonies.

26. Orpen, *op. cit.*, II, 323–24. Gwynn and Hadcock, *Medieval Religious Houses, Ireland*, 131, 142–3, 182, 360. *The Course of Irish History*, 140.

27. Orpen, *op. cit.*, 20–22. Gwynn and Hadcock, *op. cit.* 117.

28. Gwynn and Hadcock, *op. cit.*, 117.

29. *Ibid.*, 5.

30. Gwynn and Hadcock, *op. cit.*, 7–9, 218–61, 282–305, ed. Moody and Martin, *The Course of Irish History*, 140–1. On the Franciscans, Fitzmaurice and Little, *Materials for the History of the Franciscan Province of Ireland*, 1230–1450.

31. Gwynn and Hadcock, *op. cit.*, 7–9.

32. Cf. *Annals of Connacht* and *Annals of Ulster* 1528.

33. First English ed. (1705), p. 96.

34. Canice Mooney, O.F.M. *The Friars and Friary of Donegal*, in *Franciscan Donegal*, ed. Terence O'Donnell, O.F.M. 3–26. Gwynn and Hadcock, *op. cit.*, 247.

CHAPTER 14
STUDIES IN MEDIEVAL MONASTERIES

1. Mandonnet, *Art. Preachers, Catholic Encyclopedia* (1908). XII, 360–2. Rashdall, *The Universities of Europe in the Middle Ages*, Vol. I, Ch. V, sec. 2, *The Mendicants and the University*, esp. pp. 345–8, 371–2, 392–3.

2. Healy, *History of Maynooth*, 10 sqq.

3. McInerney, *History of the Irish Dominicans*, 511, 513.

4. de Burgo, *Hibernia Dominicana*, 38, 42, 184–98.

5. Portion of this Register was published by de Burgo, *op. cit.*, 233 sqq. The whole text, with introduction, was published by Fr. Ambrose Coleman, O.P., *Archivium Hibernicum*, I. 201–21. Cf. also Gwynn and Hadcock, *Medieval Religious Houses*, Ireland, 221.

6. Coleman, *op. cit.*, 213.

7. *Ibid.*, 216.

8. *Ibid.*, 219.

9. Cf. Watt, *The Church and the Two Nations in Medieval Ireland, passim.*

10. Ware, *Irish Writers*, 75–6, De Burgo, *op. cit.*, 538–9, Orpen, (*ed.*) *The Song of Dermot and the Earl*, Introd., xviii–xxix.

11. Orpen (*ed.*) *op. cit.* This title was given to it by Orpen. The page of the ms. is missing on which a title (if any) would have appeared.

12. J. F. O'Doherty, 'Historical Criticism of the Song of Dermot and the Earl', *Irish Historical Studies*, I, 4–20.

13. Orpen, *op. cit.*, xix–xxiv and xxx.

14. Little, *op. cit.*, 143.

15. *Ibid.*, 148.

16. *Ibid.*, 156.

17. *Ibid.*, 192.

18. Ed. Gleeson, 'The Annals of Nenagh'. *Analecta Hibernica* XII, 157–64.

19. Mac Niocaill, *Na Manaigh Liatha in Éirinn. Nóta ar Gníomharacht Intleachtúil na Manach*, 217–22.

20. Mac Niocaill, *op. cit.*, 217–18. The references are to *Statuta Capitulorum Generalium Ordinis Cisterciensis* I–V, ed. J. M. Canivez, II, 289–90, III, 207, 392–3, 429–35.

21. *Ibid.*, 218. ed. Salter, *Registrum Cancellarii Oxoniensis*, 305 (23 February, 1469).

22. *Ibid.*, 219, *Statuta* V, 71–2.

23. *Ibid.*, *Statuta* 72.

24. This Ms. is fully described by Charles MacNeill in *Analecta Hibernica* II (1931) 1–3. It is a valuable source of information concerning Cistercian liturgy at the time, and is illustrated by coloured sketches of ecclesiastical and lay figures.

25. Mac Niocaill, *op. cit.*, 220–22. He draws on the following sources: Macroy, *Catalogi manuscriptorum Bibliothecae Bodleianae*, V. I, II, III. Warner and Gilson, *Catalogue of Western manuscripts in the Old Royal and King's Collections* I, Abbott, *Catalogue of the Manuscripts in Trinity College, Dublin.*

26. Gwynn, *Analecta Hibernica* XVI, 316–9. The *Annals* are also briefly dealt with by Flower, *ibid.* II, 319–20. They have been printed in full by Sir John Gilbert in *Chartularies of St. Mary's Abbey, Rolls Series*, II, 241–86.

27. Gwynn and Hadcock, *op. cit.*, 30, 122, 128.

28. O'Curry, *Manuscript Materials of Ancient Irish History*, 81, 105–113.

29. O'Grady, *Catalogue of Irish Manuscripts in the British Museum*, I, 4–14. Gwynn and Hadcock, *op. cit.*, 205.

30. *Revue Celtique*, XLI, 301–330, XLII, 283–305, XLIII, 358–84, XLIV, 336–61.

31. O'Dwyer, 'The Problem of Education in the Irish Cistercian monasteries and the attempted solution of Stephen of Lexington', *The Journal of Ecclesiastical History* (Australia), Vol. XV, No. 2, 186–91. 'The Problem of Education in the Cistercian Order', *The Journal of Religious History* (Australia), Vol. 3, No. 3. The chief source for this incident is *Registrum Epistolarum Stephen de Lexington*, ed. P. Griesser in *Analecta Sacri Ordinis Cisterciensis*, ii (1946). The manuscript is in the National Library, Turin.

The whole question of the crisis in the Cistercian Order in Ireland has recently been fully dealt with by Mr. A. J. Watt, *op. cit.*, Ch. 4.

32. Registrum, 41.

33. *Ibid.*, 95, I.

34. *Ibid.*, 3.
35. *Ibid.*, 37, 47.
36. Cited Little, *op. cit.*, 190.
37. *Proceedings, Royal Irish Academy*, Vol. 22, 457–64.
38. *Irish Texts Society* Vol. XIV.
39. *Op. cit.*, i.
40. Decree 71 of the Synod of Cashel, cited later (p. 170) seems to imply this.
41. Gwynn and Gleeson. *A History of the Diocese of Killaloe*, I, 147.
42. Ed. Bliss and Twemlow, *Calendar of Entries in the Papal Registers relating to Great Britain and Ireland*, Vol. IV, 74.
43. *History of the Diocese of Raphoe*, Part I, First Volume, 82.
44. D'Alton. *History of the Archdiocese of Tuam*, II, 155.
45. The full text of these decrees will be found in Begley, *The Diocese of Limerick, Ancient and Modern*, 431–41, taken from Wilkins, *Concilia Magnae Britanniae*, 566–71. Cf. Coleman, *De Annatis Hiberniae*, Introd., cited Gwynn and Gleeson, *op. cit.*, 511–12.

CHAPTER 15
IRISH SCHOLARS ABROAD

1. Rashdall, *The Universities of Europe in the Middle Ages III*, 50–1.
2. *Cartulary of St. Frideswide's* i, 369, 370, 372; Wood's *Oxford* i, 363, 365 n., 458.
3. *Cartulary of St. Frideswide's* i. 446, 485; *Reg. Exeter College*, 364.
4. Wood's *Oxford* i. 162, 171, 181, 190, 587, 639–40; Macleane, *Pembroke College*, 48.
5. Wood's *Oxford* i, 211, 590. All cited Green, *The Making of Ireland and its Undoing*, 266–67.
6. Green, *op. cit.* 289, 301. The quotations are from Holinshed, *Antiquities VI*, 58 and *Oxford Register*, 84.
7. Cf. ed. Butler, *op. cit.*, introd. ii, and the very full account of Nicholas Maguire by A. F. Pollard in the *Dictionary of National Biography*.
8. Ware, *The Writers of Ireland*, Book I, 83. Curtis, *A History of Medieval Ireland*, 200–01.
9. The article on Fitzralph in the *Dictionary of National Biography* is full and accurate, but the most recent study of this great churchman is to be found in a series of articles by Professor Aubrey Gwynn, S.J., *Studies*, September and December, 1933, September, 1934, September and December, 1935, March, 1936, March, 1937.
10. John Venn and J. A. Venn, *Alumni Cantabrigienses, Part I, earliest times to 1751*.
11. ed. Bliss, Johnson and Twemlow, *Calendar of Entries in the Papal Registers relating to Great Britain and Ireland*. Rolls Series.
12. In the *Calendar of Entries in the Papal Registers relating to Great Britain and Ireland*, 1471–1484, ed. J. A. Twemlow, there are some similar instances of dispensations for ordination being granted with the proviso that the recipient is not bound to receive orders 'for seven years, while dwelling in any *studium* after the Manner of the Irish'. (pp. 344–5, cf. also 39, 56, 61, 300–1).
13. De Burgo, *Hibernia Dominicana*, 49–50, gives the decrees in full.
14. Ed. Bliss and Twemlow, *Calendar of entries in the Papal Registers relating to Great Britain and Ireland, Papal Letters* IV, 40. *Bullarium Franciscanum* VI, 376. Cited Little, *Materials for the history of the Franciscan Province of Ireland*, 150.
15. Pat. 49, Edw. III, *Rotulorum Patentium et Clausorum Cancellariae Hiberniae Calendarium*. p. 98, No. 274. Cited Little, *op. cit.* 157.
16. *Bullarium Franciscanum* VI, 578, Cited Little *op. cit.* 159–60.
17. Wadding, *Annales, XI*, 144.
18. *Chronicles of England, Scotland and Ireland, Vol. VI.* 62–3, (ed. 1808), published 1586.
19. Ware, III (Writers), 82.

20. I wish to acknowledge here my debt to an erudite article by Rev. M. B. Crowe, 'Peter of Ireland, Teacher of St. Thomas Aquinas', *Studies*, 1956, 443–56.

21. C. Baeumker, 'Petrus de Hibernia', Proceedings of the *Bavarian Academy*, 1920. Cited Crowe, *op. cit.*, 455.

22. M. Grabmann, *Magister Petrus von Hibernia, Mittelalterliches Geistesleben* i. 249–65, *Ibid.*

23. A. Pelzer, *Revue neo-scolastique* 23 (1922), 356. *Ibid.*

24. Holinshed *Chronicles of England, Scotland and Ireland*, Vol. VI, 62.

25. *Athenae Oxonienses*, 2nd ed. Vol. I, 10.

26. Grammar, rhetoric and dialectic, the *trivia* or first three branches of the traditional seven Liberal Arts.

27. Ware, *op. cit.*, I, (Bishops) 613–4, III, (Writers) 23–4.

28. Gwynn, 'Richard Fitzralph, Archbishop of Armagh). *Studies*, September, 1933, 399–40, March, 1936, 85.

29. Berry, *Statutes and Ordinances and Acts of the Parliament of Ireland*, Vol. I, King John to Henry V, 527.

30. *Rotuli Parliamentorum ut et Petititiones et Placita in Parliamento*, Vol. IV, 190.

31. Curtis, *A History of Medieval Ireland*, 290–1.

CHAPTER 16
EDUCATION OF LAITY IN MIDDLE AGES

1. H. Daniel-Rops, *Cathedral and Crusade. History of the Church of Christ*, III, 304–08.

2. Rashdall, *The Universities of Europe in the Middle Ages*, III, 345–52.

3. *Phases of Irish History*, 308–10.

4. Flower, *The Irish Tradition*, 77.

5. Joyce, *A Social History of Ancient Ireland* I, 409–10.

6. Orpen, IV, 253.

7. *The Making of Ireland and its Undoing* 462–3.

8. Mrs. Green gives a well-documented account of these schools. *Op. cit.* 364–71. Cf. also Joyce, *A Social History of Ancient Ireland*, I, 420–1, Corcoran, *State Policy in Irish Education*, 20–21, 45–6, 89–91. *Council of Education Reports, Primary*, 16, *Secondary*, 22.

9. Mooney, *Franciscan Donegal*, 9.

10. *A History of Medieval Ireland*, 143.

11. ed. Mills, *Calendar of the Justiciary Rolls* (1295–1303) 154–5.

12. The modern references are: Public Record Office, London, *Special Collections. Ministers' and Receivers' Accounts* (S.C. 6/1237/1–55, 1238/1–61, 1239/1–12).

13. *Journal of the Royal Society of Antiquaries in Ireland*, Vol. XXII, 50–7.

14. Hore, *History of the Town and County of Wexford*, Vol. 1, *Old and New Ross*, 5–39, 141–63. The transcripts and translations are Vol. 72 of the Hore Mss., bequeathed by Philip Hore to St. Peter's College, Wexford, where they are now preserved.

15. Hore Transcripts and Translations, 31, 294, 226a, 17, 16, 206a, 30a, 18, 119–20, 134a–35.

16. Account of John de Wympler, Provost of Ross. Hore Mss. 205. 'For hired watchman during the time of the Fair (or market) for fear of robbers 10s in this year.'

17. Account of William Passemer, keeper of the meadow of the lord Earl of Carlow, *ibid.* 36–37. 'For a certain hired carpenter to repair the roof of the great Hall where necessary for 12 days 8s, who takes 4d a day for both wages and drink.'

18. Account of David Triller, Provost of the Manor of New Ross, *ibid.* 30. 'For a certain boy hired to take care of the lambs after birth 3s 8d'.

19. See p. 153.

20. Hogan (*Onomasticon Goedelicum*, 639) lists seven places named Tobar Brighde. Brideswell, Co. Roscommon, near Athlone is the nearest to Loughrea.

21. Ed. Mills, *Calendar of Justiciar Rolls*, Part 2, 1305–7, 141–2.

22. Or Oxmantown, the area around Blackhall Place, to which the Norse of Dublin were confined after their final defeat by the Normans in 1171.

23. De Burgo, *Hibernia Dominicana*, 192–3.

24. The question of where this bridge was situated is a complicated one, and calls for only a brief consideration here. The most recent account of this school is in an article 'The Dominicans in Medieval Dublin' by Fr. B. O'Sullivan, O.P. in the *Dublin Historical Record*, Vol. IX, No. 2, June-August, 1947, pp. 41–3. Fr. O'Sullivan places St. Saviour's in the region of the Four Courts, and the 'gymnasium' of St. Thomas Aquinas at Usher's Island, where Power's distillery stands today. The bridge, therefore, must have been convenient to both these places. De Burgo identifies it with the Old Bridge, which stood where Father Mathew bridge is today, but no other authority agrees with him. Cf. Gilbert, *History of the City of Dublin* 319–27, Warburton, Whitelaw and Walsh, *History of the City of Dublin*, 1095, Fitzpatrick, *Dublin*, 95, Little, *Dublin before the Vikings*, 57–72.

25. Gwynn and Hadcock. *Medieval Religious Houses in Ireland*, 263–75.

26. Brussels Ms. 3947, presented, with introduction, by Fr. Brendan Jennings, O.F.M., *Analecta Hibernica*, No. 6. November, 1934, 12–131.

27. *Op. cit.*, 102.

28. Vol. I, 433.

29. Shirley, *Papers Relating to the Church of Ireland*, 1631–1639. Shirley remarks that this document is not signed by the bishop, but certainly emanated from him or one of his officials.

30. *Ordnance Letter from Letterkenny*, Sept. 22nd, 1835, Maguire, *op. cit.*, 434.

31. *Bishop Montgomery's Survey of the Diocese of Derry, Raphoe and Clogher. The O'Kane Papers. Analecta Hibernica* XII, 79 sqq.

32. *Rawlinson B*, 489. *Annals of Ulster*, Vol. III, 573, Vol. IV, *Introduction* iii.

33. *State Papers published under the authority of His Majesty's Commission*, Vol. III, King Henry the Eighth, Part III, continued, 130–1.

34. *Ibid.* 142–3.

35. *Annals of Ulster*.

36. *Annals of the Four Masters*.

37. *Ibid.*

38. *Annals of Ulster*.

39. *Annals of the Four Masters*.

40. *Annals of Ulster*.

41. *Ibid.*

42. *Ibid.*

43. *Annals of Ulster*. The title 'clerech' (Mod. Irish 'cléireach'), often has no religious significance, but means, as here, an educated man, or possibly a 'business manager'.

44. *Annals of Connacht*.

45. *Ibid* and *Annals of the Four Masters*.

46. *Annals of the Four Masters*.

47. *Annals of Ulster*.

48. *Annals of Ulster*.

49. *Ibid.*

50. The Marquis of Kildare, *The Earls of Kildare and their Ancestors from 1057 to 1773*, 27. *Dictionary of National Biography*, XIX, 216.

51. *Dictionary of National Biography, loc. cit.*

52. *Rotulorum Patentium et Clausorum Cancellariae Hiberniae Calendarium*, Vol. I, Pars. 1, 139 (Pat. 12 Ric. II) James is sometimes referred to as Fitzgerald, but more frequently as Fitzmaurice.

53. Ed. McLaughlan. *The Dean of Lismore's Book*. A selection of ancient Gaelic poetry. From a manuscript-collection made by Sir James McGregor, Dean of Lismore, in the beginning of the sixteenth century.

54. Details in Best, *Bibliography of Irish Philology and of Printed Irish Literature*, I, 157, 162, II, 1696, 1706–7.

55. *Studia Hibernica* 3, 1963, 7–59.

56. Flower, Introduction to T. F. O'Rahilly, *Dánta Grádha*, viii. De Blacam, *Gaelic Literature Surveyed*, 165–6.

57. Mac Niocaill, *op. cit.*, 9, 41–4.

58. Crofton Croker, *The Popular Songs of Ireland*, 287.

59. *Op. cit., loc. cit.*

60. Ed. Samuel Hayman, *Unpublished Geraldine Documents*, 3, 7, 10.

61. Gilbert, *History of the Viceroys of Ireland*, 228.

62. Ed. Brewer and Bullen, *Book of Howth, Calendar of the Carew manuscripts preserved in the Archiepiscopal Library at Lambeth*, 179–180.

63. Donough Bryan, *Gerald Fitzgerald, the Great Earl of Kildare*, 8, 9.

64. Neither Gilbert nor Bryan give any indication of the whereabouts of the original of this letter, and I have been unable to trace it. There is another letter extant, addressed to Henry VIII, which is obviously the work of a professional scribe, though signed by the Earl. Gilbert, *Facsimiles of National Manuscripts of Ireland*, III, Facsimile LXII.

65. Holinshed, *Chronicles of England, Ireland and Scotland*, (ed. 1808), V, 60, *The Description of Ireland*.

66. O'Grady, *Catalogue of Irish Manuscripts in the British Museum*, I, 149, 154, 190, 202. The second list is given in full in Bryan, *op. cit.*, Appendix 2. Both lists were published by Gilbert in Appendix to Part II of the 9th Report of the *Historical Manuscripts Commission*, 1884, 288–9. Cf. also Gilbert, *Facsimiles of National Manuscripts of Ireland* III, Introd. viii, Facsimile LXIII, Appendix IX.

67. O'Grady, *op. cit.*, 221.

68. p. 138-9.

69. *Annals of the Four Masters*, 1462 (p. 1021, Note) and 1464 (pp. 1030–1, Note).

70. *Celtica* V, 64–76, VI, 135–54.

71. *Ibid.* IX, 137–50.

72. cf. also Gilbert, *Facsimiles of National Manuscripts of Ireland*, III, xvi and Facsimile XLVII.

73. p. 189.

74. p. 191.

CHAPTER 17

EDUCATION OF LAITY IN MIDDLE AGES (continued)

1. Monck Mason, *History of the Collegiate and Cathedral Church of St· Patrick, Appendix i, No. 1*. Text of charter from ancient register '*Dignitas Decani* etc.' in *Registrum Alani* or *Black Book of Archbishop Alan*, fol. 20, p. i.

2. Lawlor, *The Fasti of St. Patrick's, Dublin*, 252.

3. *ibid.*

4. W. Monck Mason *op. cit.*, 153, 157.

5. *The Medieval Province of Armagh*, 83–4. (A study of three primatial registers preserved in the public library of Armagh).

6. Review of article 'Richard Fitzralph, Archbishop of Armagh,' by A. Gwynn, Studies, Vol. XXII, No. 87, in *Louth Archaeological Journal* VII (1932), 551–2.

7. p.168.

8. 'The Ancient Chantries of Co. Louth', *Louth Archaeological Journal* IX (1939), 181–208.

9. Murray, *op. cit.*, 202, citing diocesan register 1481.

10. Gwynn, *op. cit.*, 84.

11. Hore, *History of the Town and County of Wexford* I, 150. Mills, *Accounts of the Earl of Norfolk's Estates in Ireland, Journal of Royal Society of Antiquaries in Ireland*, XXII, 50–7.

12. There is no trace of this exact place-name in modern records. In the Index of Townlands, Census 1901 the only approximations to it are Booley, Barony of Shelburne, Parish of Templetown, New Ross, and Bowling Green, Barony of Bantry, Parish of St. Mary's, New Ross.

13. Ed. MacNeill and Otway-Ruthven, *Dowdall Deeds*, 55, 75, cited Otway Ruthven, *History of Medieval Ireland*, 143.

14. Ed. D. A. Chart, *The Register of John Swayne, Archbishop of Armagh and Primate of Ireland*, 199, cited Otway-Ruthven, *op. cit.*, 143.

15. These slates have been the subject of a detailed study by A. J. Bliss, 'The Inscribed Slates at Smarmore', *Proceedings of the Royal Irish Academy*, Vol. 64, section C, No. 2. The interpretations in the text are taken mainly from this paper.

16. Lawlor, *The Monastery of Saint Mochaoi of Nendrum*, Gwynn and Hadcock, *Medieval Religious Houses, Ireland*, 42, 104, 107, Ryan, *Irish Monasticism*, 103–4.

CHAPTER 18
UNBROKEN SUCCESSION OF NATIVE SCHOOLS

1. *Annals of the Four Masters.*
2. *ibid.*
3. *Annals of Clonmacnois.*
4. *Annals of the Four Masters.*
5. *Annals of Connacht.*
6. *Annals of Ulster.*
7. *Annals of the Four Masters.*
8. *ibid.*
9. *ibid.*
10. *ibid.*
11. *ibid.*
12. *ibid.*
13. *Annals of Ulster.*
14. *Annals of the Four Masters.*
15. *ibid.*
16. *Annals of Connacht.*
17. *Annals of Ulster.*
18. *Annals of the Four Masters.*
19. *Annals of Connacht.*
20. *Annals of the Four Masters.*
21. Hyde. *A Literary History of Ireland*, 465, sqq.
22. Ed. O'Donovan for the Irish Archaeological Society, 1862, *The Topographical Poems of John O Dughagain and Giolla na Naomh O Huidrin.* O'Donovan's introduction and notes give a wealth of information concerning Irish personal and place names. *Topographical Poems by Seaan Mor O Dubhagain and Giolla-na-naomh O Huidrin*, Ed. Carney, J., Dublin Institute for Advanced Studies, 1943.
23. *Aithdioghluim Dána* contains a hundred poems representing the work of some thirty poets. In the first volume there are valuable bibliographical notes and directions as to the whereabouts of other poems by the same writers.
24. For scholars, twelfth to fifteenth centuries, in general, see Hyde, *op. cit.*, 465–70, O'Reilly, *Irish Writers* and Eleanor Hull, *A Text-book of Irish Literature*, under the dates cited, de Blacam, *A First Book of Irish Literature*, 78–95.
25. On these and various less important Mss. cf. O'Curry, *Manuscript Materials of Ancient Irish History*, 188–92, 352–3, Hyde, *op. cit.*, 470. Hull, *op. cit.*, I, 246–8. Kenney, *Sources for the Early History of Ireland*, 24–5.
26. Ed. Standish H. O'Grady, *Caithréim Thoirdhealbhaigh, The Triumphs of Turlough.* Irish Texts Society XXVI–XXVIII. Introduction by Flower, xiv.
27. Ed. Hennessy (Vol. I) and MacCarthy (Vols. II–IV), 1887–1901. Cf. O'Curry, *op. cit.*, 83–4, Hyde, *op. cit.*, 470 and 581.
28. O'Curry, *op. cit.*, 130–8. Joyce, *A Social History of Ireland* I 523, Hyde, *op. cit.*, 206–7.
29. Ed. Bergin, *Irish Grammatical Tracts*, 1. Introductory, 2. Declensions (nouns and adjectives). 3. Irregular Verbs. 4. Abstract Nouns. 5. Metrical Faults. *Supplements to Eriu*, viii, ix, x, xiv, xvii. Ed. McKenna, *Bardic Syntactical Texts*, Dublin Institute for Advanced Studies.

30. Bergin, 'The Native Irish Grammarian', *Proceedings of the British Academy* 1938. Murphy, *Duanaire Finn, Book of the Lays of Finn, Irish Texts Society,* XXX, 190. Ó Cuív, 'Terminology in the Mediaeval Irish Bardic Tracts', *Transactions, Philological Society,* 1965. 'The Linguistic Training of the Mediaeval Irish Poet', *Celtica* X, 114–40.

31. Ó Cuív, *op. cit.,* ('Linguistic Terminology') 162.

32. Bergin, *op. cit.,* ('Native Irish Grammarian') 7.

33. Ó Cuív, *op. cit.,* ('Linguistic Training') 120–39, ('Linguistic Terminology') 143–48.

34. Bergin, *op. cit.,* 7–8.

CHAPTER 19
LAWYERS, DOCTORS, PATRONS

1. *Annals of Clonmacnois.*

2. *Annals of the Four Masters.*

3. *Annals of Ulster and Connacht.*

4. This and following obits from the *Four Masters.*

5. Gwynn and Gleeson, *History of the Diocese of Killaloe,* 147, 151, 276.

6. *Annals of the Four Masters,* 1492, Kenney, *Sources for the Early History of Ireland,* 20.

7. Westropp, 'Prehistoric Stone Forts of Northern Clare', *Journal of Royal Society of Antiquaries of Ireland,* 1897, 120–1.

8. Dr. George MacNamara, 'The O'Davorens of Cahermacnaughton, Burren, Co. Clare', *Journal of the North Munster Archaeological Society,* Vol. II, No. 2, January, 1912, 149–64.

9. Standish O'Grady, *Catalogue of Irish Manuscripts in the British Museum,* I, 109–141.

10. *Annals of the Four Masters,* Vol. I, p. 494, note by O'Donovan on medical families. Joyce, *A Social History of Ireland,* I, 600–1. Green, *The Making of Ireland and its Undoing,* 245–6, Kenney, *op. cit.,* 20–1.

11. *Annals of the Four Masters.*

12. O'Grady, *op. cit.,* I, 330.

13. *Ibid.,* 177.

14. *Annals of the Four Masters.*

15. *Ibid.*

16. Smith, *The Antient and Present State of the County and City of Cork* (1749), I, 32.

17. O'Grady, *op. cit.,* 222.

18. *Annals of the Four Masters,* Vol. II, p. 817. Note by O'Donovan. O'Grady, *loc. cit.,* Note.

19. This is O'Donovan's translation of *glas.* More probably it means 'bright [eyed]'.

20. *Annals of the Four Masters.*

21. O'Grady, *op. cit.,* I, 173–4.

22. *Ibid.,* 202–2.

23. *Ibid.,* 196.

24. *Irish Texts Society,* Vol. XXV. 1929. *Rosa Anglica,* An Early Modern Irish Translation of a section of the medieval medical textbook of John of Gaddesden, edited with Introduction, Glossary and English Version by Winifred Wulff, M.A. The title 'Rosa' has no particular significance. It was a fad of the medical doctors to give the name of a flower to their treatises.

25. *Op. cit.,* 183.

26. O'Grady, *op. cit.,* 273–74.

27. *Féil-sgríbhinn Eoin Mhic Néill.* Essays and studies presented to Professor Eoin MacNeill on the occasion of his seventieth birthday, 1938. ed. Ryan, No. 22. *Medieval Medico-Philosophical Treatises in the Irish Language.*

28. *Annals of the Four Masters.*

29. *Ibid.* and *Annals of Connacht.*

30. *Annals of the Four Masters.*

31. *Ibid.* See p. 38.
32. *Ibid.* and *Annals of Connacht.*
33. *Annals of the Four Masters.*
34. *Annals of Connacht.*
35. *Annals of the Four Masters.*
36. *Annals of Connacht, Annals of Loch Cé.*
37. *Annals of the Four Masters, Annals of Loch Cé.*
38. *Annals of the Four Masters.*
39. *Annals of Connacht.*
40. *Ibid.*
41. *Ibid.*
42. *Annals of Ulster.*
43. *Annals of the Four Masters, Annals of Connacht, Annals of Loch Cé.*
44. *Annals of Connacht.*
45. *Annals of the Four Masters.*
46. *Annals of Connacht.*
47. *Annals of Ulster.*
48. *Fear tighe naidheadh, naoidheach, aoidhedh,* etc. 'General hospitality' is O'Donovan's rendering.
49. *Annals of the Four Masters.*
50. *Annals of Connaught.*
51. *Annals of the Four Masters* and *Annals of Connacht.*
52. *Annals of the Four Masters.*
53. *Ibid.*
54. Gwynn and Gleeson, *op. cit.,* 151.

CHAPTER 20
INCHOATE UNIVERSITIES

1. Ware, *Antiquities of Ireland* (1745 ed.) Vol. II, 242–5, De Burgo, *Hibernia Dominicana,* 66, 85, 190–91. W. Monck Mason, *History and Antiquities of the Collegiate and Cathedral Church of St. Patrick near Dublin,* 100–04: a brief and not very critical account of the foundation, but of value as giving in Appendix IX–XI the texts of the bull of establishment and of the ordination setting up the university. Taylor, *History of the University of Dublin,* 2–3, Stubbs, *History of the University of Dublin* 1–3, Curtis, *History of Medieval Ireland,* 250, Orpen, *Ireland under the Normans,* IV, 210–11, and Rashdall, *Universities of Europe in the Middle Ages,* II, Appendix, 325–7, add nothing to Monck Mason. Valuable new material appeared in Fitzmaurice and Little, *Materials for the History of the Franciscan Province of Ireland,* 107–9. A definitive study with further new material is A. Gwynn, 'The Medieval University of St. Patrick's', *Dublin, Studies,* June and September, 1938.

2. *Studium Generale* was the common medieval term for a university. There is some vagueness as to what various authors meant by *generale,* but there is fairly unanimous consent that it indicated (1) admission of students from all parts – this was probably its original meaning, (2) the promotion of higher education by at least one of the higher faculties, Theology, Law or Medicine, besides Arts, and (3) a plurality of masters. *Universitas* originally meant a corporation of masters or students or of both, but by the fifteenth century had become a synonym for *studium generale.* On this the classical source in English is Rashdall, *op. cit.,* especially I, Ch. 2, *What is a University?*

3. Monck Mason, *op. cit.,* Appendix IX–X.

4. *Ibid.,* Appendix X–XI. English translation, 100–101. Ware, *De Hibernia et antiquitatibus eius,* 1658 ed., p. 77.

5. Ed. Gilbert, *Chronicles and Memorials of Great Britain and Ireland during the Middle Ages. Chartularies of St. Mary's Abbey, Dublin,* ii, 361.

6. Monck Mason, *op. cit.,* 101.

7. Ware, *The Whole Works,* Vol. II *Antiquities of Ireland* (1745 ed.), 244.

8. Rashdall, *op. cit.,* II, 326.

9. W. Monck Mason. *op. cit.,* p. 101, quoting from lost Christ Church deed, calendered in the Deputy Keeper's Report, No. 255.

10. Ed. Butler, *The Annals of Ireland by Friar John Clyn of the Convent of Friars Minor of Kilkenny whence he went to Carrick-on-Suir, and Thady Dowling, Chancellor of Leighlin.* Dowling Annals, 20.

11. Curtis, *History of Medieval Ireland,* 249–50.

12. Ware, *op. cit.,* 244–5, Ed. Tresham, *Rotulorum Patentium et Clausorum Cancellariae Hiberniae Calendarium,* Vol. I, Pars. I, 73.

13. The text of Lionel's grant is found in ed. MacNeill, *Calendar of Archbishop Alen's Register,* 216. It occurs in folio 37 of the register, preserved in the registry of the United Dioceses of Dublin, Glendalough and Kildare. For the permit of Edward III see ed. Tresham, *Cancellariae Hiberniae Calendarium* Vol. I, Pars. I, 64b.

14. *Dictionary of National Biography.*

15. Ed. W. H. Bliss, *Calendar of Entries in the Papal Registers relating to Great Britain and Ireland. Petitions to the Pope,* Vol. I, A.D. 1342–1419, 467–9.

16. *Statute Rolls of Ireland,* 5 Edw. IV, 369.

17. Hayman, *Unpublished Geraldine Documents,* 11–13. Gilbert, *History of the Viceroys of Ireland,* 378–87. Curtis, *A History of Medieval Ireland,* 326, ed. Moody and Martin, *The Course of Irish History,* 163–5.

18. Samuel Hayman, *Notes and Records of the Ancient Religious Foundations at Youghal, Co. Cork, and its Vicinity,* 33. Charles Smith, M.D., *The Ancient and Present State of the County and City of Cork,* 55–60, 83.

19. Ware, *op. cit.,* 245. The Act is 5 Edw. IV, c.6. Loftus, *Annals* (Marsh's Library) 1465. D'Alton, *History of Drogheda,* II, 149. Rashdall, *op. cit.,* II, 327–28 (Rashdall's own translation of the Act is given). Corcoran, *Selected Texts on Education Systems in Ireland,* 7, gives a slightly different Norman-French text from that of Ware.

20. Twemlow, *Calendar of Entries in the Papal Registers relating to Great Britain and Ireland,* 1471–1484, 426–7.

21. De Burgo, *op. cit.,* 67, 85, 185, 193–4.

22. Ware, *op. cit.,* 245.

23. *Ibid.,* 246.

24. Voss, *Two Bokes of the Historie of Ireland compiled by Edmund Campion,* 94–5, Ware, *Two Histories of Ireland by Edmund Campion and Meredith Hanmer* (1533 ed.), 85.

APPENDIX. MUSIC

1. There is no satisfactory history of Irish music. O'Curry (*Manners and Customs of the Ancient Irish,* II, 212–409), has amassed a large body of information, and has been drawn on by all later writers. He confines himself, however, to the ancient period. W. K. Sullivan, in his lengthy introduction to O'Curry (cccclxxxiii–dcxxxvi), gives much information regarding music in other countries, but adds little to what O'Curry states about Ireland. Joyce (*A Social History of Ancient Ireland,* I, 571–96), relies almost entirely on O'Curry. Two less well-known works are Walker, *Historical Memories of the Irish Bards,* (1786) and Armstrong, *Musical Instruments,* Part I, *The Irish and Highland Harps,* 1904. The only complete history is Grattan Flood, *History of Irish Music* (1905), an interesting, but not altogether reliable work.

There are many well-known collections of Irish music, such as Bunting, *The Ancient Music of Ireland,* 1786, 1809, 1840, Petrie, *Collection of the Ancient Music of Ireland,* 1855, Joyce, *Ancient Irish Music,* 1873, O'Sullivan, *Irish Folk Music and Song,* 1952. The few historical notes given in these are of little value.

I wish to acknowledge my indebtedness in composing this Appendix to an article 'Music in Ancient Munster and Monastic Cork' by Professor Aloys Fleischmann and Ryta Gleeson, *Journal of the Cork Historical and Archaeological Society,* Part 2, Vol. LXX, No. 212, and to an article by Professor Fleischmann, 'References to Chant in Early Irish Mss.' in *Féilscríbhinn Tórna,* ed. Pender, 43–9.

2. Macalister, ed. *Lebor Gabála* V, 417. Cf. (ed. Dinneen) Keating, *History of Ireland* II, 103.

3. O'Grady, *Silva Gadelica* II, 116.

4. *Ancient Laws*, V, 107.

5. *Ibid.*, IV, ccv, 339.

6. Colgan, *Triadis Thaumaturgae*...Acta, 536.

7. Plummer, *Lives of the Irish Saints*, II, 102–3, 112–13.

8. Stokes, ed., *Lives of the Saints from the Book of Lismore*, xiii-xv.

9. *Giraldi Cambrensis Topographia Hiberniae*, ed. James F. Dimock, London, 1867, 153–4.

10. *Ibid.*, 155.

11. O'Curry, *Manners and Customs of the Ancient Irish*, II, 270–71.

12. Bergin, ed. *'Unpublished Irish Poems'*, XXII, *Studies*, 1923, 276. Reprinted, *Irish Bardic Poetry*, ed. Greene and Kelly, text, 66–69, translation 241–2.

13. O'Curry, *op. cit.*, 259–60.

14. Stokes, ed. *Sanas Chormaic*. Cormac's Glossary. Translated and annotated by John O'Donovan. Cf. O'Curry, *op. cit.*, 359.

15. O'Curry, *op. cit.*, 363.

16. Joyce, *A Social History of Ancient Ireland*, 581.

17. Stokes, *The Destruction of Dá Derga's Hostel*, *Revue Celtique* XXII, 183–4.

18. *Journal of the Royal Society of Antiquaries of Ireland*, LXXII, (1944), 85–106.

19. O'Curry, *op. cit.*, 313–19.

20. O'Curry, *op. cit.*, II, 305–369.

21. Berry, *Register of Wills and Inventories of the Diocese of Dublin*, 1457–83, 24, 26. The term 'a pair or organs' may have referred to a double bellows to ensure continuous sound, or to a double row of pipes (Berry, *op. cit.*, 100).

22. Cited, Grattan Flood, *op. cit.*, 100.

23. Ed. Coleman 'Regestum Monasterii Fratrum Praedicatorum de Athenry', *Archivum Hibernicum* I, 118.

24. Reeves, ed. *Adamnán*, Life of St. Columba, 81.

25. O'Curry, *op. cit.*, 262.

26. The meaning of *ceis* is obscure. It has been interpreted as 'the bass strings of a harp', as a small harp played in accompaniment to the ordinary harp (cruit), and as 'a small pin which fastens the brazen string of the harp'. Cf. O'Donovan's note on this passage in the *Four Masters*, O'Curry *op. cit.*, 248–9, 252–4, Joyce, *op. cit.*, 579, Stokes on the Bodleian *Amra*, *Revue Celtique*, XX, 165.

27. Derricke, *The Image of Ireland*...with the notes of Sir Walter Scott, Bart., ed. Smal', Plate III. Harpists will be interested in the fact that the player is obviously playing with his finger nails. There are several allusions to this technique, which was apparently the usual one.

28. O'Curry, *op. cit.*, 220, 259–60, 363, 381.

29. *Ibid.*, 252.

30. Joyce, *op. cit.*, 587–9.

31. O'Curry, *op. cit.*, 390–406.

32. Sullivan, *Introduction to O'Curry's Manners and Customs of the Ancient Irish*, dxli-dcxxxvi.

33. Stokes, ed. *The Tripartite Life of St. Patrick and other documents*, II, 406–7.

34. Plummer, *Lives of the Irish Saints*, II, 20.

35. Todd, ed. *The Book of Hymns of the Ancient Irish Church*, Fasc. I, 217, 242. Ed. Bernard and Atkinson, *The Irish Liber Hymnorum*, Vol. I, 80, Vol. II, 153.

36. O'Clery, *The Martyrology of Donegal, A Calendar of the Saints of Ireland*, *trans.* O'Donovan, *ed.* with Irish text, Todd and Reeves, 225.

37. Reeves, ed. Adamnán, *Life of St. Columba*, Book i, c. 37, pp. 73–4.

38. Bernard and Atkinson, *The Irish Liber Hymnorum* II, 5.

39. Kuno Meyer, *Hibernica minora*, 31 and note 285, p. 89. Cf. O'Curry *op. cit.*, 238–9.

40. Fleischmann 'Die Iren in der Neumen und Choralforschung', *Zeitschrift für Musikwissenschaft*, 1934, 352 sqq.

41. Trans. W. J. Lawlor, *St. Bernard of Clairvaux's Life of St. Malachy of Armagh*, 17–18.

42. Gwynn and Hadcock, *Medieval Religious Houses in Ireland*, 148–52.

43. Curtis, *A History of Medieval Ireland*, 59–60.

44. For a fuller account of the history of chant see the articles of Professor Fleischmann, cited above.

45. *Annals of Clonmacnois*.

46. *Ibid*.

47. *Annals of Connacht*.

48. *Annals of Ulster*.

49. *Annals of Connacht*.

50. *Annals of the Four Masters*.

51. *Ibid*.

52. *Ibid*.

53. *Annals of Ulster*.

54. *Annals of Loch Cé*.

55. *Annals of the Four Masters*.

56. *Annals of Ulster*.

57. *Ibid*.

58. The battle of Balibragan (Bragganstown) in Louth, June 10th, 1329. Curtis, *A History of Medieval Ireland*, 203–06.

59. Butler, ed. *The Annals of Ireland by Friar John Clyn*, 20.

60. Connellan, ed. 'Imtheacht na Tromdhaimhe or the Proceedings of the Great Bardic Institution', *Transactions of the Ossianic Society*, V, 99–101. O'Curry, *op. cit.*, 235–6.

61. Bollandist *Acta Sanctorum*, 17th March, p. 595. Lanigan, *Ecclesiastical History* II, 464. Fleury, *Histoire Ecclesiastique*, Book 38, sec. 58, p. 491.

62. Ware, *Writers of Ireland*, Book I, 58. Lanigan, *op. cit.*, III, 285.

63. Berry, *op. cit.*, 33, 60.

64. *Historical Manuscripts Commission. Tenth Report. Appendix. Part V*.

65. Lawlor, *The Fasti of St. Patrick's, Dublin*, 253.

BIBLIOGRAPHY

ABBOTT, T. K. and GWYNN, E. J. *Catalogue of Irish Manuscripts in Library of Trinity College, Dublin,* Dublin and London, 1921.
Acta Sanctorum ex Codice Salmanticensi, ed. de Smedt, C. and de Backer, T., Edinburgi et Londini, 1888.
Aldhelmi Opera, Monumenta Germaniae Historica Auctorum Antiquissimorum Tomus XV, ed. Ehwald, R., Berlin, 1919.
Ancient Laws and Institutes of Ireland, Vols. I–VI. Transcript and translation by O'Donovan, J. and O'Curry, E. Ed. Hancock, W. N., O'Mahony, T., Richey, A. G., Atkinson, R., Dublin and London, 1865–1901.
ANDERSON, A. O. and M. O. *Adamnan's Life of St. Columba,* Edinburgh, 1961.
Annals of Boyle. Freeman, A. M. ed. and trans. 'The Annals in Cotton Ms. Titus A. XXV', *Revue Celtique,* vol. XLI (1924), 301–30, vol. XLII (1925), 283–305, vol. XLIII (1926), 358–84, vol. XLIV (1927), 336–61.
Annals of Clonmacnois, trans. Mageoghagan, C., ed. Murphy, D., Dublin, 1896.
Annals of Connacht: Annála Connacht, ed. Freeman, A. M., Dublin, Institute for Advanced Studies, 1944.
Annals of the Four Masters, ed. O'Donovan, J., Vols. I–VII, Dublin, 1848–51.
Annals of Inisfallen, trans. and ed. Mac Airt, S., Dublin, Institute for Advanced Studies, 1951.
Annals of Loch Cé, I–II. ed. and trans. Hennessy, W. M., Rolls Series, London, 1871.
Annals of Tigernach, ed. W. Stokes, *Revue Celtique* XVI (1895), 374–419, XVII (1896), 6–33, 119–263, 337–420, XVIII (1897), 9–59, 150–197, 267–303.
Annals of Ulster, Vol. I. ed. Hennessy, W. M., Dublin, 1887, Vols. II–IV, ed. McCarthy, B., II, 1893, III, 1895, IV, 1901.
ARCHDALL, M. *Monasticon Hibernicum,* or *An History of the Abbies, Priories and other Religious Houses in Ireland,* Dublin, 1786. (Another edition, ed. Rev. Patrick F. Moran and other antiquarians, Vols. I–II, Dublin, 1873–6).
ARMSTRONG, R. B. *Musical Instruments,* Part I, *The Irish and the Highland Harps,* Edinburgh, 1904.
ATKINSON, N. *Irish Education,* Dublin, 1969.
à WOOD, A. *Athenae Oxonienses,* ed. Bliss, P., Vols. I–IV, London, 1813–20.
BARRY, J. 'The Erenagh in the monastic Irish Church', *Irish Ecclesiastical Record,* LXXXIX, June 1958, 424–32.
BAEUMKER, C. 'Petrus de Hibernia', *Proceedings of the Bavarian Academy,* 1920.
BEDE, THE VENERABLE. *Ecclesiastical History of England,* trans. A. M. Sellar, London, 1907.
BEDE, THE VENERABLE. *Historia Ecclesiastica Gentis Anglorum,* ed. Plummer, C. Vols. I, II, Oxford, 1896.
BEGLEY, J. *The Diocese of Limerick, Ancient and Medieval,* Dublin, 1906.
BERGIN, O. 'Bardic Poetry', *Journal of the Ivernian Society* V (1913), 153–66, 203–16.
BERGIN, O. (ed.) 'Irish Grammatical Tracts', supplements to *Ériu,* VIII (1916), IX (1921–23), X (1926–8), XIV (1946), XVII (1955).
BERGIN, O. 'The Native Irish Grammarian', *Proceedings of the British Academy,* London, 1938.

BERGIN, O. (ed. Greene, D. and Kelly, F.). 'Irish Bardic Poetry', *Unpublished Irish Poems, Texts and Translations together with an Introductory Lecture,* Dublin, 1970.
BERGIN, O. and BEST, R. J. 'Tochmarc Étáine', *Ériu,* Vol. XII, (1938), 137–41, Text and Trans., 142–93.
BERNARD, J. H. and ATKINSON, R. *The Irish Liber Hymnorum,* London, Vol. I, 1895, Vol. II, 1897.
BERRY, H. F. (ed.) *Register of Wills and Inventories of the Diocese of Dublin in the times of Archbishops Tregury and Walton, 1457-83,* Dublin, 1898.
BERRY, H. F. (ed.). *Statutes and Ordinances and Acts of the Parliament of Ireland,* Vol. I, King John to Henry V, Dublin, 1907.
BEST, R. J. *Bibliography of Irish Philology and of Printed Irish Literature,* Dublin, 1913. *Bibliography of Irish Philology and Manuscript Literature,* Dublin, 1942.
BEST, R. J. and BERGIN, O. *Lebor na Huidre, Book of the Dun Cow,* Dublin, 1929.
BEST, R. J., BERGIN, O. and O'BRIEN, M. J. *The Book of Leinster formerly Lebar na Nuachongbála,* Dublin, 1954 (Vol. I), 1956 (Vol. II), 1957 (Vol. III), 1965 (Vol. IV), 1967 (Vol. V).
BIELER, L. *The Works of St. Patrick,* London, 1953.
BINCHY, D. A. 'The Background of Early Irish Literature', *Studia Hibernica,* I, 7–18. Dublin, 1961.
BINCHY, D. A. (ed.) 'Bretha Crólige', *Ériu* XII, Dublin, 1938, 1–77.
BINCHY, D. A. (ed.) 'Bretha Déin Checht', *Ériu* XX, Dublin, 1966, 1–66.
BINCHY, D. A. *Crith Gabhlach,* Dublin, 1941.
BINCHY, D. A. 'Lebor Gabála Érenn. The Book of the Taking of Ireland. Edited by R. A. Stewart Macalister'. *Celtica* II (1954), 195–209.
BINCHY, D. A. 'Patrick and his Biographers', *Studia Hibernica,* No. 2, Dublin, (1962), 7–173.
BINCHY, D. A. 'Sick Maintenance in Irish Law', *Ériu* XII, Dublin, 1938, 78–134.
BLISS, A. J. 'The Inscribed Slates at Smarmore'. *Proceedings of The Royal Irish Academy,* Vol. 64, section C, No. 2, Dublin, 1965.
BOSWELL, C. S. *An Irish Precursor of Dante,* London, 1908.
BRASH, R. R., (ed. Atkinson, G.). *The Oghum Inscribed Monuments of the Gaedhil in the British Islands,* London, 1879.
BREWER, J. S. and BULLEN, W. *Book of Howth, Calendar of the Carew manuscripts preserved in the archiepiscopal library at Lambeth,* London, Record Publications, 1867–73.
BRYAN, D. *Gerald Fitzgerald, the great Earl of Kildare,* Dublin, 1933.
BUNTING, E. *The Ancient Music of Ireland,* Dublin, 1796 and 1840, ed. O'Sullivan, D. J., London 1927–39.
BURY, J. B. *The Life of St. Patrick,* London, 1905.
BUTLER, A. (ed.) Thurston H. and Attwater, D. *The Lives of the Saints,* vols. I–XII, London, 1926–38.
BUTLER, R. (ed.) *The Annals of Ireland by Friar John Clyn of the Convent of Friars Minor of Kilkenny whence he went to Carrick-on-Suir, and Thady Dowling, Chancellor of Leighlin,* Dublin, 1849.
BYRNE, F. J. 'Seventh-century Documents', *Irish Ecclesiastical Record,* Vol. cviii, Sept., 1967, 164–82.
CALDER, J. (ed. and trans.). *Auraicept na n-Éces, The Scholar's Primer,* Edinburgh, 1917.
Calendar of Entries in the Papal Registers relating to Great Britain and Ireland. Vols. I–XIV (1198–1492), ed. Bliss, W. H., Johnson, C., Twemlow, J. A., London, 1897–1960.
Calendar of Entries in the Papal Registers relating to Great Britain and Ireland. Petitions to the Pope, Vol. I, 1342–1491, ed. Bliss, W. H., London, 1896.
CAMBRENSIS, GIRALDUS, ed. Dimock, J. F. *Topographia Hibernica,* London, 1867.

CAMBRENSIS, GIRALDUS, trans. O'Meara, J. J. *The First Version of the Topography of Ireland*, Dundalk, 1951.

CAMPION, E. ed. Vossen, A. F. *Two Bokes of the Histories of Ireland*, Assen, 1963.

CANIVEZ, J. M. (ed.). *Statuta Capitalorum Generalium Ordinis Cisterciensis ab anno 1116 ad annum 1786*, Tom. I–VIII. (Louvain, 1933–41).

CARNEY, J. *Medieval Irish Lyrics*, Dublin, 1967.

CARNEY, J. *The Problem of St. Patrick*, Dublin, 1961.

CARNEY, J. 'Society and the Bardic Poet'. *Studies*, Vol. LXII, Autumn-Winter, 1973, 233–50.

CARNEY, J. *Studies in Irish Literature and History*, Dublin, 1955.

CARNEY, J. (ed.). *Topographical Poems by Seaán Mór Ó Dubhagain and Giolla-na-naomh Ó hUidrin*, Dublin Institute for Advanced Studies, 1943.

CHADWICK, NORA K. *The Druids*, Cardiff, Univ. of Wales Press, 1966.

CHADWICK, NORA K. (ed.). *Studies in the early British Church*, Cambridge, 1958.

CHART, D. A. (ed.) *The Register of John Swayne, Archbishop of Dublin and Primate of Ireland*, Belfast, 1935.

Chronicum Scotorum, ed. and trans. Hennessy, W. M., Rolls Series, London, 1866.

CLANRICARDE, MARQUIS OF. *Memoirs*, London, 1722.

CLOSE, M. 'An Irish Astronomical Tract'. *Proceedings of the Royal Irish Academy*, Vol. XXII (1901), 457–64.

COFFEY, G. *The Bronze Age in Ireland*, Dublin, 1913.

COGAN, A. *History of the Diocese of Meath*, Vol. I, Dublin and London, 1862, Vol. II, Dublin, 1867, Vol. III, Dublin, 1870.

COLEMAN, A. (ed.). 'Regestum Monasterii Fratrum Praedicatorum de Athenry', *Archivium Hibernicum*, I, (1912) 201–21.

COLGAN, JOHN. *Triadis Thaumaturgae...Acta*, Louvain, 1647.

CONNELLAN, O. (ed.). *Imtheacht na Tromdáimhe or the Proceedings o fthe Great Bardic Institution*, Transactions of the Ossianic Institution, 5, (1860) 1–129.

CORCORAN, T. *Selected Texts on Education Systems in Ireland from the close of the Middle Ages*, Dublin, 1928.

CORCORAN, T. *State Policy in Irish Education*, A.D. 1536 to 1816, Dublin and London, 1916.

Council of Education (Ireland). *Report on the Function and Curriculum of the Primary School*, 1954. *Report on the Curriculum of the Secondary School*, Dublin, 1962.

CROKER, T. CROFTON. *The Popular Songs of Ireland*, London, 1839.

CROWE, M. B. 'Peter of Ireland, Teacher of St. Thomas Aquinas', *Studies*, 1956, 443–56.

CURTIS, E. *A History of Ireland*, London, 1936.

CURTIS, E. *A History of Medieval Ireland*, London, 1923.

CURTIS, E. 'The Spoken Languages of Medieval Ireland', *Studies*, VIII (1919) 234–54.

D'ALTON, E. A. *History of the Archdiocese of Tuam*, Vols. I, II, Dublin, 1928.

DANIEL-ROPS, H. *Cathedral and Crusade – Studies of the Medieval Church*, 1050–1350. Vol. III of *History of the Church of Christ*, trans. Warrington, J., London and New York, 1957.

DANIEL-ROPS, H. *Le Miracle Irlandais*, Paris, 1956. Trans., the Earl of Wicklow, *The Miracle of Ireland*, Dublin, 1959.

DAVIES, J. *A Discoverie of the true causes why Ireland was never entirely subdued, etc.*, London, 1612.

DE BLACAM, A. *Celtic Literature Surveyed*, Dublin, 1929.

DE BLACAM, A. *A First Book of Irish Literature*, Dublin, 1934.

DE BURGO, T. *Hibernia Dominicana*, Cologne, 1762.

DE MEZERAY, F. E., trans. Bulteel, J. *A General Chronological History of France*, London, 1683.

DE PAOR, M. and L. *Early Christian Ireland*, London, 1958.

DERRICKE, J. *The Image of Ireland*, ed. Small, J., with the notes of Sir Walter Scott, Bart., Edinburgh, 1883.
DILLON, M. *Early Irish Literature*, Chicago, 1948.
DILLON, M. (ed.). *Early Irish Society*, Dublin, 1954.
DILLON, M. 'Laud Misc. 610', *Celtica* V, 1960, 64–76, VI, 1963, 135–155.
DILLON, M. *Lebor na Cert. The Book of Rights, Irish Texts Society* xlvi, Dublin, 1962.
DILLON, M. 'On the date and authorship of the Book of Rights', *Celtica*, Vol. IV, Dublin, 1958, 239–49.
DILLON, M. and CHADWICK, N. K. *The Celtic Realms*, London, 1967.
DOWLING, P. J. *A History of Irish Education*, Cork, 1971.
DUNN, J. *The Ancient Irish Epic Tale Táin Bó Cualnge*, London, 1914.
EDWARDS, R. DUDLEY. *A New History of Ireland*, Dublin, 1972.
EMDEN, A. B. *Biographical Register of the University of Oxford to A.D. 1500*, Oxford, 1957–9.
ESPOSITO, M. 'The Knowledge of Greek in Ireland during the Middle Ages', *Studies*, Dec. 1912, 665–83.
FAHY, G. 'Geography in the early Irish Monastic Schools', *Geographical Viewpoint*, Vol. 3, 1974, 31–43.
FERGUSON, S. *Ogham Inscriptions in Ireland, Wales and Scotland*, Edinburgh, 1887.
FITZMAURICE, E. B. and LITTLE, A. G. *Materials for the history of the Franciscan Province of Ireland, A.D. 1230–1450*, Manchester, 1920.
FITZPATRICK, S. A. *Dublin, a historical and topographical account of the city*, London, 1907.
FLEISCHMANN, A. 'Die Iren in der Neumen- und Choralforschung', *Zeitschrift für Musikwissenschaft*, July–August, 1934, 352 sqq.
FLEISCHMANN, A. 'References to Chant in early Irish Mss.', *Féilscríbhinn Tórna*, ed. Pender, S., Cork, 1947, 43–9.
FLEISCHMANN, A. and GLEESON, R. 'Music in Ancient Munster and Monastic Cork', *Journal of the Cork Historical and Archaeological Society*, Part 2, Vol. LXX, No. 212 (1965), 79–98.
FLEURY, C. *Histoire Ecclésiastique, Tome I-XXXVI*, Paris, 1722, sqq.
FLOWER, R. *Catalogue of Irish Manuscripts in the British Museum*, Vols. II–III, London, 1926 and 1953, (see O'Grady).
FLOWER, R. *The Irish Tradition*, Oxford, 1947.
FLOWER, R. 'Manuscripts of Irish interest in the British Museum. Annals of St. Mary's Abbey'. *Analecta Hibernica*, Vol. II, (1931), 319–20.
GILBERT, J. T. *Chartularies of St. Mary's Abbey, Dublin...and Annals of Ireland*, Vols. I–II, Rolls Series, London, 1884.
GILBERT, J. T. *Facsimiles of National Manuscripts of Ireland*, London, Oxford, Cambridge, Edinburgh and Dublin, 1879.
GILBERT, J. T. *History of the City of Dublin*, Vols. I–III, Dublin, 1854–9.
GILBERT, J. T. *History of the Viceroys of Ireland*, Dublin, 1865.
GLEESON, D. F. (ed.). 'The Annals of Nenagh', *Analecta Hibernica*, XII (1943), 157–64.
GOUGAUD, L. *Les Chrétientés Celtiques*, Paris, 1911.
GOUGAUD, L. trans. Collins, V. *Gaelic Pioneers of Christianity*, Dublin, 1923.
GOUGAUD, L. 'The Isle of Saints', *Studies* XIII (Sept. 1924), 363–80.
GRATTAN FLOOD, W. *A History of Irish Music*, Dublin, 1903.
GREEN, ALICE STOPFORD. *History of the Irish State to 1014*, London, 1925.
GREEN, ALICE STOPFORD. *The Making of Ireland and its Undoing*, London, 1909.
GREENE, D. *The Irish Language*, Dublin, 1966.
GREGORY, AUGUSTA. *Cuchulain of Muirthemne*, London, 1902.
GRIESSER, P. (ed.). *Registrum Epistolarum Stephen de Lexington*, in *Analecta Sacri Ordinis Cisterciensis* ii, 1946.
GROSJEAN, P. 'Confusa Caligo, Remarques sur les Hesperica Famina', *Celtica* III (1956), 35–85.

272   EDUCATION IN ANCIENT AND MEDIEVAL IRELAND

GWYNN, A. 'The Annals of St. Mary's, Dublin' in 'Some unpublished texts from the Black Book of Christ Church, Dublin', *Analecta Hibernica* XVI, Dublin, 1946, 316–19.

GWYNN, A. 'The Medieval University of St. Patrick's, Dublin', *Studies,* June and September, 1938, 199–212 and 437–454.

GWYNN, A. *The Medieval Province of Armagh, 1470–1545,* Dundalk, 1946.

GWYNN, A. 'St. Malachy of Armagh', *Irish Ecclesiastical Record,* LXX, (1948), 961–78, LXXI, (1949), 134–48, 317–331.

GWYNN, A., 'Richard Fitzralph, Archbishop of Armagh', *Studies,* Sept. 1933, 389–405, Dec. 1933, 591–607, Sept. 1934, 395–411, Sept. 1935, 25–42, Dec. 1935, 558–72, March, 1936, 81–96, March, 1937, 50–67.

GWYNN, A. and GLEESON, D. *A History of the Diocese of Killaloe,* Dublin, 1962.

GWYNN, A. and HADCOCK, R. N. *Medieval Religious Houses, Ireland,* London, 1970.

GWYNN, E. J. *The Metrical Dindshenchas,* Parts I–V, Dublin, 1903–35.

GWYNN, E. J. (ed.). 'The Rule of Tallaght', *Hermathena,* No. XLIV, Second Supplementary Volume, Dublin and London, 1927. 'Teaching of Mael Ruain', 2–63, 'Rule of the Céli Dé', 64–87.

GWYNN, J. *Liber Armachanus, The Book of Armagh,* Dublin, 1913.

GWYNN, L. 'The two versions of Tochmarc Étáine', *Zeitschrift für Celtische Philologie,* Vol. IX, Halle, 1913, 353–6.

HADDAN, A. W. and STUBBS, W. *Councils and Ecclesiastical Documents relating to Great Britain and Ireland,* Vols. I–III, Oxford, 1869–78.

HARDIMAN, J. *Irish Minstrelsy,* London, 1831.

HAYMAN, S. *Notes and Records of the Ancient Religious Foundations at Youghal, Co. Cork, and its Vicinity,* Youghal, 1854.

HAYMAN, S. *Unpublished Geraldine Documents,* Vols. I–II, Dublin, 1881.

HEALY, J. *Ireland's Ancient Schools and Scholars,* Dublin, 1890.

HEALY, J. *Maynooth College: Its Centenary History,* Dublin, 1895.

HERREN, M. W. *Hisperica Famina. The Elegant Sayings.* Toronto, 1974.

Historical Manuscripts Commission Tenth Report, Appendix, Part V, London, 1885.

HOAGLAND, K. *1000 years of Irish Poetry.* New York, 1947.

HOGAN, E. *Onomasticon Goedelicum,* Dublin and London, 1910.

HOLINSHED, R. *Chronicles of England, Scotland and Ireland,* London, 1577.

HORE, P. H. *History of the Town and County of Wexford,* Vols. I–VI, London 1900–1911.

HUGHES, C. (ed.). *Shakespeare's Europe, Unpublished Chapters of Fynes Moryson's Itinerary [being the fourth part],* London, 1903.

HUGHES, KATHLEEN. *The Church in Early Irish Society,* London, 1966.

HUGHES, KATHLEEN. 'The distribution of Irish scriptoria and centres of learning from 730 to 1111', *Studies in the early British Church,* ed. Chadwick, N. K., section V.

HULL, ELEANOR. *The Cuchullin Saga in Irish History,* London, 1898.

HULL, ELEANOR. *A Text Book of Irish Literature,* Vols. I, II, Dublin and London, 1908.

HYDE, DOUGLAS. *A Literary History of Ireland,* London, 1899.

JENNINGS, B. (ed.). 'Donatus Moneyus de Provincia Hiberniae S. Francisci', *Analecta Hibernica,* No. 6, Nov. 1934, 12–131.

JONAS. *Life of St. Columbanus. Jonae vitae sanctorum Columbani, Vedastis, Johannis,* ed. Krusch, B. Script. Rer. Germ. M.G.H., Hannoverae et Lipsiae, 1905.

JOYCE, P. W. *Ancient Irish Music,* Dublin, 1873.

JOYCE, P. W. *A Social History of Ancient Ireland,* Vols. I, II, London, 1903.

JUBINAL, A. *La Légende Latine de S. Brendaines, avec une traduction inédite en prose et en poésie romaines,* Paris, 1836.

KEATING, G. *History of Ireland,* ed. and trans. D. Comyn and P. S. Dinneen. Irish Texts Society, IV, VIII, IX, XV, London, 1902–14.

KEARY, C. F. *The Vikings of Western Christendom, from A.D. 789 to A.D. 888,* London, 1891.

KENDRICK, T. D. *The Druids,* London, 1927.

KENDRICK, T. D. *A History of the Vikings,* London, 1930.

KENNEY, J. F. 'The Legend of St. Brendan', *Transactions of the Royal Society of Canada,* 1920, Sect. II, 51–71.

KENNEY, J. F. *The Sources for the Early History of Ireland,* New York, 1929.

KILDARE, THE MARQUIS OF. *The Earls of Kildare and their Ancestors from 1057 to 1773,* Dublin, 1857.

KNOTT, E. 'Filidh Eireann go haointeach', *Ériu* V (1911), 50–69.

KNOTT, E. 'Irish Classical Poetry', in Knott, E. and Murphy, G. *Early Irish Literature,* London, 1966.

LANIGAN, J. *An Ecclesiastical History of Ireland,* Dublin, 1822.

LAWLOR, H. C. *The Monastery of Saint Mochaoi of Nendrum,* Belfast, 1925.

LAWLOR, H. J. *The Fasti of St. Patrick's, Dublin,* Dundalk, 1930.

LAWLOR, H. J. (trans. and ed.). *St. Bernard of Clairvaux's Life of St. Malachy of Armagh,* London and New York, 1920.

LEAHY, A. H. *Heroic Romances of Ireland,* Vols. I, II, London, 1905–6.

LE ROUX, FRANÇOISE. *Les Druides,* Paris, 1961.

LITTLE, A. G. *Materials for the History of the Franciscan Province of Ireland,* Manchester, 1920.

LITTLE, G. A. *Dublin before the Vikings,* Dublin, 1957.

LYNCH, J. *Cambrensis Eversus.* St. Omer, 1662. Ed., trans., and notes, Kelly, M., Vols. I–III, Dublin, Celtic Society, 1848–52.

MABILLON, J. *Armarium Solesmense. Acta Sanctorum Ordinis St. Benedicti,* Mâcon, vol. I, 1935, vol. II, 1939.

MACALISTER, R. A. S. *The Archaeology of Ireland,* London, 1928.

MACALISTER, R. A. S. *Ireland in pre-Celtic Times,* Dublin, 1921.

MACALISTER, R. A. S. (ed. and trans.). *Lebor Gabála Érenn, The Book of the Taking of Ireland,* Dublin, Irish Texts Society, Part I, 1938, Part II, 1939, Part III, 1940, Part IV, 1941.

MACALISTER, R. A. S. *Studies in Irish Epigraphy,* London, Part I 1897, Part II 1902, Part III 1907.

MAC CANA, P. *Celtic Mythology,* London, 1970.

MAC CANA, P. 'The Rise of the later schools of Filidheacht', *Ériu,* Vol. XXV, Dublin, 1974, 126–146.

McCARTHY, B. 'The Litany of Oengus Céile De', *Irish Ecclesiastical Record,* Vol. III, May, 1867, 385–97, 468–77.

MAC EOIN, G. 'The date and authorship of Saltair na Rann', *Zeitschrift für Celtische Philologie* XXVIII (1960–61), 51–67.

McINERNEY, M. H. *A History of the Irish Dominicans,* Vol. I, Dublin, 1916. (Vol. II not published).

McKENNA, L. *Aithdioghluim Dána,* Vols. I and II. Irish Texts Society XXXVII, XL, Dublin, 1939, 1940.

McKENNA, L. (ed.), *Bardic Syntactical Texts,* Dublin, 1944.

McKENNA, L. *Dán Dé: the poems of Donnchadh Mór Ó Dálaigh and the religious poems in the Duanaire of the Yellow Book of Lecan,* Dublin, 1922.

McKENNA, L. *Dioghluim Dána,* Dublin, 1938.

McKENNA, L. *Iomarbhágh na bhFile, Contention of the Bards,* Irish Texts Society, XX, XXI, 1918 [20].

McLAUGHLAN, T. (ed.). *The Dean of Lismore's Book,* Edinburgh, 1862.

MacNAMARA, G. 'The O'Davorens of Cahermacnaughton, Burren, Co. Clare', *Journal of the North Munster Archaeological Society,* Vol. II, No. 2, Jan. 1912, 63–93, 149–64.

Mac NEILL, C. *Calendar of Bishop Alen's Register,* Dublin, Royal Society of Antiquaries of Ireland, 1950.

Mac NEILL, C. 'Rawlinson Manuscripts, C. 32. Ordinale of Rosglas Abbey'. *Analecta Hibernica* Vol. II, (1931), 1–3.

Mac NEILL, C. and OTWAY-RUTHVEN, A. J. *Dowdall Deeds,* Dublin, 1960.

Mac NEILL, E. 'Ancient Irish Law: The Law of Status or Franchise', *Proceedings of the Royal Irish Academy*, Vol. XXXVI, (1923), 265–316.

Mac NEILL, E. *Celtic Ireland*, Dublin, 1921.

Mac NEILL, E. *Early Irish Laws and Institutions*, London, 1935.

Mac NEILL, E. ed. Ryan J. *Saint Patrick*, Dublin, 1964.

Mac NEILL, E. 'A Pioneer of Nations', *Studies*, Vol. XI, 1922, 13–28, 435–46.

MAC NIOCAILL, G. 'Duanaire Ghearóid Iarla', *Studia Hibernica*, No. 3, 1963, 7–59.

MAC NIOCAILL, G. *Na Manaigh Liatha in Éirinn, 1142–1600*, Dublin, 1959.

MAC NIOCAILL, G. *The Red Book of the Earls of Kildare*, Historical Manuscripts Commission, Appendix to Part II of 9th Report, Dublin, 1964.

MAC WHITE, E. 'Irish Bronze Age Trumpets', *Journal of the Royal Society of Antiquaries of Ireland*, Vol. LXXV (1945), 85–106.

MAGUIRE, E. *History of the Diocese of Raphoe*, Vols. I, II, Dublin, 1920.

MASON, W. MONCK. *History and Antiquities of the Collegiate and Cathedral Church of St. Patrick near Dublin, from...1190 to...1819*, Dublin, 1820.

MEYER, K. (ed. and trans.). *Cain Adamnáin, an Old Irish treatise on the Law of Franchise*, Oxford, Clarendon Press, 1905.

MEYER, K. *Hibernica Minora, being a fragment of an Old-Irish treatise on the Psalter...* Oxford, 1894.

MEYER, K. *The Instructions of King Cormac mac Airt (Tecosca Cormaic)*. *Royal Irish Academy: Todd Lecture series*, Vol. XV, Dublin, 1909.

MEYER, K. (ed.). *Sanas Cormaic, an Old-Irish Glossary* (from *Yellow Book of Lecan*), *Anecdota from Irish Manuscripts* ed. Bergin, Best, Meyer, O'Keefe, Vol. IV, Halle and Dublin, 1912.

MEYER, K. 'The Wooing of Emer', *Archaeological Review* Vol. I (1888), 68–75, 150–55, 231–5, 298–307.

MEYER, K. and NUTT, A. (ed.) *The Voyage of Bran*, London, 1895.

MILLER, A. W. K. 'Glossary of Michael O'Clery', *Revue Celtique*, Vol. IV (1879–80), 349–428, Vol. V (1881–3), 1–69.

MILLS, J. 'Accounts of the Earl of Norfolk's Estates in Ireland, 1279–1294', *Journal of the Royal Society of Antiquaries of Ireland*, Vol. XXII (1892), 50–57.

MILLS, J. (ed.). *Calendar of the Justiciary Rolls* (1295–1303), parts i–ii, Dublin, Public Record Office, 1905–14.

MOODY, T. W. and MARTIN, F. X. (ed.). *The Course of Irish History*, Cork, 1967.

MOONEY, C. 'The Friars and Friary of Donegal, 1474–1840', in *Franciscan Donegal*, ed. O'Donnell, T., Ros Nuala, 1952.

MORYSON, FYNES. *An History of Ireland from...1599 to 1603. To which is added a description of Ireland*. A reprint of Pt. II and of Pt. III, Bk. 3, Ch. 5, of the Itinerary, Vols. I–II, Dublin 1773.

MORYSON, FYNES. *An itinerary...containing his ten yeeres travell etc.*, Parts I–III, London, 1617.

MULCHRONE, K. *Betha Phátraic* I. *Text and Sources*, Dublin, London, 1939.

MURPHY, G. 'Baile Chuind and the date of Cin Dromma Snechtai', *Ériu*, Vol. XVI (1952), 145–51.

MURPHY, G. *Duanaire Finn. The Book of the Lays of Finn*, Part II, Irish Texts Society, Vol. XXVIII, Dublin, 1933.

MURPHY, G. *Early Irish Metrics*, Dublin, 1961.

MURRAY, A. J. 'The Ancient Chantries of Co. Louth', *Louth Archaeological Journal* IX (1939), 181–208.

MURRAY, A. J. Review of article 'Richard Fitzralph, Archbishop of Armagh', by A. Gwynn, *Studies*, Vol. XXII, No. 87, in *Louth Archaeological Journal*, IX (1939), 181–208.

NERNEY, D. 'Johannes Scottus Eriugena', *Studies*, Vol. XXIV, Sept. 1935, 415–32.

NIC ÉNRI, U. and MAC NIOCAILL, G. 'The Second Recension of the Evernew Tongue', *Celtica*, Vol. IX (1971), 1–59.

O'CLERY, M. *Irish Glossary*, ed. and trans. Miller, A. W. K. *Revue Celtique* Vol. IV, (1879–80), 349–428, Vol. V (1881–3), 1–69.

O'CLERY, M. *The Martyrology of Donegal, A Calendar of the Saints of Ireland*, trans. O'Donovan, J., ed. with Irish text, Todd, J. H. and Reeves, W., Dublin, 1864.

Ó CORRÁIN, D. *Ireland before the Normans*, Dublin and London, 1972.

Ó CUÍV, B. 'Linguistic Terminology in the Mediaeval Irish Bardic Tracts', *Transactions of the Philological Society*, 1965, 158–59.

Ó CUÍV, B. 'The Linguistic Training of the Mediaeval Irish Poet', *Celtica*, X, (1973), 114–40.

Ó CUÍV, B. (ed.). *Seven Centuries of Irish Learning*, Radio Éireann Thomas Davis Lectures, Dublin, 1961.

O'CURRY, E. Translation of *Filidh Eireann go haointeach*, by Gofraidh Fionn Ó Dálaigh, *Proceedings of the Royal Irish Academy*, Vol. VI, 1858, 44–54.

O'CURRY, E. *Manners and Customs of the Ancient Irish*, Vol. II (Vol. I is Introduction by W. K. Sullivan), London and Dublin, 1873.

O'CURRY, E. *Lectures on the Manuscript Materials of Ancient Irish History*, Dublin, 1861.

O'CURRY, E. 'The Sick-bed of Cuchulainn and the only Jealousy of Eimer' [quoted from the "Yellow Book of Slane" in Leabhar na h-Uidre], *Atlantis*, Vol. I, (1858), 362–92, Vol. II, (1859), 98–124.

O'DOHERTY, J. F. 'Historical Criticism of the Song of Dermot', *Irish Historical Studies*, I, 4–20.

O'DONOVAN, J. *A Grammar of the Irish Language*, Dublin, 1845.

O'DONOVAN, J. (ed.). *Leabhar na gCeart*, or *The Book of Rights*, Dublin, 1847.

O'DONOVAN, J. *The Topographical Poems of John Ó Dubhagain and Giolla na Naomh Ó hUidrin*, Dublin, 1851.

O'DONOVAN, J. (ed.) *The Tribes and Customs of Hy Many from the Book of Lecan and the genealogical MSS. of Dubhaltaigh Mac Fírbhisigh*, Dublin, Irish Archaeological Society, 1843.

O'DONOVAN, J. and STOKES, W. (ed. and trans.), *Sanas Chormaic, Cormac's Glossary*, Dublin, Irish Archaeological and Celtic Society, 1868.

O'DWYER, B. 'The Problem of Education in the Cistercian Order', *The Journal of Religious History (Australia)*, Vol. 3, No. 3.

O'DWYER, B. 'The Problem of Education in the Irish Cistercian monasteries and the attempted solution of Stephen of Lexington', *The Journal of Ecclesiastical History (Australia)*, Vol. XV, No. 2, 186–91.

Ó FIAICH, T. *Columbanus in his own words*, Dublin, 1974.

Ó FIAICH, T. 'St. Patrick and Armagh', *Irish Ecclesiastical Record*, Vol. LXXIX, 1958, 153–70.

O'FLAHERTY, R. *A Chorographical Description of West or Iar-Connacht*, ed. Hardiman, J., Dublin, Irish Archaeological Society, 1846.

O'FLAHERTY, R. *Ogygia or a Chronological Account of Irish Events*, London and Dublin, 1685. English trans. Hely, J., Vols. I–II, Dublin, 1793.

O'GRADY, S. H. *Caithréim Thoirealbhaigh, The Triumphs of Turlough*, Irish Texts Society, Vols. XXVI–XXVII, London, 1929.

O'GRADY, S. H. *Catalogue of Irish Manuscripts in the British Museum*, Vol. I, London, 1926. (See Flower).

O'GRADY, S. H. *Silva Gadelica*, Vol. I (Irish text), Vol. II (translation and notes), London, 1892.

O'HALLORAN, S. *An Introduction to the Study of the History and Antiquities of Ireland*, Dublin, 1772.

O'HANLON, J. *Lives of the Irish Saints*, Vols. I–X, Dublin, London and New York, 1875.

'The O'Kane Papers, II, Bishop Montgomery's Survey of the Bishoprics of Derry, Raphoe and Clogher'. Presented by Alexander, A. F. O'D., *Analecta Hibernica* No. 12, Jan. 1943, 79–111.

O'KEEFE, J. G. 'Riagail Pátraic: The Rule of Patrick', *Ériu*, Vol. I, (1904), 216–24.

O'KELLEHER, A. and SCHOEPPERLE, G. *Betha Colaim Chille. Life of Columcille, compiled by M. O'D. in 1532,* University of Illinois, 1918.

OLDEN, T. 'On the Geography of Ros Ailithir', *Proceedings of the Royal Irish Academy,* Second Series, Vol. II, 1884, 219–49.

O'RAHILLY, CECILE. *Five Seventeenth-Century Political Poems,* Dublin, 1952.

O'RAHILLY, CECILE. *Táin Bó Cualgne, from the Book of Leinster,* Dublin, 1967, Irish Texts Society, Vol. XLIX.

O'RAHILLY, T. F. *Dánta Grádha, an anthology of Irish love poetry of the sixteenth and seventeenth centuries,* Dublin, 1916.

O'RAHILLY, T. F. *Early Irish History and Mythology,* Dublin, 1946.

O'RAHILLY, T. F. 'The Goidels and their Predecessors', *Proceedings of the British Academy,* Vol. XXI (1935).

O'RAHILLY, T. F. *The Two Patricks,* Dublin, 1942.

Ó RAITHBHEARTAIGH, T. *Irish Manuscripts Commission, Genealogical Tracts I,* Dublin, 1932.

O'REILLY, E. *Irish Writers. A chronological account of nearly four hundred Irish writers.* Transactions, Iberno-Celtic Society, Vol. I, Part I. Dublin, 1820.

Ó RÍORDÁIN, S. *Antiquities of the Irish Countryside,* Cork Univ. Press, 1942.

ORPEN, G. H. *Ireland under the Normans,* Oxford, 1911 (Vols. I, II), 1920 (Vols. III, IV).

ORPEN, G. H. *The Song of Dermot and the Earl.* Oxford, Clarendon Press, 1892.

O'SULLIVAN, A. and W. 'Three Notes on Laud Misc. 610 (or The Book of Pottlerath'. *Celtica,* Vol. IX (1971), 133–51.

O'SULLIVAN, D. *Irish Folk Music and Song,* Dublin, 1952.

OTWAY-RUTHVEN, A. J. *A History of Medieval Ireland,* London, 1968.

PETRIE, G. *Collection of the Ancient Music of Ireland,* Dublin, 1855–82.

PETRIE, G. 'On the history and antiquities of Tara Hill', *Transactions of the Royal Irish Academy,* Vol. XVIII, part II (1839), 25–232.

PLOWDEN, F. P. *An Historical Review of the State of Ireland from the invasion of that country under Henry II to its Union with Great Britain,* Egerton, 1801.

PLUMMER, C. *Bethada Náem nErenn, Lives of the Irish Saints,* Vols. I and II, Oxford, 1922.

PLUMMER, C. 'On the colophons and marginalia of Irish scribes', *British Academy Proceedings* XII, 11–14.

PLUMMER, C. *Vitae Sanctorum Hiberniae,* Vols. I and II, Oxford, 1910.

PLUMMER, C. *Litany of Oengus Céli Dé,* Henry Bradshaw Society Vol. LXII, *Irish Litanies,* XX, 161–75.

POWER, MAURA (ed.). *An Irish Astronomical Tract,* Irish Texts Society, Vol. XIV, London, 1914.

QUIGGIN, E. C. 'Prolegomena to the study of the Later Irish Bards 1200 to 1500' from the *Proceedings of the British Academy,* Vol. V, London, 1913.

RAFTERY, J. *Prehistoric Ireland,* London, 1951.

RASHDALL, H. *The Universities of Europe in the Middle Ages,* Oxford, 1895, new edition ed. Powicke and Emden, 1936.

Red Book of Ossory. Historical Manuscripts Commission, 10th Report, Appendix, Part V, 244.

REEVES, W. *The Life of St. Columba...by Adamnan,* Dublin, 1857.

REEVES, W. 'On the Céli-dé, commonly called Culdees', *Proceedings of the Royal Irish Academy,* Vol. XXIV, 1864, 119–263.

REEVES, W. 'Prose Rule of the Céli Dé', *Transactions, Royal Irish Academy,* Vol. XXIX (1864), 213.

Rotuli Parliamentorum ut et Petitiones et Placita in Parliamento tempore Edw. III... Henry VI. Collected by R. Blyke, P. Morant, T. Astle and J. Topham, ed. by J. Strachey, Vols. I–VI, London, 1767–72.

RYAN, J. *The Cáin Adomnáin.* No. 7 in ed. Thurneysen and others, *Studies in Early Irish Laws,* 269–76, Dublin, 1936.

RYAN, J. *Clonmacnois,* Dublin, 1976.

RYAN, J. 'The Convention of Druim Ceat (A.D. 575)', *Journal of the Royal Society of Antiquaries of Ireland*, Vol. LXXVI, (1946), 35–55.

RYAN, J. (ed.). *Féil-Sgríbhinn Eóin Mhic Néill, Essays and Studies presented to Professor Eóin Mac Neill, D.Litt. on the occasion of his seventieth birthday*, Dublin, 1940.

RYAN, J. *Irish Monasticism*. Dublin, 1931.

SALTER, H. E. (ed.). *Registrum Cancellariae Oxoniensis*, 1434–69, Oxford, Clarendon Press, 1932.

SCHRÖDER, C. *Sankt Brandan. Ein lateinischer und drei deutsche Texte*, Erlangen, 1871.

SELMER, C. (ed.). *Navigatio S. Brendani*. Publications in Medieval Studies, Vol. XVI, Indiana, University of Notre Dame, 1959.

SHAW, F. *Irish Medical Men and Philosophers*. No. VI in ed. Ó Cuív, B. *Seven Centuries of Irish Learning*, Dublin, 1961.

SHAW, F. 'Medieval Medico-Philosophical Treatises in the Irish language'. No. 22, *Féil-sgríbhinn Eoin Mhic Neill, Essays and Studies presented to Professor Eoin Mac Neill on the occasion of his seventieth birthday*, ed. Ryan, J., Dublin, 1940.

SHEEHY, M. *Pontificia Hibernica, Medieval Papal Chancery Documents concerning Ireland, 640–1261*, Dublin, 1962.

SHIRLEY, E. P. *Original Letters and Papers relating to the history of the Church in Ireland during the reign of Edward VI, Mary and Elizabeth*, London, 1851.

SMITH, C. *The Antient and Present State of the County and City of Cork*, 1749, ed. Day, R. and Copinger, W. A., Cork (Vol. I), 1893, (Vol. II), 1894.

SMITH, W. and WACE, H. *A Dictionary of Christian Biography, Literature, Sects and Doctrines*, Vols. I–IV, London 1877–87.

SPENSER, E. *View of the Present State of Ireland*, 1596 (ed. Renwick, W. L.), Oxford, 1970.

STEVENSON, J. (ed.), *Gildas De Excidio Britanniae* [with *V. de S. Gildas* ascribed to Caradoc of Llancarfan] English History Society, 1838.

STOKES, G. T. 'The Knowledge of Greek in Ireland between 500 and 900 A.D.', *Proceedings of the Royal Irish Academy, May, 1892*.

STOKES, W. 'Amra Senáin', *Zeitschrift für Celtische Philologie*, Vol. III (1901), 220–25.

STOKES, W. 'The Bodleian *Amra Choluimb Chille*', *Revue Celtique*, Vol. XX (1899), 248–89, Vol. XXI (1900), 133–6.

STOKES, W. (ed.). 'The Destruction of Dá Derga's Hostel', *Revue Celtique*, Vol. XXII, 1901, 164–215, 390–437.

STOKES, W. (ed.). 'The Evernew Tongue, Tenga Bithnua'. *Ériu*, Vol. II, London, 1905, 96–162.

STOKES, W. (ed.). *Féilire Oengusso Céli Dé. The Martyrology of Oengus the Culdee*, London, Henry Bradshaw Society, Vol. XXIX, 1905.

STOKES, W. '*Immacallam In Da Thuarad*, The Colloquy of the Two Sages', *Revue Celtique*, XXVI (1905), 51.

STOKES, W. 'The Life of Fursa', *Revue Celtique*, Vol. XXV (1904), 385–401.

STOKES, W. *Lives of the Saints from the Book of Lismore*, Oxford, 1890.

STOKES, W. 'On the Calendar of Oengus' *Transactions of the Royal Irish Academy*, Vol. I, 1870, Part i, cxli.

STOKES, W. (ed.). *Saltair na Rann. A Collection of Early Irish Poems*, Oxford, 1883.

STOKES, W. 'Sanas Cormaic (from Ms. in R.I.A.)' included in *Three Irish Glossaries*, 13.

STOKES, W. *Three Irish Glossaries*, London and Edinburgh, 1862.

STOKES, W. *Three Middle Irish Homilies (from Lebor Brecc) on the Lives of Saints Patrick, Brigit and Columba*, Calcutta, 1877.

STOKES, W. *The Tripartite Life of St. Patrick and other documents relating to that Saint*, Rolls series, Parts I–II, London, 1887.

STOKES, W. and STRACHAN, J. *Thesaurus Palaeohibernicus*, Cambridge, Vol. I, 1901, Vol. II, 1903.

STOKES, W. and WINDISCH, E. (ed.). 'Mittelirische Verslehren', *Irische Texte, Dritte Serie, 1. Heft*, Leipzig, 1891.

SULLIVAN, W. K. Introduction to (or Vol. I of) O'Curry's *Manners and Customs of the Ancient Irish*, London and Dublin, 1873.

THURNEYSEN, R. 'Aus dem Irischen Recht, IV (1926). Zu Ancient Laws und Senchas Mar', *Zeitschrift für Celtische Philologie*, XVI Band, 1 Heft, 166–196.

THURNEYSEN, R. 'Zur Irischen Accent- und Verslehre', *Revue Celtique*, Tome V, (1881–3), 326–47.

TIERNEY, J. J., with contributions by Bieler, L. *Dicuili Liber de Mensura Orbis Terrae*, Dublin Institute for Advanced Studies, 1967.

TODD, J. H. *The Book of Hymns of the ancient Church of Ireland*, Dublin, 1855–69.

TODD, J. H. *Cogadh Gaedhel re Gallaibh, The War of the Gaedhil with the Gaill*, London, 1867.

TODD, J. H. (ed.). *Leabhar Breathnach Annso Sis*, The Irish Version of the *Historia Britonum* of Nennius, Dublin, 1848.

TOMMASINI, A. N. (trans. Scanlan, J. F.). *Irish Saints in Italy*, London, 1937·

TRAUBE, L. *Monumenta Germaniae Historica, Poetae Aevi Carolini*, Berlin, 1886–96.

TRAUBE, L. *O Roma Nobilis. Philologische Untersuchungen aus dem Mittelalter*, Munich, 1891.

TRESHAM, E. (ed.). *Rotulorum Patentium et Clausorum Cancellariae Hiberniae Calendarium*, Vol. I, Pars. i, Henry II – Henry VII, Dublin, 1828.

USSHER, J. *Britannicarum Ecclesiarum Antiquitates*, Dublin, 1639.

USSHER, J. *Veterum Epistolarum Hibernicarum Sylloge*, Dublin, 1632.

VENN, JOHN and J. A. *Alumni Cantabrigienses*, Cambridge, 1921.

VOSSEN, A. F. (ed.). *Two Bokes of the Historie of Ireland, compiled by Edmund Campion*, Assen, 1963.

WALKER, G. S. M. *Sancti Columbani Opera. Scriptores Latini Hiberniae*, ii, Dublin, 1957.

WALKER, J. C. *Historical Memoirs of the Irish Bards*, Vol. 1, Dublin, 1818.

WALSH, P. *Irish Men of Learning*, Dublin, 1947.

WARBURTON, J., WHITELAW, J., and WALSH, R. *History of the City of Dublin*, Vols. I–II, London, 1818.

WARE, J. *De Hibernia et Antiquitatibus eius Disputationes*, London, 1654.

WARE, J. *The Whole Works of Sir James Ware*, ed. Harris, W., Dublin, Vol. I, (1739), Vol. II (1745), Vol. III (1746).

WARE, J. (ed.). *Two histories of Ireland by Edmund Campion and Meredith Hanmer*, Dublin, 1633.

WARNER, G. F. and GILSON, J. P. *Catalogue of western manuscripts in the old Royal and King's Collections*, Vols. I–IV. London, 1921.

WATKINS, C. 'Indo-European Metrics and Archaic Irish Verse', *Celtica* VI, (1963), 194–249.

WATT, J. A. *The Church and the Two Nations in Medieval Ireland*, Cambridge, 1970.

WESTROPP, T. J. *The Ancient Forts of Ireland* (reprint from *Transactions of the Royal Irish Academy*, Vol. XXXI), Dublin, 1902.

WESTROPP, T. J. 'Prehistoric Stone Forts of Northern Clare', *Journal of Royal Society of Antiquaries of Ireland*, (1897), 120–21.

WHITE, S. *Apologia pro Hibernia adversus Cambri columnias, nunc primum edita cura Matthaei Kelly*, Dublin, 1849.

WINDISCH, E. *Mittelirische Verslehren. Irische Texte, Dritte Serie, erstes Heft*, 1–182, Leipzig, 1891.

WINDISCH, E. (Ed.). *Tochmarc Etáine, Irische Texte, Erste Serie, Erstes Heft*, 113–33, Leipzig, 1880.

WULFF, WINIFRED (ed.). *Rosa Anglica, An Early Modern Irish Translation of a section of the mediaeval medical textbook of John of Gaddesden*, Irish Texts Society, Vol. XXV, London, 1929.

ZIMMER, H. *Pelagius in Irland. Texte und Untersuchungen zur patristischen Literatur*, Berlin, 1901.

INDEX